COMMISSIONED REVIEWS OF 250 PSYCHOLOGICAL TESTS

COMMISSIONED REVIEWS OF 250 PSYCHOLOGICAL TESTS

Volume 2

Edited by
John Maltby
Christopher Alan Lewis
Andrew Hill

Mellen Studies in Psychology
Volume 2b

The Edwin Mellen Press
Lewiston•Queenston•Lampeter

Library of Congress Cataloging-in-Publication Data

Commissioned reviews of 250 psychological tests / edited by John Maltby, Christopher Alan Lewis, Andrew Hill.
    p. cm. -- (Mellen studies in psychology ; v. 2b)
    Includes bibliographical references and indexes.
    ISBN 0-7734-7452-8 (v.1) 0-7734-7454-4 (v. 2)
    1. Psychological tests--Evaluation. I. Maltby, John, 1969- II. Lewis, Christopher Alan.
III. Hill, Andrew, 1969- IV. Series.

BF176 .C65 2000
150' .28'7--dc21

00-052519

This is volume 2b in the continuing series
Mellen Studies in Psychology
Volume 2b ISBN 0-7734-7454-4
MSPs Series ISBN 0-7734-7529-X

A CIP catalog record for this book is available from the British Library.

The Edwin Mellen Press
Box 450
Lewiston, New York
USA 14092-0450

The Edwin Mellen Press
Box 67
Queenston, Ontario
CANADA L0S 1L0

The Edwin Mellen Press, Ltd.
Lampeter, Ceredigion, Wales
UNITED KINGDOM SA48 8LT

Printed in the United States of America

TABLE OF CONTENTS

CHAPTER 4

SOCIAL PSYCHOLOGY: ATTITUDES, BELIEFS, AND INTERPERSONAL RELATIONSHIPS

4.01: ATTITUDES TOWARD SEXUALITY INVENTORY, THE REVISED.
AUTHORS: Patton and Mannison.

VARIABLE: Attitudes toward sexuality.

DESCRIPTION: A 40-item attitude scale that looks at sexuality issues, with a particular focus on sexual coercion. 35 items reflect broad issues in sexuality including masturbation, sexuality in children and the aged, sexual coercion and assault in childhood and adulthood, homosexuality, abortion, and contraception. Five items that focus on attitudes toward women are also included. Respondents reply to a 6-point scale ranging from *Strongly agree* through to *Strongly disagree*. The 6-point format was chosen in order to avoid a midpoint and invite a choice for one side or the other. The inventory requires approximately 5-10 minutes to complete. Items are worded to counter a tendency to simply agree or disagree with all of them. As a result, items 4, 7,13, 15, 19, 20, and 23 are reverse scored.

SAMPLE: The inventory is designed to be used with older adolescents and adults. The scale development was conducted with first year university students (18-20 years), teachers and nurses completing a university sexuality unit, and with school based sexuality educators.

RELIABILITY: **Internal consistency:** Cronbach's alpha for the overall revised inventory was .85. A factor analysis found three reliable and clear factors. Two additional factors were less clear (Patton & Mannison, 1995). The three factors were Attitudes toward Sexual Coercion and Assault (Items 2, 5, 6, 13, 17, 18, 25, 27, 29, 33, 37, 38), Attitudes toward Sexuality Issues (Items 4, 7, 8, 15, 19, 20, 23, 35), and Attitudes toward Gender Role (Items 9, 28, 31, 32, 35). For the three clear factors, the alphas were .85, .79, and .68 respectively (Patton & Mannison, 1995).

VALIDITY: The initial version of the Attitudes toward Sexuality Inventory was used to evaluate attitude change following a university course. Pre and post-test data were received from 115 students (Patton & Mannison, 1993). Patton and Mannison (1994) also used the initial version of the inventory in a study designed to measure attitude and behaviour change (measured by responses to problem situations) following a university human sexuality course. Analyses conducted by Patton and Mannison (1995) found significant gender differences on 19 of the 25 individual items in the three clear factors. In addition, analyses of variance performed on the summed factor scores for the three reliable factors also found that these gender differences generally remained for the total factor score, with Factors 1 and 3 showing significant gender differences.

LOCATION: Patton, W., & Mannison, M. (1997). The Revised Attitudes toward Sexuality Inventory. In C.M. Davis, W.L. Yarber, R. Bauserman, G. Scheer, & S.

L. Davis (Eds.), *Handbook of Sexuality Related Measures* (pp. 85-87). Newbury Park, CA: Sage.

COMMENT: Patton and Mannison (1995) reported that additional redefinition of the measure is necessary. However, analyses found three reliable and clear factors and two other factors that were less clear. The overall scale reliability was strong, and reliability of three of the factors was above .68. The first two factors may be used as independent measures, yet accepting the multidimensional complexity of attitudes toward sexuality suggests further refinement while continuing to include a wide range of content.

REFERENCES:

Patton, W., & Mannison, M. (1993). Effects of a university subject on attitudes towards human sexuality. *Journal of Sex Education and Therapy, 19,* 93-107.

Patton, W., & Mannison, M. (1994). Investigating attitudes towards sexuality: Two methodologies. *Journal of Sex Education and Therapy, 20,* 185-197.

Patton, W., & Mannison, M. (1995). Sexuality attitudes: A review of the literature and refinement of a new measure. *Journal of Sex Education and Therapy, 21,* 268-295.

Patton, W., & Mannison, M. (1997). The Revised Attitudes toward Sexuality Inventory. In C.M. Davis, W.L. Yarber, R. Bauserman, G. Scheer, & S.L. Davis (Eds.), *Handbook of Sexuality Related Measures* (pp. 85-87). Newbury Park, CA: Sage.

REVIEWER: Wendy Patton, School of Learning and Development, Queensland University of Technology, Kelvin Grove Campus, Brisbane, Queensland 4059, Australia. E-mail: w.patton@qut.com

4.02: BATTERED WOMAN SCALE (BWS), THE.

AUTHORS: Schwartz and Mattley.

VARIABLE: Gender role trait ascriptions as an aspect of self-concept.

DESCRIPTION: The Battered Woman Scale consists of seven items derived from the Personal Attributes Questionnaire (PAQ; Spence, Helmreich, & Stapp, 1974), with one item from the PAQ Masculinity subscale, two from the Femininity subscale, and four from the Masculinity-Femininity subscale. These seven items, embedded with 17 distracter items, were selected based upon characteristics of battered women in the literature. PAQ items are semantic differential; the BWS items were converted to Likert style for ease of understanding by readers of the scale.

SAMPLE: The authors designed the BWS for use with battered women in shelter houses: 1) as a research instrument with items particularly salient to battered women's experiences, and; 2) as an evaluation instrument for shelter programming designed to change women's self-concept as they emerge from the battering experience.

RELIABILITY: No reliability information was provided for the BWS. The PAQ has satisfactory internal consistency reliability (Helmreich, Spence, & Wilhelm, 1981; Yoder, Rice, Adams, Priest, & Prince, 1982) and test-retest reliability (Yoder *et al.*, 1982).

VALIDITY: Convergent: Several college classes, responding to the test items in the original semantic differential form and in the revised Likert scale form, gave "virtually identical results" (Schwartz & Mattley, 1993, p. 279). **Discriminant:** A sample of 117 shelter women scored significantly higher on the BWS than 132 non-shelter, non-battered women of similar ethnicity and socioeconomic status. Further, the subgroups of White and Black shelter women scored higher than the control subgroups of White and Black women, indicating the Scale's usefulness with both ethnicities (Mattley & Schwartz, 1990). A discriminant function analysis with BWS score as the predictor variable correctly classified 77.51% of the women into shelter and control groups. The canonical correlation was .56 (Schwartz & Mattley, 1993). Adding ethnicity to the equation resulted in 79.12% corrrect classifications (Mattley & Schwartz, 1990).

LOCATION: Schwartz, M. D., & Mattley, C. L. (1993). The Battered Woman Scale and gender identities. *Journal of Family Violence, 8,* 277-287.

COMMENT: From a theoretical perspective, Mattley and Schwartz (1990; Schwartz & Mattley, 1993) view battered women's trait ascriptions as the result of their battering, not as a cause of their battering. Consequently they expect a change in scores after time spent in a supportive shelter environment. This may be the best use of the BWS, as a before and after measure upon entering and leaving shelter. The scoring of items is somewhat illogical, suggesting responses to individual items may be more useful than the total BWS score. Reliability data are needed. The BWS has not been widely used as a research tool. A search of the Social Sciences Citation Index yielded just three additional references to the two BWS articles (Ellington & Marshall, 1997; Holtzworth-Monroe, Smutzler, & Sandlin, 1997; Rhodes & McKenzie, 1998); all cited the authors' findings rather than using the scale for research purposes.

REFERENCES:

Ellington, J.E., & Marshall, L.L. (1997). Gender role perceptions of women in abusive relationships. *Sex Roles, 36,* 349-369.

Helmreich, R.L., Spence, J.T., & Wilhelm, J.A. (1981). A psychometric analysis of the Personal Attributes Questionnaire. *Sex Roles, 7*, 1097-1108.

Holtzworth-Munroe, A., Smutzler, N., & Sandin, E. (1997). A brief review of the research on husband violence. Part II. The psychological effects of husband violence on battered women and their children. *Aggression and Violent Behavior, 2*, 179-213.

Mattley, C., & Schwartz, M.D. (1990). Emerging from tyranny: Using the Battered Woman Scale to compare the gender identities of battered and non-battered women. *Symbolic Interaction, 13*, 281-289.

Rhodes, N.R., & McKenzie, E.B. (1998). Why do battered women stay? Three decades of research. *Aggression and Violent Behavior, 3*, 391-406.

Schwartz, M.D., & Mattley, C.L. (1993). The Battered Woman Scale and gender identities. *Journal of Family Violence, 8*, 277-287.

Spence, J.T., Helmreich, R., & Stapp, J. (1974). *JSAS Catalog of Selected Documents in Psychology, 4*, 43.

Yoder, J.D., Rice, R.W., Adams, J., Priest, R.F., & Prince, H.T., II. (1982). Reliability of the Attitudes Toward Women Scale (AWS) and the Personal Attributes Questionnaire (PAQ). *Sex Roles, 8*, 651-657.

REVIEWER: Jane Elizabeth Ellington, Department of Psychology, Sociology, and Anthropology, Austin College, Sherman, Texas 75090-4440, U.S.A. E-mail: jellington@austinc.edu

4.03: BELIEFS IN A JUST WORLD QUESTIONNAIRE.

AUTHORS: Dalbert, Montada, and Schmitt.

VARIABLE: General belief in a just world and personal belief in a just world.

DESCRIPTION: The Beliefs in a Just World Questionnaire consists of the General Belief in Just World Scale (Dalbert, Montada, & Schmitt, 1987; its English version first published in: Dalbert & Yamauchi, 1994) and the Personal Belief in a Just World Scale (Dalbert, in press) and contains 13 items. Of these, 6 items are designed to measure the belief that the world in general is a just place and 7 items depict the belief that, overall, events in one's life are just. Each item is to be rated on a 6-point Likert-type scale ranging from (1) *Strongly disagree* to (6) *Strongly agree*.

SAMPLE: Dalbert, Montada and Schmitt (1987) and Dalbert (in press) intended the scales to be used for the assessment of beliefs in a just world in non-psychiatric populations.

RELIABILITY: Internal consistency: For the General Belief in a Just World Scale, the 1-factor-model was successfully tested by confirmatory factor analyses (Dalbert, 1992; Dalbert & Katona-Sallay, 1996; Dalbert & Yamauchi, 1994) and the scale demonstrated satisfactory levels of internal reliability (Dalbert, 1993a, in press; Dalbert, Montada, & Schmitt, 1987; Dalbert & Warndorf, 1996; Dalbert & Yamauchi; 1994; Lipkus, Dalbert, & Siegler, 1996; Montada, Schmitt, & Dalbert, 1986) ranging from $\alpha=.66$ (Dalbert, 1993a) to $\alpha=.88$ (Montada, Schmitt, & Dalbert, 1986). The Personal Belief in a Just World Scale demonstrated a good level of internal reliability, ranging from $\alpha=.82$ to $\alpha=.87$ (Dalbert, in press). **Test-retest:** For the General Belief in a Just World Scale, Dalbert and Schneider (1995) reported a test-retest correlation of $r_{manifest}=.73$ /$r_{latent}=.82$ among $n=425$ German adults after a 3 month interval. Moreover, a latent state-trait-model showed that the main variance for both assessments could be explained by a common trait factor. For the Personal Belief in a Just World Scale there is none.

VALIDITY: **Convergent:** The General Belief in a Just World Scale demonstrated satisfactory convergent validity with various other measures of beliefs in a just world (Lipkus, Dalbert, & Siegler, 1996). For the Personal Belief in a Just World Scale there is none. **Discriminant:** The General Belief in a Just World Scale demonstrated good discriminant validity compared to authoritarianism (Dalbert, 1992), optimism (Dalbert, 1996), and personal belief in a just world (Dalbert, in press). Both just world scales demonstrated good discriminant validity compared to the fairness related self-concept (Dalbert, in print). **Construct:** The construct validity of the General Belief in a Just world Scale was demonstrated by its significant relationships with justice judgements (Dalbert & Yamauchi, 1994; Dalbert, Fisch, & Montada, 1992), religiosity (Dalbert & Katona, Sallay, 1996), disdain of the disadvantaged (Montada, Schmitt, & Dalbert, 1986), political orientation (Dalbert, 1992; 1993b), solidarity (Schmitt, 1998), attitudes towards charity (Furnham, 1995), prosocial behavior (Bierhoff, Klein, & Kramp, 1991), social responsibility (Bierhoff, 1994), claiming for compensation (Dalbert & Warndorf, 1996), well-being and self-esteem (Dalbert, 1993a), and coping with an unjust fate (Dalbert, 1997, 1998). The construct validity of the Personal Belief in a Just World Scale was supported by its significant relationship with well-being and self-esteem (Dalbert, in press).

LOCATION: **English version/general:** Dalbert, C., & Yamauchi, L. (1994). Belief in a just world and attitudes toward immigrants and foreign workers: A cultural comparison between Hawaii and Germany. *Journal of Applied Social Psychology*, *24*, 1612-1626. **German version/general:** Dalbert, C., Montada, L., & Schmitt, M. (1987). Glaube an eine gerechte Welt als Motiv: Validierungskorrelate zweier

Skalen. *Psychologische Beiträge*, *29*, 596-615. **English version/general and personal:** Dalbert, C. (in press). The world is more just for me than generally: About the Personal Belief in a Just World Scale's validity. *Social Justice Research*.

COMMENT: There is strong evidence for the General Belief in a Just world Scale's satisfactory psychometric properties and construct validity in different cultures as Germany, U.S.A., Great Britain, Hungary, Slovakia, Slovenia, Spain. However, it was expected that the belief in a personal just world compared to a general belief could better predict mental health and coping. The psychometric properties and validity of the Personal Belief in a Just World Scale was supported in a first series of three questionnaires studies and an experiment.

REFERENCES:

Bierhoff, H.W. (1994). Verantwortung und altruistische Persönlichkeit. *Zeitschrift für Sozialpsychologie*, *25*, 217-226.

Bierhoff, H.W., Klein, R., & Kramp, P. (1991). Evidence for the altruistic personality from data on accident research. *Journal of Personality*, *59*, 263-280.

Dalbert, C. (1992). Der Glaube an die gerechte Welt: Differenzierung und Validierung eines Konstrukts. *Zeitschrift für Sozialpsychologie*, *23*, 268-276.

Dalbert, C. (1993a). Gefährdung des Wohlbefindens durch Arbeitsplatzunsicherheit: Eine analyse der einflußfaktoren selbstwert und Gerechte-Welt-Glaube. *Zeitschrift für Gesundheitspsychologie*, *1*, 235-253.

Dalbert, C. (1993b). Psychisches Wohlbefinden und Persönlichkeit in Ost und West: Vergleich von Sozialisationseffekten in der früheren DDR und der alten   BRD.   *Zeitschrift   für   Sozialisationsforschung   und Erziehungssoziologie*, *1*, 82-94.

Dalbert, C. (1996). *Über den Umgang mit Ungerechtigkeit*. Bern: Huber.

Dalbert, C. (1997). Coping with an unjust fate: The case of structural unemployment. *Social Justice Research; Special Issue "Job Loss, Unemployment and Social Injustices"*, *10*, 175-189.

Dalbert, C. (1998). Belief in a just world, well-being, and coping with an unjust fate. In L. Montada, & M.J. Lerner (Eds.), *Responses to Victimizations and Belief in a Just World* (pp. 87-105). New York: Plenum Press.

Dalbert, C. (in press). The world is more just for me than generally: About the Personal Belief in a Just World Scale's validity. *Social Justice Research*.

Dalbert, C., Fisch, U., & Montada, L. (1992). Is inequality unjust? Evaluating women's career chances. *European Review of Applied Psychology*, *42*, 11-17.

Dalbert, C., & Katona-Sallay, H. (1996), The "belief in a just world" construct in Hungary. *Journal of Cross-Cultural Psychology*, *27*, 293-314.

Dalbert, C., Montada, L., & Schmitt, M. (1987). Glaube an eine gerechte Welt als Motiv: Validierungskorrelate zweier Skalen. *Psychologische Beiträge*, *29*, 596-615.

Dalbert, C., & Schneider, A. (1995). Die Allgemeine Gerechte-Welt-Skala: Dimensionalität, Stabilität und Fremdurteiler-Validität. (*Berichte aus der Arbeitsgruppe "Verantwortung, Gerechtigkeit, Moral" Nr. 86*). Trier: Universität Trier, FB I - Psychologie.

Dalbert, C., & Warndorf, P.K. (1996). Ein behindertes Kind - Eine Familienentwicklungsaufgabe: Überprüfung eines dreidimensionalen Gerechtigkeitsmodells familialer Belastungen. *Zeitschrift für Entwicklungspsychologie und Pädagogische Psychologie*, *28*, 336-356.

Dalbert, C., & Yamauchi, L. (1994). Belief in a just world and attitudes toward immigrants and foreign workers: A cultural comparison between Hawaii and Germany. *Journal of Applied Social Psychology, 24*, 1612-1626.

Furnham, A. (1995). The just world, charitable giving, and attitudes to disability. *Personality and Individual Differences, 19*, 577-583.

Lipkus, I.M., Dalbert, C., & Siegler, I.C. (1996). The importance of distinguishing the belief in a just world for self versus others. *Personality and Social Psychology Bulletin, 22*, 666-677.

Montada, L., Schmitt, M., & Dalbert, C. (1986). Thinking about justice and dealing with one's own privileges: A study of existential guilt. In H.W. Bierhoff, R. Cohen, & J. Greenberg (Eds.), *Justice in Social Relations* (pp. 125-143). New York: Plenum Press.

Schmitt, M. (1998). Gerechtigkeit und Solidarität im wiedervereinigten Deutschland. In B. Reichle, & M. Schmitt (Eds.), *Verantwortung, Gerechtigkeit, Moral* (pp. 87-98). Weinheim. Juventa.

REVIEWER: Claudia Dalbert, Department of Educational Psychology, Martin-Luther-University Halle-Wittenberg, Halle, Germany.

5.04: BERKELEY EXPRESSIVITY QUESTIONNAIRE, THE.
AUTHORS: Gross and John.

VARIABLE: Emotional expressivity.

DESCRIPTION: Self report measure of individual differences in emotional expressivity, defined as "the behavioral (*e.g.*, facial, postural) changes that typically accompany emotion, such as smiling, frowning, crying, or storming out of the room" (Gross & John, 1997, p. 435). Respondents indicate their agreement or disagreement regarding 16 items using a 7-point Likert scale on which 1=*Strongly agree*, 4=*Neutral*, and 7=*Strongly agree*. Three items are reverse scored. Higher scores indicate greater expressivity. In addition to a Total scale score, there are three sub-scales. Negative Expressivity is defined by 6 items, Positive Expressivity by 4 items, and Impulse Strength by 6 items.

SAMPLES: Gross and John (1995) intended the scale to be used in normal populations.

RELIABILITY: Internal consistency: Internal consistency for the Total scale has ranged from .82 to .86. Internal consistencies for the sub-scales have ranged from .68 to .74 for Negative Expressivity .65 to .71 for Positive Expressivity; and, .73 to .80 for Impulse Strength (Gross & John, 1995, 1997, 1998). Test-retest: Gross and John (1995) reported test-retest reliabilities of r=.86 (Total scale), r=.78 (Negative Expressivity), r=.71 (Positive Expressivity), and r=.82 (Impulse Strength) in a sample of 68 college students. The test-retest interval was 2 to 3 months.

VALIDITY: Convergent: Self reported expressivity shows impressive convergent relations with peer rated expressivity (r=.53), as well as with emotion-expressive behavior during film viewing (Gross & John, 1997). Negative Expressivity and Positive Expressivity also were related to (a) typical emotion expression in peer relationships, (b) ability to pose emotions in the laboratory, (c) interpersonal consequences (*e.g.*, likeability), and (d) regulation of emotion and mood (Gross & John, 1998). Discriminant: Although Negative and Positive Expressivity scales are correlated, Negative Expressivity predicts behavioural expressions of sadness (but not amusement), and Positive Expressivity predicts behavioural expressions of amusement (but not sadness). Emotional expressivity is essentially unrelated to socioeconomic status, social desirability, or self esteem (Gross & John, 1997).

LOCATION: Gross, J.J., &, John, O.P. (1997). Revealing feelings: Facets of emotional expressivity in self reports, peer ratings, and behavior. *Journal of Personality and Social Psychology, 72,* 435-44.

COMMENT: Individual differences in emotional expressivity may be measured at a number of levels, ranging from general expressivity to the expressivity of specific emotions such as anger. The Berkeley Expressivity Questionnaire permits valid and reliable assessment of three core facets of emotional expressivity.

REFERENCES:

Gross, J.J., & John, O.P. (1995). Facets of emotional expressivity: Three self report factors and their correlates. *Personality and Individual Differences, 19,* 555-568.

Gross, J.J., & John, O.P. (1997). Revealing feelings: Facets of emotional expressivity in self reports, peer ratings, and behavior. *Journal of Personality and Social Psychology, 72,* 435-448.

Gross, J.J., & John, O.P. (1998). Mapping the domain of emotional expressivity: Multi-method evidence for a hierarchical model. *Journal of Personality and Social Psychology, 74,* 170-191.

Gross, J.J., John, O.P., & Richards, J.M. (2000). The dissociation of emotion expression from emotion experience: A personality perspective. *Personality and Social Psychology Bulletin, 26,* 712-726.

REVIEWER: James J. Gross, Department of Psychology, Stanford University, Stanford, California, 94305 2130, U.S.A.

4.05: BODY SHAPE QUESTIONNAIRE-REVISED-10 (BSQ-R-10), THE.
AUTHOR: Mazzeo.

VARIABLE: Body Image Preoccupation/Concern.

DESCRIPTION: The Body Shape Questionnaire-Revised (BSQ-R-10; Mazzeo, 1999) is a 10-item self-report scale designed to measure body image preoccupation based on the Body Shape Questionnaire (Cooper, Taylor, Cooper, & Fairburn, 1987). Items are rated on a 6-point scale: *Never* (1), *Rarely* (2), *Sometimes* (3), *Often* (4), *Very often* (5), and *always* (6). Higher scores indicate greater body image preoccupation.

SAMPLE: The BSQ-R-10 was developed in a sample of 302 female undergraduates, and cross-validated in another sample of 212 female undergraduates (Mazzeo, 1999). The original BSQ has been used in samples of female patients with bulimia nervosa, females attending a family planning clinic, and female occupational therapy students (Cooper *et al.*, 1987). Bunnell and colleagues (Bunnell, Cooper, Hertz, & Shenker, 1992) used the original BSQ in samples of both eating disordered and non-eating disordered adolescents. The original BSQ has also been used in a sample of obese male dieters (Rosen, Jones, Ramirez, & Waxman, 1996).

RELIABILITY: Internal consistency: The BSQ-R-10 yields internally consistent scores across samples of female undergraduates (Cronbach's alpha coefficient was .96 in two samples Mazzeo, 1999). **Test-retest:** The stability of the BSQ-R-10 has not yet been investigated; however, Rosen *et al.* (1996) reported a test-retest correlation of .88 for the original BSQ in a sample of 33 female undergraduates.

VALIDITY: **Construct Validity:** A confirmatory factor analysis of the BSQ-R-10 supported the proposed one factor model (Mazzeo, 1999). **Criterion Validity:** The BSQ-R-10 demonstrated criterion validity with two measures of disordered eating, the EAT-26 and BULIT-R (Mazzeo, 1999). In addition, correlations between the BSQ-R-10 and measures of disordered eating were found to be significantly stronger than the correlations between measures of body image satisfaction (the Multidimensional Body-Self Relations Questionnaire-Appearance Evaluation Subscale and the Body Esteem Scale) and disordered eating. **Discriminant Validity:** The BSQ-R-10 was found to be only moderately correlated with the Body Esteem Scale Physical Condition subscale (r=-.30) and Sexual Attractiveness subscale (r=-.26; Mazzeo, 1999).

LOCATION: Mazzeo, S.E. (1999). Modification of an existing measure of body image preoccupation and its relationship to disordered eating in female college students. *Journal of Counseling Psychology, 46,* 42-50.

COMMENT: The BSQ-R-10, a modification of the BSQ, is an efficient measure of body image preoccupation that is strongly associated with disordered eating; yields internally consistent scores, and is unidimensional. Future research should investigate its utility with clinical samples.

REFERENCES:

Bunnell, D.W., Cooper, P.J., Hertz, S., & Shenker, I.R. (1992). Body shape concerns among adolescents. *International Journal of Eating Disorders, 11,* 79-83.

Cooper, P.J., Taylor, M.J., Cooper, Z., & Fairburn, C.G. (1987). The Development and validation of the body shape questionnaire. *International Journal of Eating Disorders, 6,* 485-494.

Mazzeo, S.E. (1999). Modification of an existing measure of body image preoccupation and its relationship to disordered eating in female college students. *Journal of Counseling Psychology, 46*, 42-50.

Rosen, J.C., Jones, A., Ramirez, E., & Waxman, S. (1996). Body shape questionnaire: Studies of reliability and validity. *International Journal of Eating Disorders, 20*, 315-319.

REVIEWER: Suzanne E. Mazzeo, University of Illinois at Urbana-Champaign, Department of Educational Psychology, 230 Education Building, 230 S. Sixth Street Champaign, IL 61820, U.S.A. E-mail: mazzeo@students.uiuc.edu

4.06: CENTRAL RELATIONSHIP QUESTIONNAIRE (CRQ), THE.

AUTHORS: Barber, Foltz and Weinryb.

VARIABLE: Central relationship patterns, or people's characteristic ways of relating to significant others in terms of their wishes (Wish), their perceptions of others' responses to them (Response of Other, RO), and their own responses to both of these (Response of Self, RS).

DESCRIPTION: The Central Relationship Questionnaire (CRQ; Barber, Foltz, & Weinryb, 1998) was derived from the clinician-rated Core Conflict Relationship Theme method (Luborsky, 1977; Luborsky & Crits-Christoph, 1990) to measure central relationship patterns, specifically Wishes, ROs and RSs. The CRQ consists of 7 Wish subscales (65 items), 7 RO subscales (51 items) and 8 RS subscales (64 items). Each item is rated on a 7-point scale which is anchored by *Never true or typical of me* (1) and *Always true or typical of me* (7). Participants complete the CRQ in reference to a specific relationship and rate the relationship when it is at its worst.

SAMPLE: The CRQ can be used in both patient and nonpatient samples. It has been used with adolescent and adult samples.

RELIABILITY: Internal consistency: The CRQ subscales were empirically identified from factor analysis and Cronbach's alpha coefficients ranged from .78 to .95 for the 7 Wish subscales (Mdn=.90), .82 to .95 for the 7 RO subscales (Mdn=.88), .71 to .94 for the 8 RS subscales (Mdn=.89). Similar coefficients for the CRQ subscales have been found in subsequent unpublished studies. **Test-retest:** Barber *et al.* (1998) reported average test-retest correlations (rs) of .65 for the Wish subscales, .66 for the ROs and .63 for the RSs among 54 adults over a 1 year period. The test-retest data are consistent with the notion that the construct underlying the CRQ is relatively stable. **Self-observer reports:** 96 Romantic partners evidenced significant self-observer agreement on the CRQ for ROs and RSs, but not for Wishes (Foltz & Barber, 1999, submitted).

VALIDITY: The CRQ demonstrated preliminary convergent and divergent validity with measures of interpersonal problems and symptomatology (Barber *et al.*, 1998). The CRQ broadly discriminated between a group of students and a group of individuals who met DSM diagnostic criteria for psychiatric disorders (Barber *et al.*, 1998). A moderate level of consistency in central relationship patterns across different types of significant others has also been reported (Foltz, Barber, Weinryb, Morse, & Chittams, 1999). The CRQ also discriminated between offspring of Holocaust survivors characterised by different parental communication patterns about Holocaust trauma as well as a control group (Wiseman *et al.*, 1999).

FURTHER EMPIRICAL USES: Researchers are increasingly recognizing the importance of having theoretically relevant outcome measures (*e.g.*, Imber *et al.*, 1990) to adequately test the efficacy of dynamic psychotherapy (*e.g.*, Barber, 1994), where change in maladaptive relationship patterns (and not only symptom reduction) is a primary aim of treatment. The CRQ might also be used as a measure of intrapsychic conflict - a core concept of psychodynamic theory - given that the CRQ, unlike other existing self-report measures of interpersonal patterns, assesses wishes and responses of self and others, and the relationships among those components.

LOCATION: Barber, J.P., Foltz, C., & Weinryb, R.M. (1998). The Central Relationship Questionnaire: Initial report. *Journal of Counseling Psychology, 45*, 131-142.

COMMENT: Although there are some limitations to capturing central relationship patterns by the CRQ, a self-report questionnaire, it could provide both a cost-efficient measure of central relationship patterns and more readily permit clinicians to empirically address questions about psychodynamic theory and therapy.

REFERENCES:

Barber, J.P. (1994). Efficacy of short-term dynamic psychotherapy: Past, present and future. *Journal of Psychotherapy, Practice and Research, 3*, 108-121.

Barber, J.P., Foltz, C., & Weinryb, R.M. (1998). The Central Relationship Questionnaire: Initial report. *Journal of Counseling Psychology, 45*, 131-142.

Foltz, C., & Barber, J.P. (June, 1999). *Self and observer ratings on the Central Relationship Questionnaire: Issues of self-observer agreement and assumed similarity*. Paper presented at the annual meeting of Society for Psychotherapy Research Conference, Braga, Portugal.

Foltz, C., & Barber, J.P. (submitted). Self-observer agreement and projection in central relationship patterns. *Journal of Social and Clinical Psychology*.

Foltz, C., Barber, J. P., Weinryb, R. M., Morse, J.Q., & Chittams, J. (1999). Consistency of themes across interpersonal relationships. *Journal of Social and Clinical Psychology, 18*, 204-222.

Imber, S.D., Pilkonis, P.A., Sotsky. S.M., Elkin, I., Watkins, J.T., Shea, M.T., Glass, D.R., Collins, J.F., & Leber, W.R. (1990). Mode specific effects among three treatments of depression. *Journal of Consulting and Clinical Psychology, 54*, 95-105.

Wiseman, H., Barber, J.P., Raz, A., & Yam, I. (May, 1999). *Parental communication of holocaust experiences and central relationship themes among offspring of holocaust survivors*. Paper presented at the biennial meeting of the Society for Research in Child Development, Albuquerque, New Mexico.

REVIEWERS: Carol Foltz and Jacques P. Barber, Center for Psychotherapy Research, Department of Psychiatry, University of Pennsylvania School of Medicine, Suite 704, 3600 Market Street, Philadelphia, PA 19104-2648, U.S.A.

4. 07: CLOSE PERSONS QUESTIONNAIRE.

AUTHORS: Stansfeld, Marmot and Fuhrer.

VARIABLE: Types of social support.

DESCRIPTION: Self-report scale containing 15 items measuring three types of social support: Confiding/emotional support; Practical support; and Negative aspects of close relationships (formerly negative aspects of support) from up to five sources of support. Sources of support are nominated by the respondent as the closest person and up to four other close persons. Respondents rate the amount of support provided by the close person for each item over the last 12 months on a four point scale from *Not at all* to *A great deal*. Additionally, there are questions measuring social networks drawn from Berkman and Syme including frequency of contact with relatives and friends and social contacts with workmates, membership of and attendance at clubs and social organisations and engagement in voluntary service.

SAMPLE: The scale is intended for use in general population samples.

RELIABILITY: Internal consistency: Cronbach's alpha was .85 for the 7-item confiding/emotional support scale, .82 for the 3-item practical support scale and .63 for the 4-item negative aspects of close relationships scale.

VALIDITY: Construct: Confiding/emotional and practical support scores vary appropriately with frequency and proximity of contact with the source of support. Confiding/emotional support is usually associated with the Rosenberg Self Esteem Scale but not with Eysenck Personality Questionnaire extraversion. Confiding/emotional support and practical support are negatively associated with Eysenck Personality Questionnaire neuroticism. Negative aspects of close relationships are weakly associated with neuroticism on the Eysenck Personality Questionnaire and hostility on the Cook-Medley Hostility Scale. **Criterion:** Validity was tested in 201 middle-aged civil servants against the Self Evaluation and Social Support Interview, a detailed semistructural standardised interview measure of social support (SESS). Confiding/emotional support shows moderate agreement with appropriate scales from the SESS. Practical support agreed well with SESS interview items only in non-married people. There were relatively low correlations between negative aspects of close relationships and negative interaction items from the SESS.

LOCATION: Details of the questionnaire and scoring instructions are available from the reviewer.

COMMENT: The questionnaire has been used in the Whitehall II Study as a predictor of psychiatric disorder and health functioning and is beginning to be used in other studies. Social support from both the closest person alone and from up to four close persons has been used.

REFERENCES:

Fuhrer, R., Stansfeld, S.A., Hudry-Chemali, J., & Shipley, M. (1999). Gender, social relations and mental health: Prospective findings from an occupational cohort (Whitehall II study). *Social Science and Medicine*, 48, 77-87.

Rael, E.G.S., Stansfeld, S.A., Shipley, M., Head, J., Feeney, A., & Marmot, M. (1995). Sickness absence in the Whitehall II study, London: The role of social supports and material problems. *Journal of Epidemiology and Community Health*, 49, 474-481.

Stansfeld, S.A., Bosma, H., Hemingway, H., & Marmot, M.G. (1998). Psychosocial work characteristics and social support as predictors of SF-

36 health functioning: The Whitehall II study. *Psychosomatic Medicine*, *60*, 247-255.

Stansfeld, S.A., Fuhrer, F., & Shipley, M. (1998). Types of social support as predictors of psychiatric morbidity in a cohort of British Civil Servants (Whitehall II study). *Psychological Medicine, 28*, 881-892.

Stansfeld, S.A., Head, J., & Marmot, M.G. (1998). Explaining social class differences in depression and well-being. *Social Psychiatry and Psychiatric Epidemiology, 33*, 1-9.

Stansfeld, S., & Marmot, M. (1992). Deriving a survey measure of social support: the reliability and validity of the Close Persons Questionnaire. *Social Science and Medicine, 35*, 1027-1035.

Stansfeld, S.A., Rael, *E.G.*S., Head, J., Shipley, M., & Marmot, M.G. (1997). Social support and psychiatric sickness absence: A prospective study of British civil servants. *Psychological Medicine, 27*, 35-48.

REVIEWER: Stephen A. Stansfeld, Department of Psychiatry, St. Bartholomew's and the Royal London School of Medicine and Dentistry, BMS Building, Queen Mary & Westfield College, Mile End Road, London E1 4NS, England, U.K. E-mail: S.A.Stansfeld@qmw.ac.uk.

4.08: COLLECTIVISM SCALE
AUTHORS: Kashima, Yamaguchi, Kim, Choi, Gelfand and Yuki.

VARIABLE: Individualistic/collective dimensions of self-construal.

DESCRIPTION: The Collectivism Scale is a modified version of an earlier scale devised by Yamaguchi (1994) to be used in a Japanese context. In addition to the

14 original items, a further 16 items were devised. Items describe situations for which a response can be categorised as supporting either personal or group interests, *e.g.* "I stick with my group even through difficulties". The eventual scale consists of 30 statements, with which respondents agree or disagree using a 5-point Likert scale ranging from *Describes me very well* to *Does not describe me at all*. The original items were in Japanese; later versions have translated these into English and Korean.

SAMPLE: Intended for cross-cultural comparisons of undergraduate respondents. In the Kashima *et al.* study (1995) five separate samples were used, consisting of undergraduates from Australia (*n*=158), the United States (*n*=134), Hawaii (*n*=209), Japan (*n*=256) and Korea (*n*=254).

RELIABILITY: The earlier scale (Yamaguchi, 1994) was administered to a total of 608 Japanese respondents and alpha coefficients ranged from .77 to .88. In a study consisting of Japanese, Korean and US students (Yamaguchi, Kuhlman, & Sugimori, 1995), coefficients ranged from .69 and .72 in the US samples to .77 in the Japanese sample. Again this study only used the 14 original items.

VALIDITY: Convergent: In the Kashima *et al.* (1995) study, factor analysis identified three factors, of which the most highly loaded (12.9%) was termed *collectivism*. Collectivism was found to have significant positive correlations with measures of relatedness, or "Kanjin-shugi" (translated literally as "between-people-ism"; Hamaguchi, 1987); a measure of friendship group cohesion (Knoke & Kulinski, 1982); allocentrism, a construct related to, though not identical to, collectivism (Triandis, McCusker, Betancourt, Iwao, Leung, Salazar, Setiada, Sinha, Touzard, & Zaleski, 1993); and an original measure of self-other similarity. Discriminant: Kashima *et al.* (1995) found that Korean and Japanese respondents achieved significantly higher collectivism scores than Australian and US respondents (F=13.5, p<.005). Using the 14 original scale items, Yamaguchi *et al.* (1995) found that only the Korean sample achieved a significantly higher score than Japanese and US samples (F=17.4, p<.0001), but that a within-sample comparison of Asian American and Caucasian American undergraduates found higher scores among Asian Americans (F=5.4, p<.03). However, since the latter group comprised only 19 respondents, the effect is likely to be very small.

LOCATION: Kashima, Y., Yamaguchi, S., Kim, U., Choi, S., Gelfand, M. J., & Yuki, M. (1995). Culture, gender and self: A perspective from individualism-collectivism research. *Journal of Personality and Social Psychology*, *69*, 925-937.

COMMENT: There is still considerable confusion in the field of cultural psychology over what is the best way to conceptualise self-construal from a cultural perspective. Collectivism is essentially a socio-economic phenomenon; the relation between this and individual social cognition is obviously a matter of conjecture. Singelis (1994) argues that independence and interdependence can be treated as separate self-construals that operate independently within an individual's set of cognitions at any given time; Triandis *et al.*'s (1993) idiocentrism/allocentrism scale works from similar assumptions. As yet no-one has successfully knitted all these approaches together into a single psychometric instrument. Whether this is possible, or even desirable, remains to be seen.

REFERENCES:

Hamaguchi, E. (1987). *Nihonjin no kihonteki kachikan ni kansuru jikken-chosa kenkyu.* (Experimental and survey research on the Japanese basic value). Unpublished manuscript, Osaka University.

Kashima, Y.,Yamaguchi, S., Kim, U., Choi, S., Gelfand, M. J., & Yuki, M. (1995). Culture, gender and self: A perspective from individualism-collectivism research. *Journal of Personality and Social Psychology*, *69*, 925-937.

Knoke, D., & Kulinksi, J.H. (1982). *Network Analysis*. Newbury Park, CA: Sage.

Singelis, T.M. (1994). The measurement of independent and interdependent self-construals. *Personality and Social Psychology Bulletin*, *20*, 580-591.

Triandis, H.C., McCusker, C., Betancourt, H., Iwao, S., Leung, K., Salazar, J.M., Setiada, B., Sinha, J.B.P., Touzard, H., & Zaleski, Z. (1993). An etic-emic analysis of individualism-collectivism. *Journal of Cross-Cultural Psychology*, *24*, 366-383.

Yamaguchi, S. (1994). Collectivism among the Japanese: A perspective from the self. In U. Kim, H.C. Triandis, C. Kagitcibasi, S.C. Choi, & G.Yoon (Eds.) *Individualism and Collectivism* (pp. 175-188). Newbury Park, CA: Sage.

Yamaguchi, S., Kuhlman, D.M., & Sugimori, S. (1995). Personality correlates ofallocentric tendencies in individualist and collectivist cultures. *Journal of Cross-Cultural Psychology*, *26*, 658-672.

REVIEWER: David Giles, Department of Psychology, Coventry University, Coventry, CV1 5FB, England, U.K.

4.09: COMMUNITY ORGANIZATION SENSE OF COMMUNITY SCALE (COSOC), THE.

AUTHORS: Hughey, Speer, and Peterson.

VARIABLE: Sense of community in community organisations.

DESCRIPTION: The Community Organization Sense of Community scale (COSOC; Hughey, Speer, & Peterson, 1999) consists of 15 items. The scale is designed to measure different facets of sense of community across four domains: 1) Relationship to the Organization; 2) Organization as Mediator; 3) Influence of the Community Organization; and 4) Bond to the Community. Respondents are asked about their perceptions of the community Organization in which they are involved. Items are rated on a 5-point Likert-type scale: *Strongly agree* (1), *Agree* (2), *Unsure* (3), *Disagree* (4), *Strongly disagree* (5). Seven items are reverse scored. Lower scores on the scale indicate a stronger sense of community. Civic organisations, religious congregations, political groups, policy organisations, environmental organisations, feminist organisations, professional organisations and the like are appropriate for the instrument.

SAMPLE: Hughey, Speer, and Peterson (1999) intended the scale to be used with participants in a variety of community organisations. This instrument is best used with community organisations that have some contact with other community entities. Thus, social support groups and the like would not be appropriate target groups for the instrument.

RELIABILITY: Internal consistency: Item-total correlations indicate that the COSOC scale demonstrated satisfactory levels of internal reliability (Hughey, Speer, & Peterson, 1999). Cronbach's alphas of .82, .86, and .87 were detected.

VALIDITY: Convergent: demonstrated satisfactory convergent validity with two other measures of psychological sense of community - the Sense of Community Index (McMillan & Chavis, 1986), and the Sense of Community Scale (Bachrach & Zautra, 1985). The instrument also exhibited appropriate correlation with community involvement (Rothenbuhler, 1991) and political participation (Davidson & Cotter, 1989).

LOCATION: Hughey, J., Speer, P., & Peterson, A. (1999). Sense of community in community organizations: Structure and evidence of validity. *Journal of Community Psychology, 27,* 97-113.

COMMENT: The proposed framework for sense of community in community organizations was refined and generally supported across multiple community samples (Hughey, Speer, & Peterson, 1999), involving about 1700 community participants. The patterns of relationship among the dimensions of the COSOC and other measures of sense of community as well as related variables provided strong evidence for validity of the measure. Although it was not initially clear how many factors would consistently emerge, replication of findings on multiple samples supports the conclusion that three or four factors can sufficiently encompass the concept for community organizations. Perhaps owing to the context of community organizations, the use of a measure that employs multiple referents is recommended by these findings. Depending on context, users of the scale should probably use the three factor solution that folds together Relationship to Organization with Influence of the Organization into a 5-item scale. Two other scales are: Organization as Mediator and Bond to the Community (3 items).

REFERENCES:

Hughey, J., Speer, P., & Peterson, A. (1999). Sense of community in community organizations: Structure and evidence of validity. *Journal of Community Psychology, 27,* 97-113.

Bachrach, R.M., & Zautra, A.J. (1985). Coping with a community stressor: The threat of a hazardous waste facility. *Journal of Health and Social Behavior, 26,* 127-141.

Davidson, W.B., & Cotter, P. (1989). Sense of community and political participation. *Journal of Community Psychology, 17,* 119-125.

McMillan, D.W., & Chavis, D.M. (1986). Sense of community: A definition and theory. *Journal of Community Psychology, 14,* 6-23.

Rothenbuhler, E.W. (1991). The process of community involvement. *Communication Monograph, 58,* 63-78.

REVIEWER: J. Hughey, College of Arts and Sciences, University of Missouri, Kansas City, Kansas City, Missouri 64110, U.S.A.

4.10: COUPLES CRITICAL INCIDENTS CHECK LIST (CCICL).

AUTHORS: Piedmont and Piedmont.

VARIABLE: A wide range of interpersonal issues .

DESCRIPTION: The Couples Critical Incidents Check List (CCICL; Piedmont & Piedmont, 1996) contains 133-items, designed to assess the extent and type of dissatisfaction an individual is experiencing with one's spouse. One-item scale assesses person's global level of dissatisfaction within the current relationship, ranging from (1) *Very little or no dissatisfaction* to (7) *Extreme dissatisfaction or very unhappy.* The CCICL items reflect problems that are linked to motivational dynamics from the five-factor model of personality. The CCICL assesses 6 aspects of interpersonal conflicts that an individual may be experiencing with his or her spouse. Namely, the area of: *Emotional* (24 items) assessing difficulties linked to neuroticism scores, *Interpersonal* (25 items), is a category that reveals marital issues connected to extraversion, *Flexibility* (22 items), is a facet dealing with issues which are associated with the facet of openness, *Cooperativeness* (26 items), captures issues which relate to agreeableness, *Personality reliability* (19 items), is linked with the dimension of conscientiousness, and *Miscellaneous* (12 items), contain behaviors that could not be unambiguously classified in one of the previously listed categories, but represent salient issues that warrant their being included.

SAMPLE: Kosek (1996) intended the scale to be used in marriage counseling settings.

VALIDITY: Discriminant: The correlations between the self-reports for both genders between the scores of their self-reports on the five-factor model (FFM) and their respective rating on the CCICL showed patterns of insignificant correlations indicated that the manner in which the spouses rated their partners on specific problem behaviors on the CCICL was independent from their own self-reported personality (Kosek, 1996). **Convergent:** The correlations between the scores of the spousal self-reports on the FFM of personality and the kind of marital issues identified on each of the five sections of the CCICL, which lists particular areas of conflict that the rater experiences with the spouse, were highly significant for both genders. The correlations ranged from .50 to .20 for women and for .47 to .22 for men (Kosek, 1998).

LOCATION: Piedmont, R.L., & Piedmont, R.I (1996). *Couples Critical Incidents Check List, Manual.* Baltimore: Author.

COMMENT: Despite the CCICL's great attribute for assessment of interpersonal issues, the tabulation of the scores may become a cumbersome task. For example, to obtain a total score for the EMOTIONAL category, items describing high Neurotic characteristics, (*e.g.*, one who "never shows weakness" or is "too calm") were subtracted from items describing low neurotic characteristics, (*e.g.*, one who whines or "falls apart under stress").

REFERENCES:

Kosek, R.B. (1998). Couples Critical Incidents Checklist. *Journal of Clinical Psychology, 54,* 785-794.

Piedmont, R.L. (1999). *The Revised NEO Personality Inventory: Clinical and Research Applications.* New York: Plenum Press.

Piedmont, R.L., & Piedmont, R.I (1996). *Couples Critical Incidents Check List, Manual.* Baltimore: Author.

REVIEWER: Robert B. Kosek, St. John's Healing Center, 45 Victoria Road N Guelph, ON N1E 5G9, Canada

4.11: DIFFERENTIATION OF SELF INVENTORY, THE.
AUTHORS: Skowron and Friedlander.

VARIABLES: Emotional reactivity, emotional cutoff, 'I' position and fusion with others.

DESCRIPTION: The Differentiation of Self Inventory (DSI; Skowron & Friedlander, 1998) consist of 43 item designed to measure the four factors of the adults self-differentiation. 'Emotional Reactivity' measuring of intrapsychic or emotional reaction to interpersonal conditions, 'Emotional Cutoff' indicative of ongoing problematical interpersonal relations outside as well as within one's family of origin, 'I Position', indicative of Bowen's (1978) concept of self and of one's convictions, and 'Fusion with Others' indicative of extreme emotional attachment, and projection of parental values. Responses are rated from 1 (*Not at all true of me*) to 6 (*Very true of me*), with the higher scores reflecting greater differentiation.

SAMPLE: Skowron and Friedlander (1998) foresee the scale to be utilised in family therapy.

RELIABILITY: Internal Reliability: Kosek (1998) and Skowron and Friedlander (1998) demonstrated satisfactory internal reliability for the entire DSI (.88) and for the four subscales ranging from .70 to .88. **Internal consistency:** The four factor analysis of the scale demonstrated a good fit (Skowron & Friedlander, 1998).

VALIDITY: Convergent: The DSI demonstrated a high convergent validity with various measures of feelings of distress, performance difficulties, somatic distress (Skowron, 1995; Tuason & Friedlander, 2000). **Discriminant:** The validity of the

DSI is also supported by its discriminatory powers in distinguishing individuals enjoying greater marital satisfaction from the dissatisfied ones (Skowron & Friedlader, 1998).

LOCATION: Skowron, E.A., & Friedlader, M.L. (1998). The Differentiation of Self Inventory: Development and initial validation. *Journal of Counseling Psychology, 45,* 235-246.

COMMENT: The DSI is a successful empirical attempt to measure Bowen's (1978) self differentiation constructs. Since the scale does not account for gender differences, the clinician must be cautious in interpreting the results (Kosek, 1998).

REFERENCES:

Bowen, M. (1978). *Family Therapy in Clinical Practice.* New York: Jason Aronson.

Kosek, R.B. (1998). Self-Differentiation within couples. *Psychological Reports, 83,* 275-279.

Tuason, M.T., & Friedlander, M.L. (2000). Do parents' differentiation levels predict those of their adult children. *Journal of Counseling Psychology, 47,* 27-35.

Skowron, E.A. (1995). *Using differentiation of self to predict psychological adjustment and marital satisfaction.* Unpublished doctoral dissertation, State University of New York, Albany, NY.

Skowron, E.A., & Friedlader, M.L. (1998). The Differentiation of Self Inventory: Development and initial validation. *Journal of Counseling Psychology, 45,* 235-246.

REVIEWER: Robert B. Kosek, St. John's Healing Center, 45 Victoria Road N, Guelph, ON, N1E 5G9, Canada.

4.12: DIMENSIONS OF COMMITMENT INVENTORY, THE.

AUTHORS: Adams and Jones.

VARIABLE: Three dimensions of interpersonal commitment.

DESCRIPTION: The Dimensions of Commitment Inventory (DCI; Adams & Jones, 1997) measures three underlying dimensions of interpersonal commitment: Commitment to Spouse (commitment based on personal dedication and devotion to one's spouse), Commitment to Marriage (commitment based on one's feelings of moral responsibility), and Feelings of Entrapment (commitment based on the perception of barriers that make leaving the relationship difficult). The DCI consists of 45 items that are divided into three subscales with 15 items each. Responses are scored on a 5-point scale ranging from 1 (*Strongly disagree*) to 5 (*Strongly agree*).

SAMPLES: The DCI was designed for use in research on the relationships of married couples; however, it also may be used in clinical settings as a diagnostic tool.

RELIABILITY: **Internal consistency:** The three subscales of the DCI have demonstrated high internal consistency in several studies. Values of coefficient alpha for Commitment to Spouse, Commitment to Marriage, and Feelings of Entrapment range from .84 to .91, .84 to .89, and .81 to .86, respectively (Adams, 1994; Adams & Jones, 1997; Adams & Marsil, 1995). **Test-retest:** Adams (1994) reported six-month test-retest correlations of .23, .84, and .73 for Commitment to Spouse, Commitment to Marriage, and Feelings of Entrapment, respectively, among 439 married individuals.

VALIDITY: **Convergent:** Adams and Jones (1997) reported extensive validity data on the DCI. The Commitment to Spouse subscale is positively related to marital adjustment, love, marital goal orientation, primacy of the relationship, and other measures of personal commitment; the Commitment to Marriage subscale is positively related to measures of moral standards, intrinsic religiosity, and church attendance; and the Feelings of Entrapment subscale is positively related to emotional reliance on others, lack of self confidence, and social pressure to remain married. **Discriminant:** Commitment to Spouse is inversely related to loneliness, guilt, shyness, and marital instability; Commitment to Marriage is inversely related to the number of times married; and Feelings of Entrapment are inversely related to the tendency to make commitments (Adams & Jones, 1997). **Other validity evidence:** As reported by Adams and Jones (1997), the three subscales of the DCI discriminate among couples at different stages of relationship development (dating, engaged, married, divorced), and show a stable factor structure across samples.

LOCATION: Adams, J.M., & Jones, W.H. (1997). The conceptualization of marital commitment: An integrative analysis. *Journal of Personality and Social Psychology, 72,* 1177-1196.

COMMENT: The structure of the DCI is consistent with various theoretical models of interpersonal commitment and is the only measure of interpersonal commitment to be thoroughly validated. The DCI has been translated into several languages (including Spanish, Portuguese, Afrikaans, French, and Punjabi) and may be used in cross-cultural research.

REFERENCES:

Adams, J.M. (1994, August). *The psychometric assessment of marital commitment: A comparison of definitions.* Paper presented at the annual meeting of the American Psychological Association, Los Angeles, CA.

Adams, J.M., & Marsil, D.F. (1995, August). *Attachment style as a predictor of marital commitment.* Paper presented at the annual meeting of the American Psychological Association, New York, NY.

Adams, J.M., & Jones, W.H. (1997). The conceptualization of marital commitment: An integrative analysis. *Journal of Personality and Social Psychology, 72,* 1177-1196.

REVIEWER: Jeffrey M. Adams, Department of Behavioral Sciences, High Point University, High Point, North Carolina, NC 27262, U.S.A.

4.13: FAMILY ALLOCENTRISM SCALE.

AUTHORS: Lay, Fairlie, Jackson, Ricci, Eisenberg, Sato, and Melamud.

VARIABLE: Family Allocentrism.

DESCRIPTION: The Family Allocentrism Scale is designed to measure an individual's connectedness to his or her family. Family allocentrism (-

idiocentrism) is a within culture individual difference variable equivalent to the cross-cultural construct of individualism-collectivism (Hofstede, 1980; Triandis, 1995). The Family Allocentrism Scale is a self-report scale which contains 21 items representing a mix of cognitive and emotional experiences. Eight of the items are emotionally oriented while 13 of the items are cognitively oriented. Six items are reverse keyed. Respondents are asked to indicate the extent to which they agree to each of the items on a 5-point scale from *Strongly disagree* (1) to *Strongly agree* (5). Total scores can range from 21 to 105. Higher scores indicate high family allocentrism and lower scores indicate high family idiocentrism.

SAMPLE: Primarily constructed and validated with undergraduate university student samples but has been found to be reliable with non-student adult samples (17-45 years) as well (Lay *et al.*, 1998).

RELIABILITY: **Internal consistency:** Good internal consistency values have been obtained in numerous studies with alpha coefficients ranging from .73 to .85 (Lay *et al.*, 1998; Sato, 1999a,b).

VALIDITY: **Convergent:** It demonstrated satisfactory convergent validity with identity style, ethnic identity, & acculturation in Canada (Lay *et al.*, 1998). **Discriminant:** It demonstrated satisfactory discriminant validity from self-deceptive enhancement and impression management (Paulhus, 1991) and from allocentrism with classmates and friends (Lay *et al.*, 1998).

LOCATION: Lay, C., Fairlie, P., Jackson, S., Ricci, T., Eisenberg, J., Sato, T.A., & Melamud, A. (1998). Domain-specific allocentrism-idiocentrism: A measure of family connectedness. *Journal of Cross-Cultural Psychology*, *29*, 434-460.

COMMENT: Due to the recency of its scale construction, little work using this scale has been published. There is growing evidence, however, for the satisfactory psychometric properties of the Family Allocentrism Scale. It's relationships with other prominent cross-cultural constructs need to be further examined.

REFERENCES:

Hofstede, G.H. (1980). *Culture's Consequences: International Differences in Work-Related Values*. Beverly Hills: Sage Publications.

Lay, C., Fairlie, P., Jackson, S., Ricci, T., Eisenberg, J., Sato, T.A., & Melamud, A. (1998). Domain-specific allocentrism-idiocentrism: A measure of family connectedness. *Journal of Cross-Cultural Psychology, 29,* 434-460.

Paulhus, D.L. (1991). Measurement and control of response bias. In J.P. Robinson, P.R. Shaver, & L.S. Wrightsman (Eds.), *Measures of Personality and Social Psychological Attitudes* (pp. 17-59). New York: Academic Press.

Sato, T. (1999a). *Family allocentrism and its relationship with measures of other cross-cultural constructs*. Manuscript in preparation.

Sato T. (1999b). *Family allocentrism and its relationship with interpersonal schemata*. Manuscript in preparation.

Triandis, H.C. (1995). *Individualism and Collectivism*. Boulder: Westview Press.

REVIEWER: Toru Sato, Dept. of Psychology, 601-I Ginger Hall, Morehead State University, Morehead, Kentucky 40351-1689, U.S.A.

4.14: GENDER IDENTITY QUESTIONNAIRE, THE.

AUTHORS: Willemsen and Fischer.

VARIABLE: Gender identity, femininity, masculinity.

DESCRIPTION: Self-report scale, consisting of 30 personality traits and 28 items related to behaviours and preferences in the areas of social relations, leisure time, the expression of emotions and gender roles. The questionnaire consists of two scales, Femininity and Masculinity, and comprises four subscales, called Feminine traits (FT, 15 items), Masculine traits (MT, 15 items), Feminine behaviours (FB, 14 items) and Masculine behaviours (MB, 14 items). The personality traits are presented first, in alphabetical order. Responses are given on a 5-point scale, ranging from [I am] *not*, which is scored as 1, and [I am] *very*, which is scored as 5, with the answers in between scored as 2, 3 and 4 respectively. The next 28 questions (14 FB, 14 MB) are presented in a fixed order. Each question has five responses, also scored from 1 to 5. Higher scores reflect stronger Femininity and Masculinity respectively. Subscale scores are expressed as an average of the item scores.

SAMPLE: The scale was developed for use in normal, adult populations.

RELIABILITY: Internal consistency: Willemsen and Fischer (1997, 1999) report the following values for Cronbach's alpha, based on a representative sample of 314 male and 451 female respondents: Feminine traits .71; Feminine behaviours .69; Femininity .80; Masculine traits .69; Masculine behaviours .67; Masculinity .78. Severiens and Ten Dam (1997) report values of .76 for Femininity and .80 for Masculinity. **Test-retest:** No test-retest correlations are available. However, in studies by Van Goozen, Cohen-Kettenis, Gooren, Frijda, and Van de Poll (1995) and by Slabbekoorn, Van Goozen, Gooren, and Cohen-Kettenis (1999), who studied samples of transsexuals before and after 3 months of cross-sex hormone treatment, no test-retest differences were found on any of the subscale scores for any of the groups tested (the Van Goozen *et al.*, 1995 study included control groups of normal adults, with the same time lag between the two administrations of the questionnaire). This demonstrates stability of the scores.

VALIDITY: Construct: The M and F scales are independent ($r=-.07$, n.s.). Women score higher on Feminine traits and Feminine behaviours than men, and men score higher on Masculine traits and Masculine behaviours than women (Severiens & Ten Dam, 1997; Willemsen & Fischer, 1999). For women, Masculinity scores correlate negatively with participation in household tasks and positively with hours of paid work; for men, higher Femininity scores correlate positively with participation in household tasks (Willemsen & Fischer, 1999). In a separate study, reported in Willemsen and Fischer (1997), in which the GIQ was administered together with (a Dutch translation of) the BSRI (Bem, 1974), that consists only of personality traits, correlation between BSRI-Femininity and GIQ-FT was .62, between BSRI-Masculinity and GIQ-MT .67.

LOCATION: Both the original test, in Dutch, and translations in English, German or French are available from Willemsen at Tilburg University (address at the end of the review).

COMMENT: The scale measures stereotypic masculinity and femininity. The traits and behaviours of the scale are all gender stereotypical, as was determined in pretests. At present, only results for Dutch samples are available. In the Netherlands, the questionnaire gives satisfactory results. It is to be expected that also in other countries this test, in its present form or adapted to the cultural context, can be a useful alternative for gender identity or sex role scales that are only based on personality traits or that are outdated.

REFERENCES:

Bem, S.L. (1974). The measurement of psychological androgyny. *Journal of Consulting and Clinical Psychology, 42*, 155-162.

Severiens, S., & Ten Dam, G. (1997). Gender and gender identity differences in learning styles. *Educational Psychology, 17*, 79-93.

Slabbekoorn, D., Van Goozen, S.H.M., Gooren, L.J.G., & Cohen-Kettenis, P.T. (1999). *Effects of cross-sex hormone treatment on emotionality in transsexuals.* Manuscript submitted for publication.

Van Goozen, S.H.M., Cohen-Kettenis, P.T., Gooren, L.J.G., Frijda, N.H., & Van de Poll, N.E. (1995). Gender differences in behaviour: Activating effects of cross-sex hormones. *Psychoneuroendocrinology, 20*, 343-363.

Willemsen, T.M., & Fischer, A.H. (1997). De Nederlandse Sekse-Identiteit Vragenlijst (NSIV) (The Dutch Gender Identity Questionnaire. [NSIV]). *Nederlands Tijdschrift voor de Psychologie, 52*, 126-130.

Willemsen, T.M., & Fischer, A.H. (1999). Assessing multiple facets of gender identity: The Gender Identity Questionnaire. *Psychological Reports, 84*, 561-562.

REVIEWER: Tineke M. Willemsen, Department of Women's Studies, Tilburg University, P.O. Box 90153, 5000, LE Tilburg, The Netherlands. E-mail t.m.willemsen@kub.nl

4.15: GENDER ROLE JOURNEY MEASURE (GRJM).
AUTHORS: O'Neil, Egan, Owen, and Murry McBride.

VARIABLE: Phases of the Gender Role Journey (Acceptance of Traditional Gender Roles; Gender Role Ambivalence, Confusion, Anger, and Fear; Personal-Professional Activism).

DESCRIPTION: The Gender Role Journey Measure (GRJM) is a self-report scale consisting of 34 items that assesses the phases of men's and women's gender role journeys. The scale consists of three subscales representing the following phases of the gender role journey: Acceptance of Traditional Gender Roles (10 items); Gender Role Ambivalence, Confusion, Anger, and Fear (11 items); Personal-Professional Activism (13 items). Six items are reversed scored and respondents are asked to assess the degree that they endorse the different gender role journey phases using a 6-point Likert-type scale (*Strongly agree* to *Strongly disagree*) A high score on any of the subscales reflects endorsement of one of the phases of the gender role journey.

SAMPLE: O'Neil, Egan, Owen, and Murry McBride (1993) have normed the GRJM to be used with both males and female students and adults.

RELIABILITY: **Internal consistency:** Reliabilities for the three factors have been calculated in two studies (O'Neil *et al.*, 1993; Kaplan, 1992). The alphas for the three factors were Acceptance of Traditional Gender Roles (.87 and .84), Gender Role Ambivalence, Confusion, Anger, and Fear (.76 and .72), and Personal-Professional Activism (.89 and .81). **Test-retest:** Reliabilities for the three factors include Acceptance of Traditional Gender Roles (.75), Gender Role Ambivalence, Confusion, Anger, Fear (.53), Personal-professional Activism (.77) (O'Neil *et al.*, 1993).

VALIDITY: The validity of the GRJM's three subscales was established through a exploratory principal factor analysis (O'Neil *et al.*, 1993). The results indicated that: 76% of the variance was explained; all factor loadings exceeded .35; and all loadings did not cross load on any other factor. Two studies have shown that educational interventions can change students' phase of the gender role journey (Egan, 1992; Gertner, 1994). Sex differences on the subscales has been found in three studies (O'Neil *et al.*, 1993; Plante, 1998; Sweet, 1995). Rynkiewicz (1998) found one phase of the gender role journey significantly predicted more positive views and satisfaction with a female dominated graduate program. Different phases of the gender role journey have been significantly correlated with men's gender role conflict, hypermasculinity, hostility toward women, sexually aggressive experiences, and likelihood of forcing sex (Kaplan, 1992; Kaplan, O'Neil, & Owen, 1993). For adult women, the different phases of the gender role journey have been significantly correlated with positive and negative affect, depression, religious well being, and emotional distress (Mock, 1995). O'Neil *et al.* (1993) also found significant interactions of sex and gender role orientation on two of the gender role journey subscales.

LOCATION: O'Neil, J.M., Egan, J., Owen, S.V., & Murry McBride, V. (1993). The gender role journey measure: Scale development and psychometric evaluation. *Sex Roles, 28,* 167-185. Also see O'Neil (1998) for the gender role conflict and gender role journey research program.

COMMENT: The initial theory on the gender role journey concepts (O'Neil & Egan, 1992a,b) have been given some empirical support through GRJM. Although more psychometric work needs to be completed on the GRJM, the initial results are promising in assessing men's and women's gender role journeys. The data gathered give further support for the practical application of the gender role journey concept in educational interventions (Egan, 1992; Goldberg &

O'Neil, 1997; O'Neil, 1995; O'Neil & Roberts Carroll, 1988a,b) and for helping men and women understand each other (Philpot, Brooks, Lusterman, & Nutt, 1997).

REFERENCES:

Egan, J. (1992). Gender role development as a function of transition coping skills. (Doctoral dissertation, University of Connecticut). *Dissertation Abstracts International, 54/01*, 59.

Gertner, D.M. (1994). Learning men: Effects of a semester academic course in men's studies on gender role conflict and gender role journey of male participants. (Doctoral dissertation, University of Northern Colorado). *Dissertation Abstracts International, 55/01*, 0046.

Goldberg, J.L., & O'Neil, J.M. (1997). Marilyn Monroe's gender role journey: Promoting women's development. *Journal of College Student Development, 38*, 543-545.

Kaplan, R. (1992). Normative masculinity and sexual aggression among college males. (Doctoral dissertation, University of Connecticut). *Dissertation Abstracts International, 53/08*, 3005.

Kaplan, R. O'Neil, J.M., & Owen, S.V. (1993, August). Sexist, normative, and progressive masculinity and sexual assault: Empirical research. In J.M. O'Neil (Chair) *Research on Men's Sexual Assault and Constructive Gender Role Interventions.* Symposium conducted at the American Psychological Association Toronto, Canada.

Mock, J.F. (1995). Influence of gender role journey and balance of power in the marital relationship, on the emotional and spiritual well-being of mid-life married women. (Doctoral dissertation, Loyola College in Maryland). *Dissertation Abstracts International, 56/05*, 2002.

O'Neil, J.M. (1995). The gender role journey workshop: Exploring sexism and gender role conflict in a coeducational setting. In M. Andronico (Ed.)

Men in Groups: *Insights, Interventions, Psychoeducational Work.* Washington, D.C.: APA Books.

O'Neil, J.M. (1998). Gender role conflict and gender role journey research program (1978-present) [on line]. School of Family Studies, University of Connecticut, Storrs, CT, U.S.A. Available: www.familystudies.uconn.edu/oneil.htm

O'Neil, J.M., & Egan, J. (1992a). Men and women's gender role journies: A metaphor for healing, transition, and transformation. In B. Wainrib (Ed.) *Gender Issues across the Life Cycle.* New York: Springer Publishing Company.

O'Neil, J.M., & Egan, J. (1992b). Men's gender role transitions over the lifespan: Transformation and fears of femininity. *Journal of Mental Health Counseling, 14,* 306-324.

O'Neil, J.M., Egan, J., Owen, S.V., & Murry McBride, V. (1993). The gender role journey measure (GRJM): Scale development and psychometric evaluations. *Sex Roles, 28, 167-185.*

O'Neil, J.M., & Roberts Carroll, M. (1988a). A gender role workshop focused on sexism, gender role conflict, and the gender role journey. *Journal of Counseling and Development, 67, 193-197.*

O'Neil, J.M., & Roberts Carroll, M. (1988b, September). *Evaluation of gender role workshop: Three years of follow-up data.* Paper presented at the 95th annual convention of the American Psychological Association, New York, New York (ERIC Document Reproduction Service No. ED020250).

Philpot, C.L., Brooks, G. R., Lusterman, D., & Nutt, R.L. (1997). *Bridging Separate Gender Worlds: Why Men and Women Cash and How Therapists Can Bring Them Together.* Washington, D.C.: American Psychological Association Press.

Plante, J.M. (1998). *Gender role stereotypes and expectations for gender role stereotypic strategies for depression. A senior comprehensive project.* Department of Psychology, Allegheny College, Meadville, PA.

Rynkiewicz, D.J. (1998). *Males' satisfaction with a female-dominated graduate program as a function of gender role journey.* (Master thesis, Immaculata College). Psychology Department, Immaculata, Pennsylvania.

Sweet, H.B. (1995). Perception of undergraduate male experiences in heterosexual romantic relationships: A sex role norm analysis. (Doctoral dissertation, Boston College). *Dissertation Abstracts International, 57/01,* 767.

REVIEWER: James M. O'Neil, School of Family Studies, Box U-58, 348 Mansfield Road, University of Connecticut, Storrs, CT., U.S.A. 06269-2058. E-mail: oneil@uconnvm.uconn.edu

4.16: INFORMAL PEERGROUPS IN ADOLESCENCE, A GROUP-CULTURE MEASUREMENT SCALE FOR.
AUTHOR: Busch.

VARIABLE: Group culture.

DESCRIPTION: A self-report scale consisting of 7 items that represent the following aspects of social climate in informal adolescent peergroups: hierarchical structure; group pressure and emphasis on group solidarity; quality of group boundaries; provocative and risky group activities. Respondents are asked if statements about group-culture are true for their peer-group. They can rate each item on a 4-point scale: (1) *Clearly not true*; (2) *Kind of not true*; (3) *Kind of true*; (4) *Absolutely true*.

SAMPLE: The scale was developed as a part of an extensive questionnaire, covering multiple aspects concerned with aggressive behavior in schools. During a longitudinal study (1994 to 1996) it was presented once a year to 1600-1800 pupils grade 5 to 9 from three comprehensive schools in a rural area in Germany.

RELIABILITY: Internal consistency: The scale demonstrated a fairly good internal consistency. For each of the three measurement points an internal consistency of Cronbach's α=.79 was found.

VALIDITY: Substantial correlations with physical aggression, verbal aggression, indirect aggression, vandalism and anti-democratic political orientation were found as proposed (Busch, 1998a,b).

LOCATION: Busch, L. (1998). Gruppenkultur als Indikator für eine deviante Orientierung von Cliquen im Jugendalter: Entwicklung einer Skala zur Erfassung der Gruppenkultur. *Gruppendynamik, 29*, 421-432.

COMMENT: The results show that the scale is measuring an important aspect of peergroups in adolescence in a very economic way. It can be used as a part of more extensive questionnaires, concerned with research on various aspects of youth and adolescence.

REFERENCES:

Busch, L. (1998a). Gruppenkultur als Indikator für eine deviante Orientierung von Cliquen im Jugendalter: Entwicklung einer Skala zur Erfassung der Gruppenkultur. *Gruppendynamik, 29*, 421-432.

Busch, L. (1998b). *Aggression in der Schule*: *Präventionsorientierte und differentielle Analyse von Bedingungsfaktoren aggressiven Schülerverhaltens*. Wettenberg: Selbstverlag.

Busch, L. (in press). Jugendcliquen und aggressives Verhalten in der Schule: Die Bedeutung der Gruppenkultur. *Empirische Pädagogik*

REVIEWER: L. Busch, Staatl Schulamt Hochtaunus & Wetteraukreis Schulpsycholog, Diemt, Mainzer-Tor-Anlage, D-1169, Friedberg, Germany.

4.17: INTERPERSONAL BETRAYAL SCALE.
AUTHORS: Jones and Burdette.

VARIABLE: Tendency to betray relationship partners (*i.e.*, to violate the expectations, trust, and commitment of close personal relationships).

DESCRIPTION: The Interpersonal Betrayal Scale (IBS) is a 15-item self-report scale designed to determine the relative frequency with which an individual undermines his/her relationship partners through commonplace types of interpersonal transgression and harm-doing (*e.g.*, gossiping, lying, cheating, ignoring, avoiding, betraying a confidence, etc.). Responses are rendered on a 5-point Likert-type scale verbally anchored as follows: 1=*I have never done this*; 2=*I have done this once*; 3=*I have done this a few times*; 4=*I have done this several times*; 5=*I have done this many times*. Scores may vary from 15 to 75 with higher scores reflecting more frequent betrayals of relationship partners.

SAMPLE: Jones and Burdette (1994) reported analyses involving over 1,000 adult respondents. In order to study betrayal and related constructs, the IBS was administered across several studies to various sample populations, including college students (Couch & Jones, 1997), the elderly (Hansson, Jones, & Fletcher, 1990), and both institutionalised and 'normal' children and adolescents (Jones, Cohn, & Miller, 1991).

RELIABILITY: **Internal consistency:** Estimates of internal consistency (coefficient alpha) for IBS scores have varied from .87 to .89.

VALIDITY: **Convergent:** The IBS significantly predict alternative procedures for measuring betrayal. Specifically, scores on IBS significantly relate to assessments of moral standards, self-control, well-being, responsibility, and tolerance, and to self-selected adjective self-descriptions including envious, cynical, exploitative, jealous, suspicious, and gossipy. Furthermore, scores on the IBS inversely correlate with paranoid, histrionic, and passive-aggressive personality disorder dimensions and with self-selected adjective self-descriptors such as trusting, courageous, and truthful. **Discriminant:** There is evidence that IBS scores do not simply reduce to delinquency or moral standards.

LOCATION: Jones, W.H., & Burdette, M.P. (1994). Betrayal in close relationships. In A.L. Weber, & J. Harvey (Eds.). *Perspectives on Close Relationships* (pp. 243-263). Boston: Allyn and Bacon.

COMMENT: The IBS appears to be a useful means of operationalising the self-reported tendency to betray relationship partners. Subsequent to its publication, a companion scale with 15 items was developed to assess the self-report of having been betrayed by relationship partners using the same items with the perspective reversed. These items are available from the author.

REFERENCES:

Hansson, R.O., Jones, W.H., & Fletcher, W.L. (1990). Troubled relationships in later life: Implications for support. *Journal of Social and Personal Relationships, 7,* 451-463.

Jones, W.H., & Burdette, M.P. (1994). Betrayal in close relationships. In A. L. Weber & J. Harvey (Eds.). *Perspectives on Close Relationships* (pp. 243-263). Boston: Allyn and Bacon.

Jones, W.H., Cohn, M.G., & Miller, C.E. (1991). Betrayal among children and adults. In K.J. Rotenberg (Ed.). *Children's Interpersonal Trust: Sensitivity to Lying, Deception, and Promise Violations* (pp. 118-134). New York: Springer-Verlag.

REVIEWERS: Laura A. Negel and Rebecca L. Jobe, Department of Psychology, University of Tennessee at Knoxville, Knoxville, TN 37996, U.S.A.

4.18: JOINERS' SCALE, THE.
AUTHORS: Wann and Hamlet.

VARIABLE: Assesses social complexity, that is, one's desire to join and maintain memberships in diverse groups.

DESCRIPTION: The Joiners' Scale (Wann & Hamlet, 1994) is a single factor scale that consists of seven items designed to measure an individual's social complexity, that is, his or her desire to join and maintain memberships in diverse groups. Response options to the Likert-style items range from 1 (*Low social complexity*) to 9 (*High social complexity*). Four items are reverse scored, leading to a scale range of 7 to 63, with higher numbers indicating greater social complexity

SAMPLE: Scale was designed to assess the social complexity of non-clinical (*i.e.*, normal) populations.

RELIABILITY: **Internal consistency:** Wann and Hamlet (1994) reported that the internal consistency of the scale ranged from .81 to .90 across the four samples tested (*n*s ranged from 63 to 125). **Test-retest:** Wann and Hamlet (1994) reported that the ten-week test-retest correlation for the scale was .85 (*n*=63).

VALIDITY: **Criterion:** The criterion validity of the scale was documented by data revealing positive relationships between scale scores and the frequency in which participants experienced positive emotions, personal self-esteem, and collective self-esteem (see Wann & Hamlet, 1994). Further, negative relationships were found between scores on the instrument and experiences of negative emotions, stress, and loneliness. **Discriminant:** Wann and Hamlet (1994) documented the discriminant validity of the Joiners' Scale by examining the relationship between scale scores and tendencies toward sensation seeking and social desirability. In support of the scale's validity, no significant positive relationships were found.

LOCATION: Wann, D.L., & Hamlet, M.A. (1994). The Joiners Scale: Validation of a measure of social-complexity. *Psychological Reports, 74*, 1027-1034.

REFERENCES:

Hamlet, M.A. (1993). *Effects of increasing social-complexity on the acclimation of first-semester college students to a university environment.* Unpublished Master's thesis, Murray State University, Murray, KY.

Wann, D.L., & Hamlet, M.A. (1994). The Joiners Scale: Validation of a measure of social-complexity. *Psychological Reports, 74*, 1027- 1034

Wann, D.L., & Hamlet, M.A. (1996). Being a "joiner" and psychological well-being. *Psychological Reports, 79*, 1186.

REVIEWER: Daniel L. Wann, Department of Psychology Murray State University Murray, KY 42071, U.S.A.

4.19: KNOWLEDGE ABOUT MENTAL RETARDATION (KAMR), TEST OF.
AUTHOR: Antonak.

VARIABLE: Attitudes toward persons with mental retardation.

DESCRIPTION: The error-choice test, an indirect measure of attitudes, was first described by Newcomb (1946) and first operationalised by Hammond (1948). Hammond's 'error-choice' items concerned labour-management relations and required respondents to select from among *incorrect* alternatives. In some cases, the alternatives represented errors equidistant in opposite directions from the truth that was determinable; in other cases, representing controversial issues, the alternatives offered opposing views. To disguise the true purpose of the instrument, difficult general information items with the correct answers were interspersed with the error-choice items. The constancy and direction of the respondents' *errors* were interpreted as a measure of their attitude. Because the respondent is duped into believing that the purpose of the investigation is other than what it is, threats to the validity of the resultant measurements (*i.e.*, faking, sensitisation, reactivity, response styles) were reduced. Principles for the construction of an error-choice test have been provided elsewhere (Antonak &

Livneh, 1995). Only 11 research studies since 1948 have used the error-choice method (Buttery, 1978; Campbell & Damarin, 1961; Jacobs, 1972; Kubany, 1953; Parish & Campbell, 1953; Rankin & Campbell, 1955; Weschler, 1950a,b,c; Wilde & deWit, 1970; Wilde & Fortuin, 1969). Arguing that an indirect measure of attitudes toward persons with mental retardation would be particularly useful for research in which responses to a direct attitude instrument may yield biased data, Antonak (1994) developed the error-choice KAMR. The instrument consists of 20 error-choice items with 4 *incorrect* alternatives and 20 difficult items of general knowledge about mental retardation to disguise the true purpose of the test. The format is a typical four-alternative multiple-choice test familiar to everyone from his or her school experience. Directions state that there *are* right and wrong answers to each question, that the test is difficult but that respondents should strive to do their best, and that respondents should answer as rapidly as possible and to guess intelligently on questions to which they do not know the answer because there is no penalty for guessing.

SAMPLE: Antonak (1994) intended the KAMR to be used primarily with special service providers, such as regular and special educators, physicians, nurses, and rehabilitation counselors, although it could also be used with non human-service providers, as well as with the general public.

RELIABILITY: Antonak (1994, submitted) reported Spearman-Brown corrected KR-20 split-half reliability estimates of .55 (SEE=1.94) and .60 (SEE=2.56). These values are reasonable for a measure composed of 20 dichotomous items with unequal item difficulties.

VALIDITY: Iterative alpha factor analyses yielded one factor with eigenvalue greater than one, hypothesized to be attitude toward persons with mental retardation (Antonak, 1994). Factor loadings for the items supported a conclusion of item homogeneity. A nearly identical factor analytic result was reported in a subsequent study (Antonak, submitted). Antonak (submitted) related KAMR scores to scores on the Mental Retardation Attitude Inventory (MRAI), a self-report summated rating instrument (Antonak & Harth, 1994). Scores on the KAMR in a sample of 202 individuals were found to be significantly related to overall scores on the MRAI (r=.15, p<.05) and to scores on the Integration-Segregation (r=.16, p<.05) and Subtle Derogatory Beliefs (r=.27, p<.01) scales of the MRAI. Multivariate multiple regression analysis and discriminant function analyses explored the associations of sociodemographic and experiential variables with the KAMR and MRAI scores (Antonak, submitted). Although the KAMR and the MRAI are related measures of attitudes toward persons with mental retardation, they appear to be tapping somewhat different dimensions of this construct. The KAMR is unidimensional and the construct being measured is not merely knowledge of mental retardation. KAMR scores were significantly related in the predicted direction to age, to a composite variable representing familiarity with persons with mental retardation, and to professional training and experience in special services; scores were not related to respondent ethnic group, sex, or marital status (Antonak submitted; Antonak & Harth, 1994).

LOCATION: Antonak, R.F. (1994). Development and psychometric analysis of an indirect measure of attitudes toward persons with mental retardation using the error-choice method. *Mental Retardation, 32*, 347-355.

COMMENT: The item characteristics of the 20-item error-choice KAMR were found adequate, and the measure's reliability was judged acceptable. Factor analyses confirmed the homogeneity of the items and suggested that the instrument measured a single construct hypothesized to be attitudes toward persons with mental retardation. Partial support for the validity of the measure was found in the analyses of the relations of KAMR scores with respondent demographic and experiential variables, and with scores on the summated rating MRAI. Additional validity investigations are needed to relate KAMR scores to other respondent personality characteristics (*e.g.*, ethnocentrism, acquiescence, self-concept) and, what is more important, to behavioral indicators of attitudes (*e.g.*, working with or serving persons with mental retardation). If it can be shown that the KAMR is a valid predictor of attitudes toward persons with mental retardation, then it should be useful as a supplement to the more traditional direct attitude instruments for the investigation of questions concerning the integration of persons with mental retardation into society's schools, workplaces, and neighbourhoods. Many special education, psychology, and pediatrics training programs expose their trainees to the study of attitudes toward persons with mental retardation. Administered in conjunction with one of the direct scales, an indirect measure such as an error-choice test may point out discrepancies between trainees' professed attitudes as tapped by the direct measure and those that surface in response to an indirect measure. When discrepancies occur, they may also serve as a basis for the trainee's self-awareness and self-growth. Moreover, data from a less biased, indirect measure, such as an error-choice test, may prove useful in an evaluation study of a program to train mental retardation professionals that includes attitude change as one criterion of success.

Antonak, R.F. (1994). Development and psychometric analysis of an indirect measure of attitudes toward persons with mental retardation using the error-choice method. *Mental Retardation, 32,* 347-355.

Antonak, R.F. (submitted). *Validation of an indirect measure of attitudes: The error-choice Test of Knowledge About Mental Retardation.*

Antonak, R.F., & Harth, R. (1994). Psychometric analysis and revision of the Mental Retardation Attitude Inventory. *Mental Retardation, 32,* 272-280.

Antonak, R.F., & Livneh, H. (1995). Direct and indirect methods to measure attitudes toward persons with disabilities, with an exegesis of the error-choice method. *Rehabilitation Psychology, 40,* 3-24.

Buttery, T.J. (1978). Pre-service teachers' attitude regarding gifted children. *College Student Journal, 12,* 288-289.

Campbell, D.T., & Damarin, F.L. (1961). Measuring leadership attitudes through an information test. *Journal of Social Psychology, 55,* 159-176.

Hammond, K.R. (1948). Measuring attitudes by error-choice: An indirect method. *Journal of Abnormal and Social Psychology, 43,* 38-48.

Jacobs, J.C. (1972). Teacher attitude toward gifted children. *Gifted Child Quarterly, 16,* 23-26.

Kubany, A.J. (1953). A validation study of the error-choice technique using attitudes on National Health Insurance. *Educational and Psychological Measurement, 13,* 157-163.

Newcomb, T.M. (1946). The influence of attitude climate upon some determinants of information. *Journal of Abnormal and Social Psychology, 41,* 291-302.

Parish, J.A., & Campbell, D.T. (1953). Measuring propaganda effects with direct and indirect attitude tests. *Journal of Abnormal and Social Psychology, 48,* 3-9.

Rankin, R.E., & Campbell, D.T. (1955). Galvanic skin response to Negro and white experimenters. *Journal of Abnormal and Social Psychology, 51,* 30-33.

Weschler, I.R. (1950a). A follow-up study on the measurement of attitudes toward labor and management by means of the error-choice method. *Journal of Social Psychology, 32,* 63-69.

Weschler, I.R. (1950b). An investigation of attitudes toward labor and management by means of the error-choice method. *Journal of Social Psychology, 32,* 51-62.

Weschler, I.R. (1950c). The personal factor in labor mediation. *Personnel Psychology, 3*, 113-133.

Wilde, G.J.S., & deWit, O.E. (1970). Self-report and error-choice: Inter-individual differences in the operation of the error-choice principle and their validity in personality questionnaire tests. *British Journal of Psychology, 61*, 219-228.

Wilde, G.J.S., & Fortuin, S. (1969). Self-report and error-choice: An application of the error-choice principle to the construction of personality test items. *British Journal of Psychology, 60*, 101-108.

REVIEWER: Richard F. Antonak, Associate Vice President for Academic Affairs, Indiana State University, Terre Haute, IN 47809, U.S.A. E-mail: rantonak@indstate.edu.

4.20: LIFE VALUES INVENTORY, THE.

AUTHORS: Brown and Crace

VARIABLE: Life Values for decisions regarding work, education, relationships, and leisure.

DESCRIPTION: The Life Values Inventory (LVI; Brown & Crace, 1996) contains 42 items that measure 14 sub-scales. The values measured by the LVI include Achievement, Belonging, Concern for the Environment, Concern for Others, Creativity, Financial Prosperity, Health and Activity, Humility, Independence, Loyalty to Family or Group, Privacy, Responsibility, Scientific Understanding, and Spirituality. The LVI was designed to serve as an aid in making decisions about life roles through a values clarification process. The first section of the questionnaire contains self-report items, while the latter sections contain qualitative exercises designed to help people clarify their values.

SAMPLE: Brown and Crace (1996) developed and validated the scale in several studies that included samples of 350 high school, 800 university, community college and technical school students, 350 adults from six states, and 225 corporate employees.

RELIABILITY: Internal consistency: Cronbach's alphas computed for each of the factors ranged from .63 for the Independence scale to .90 for the Spirituality scale (Brown & Crace, 1996, LVI Manual and User's Guide). Test-retest: Brown and Crace (1996) report several studies of the temporal stability of the LVI. Retest coefficients for adults ranged from .57 on Concern for Others to .90 on Spirituality. Coefficients for high school students ranged from .49 on the Privacy scale to .75 on the Belonging scale.

VALIDITY: Convergent: Convergent validity was assessed by correlating LVI scale scores with items from a rating scale version of the Rokeach Values Survey (Brown & Crace, 1996). Correlations between five analogous scales on the LVI and RVS ranged from .39 to .66 (M=. 53). Discriminant: Discriminant validity was assessed for the adult sample by correlating LVI scores with the Crowne-Marlowe Social Desirability Scale. Correlations ranged from -.04 to .28, suggesting that the impact of social desirability on LVI score is minimal (Brown & Crace, 1996).

LOCATION: Brown, D., & Crace, R.K. (1996). *Life Values Inventory*. Published by Life Values Resources, 620 Bayberry Dr., Chapel Hill, NC 27514 , U.S.A.

COMMENT: Several thesis research projects have been completed and are underway using the LVI. A Form B of the LVI has been developed for use with businesses as part of a values-based intervention program for team building (Crace & Hardy, 1997). The LVI is currently being revised to include two rating scales per item. These scales will be used to develop a two axis grid with the 14 sub-scales plotted according to four areas: (1) high importance, frequent guide to behavior; (2) high importance, infrequent guide to behavior; (3) low importance, frequent guide to behavior; (4) low importance, infrequent guide to behavior. With each area, there will be a description of the implications of these values for functions such as decision making, stress management, and role satisfaction. Validation and reliability studies are being conducted. The revised scale will have application to contexts in which career counseling, values clarification, team building, stress management, and other student or employee development activities are appropriate.

REFERENCES:

Brown, D. (1995). A values-based approach to career transitions. *Career Development Quarterly, 44*, 4-11.

Brown, D. (1996). A holistic, values-based model of life role decision making and satisfaction. In D. Brown & L. Brooks and Associates. *Career Development Choice and Development* (pp. 337-372).

Brown, D., & Brooks, L. (1991). Assessing values. In D. Brown & L. Brooks, *Career Counseling Techniques*. Boston, MA: Allyn & Bacon.

Brown, D., & Crace, R.K. (1996a). Values in life role choices and outcomes: A conceptual model. *Career Development Quarterly, 41*, 210-222.

Brown, D., & Crace, R.K. (1996b). *Life Values Inventory: Manual and User's Guide*. Chapel Hill, NC: Life Values Resources

Crace, R.K., & Hardy, C.J. (1997). Individual values and the team building process. *Journal of Applied Sport Psychology, 9*, 41-60.

Shean, G.D., & Shei, T. (1995). The values of student environmentalists. *Journal of Psychology, 129*, 559-564.

REVIEWER: Glenn D. Shean, Department of Psychology, College of William & Mary, PO Box 8795, Williamsburg, VA 23187-8795, U.S.A.

4.21: MODERN RACISM SCALE, THE.
AUTHOR: McConahay.

VARIABLE: The scale is concerned with symbolic racism, and assesses the degree to which Caucasian individuals hold negative attitudes toward African Americans.

DESCRIPTION: The Modern Racism Scale is an update of the Old Fashioned Racism Scale (Greeley & Sheatsley, 1971). According to McConahay (1986), modern racism consists of the idea that "(1) discrimination is a thing of the past because blacks now have the freedom to compete in the marketplace and to enjoy those things they can afford, (2) Blacks are pushing too hard, too fast, and into places where they are not wanted, (3) these tactics and demands are unfair, and (4) recent gains are undeserved and the prestige granting institutions of society are giving blacks more attention and the concomitant status than they deserve" (p. 93). Most importantly, "individuals who endorse these beliefs do not define their own beliefs and attitudes as racist" (p. 93). In developing the Modern Racism Scale, McConahay maintained that open expressions of racist attitudes had become less socially acceptable, and thus it was important to have a less reactive measure of these attitudes. The scale can have six items (adult version) or seven items (college student version) on a 4-point or 5-point scale (ranging from *Strongly disagree* to *Strongly agree*), depending on the population used in the study. Higher scores on the scale indicate higher levels of modern racism in the individual's beliefs.

SAMPLE: The scale is intended for use with Caucasian college-age or adult populations.

RELIABILITY: **Internal Consistency**: Recent studies have demonstrated high internal reliability. Monteith, Deneen, and Tooman (1996) reported an alpha of .87 with a college population. Swim, Aikin, Hall, and Hunter (1995) reported an alpha of .85 with a similar population. **Test-retest:** In a variety of samples, test-retest reliability has been reported between .72 and .93 (for a summary of these studies, see McConahay, 1986).

VALIDITY: **Convergent:** The Modern Racism Scale correlates negatively (-.30) with the Scale of Sympathetic Identification with the Underdog (Schuman & Harding, 1963), and positively (.38) with anti-black sentiment, assessed with the Feeling Thermometer (Campbell, 1971). These correlations demonstrate moderately high internal consistency. Sabnani and Ponterotto (1992) presented additional information regarding evidence for concurrent validity and construct validity of the Modern Racism Scale.

LOCATION: McConahay, J. B. (1986). Modern racism, ambivalence, and the modern racism scale. In J. F. Dovidio & S. L. Gaertner (Eds.), *Prejudice, Discrimination, and Racism* (pp. 91-125). Orlando, FL: Academic Press.

COMMENT: The Modern Racism Scale is considered a satisfactory measure of racist attitudes in the context of a contemporary atmosphere in which it has become socially undesirable to endorse such attitudes. The one weakness with the scale appears to be that the items tap into political conservatism. According to

Fazio, Jackson, Dunton, and Williams (1995), "it would be difficult for a political conservative - one who does not value government intervention - to score at the low-prejudiced end of the scale" (p. 1021). Thus, researchers should take care to include measures that will allow for the teasing apart of modern racist attitudes and politically conservative beliefs.

REFERENCES:

Campbell, A. (1971). *White Attitudes toward Black People.* Ann Arbor, MI: Institute for Social Research.

Fazio, R. H., Jackson, J. R., Dunton, B. C., & Williams, C. J. (1995). Variability in automatic activation as an unobtrusive measure of racial attitudes: A bona fide pipeline? *Journal of Personality and Social Psychology, 69,* 1013-1027.

Greeley, A. M., & Sheatsley, P. B. (1971). Attitudes toward racial integration. *Scientific American, 225,* 13-19.

McConahay, J. B. (1986). Modern racism, ambivalence, and the modern racism scale. In J.F. Dovidio & S.L. Gaertner (Eds.), *Prejudice, Discrimination, and Racism* (pp. 91-125). Orlando, FL: Academic Press.

Monteith, M. J., Deneen, N. E., & Tooman, G. D. (1996). The effect of social norm activation on the expression of opinions concerning gay men and Blacks. *Basic and Applied Social Psychology, 18,* 267-288.

Sabnani, H. B., & Ponterotto, J. G. (1992). Racial/ethnic minority-specific instrumentation in counseling research: A review, critique, and recommendations. *Measurement and Evaluation in Counseling and Development, 24,* 161-187.

Schuman, H., & Harding, J. (1963). Sympathetic identification with the underdog. *Public Opinion Quarterly, 27,* 230-241.

Swim, J. K., Aikin, K. J., Hall, W. S., & Hunter, B. A. (1995). Sexism and racism: Old-fashioned and modern prejudices. *Journal of Personality and Social Psychology, 68,* 199-214.

REVIEWER: Jonathan Iuzzini, Department of Psychology, Texas A&M University, College Station, TX 77840, U.S.A. E-mail: jon-iuzzini@tamu.edu.

4.22: NEIGHBORING (MMN), A MULTI-DIMENSIONAL MEASURE OF.
AUTHORS: Skjæveland, Gärling, and Mæland.

VARIABLES: Four subscales of neighbouring labeled Supportive Acts, Annoyance, Neighbourhood Attachment, and Weak Social Ties.

DESCRIPTION: A self-report scale consisting of 14 items measuring four non-orthogonal dimensions of social life within neighborhoods: supportive acts of neighboring (6 items), neighbor annoyance (3 items), neighborhood attachment (3 items), and weak social ties (2 items). Respondents are asked to rate attributes of observable social interaction and exchange of help and goods as well as of perceptions of the neighborhood. Response categories include frequency ratings of neighboring acts mixed with 4-point Likert scales. By summing across items, a subscale score is obtained for each of the dimensions of neighboring. The original items are in Norwegian but have been appropriately translated into English.

SAMPLE: Adult residents of neighborhoods.

RELIABILITY: **Internal consistency:** Cronbach's alpha ranges from .70 to .86 for each of the four subscales. **Test-retest:** Two-month test-retest reliability ranges from .58 to .73, and six-month test-retest reliability from .62 to .70. **Factor Reliability:** Correlations between factors from different factor analyses are in the order of .98. Invariance tests showed that five of 12 coefficients were higher than .95, and only one coefficient was lower than .80. Also the factorial structure remained stable in various samples (Gorsuch, 1974).

VALIDITY: Construct: Factor analyses confirm four factors corresponding to theoretically derived dimensions of neighboring. Factor analyses also show that measures of social activities not to reflecting neighboring are unrelated to the neighboring dimensions. Correlations with a dimension named 'other social relations' were insignificant or very low, whereas residential satisfaction and intentions of future residency displayed a pattern of significant correlations ranging from very low to extensive. **Convergent:** The Neighborhood Cohesion Index (NCI; Buckner, 1988) shows expected correlations with each subscale. **Discriminant:** All subscales discriminate between sociodemographic groups hypothesized to differ in neighboring.

LOCATION: Skjaeveland, O., Gärling, T., & Maeland, J. (1996). A multidimensional measure of neighboring. *American Journal of Community Psychology, 24,* 413-435.

COMMENT: The theoretical background is described in Skjaeveland and Gärling (in press). All psychometric data are reported in Skjaeveland, Maeland, and Gärling (1996). Additional observations are that the questionnaire can be answered in approximately 10 minutes individually, in groups, or by mail. Since MMN measures four dimensions of neighboring, it is furthermore sufficiently sensitive to detect changes over time, changes of the physical environment, and group differences (Skjaeveland, in press; Skjaeveland & Gärling, 1997).

REFERENCES:

Buckner, J.C. (1988). The development of an instrument to measure neighborhood cohesion. *American Journal of Community Psychology*, *16*, 771-791.

Gorsuch, R.L. (1974). *Factor Analysis*. Philadelphia: Saunders.

Skjaeveland, O. (in press). Effects of street parks on social interactions among neighbors: A place perspective. *Journal of Architecture and Planning Research*.

Skjaeveland, O., & Gärling, T, (1997). Effects of interactional space on neighbouring. *Journal of Environmental Psychology*, *17*, 181-198.

Skjaeveland, O., & Gärling, T. (in press). Spatial-physical neighborhood attributes affecting social interaction among neighbors. In Aragonés, J.I., Francescato, G., & Gärling, T. (Eds.), *Residential Environments: Choice, Satisfaction, and Behavior*. Westport, CT: Greenwood.

REVIEWERS: Oddvar Skjaeveland, Research Center of Health Promotion, Environment, and Lifestyle (HEMIL), University of Bergen, 5000 Bergen, **and** Tommy Gärling, Department of Psychology, Göteborg University, P. O. Box 500, SE-40530 Göteborg, Sweden

4.23: PERSONAL OPINIONS QUESTIONNAIRE (POQ), THE: A MEASURE OF INTRAPERSONAL EMPOWERMENT.

AUTHORS: Bolton and Brookings.

VARIABLE: Four aspects of intrapersonal empowerment and a total score.

DESCRIPTION: The POQ consists of 64 true/false items that are scored on four sub scales: Personal Competence (24 items), Group Orientation (15 items), Self-Determination (14 items), and Positive Sense of Identity as a Person with a Disability (11 items). A total score is also obtained. Norms are available for two samples: college students with disabilities and vocational rehabilitation clients.

SAMPLE: The POQ was developed for use with people with disabilities in educational and rehabilitation settings.

RELIABILITY: Internal consistency: Reliability estimates derived from the two normative samples for the four POQ sub scales and the total score averaged .88, .82, .77, .81, and .94, respectively.

VALIDITY: A thorough review of the empowerment literature established the conceptual foundation for the POQ. A factor analysis of 20 primary facets of empowerment identified the four POQ sub scales. Correlational analysis with the Sixteen Personality Factor Questionnaire (16 PF) supported the trait validity of the four POQ sub scales. A subsequent confirmatory factor analysis supported the factorial validity of the four POQ sub scales and the total score as measures of intrapersonal empowerment.

LOCATION:

Bolton, B., & Brookings, J B. (1998). Development of a measure of intrapersonal empowerment. *Rehabilitation Psychology, 43,* 131-142.

Brookings, J.B., & Bolton, B. (2000). Confirmatory factor analysis of a measure of interpersonal empowerment. *Rehabilitation Psychology, 45.*

COMMENT: The POQ is the only multidimensional instrument developed for use with people with disabilities that comprehensively measures the extent to which the values and attitudes associated with empowerment have been incorporated into the respondent's personal world view as a foundation for action.

REFERENCES:

Bolton, B., & Brookings, J. B. (1996). Development of a multifaceted definition of empowerment. *Rehabilitation Counseling Bulletin, 39,* 256-264.

Bolton, B., & Brookings, J B. (1998). Development of a measure of intrapersonal empowerment. *Rehabilitation Psychology, 43,* 131-142.

Brookings, J.B., & Bolton, B. (2000). Confirmatory factor analysis of a measure of interpersonal empowerment. *Rehabilitation Psychology, 45.*

REVIEWER: Brian Bolton, Department of Rehabilitation Education and Research, University of Arkansas, Fayetteville, Arkansas 72701, U.S.A.

4.24: SPEAKING EXTENT AND COMFORT SCALE (SPEACS), THE.
AUTHORS: Lyons and Spicer.

VARIABLE: The extent and comfort of general conversations and conversations about the self.

DESCRIPTION: The Speaking Extent and Comfort Scale (SPEACS; Lyon & Spicer, 1999) is a 20-item self-report scale which assesses four aspects of past conversational experience, namely the frequency of general conversations and conversations about oneself, and how comfortable the respondent feels during general conversations and conversations about oneself. Respondents consider the frequency of their conversations, and how comfortable they feel during these conversations, for five target persons/groups: partner/spouse, best friend, other friends, relatives and acquaintances. Seven response categories are available for the 10 frequency items: not applicable/never, 11 or more times per day, 6-10 times per day, 1-5 times per day, several times per week, several times per month, several times per year. These categories are coded from 0-6 and summed to provide an overall frequency score, and by summing the relevant 5 items can also provide a frequency of *general* conversations score and a frequency of *self* conversations score. Comfort items ask the respondent to rate how comfortable they feel when talking to the target person(s) generally, and about themselves, on a 7-point scale from not at all comfortable to very comfortable. The mean response to the comfort items is calculated to provide an overall comfort score, as well as average comfort scores during general conversations and conversations specifically about the self.

SAMPLE: Lyons and Spicer (1999) intended the scale to be used to assess conversational experience in non-psychiatric populations. It was developed in a psychophysiological setting, to quantify aspects of conversational experience to investigate relationships with cardiovascular functioning.

RELIABILITY: Internal consistency: The extent subscales demonstrated moderate to low internal consistency (for general conversation, r=.22, for self-conversation, r=.58) as might be expected, given that a specific behaviour is being measured across diverse situations. The comfort subscales showed moderate levels of internal consistency (rs=.67 & .70). **Test-retest:** Lyons and Spicer (1999) report test-retest correlations for the subscales ranging between .66 and .79 among 146 University students over a three week interval.

VALIDITY: The SPEACS subscales have been found to have weak to moderate, positive relationships with various measures of social experience, including the perceived availability of someone to talk to comfortably about one's problems, social competence, self-disclosure and assertiveness. Conversely, all of the SPEACS subscales have demonstrated weak, negative relationships with measures of social distress and avoidance, while the comfort subscales show negative relationships with social anxiety (Lyons & Spicer, 1999).

LOCATION: Lyons, A.C., & Spicer, J. (1999). A new measure of conversational experience: The speaking extent and comfort scale (SPEACS). *Assessment, 6,* 189-202.

COMMENT: The SPEACS was developed in a research setting to try and capture the notion of past conversational experience as a resource. In their work on the effects of self-talk on cardiovascular responses, the authors theorised that how individuals negotiate conversational episodes will depend on their past conversational history. Findings from this work showed that the difference in blood pressure reactivity across three conversations on various topics depended upon both the usual extent, and comfort, of conversing (Lyons, Spicer, Tuffin, & Chamberlain, 2000). This provides some indication of criterion validity of the SPEACS.

REFERENCES:

Lyons, A.C., & Spicer, J. (1999). A new measure of conversational experience: The Speaking Extent and Comfort Scale (SPEACS). *Assessment, 6,* 189-202.

Lyons, A.C., Spicer, J, Tuffin, K., & Chamberlain, K. (2000). Does cardiovascular reactivity during speech reflect self-construction processes? *Psychology and Health, 14,* 1123-1140.

REVIEWER: Antonia Lyons, School of Psychology, University of Birmingham, Edgbaston, Birmingham B15 2TT, England, U.K. E-mail a.c.lyons@bham.ac.uk

4.25: SELF-CONSTRUAL SCALE.
AUTHOR: Singelis.

VARIABLE: Independent/interdependent self-image.

DESCRIPTION: The self-construal scale (SCS; Singelis, 1994), comprises 45 statements (refined to 24 following exploratory factor analysis), with which respondents are asked to agree or disagree using a 7-point Likert scale. The items relate to aspects of self-image with varying degrees of dependence upon others, *e.g.* "I act the same way no matter who I am with". Items were drawn from a number of related tests (*e.g.*, Bhawuk & Brislin, 1992) and rewritten for a student population.

SAMPLE: Intended for cross-cultural comparisons of undergraduate respondents, with an expectation based on previous research that Eastern respondents would favour *interdependent* construals of self and Western respondents would favour *independent* construals of self. In the original study (Singelis, 1994), two samples were used. The first sample consisted of a total of 360 undergraduates from the University of Hawaii; for discriminant validity purposes, these were roughly classified as 'Asian Americans' (n=210) and 'Caucasian Americans' (n=49). The second consisted of 165 undergraduates (93 Asian Americans and 32 Caucasian Americans).

RELIABILITY: The final 24 items were divided into 2 subscales - independent items and interdependent items - on the basis of principal components factor analysis of the first sample. Split-half reliability was measured for each subscale in both samples and was found to be consistent, if not particularly high (α=.73 and .74 for the interdependent items, and .69 and .70 for the independent items). Subsequent uses of the scale have produced similar coefficients, although a recent study of over 600 respondents (Singelis, Bond, Sharkey & Lai, 1999) produced quite low figures (.66 and .61 respectively)

VALIDITY: Discriminant validity was found to be similar to other measures; for example, Asian American respondents had higher interdependent scores than Caucasian Americans (p<.01) and the reverse was true with regard to independent scores (p<.01 and<.05 for samples 1 and 2 respectively). These findings are in line with Markus and Kityama (1991), and have been reproduced in a cross-cultural comparison of US and Japanese respondents (Ozawa, Crosby & Crosby, 1996). Construct validity is harder to establish, since the independent/interdependent distinction has a number of parallels (*e.g.* individualist/collectivist, idiocentric/allocentric) which may, or may not, be said to measure the same phenomenon. On other measures of aspects of self, both subscales have been found to contribute to embarrassability (how easily an individual can become embarrassed) (Singelis & Sharkey, 1995), though not to self-esteem (Singelis *et al.*, 1999).

FURTHER EMPIRICAL USES: Nine items from the SCS were added to the item pool of a study of family allocentrism by Lay, Fairlie, Jackson, Ricci, Eisenberg, Sato, Teeäär and Melamud (1998).

LOCATION: Singelis, T.M. (1994). The measurement of independent and interdependent self-construals. *Personality and Social Psychology Bulletin, 20*, 580-591.

COMMENT: In an unpublished study by the reviewer, this scale was found to have low correlation among British undergraduates with a long-established measure of 'independence/autonomy', the Twenty Statements Test (Kuhn & McPartland, 1954). There was also low (positive) correlation between the independence and interdependence subscales, a finding reported by Singelis himself in the original study (Singelis, 1994). However, Singelis and Sharkey (1995) report a slightly higher correlation ($r=.19$, $p<.001$). There are many issues worth considering which relate to the independence/interdependence dimension, including the argument that these may be two separate construals of self residing in an individual's broad self-concept (see Singelis *et al.*, 1999, for a fuller discussion).

REFERENCES:

Bhawuk, D.P.S., & Brislin, R.W. (1992). The measurement of intercultural sensitivity using the concepts of individualism and collectivism. *International Journal of Intercultural Relations, 16*, 413-436.

Kuhn, M.H., & McPartland, T. (1954). An empirical investigation of self-attitudes. *American Sociological Review, 19*, 58-76.

Lay, C., Fairlie, P., Jackson, S., Ricci, T., Eisenberg, J., Sato, T., Teeäär, A., & Melamud, A. (1998). Domain-specific allocentrism-idiocentrism: A measure of family connectedness. *Journal of Cross-Cultural Psychology, 29*, 434-460.

Markus, H.R., & Kityama, S. (1991). Culture and the self: Implications for cognition, emotion and motivation. *Psychological Review, 98*, 224-253.

Ozawa, K., Crosby, M., & Crosby, F. (1996). Individualism and resistance to affirmative action: A comparison of Japanese and American samples. *Journal of Applied Social Psychology, 26*, 1138-1152.

Singelis, T.M. (1994). The measurement of independent and interdependent self-construals. *Personality and Social Psychology Bulletin, 20*, 580-591.

Singelis, T.M., Bond, M.H., Sharkey, W.F., & Lai, C.S.Y. (1999). Unpacking culture's influence on self-esteem and embarrassability: The role of self-construals. *Journal of Cross-Cultural Psychology, 30*, 315-341.

Singelis, T.M., & Sharkey, W.F. (1995). Culture, self-construal and embarrassability. *Journal of Cross-Cultural Psychology, 26*, 622-644.

REVIEWER: David Giles, Department of Psychology, Coventry University, Coventry, CV1 5FB, England, U.K.

4.26: SPORT SPECTATOR IDENTIFICATION SCALE, THE.

AUTHORS: Wann and Branscombe.

VARIABLE: Assesses one's level of identification with (*i.e.*, attachment to and psychological connection with) a sport team.

DESCRIPTION: The Sport Spectator Identification Scale (Wann & Branscombe, 1993) is a single factor scale that consists of seven items designed to measure an individual's identification with a sport team, that is, his or her attachment to and psychological connection with the team. Response options to the Likert-style items range from 1 (*low identification*) to 8 (*high identification*). Scale scores range from 7 to 56 with higher numbers indicating greater levels of team identification.

SAMPLE: Scale was designed to assess the team identification of non-clinical (*i.e.*, normal) populations.

RELIABILITY: Internal consistency: Data collected by Wann and Branscombe (1993) revealed that the internal consistency of the scale exceeded .90. Other authors have replicated this level of' reliability (*e.g.*, Wann, Brewer, & Royalty, 1999; Wann, Inman, Ensor, Gates, & Caldwell, 1999). **Test-retest:** Wann and Branscombe (1993) reported that the one-year test-retest correlation for the scale was .60 (*n*=49).

VALIDITY: Criterion: The criterion validity of the scale was documented by data revealing positive relationships between scale scores and the number of games subjects attended, how long they had been a fan of the team, how much they were willing to pay for a ticket, how long they were willing to wait in line for a ticket, and the percentage of their friends who were also fans of the team

LOCATION: Wann, D.L., & Branscombe, N.R. (1993). Sports fans: Measuring degree of identification with the team. *International Journal of Sport Psychology*, *24*, 1-17.

REFERENCES:

Wann, D.L., Brewer, K.B., & Royalty, J.L. (1999). Sport fan motivation: Relationships with team identification and emotional reactions to sporting events. *International Sports Journal, 3*, 8-18.

Wann, D.L., Inman, S., Ensor, C.L, Gates, R.D., & Caldwell, D.S. (1999) Assessing the psychological well-being of sport fans using the Profile of Mood States: The importance of team identification. *International Sports Journal, 3*, 81-90.

Wann, D.L., & Branscombe, NR. (1993). Sports fans: Measuring degree of identification with the team. *International Journal of Sport Psychology*, *24*, 1-17.

REVIEWER: Daniel L. Wann, Department of Psychology Murray State University Murray, KY 42071, U.S.A.

CHAPTER 5

PSYCHOLOGICAL WELL-BEING

5.01: ALBANY PANIC AND PHOBIA QUESTIONNAIRE, THE.
AUTHORS: Rapee, Craske, and Barlow.

VARIABLE: Fear of activities and situations that produce fearful interoceptive sensations.

DESCRIPTION: The Albany Panic and Phobia Questionnaire (APPQ) is a 27-item measure of situational and interoceptive fear comprised of three subscales: *agoraphobic situations*, *social-phobic situations*, and *interoceptive-sensations-producing situations*. Fear of interoceptive cues and self-focused attention are considered key variables in panic disorder and social phobia, respectively. Participants are asked to indicate the amount of fear that they *think* they would experience in 27 different situations if they were to occur in the next week. Each item is rated on an 8-point Likert-type scale, ranging from *No fear* (0) to *Extreme fear* (8). Scoring involves adding the scores for each item within each subscale.

SAMPLE: Rapee *et al.* (1994-1995) intended the scale to be used among individuals who have been diagnosed with panic disorder (with or without agoraphobia) or social phobia.

RELIABILITY: **Internal consistency:** Analysis were performed on the scores of 405 individuals who had been diagnosed with various anxiety disorders and 33 individuals with no such disorder (Rapee *et al.*, 1994-1995). The results of factor analysis suggested three distinct factors: interoceptive, agoraphobia, and social phobia. Cronbach's alpha of these subscales were .87, .90, and .91, respectively. The interoceptive and the agoraphobia subscales were strongly correlated (r=.66). **Test-retest:** Rapee *et al.* (1994-1995) reported a test-retest correlation of .68, .80, and .84 for the interoceptive, agoraphobia, and social phobia subscale, respectively. These analyses were performed on the scores of 45 individuals with panic disorder (with no or mild agoraphobia) at 10.9 weeks interval (2.4 to 25.0) prior to their participation in a treatment program.

VALIDITY: To demonstrate **construct validity**, Rapee *et al.* (1994-1995) compared the APPQ subscale scores of participants with social phobia, panic disorder, or agoraphobia diagnosis. The APPQ subscales were found to discriminate among relevant diagnostic groups. **Convergent validity** was assessed by correlating several anxiety-related questionnaires with the APPQ subscales. Of interests, correlation coefficients between the APPQ subscales (agoraphobia, interoceptive, and social phobia) and a measure of fear of physical sensations (Anxiety Sensitivity Index; Reiss, Peterson, Garsky, & McNally, 1986) were .50, .47, and .34, respectively (Rapee *et al.*, 1994-1995). Further, correlation coefficients between a measure of fear of social interaction situations (Social Interaction Anxiety Scale; Mattick, Peters, & Clarke, 1989) and the APPQ subscales (agoraphobia, interoceptive, and social phobia) were .18, .14, and .76, respectively.

COMMENT: The Albany Panic and Phobia Questionnaire was developed to complement more traditional measures of agoraphobic fears. The intent was for the interoceptive subscale to measure a construct that is distinct from other well-researched constructs, such as fear of internal sensations, experience with panic attacks, and fear of avoidance of external situations. Finally, the APPQ was associated with favourable level of sensitivity to change following a 12-week cognitive behavioral treatment for panic disorder (Rapee *et al.*, 1994-1995).

LOCATION: Rapee, R.M., Craske, M.G., & Barlow, D.H. (1994-1995). Assessment instrument for panic disorder that includes fear of sensation-producing activities: The Albany Panic and Phobia Questionnaire. *Anxiety, 1*, 114-122.

REFERENCES:

Mattick, R.P., Peters, L., & Clarke, J.C. (1989). Exposure and cognitive restructuring for social phobia: A controlled study. *Behavior Therapy, 20*, 3-23.

Rapee, R.M., Craske, M.G., & Barlow, D.H. (1994-1995). Assessment instrument for panic disorder that includes fear of sensation-producing activities: The Albany Panic and Phobia Questionnaire. *Anxiety, 1*, 114-122.

Reiss, S., Peterson, R.A., Garsky, D.M., & McNally, R.J. (1986). Anxiety sensitivity, anxiety frequency, and the prediction of fearfulness. *Behaviour Research and Therapy, 24*, 1-8.

REVIEWERS: Marie-Claude Laplante, School of Psychology, University of Ottawa, Ottawa, Ontario, K1N 6N5, Canada   **and** Stéphane Bouchard' Département de Psychoéducation, Université du Québec à Hull, Hull, Québec, J8X 3X7, Canada.

5.02: ANXIETY SENSITIVITY INDEX.

AUTHORS: Reiss, Peterson, Gursky, and McNally.

VARIABLE: Anxiety sensitivity (fear of anxiety).

DESCRIPTION: Anxiety sensitivity (AS) is the fear of anxiety-related sensations, such as fears of palpitations, dizziness, and chest tightness. These fears arise from beliefs that the sensations have harmful somatic, psychological, or social consequences (Reiss, 1991). People with high AS, for example, tend to believe that palpitations will lead to heart attacks; people with low AS tend to believe that palpitations are harmless sensations. According to Reiss' (1991) expectancy theory, anxiety sensitivity amplifies anxiety reactions. That is, when a person experiences an anxiety-evoking event, his or her anxiety sensitivity will amplify the anxiety reaction. Anxiety sensitivity is thought to play a role in a variety of anxiety reactions, particularly panic attacks. The Anxiety Sensitivity Index (ASI) was developed by Reiss and colleagues (1986) to measure anxiety sensitivity. The ASI is a 16-item self-report scale in which the respondent rates the extent to which he or she agrees with a given item (*e.g.*, "It scares me when I become short of breath"). Each item is rated on a 5-point scale ranging from 0 (*Very little*) to 4 (*Very much*). The ASI total score is computed by adding the item scores.

SAMPLE: The scale was intended for use with normal and psychiatric adult populations.

RELIABILITY: The ASI has acceptable internal consistency, with coefficients α being>.80 in most studies. Test-retest reliability correlations have been reported to be>.64 for retest intervals ranging from 2 weeks to 3 years. Reliability data are reviewed in detail in the chapters in Taylor (1999).

VALIDITY: There have been numerous tests of the validity of the ASI, as reviewed in the chapters in Taylor (1999). The ASI has performed well on tests of convergent, discriminant, concurrent, known-groups, incremental, and predictive validity. To illustrate, ASI scores tend to be high in people with panic disorder, compared to people with other anxiety disorders and normal controls (known-groups validity). ASI scores also predict the occurrence of panic attacks in stressful situations, even for people who have never previously panicked (convergent validity). ASI scores predict panic and anxiety, even after controlling for conceptually related variables such as trait anxiety (incremental validity). Recent research provides mixed support for the ASI's factorial validity. Although the ASI was intended to be a unidimensional measure, research suggests it consists of three correlated factors: (1) fear of somatic sensations, (2) fear of cognitive dyscontrol, and (3) fear of publicly observable anxiety reactions. These factors load on a single higher-order factor (Taylor, 1999).

FURTHER EMPIRICAL USES: The ASI has been used to test Reiss' (1991) theory and to explore the relationship between anxiety sensitivity and many forms of psychopathology, including chronic pain, substance abuse, and depression. The

ASI also has been used in treatment outcome studies to investigate the relationship between changes in anxiety sensitivity and changes in anxiety symptoms and disorders (see Taylor, 1999).

LOCATION: **Test manual**: Peterson, R.A., & Reiss, S. (1992). *Anxiety Sensitivity Index Manual* (2nd ed.). Worthington, OH: International Diagnostic Systems. **Available from**: Steven Reiss, Ohio State University, Nisonger Center, 1581 Dodd Drive, Columbus, Ohio, 43210-1296, U.S.A.

COMMENT: Norms are available for the ASI total score in English (Peterson & Reiss, 1992) and preliminary norms are available for a Spanish version of the ASI (Sandin *et al.*, 1996). The Childhood Anxiety Sensitivity Index has been developed for assessing school-aged children and adolescents (6-17 years) and has performed generally well on tests of reliability and validity (Silverman & Weems, 1999). To better assess the multiple dimensions of anxiety sensitivity in adults, two new measures have been recently developed (Taylor & Cox, 1998a,b). Preliminary data on their reliabilities and validities are encouraging, but further evaluation is required.

REFERENCES:

Peterson, R.A., & Reiss, S. (1992). *Anxiety Sensitivity Index Manual* (2nd ed.). Worthington, OH: International Diagnostic Systems.

Reiss, S. (1991). Expectancy theory of fear, anxiety, and panic. *Clinical Psychology Review, 11*,141-153.

Reiss, S., Peterson, R.A., Gursky, M., & McNally, R.J. (1986). Anxiety sensitivity, anxiety frequency, and the prediction of fearfulness. *Behaviour Research and Therapy, 24*, 1-8.

Sandin, B., Chorot, P., & McNally, R. J. (1996). Validation of the Spanish version of the Anxiety Sensitivity Index in a clinical sample. *Behaviour Research and Therapy, 34*, 283-290.

Silverman, W.K., & Weems, C.F. (1999). Anxiety sensitivity in children. In S. Taylor (Ed.), *Anxiety Sensitivity*, (239-268). Mahwah, NJ: Erlbaum.

Taylor, S. (1999). *Anxiety Sensitivity*. Mahwah, NJ: Erlbaum.

Taylor, S., & Cox, B.J. (1998a). An expanded Anxiety Sensitivity Index: Evidence for a hierarchic structure in a clinical sample. *Journal of Anxiety Disorders, 12*, 463-484.

Taylor, S., & Cox, B.J. (1998b). Anxiety sensitivity: Multiple dimensions and hierarchic structure. *Behaviour Research and Therapy, 36*, 37-51.

REVIEWER: Steven Taylor, Department of Psychiatry, 2255 Wesbrook Mall, University of British Columbia, Vancouver, B.C. V6T 2A1, Canada. E-mail taylor@unixg.ubc.ca

5.03: ANXIOUS THOUGHTS INVENTORY (AnTI), THE.
AUTHOR: Wells.

VARIABLE: Individual vulnerability to three dimensions of generalised worry.

DESCRIPTION: The Anxious Thoughts Inventory (AnTI; Wells, 1994a) is a self-report measure that consists of items derived from interviews with patients with generalised anxiety. After a series of factor analyses (FA) a 3-factor structure, which was invariant in both sexes, was obtained (Wells, 1994a). The final version, based on the FA results, contains 22 items. Of these, 9 measure 'Social Worry' (SW), 6 measure 'Health Worry' (HW) and 7 of measure 'Meta-Worry' (M-W;

worries about the controllability of thought processes). The three scales are positively correlated. Responses are required on a four-point scale ranging from *Almost never* to *Almost always*.

SAMPLE: The AnTI measures proneness to non-pathological Worry and is mainly intended to be used in non-psychiatric populations. However, the inventory has also been used in samples of patients with different clinical disorders.

RELIABILITY: Internal consistency: Wells (1994a,b) reported alpha estimates of α=.84 (SW), α=.81 (HW) and α=.75 (M-W) from a sample of 239 subjects. Ferrando (1995) used a Spanish adaptation of the AnTI and replicated the 3-factor structure obtained by Wells. From a sample of 834 undergraduate students, Ferrando obtained alpha estimates of α=.84 (SW), α=.79 (HW) and α=.77 (M-W). Test-retest: Wells (1994a,b) reported test-retest correlations of r=.76 (SW), r=.84 (HW) and r=.77 (M-W) from 64 undergraduate students after a six-week interval.

VALIDITY: Convergent: The AnTI showed satisfactory convergent validity with various personality measures, including self-consciousness, trait anxiety, neuroticism, and extraversion (Wells, 1992, 1994a).

LOCATION: Wells, A. (1994). A multidimensional measure of Worry: Development and preliminary validation of the Anxious Thoughts Inventory. *Anxiety, Stress and Coping, 6*, 289-299.

FURTHER EMPIRICAL USES: Wells (1994a) explored the power of the AnTI scales to discriminate among patients with different anxiety disorders, patients with major depression and normal subjects. In general, the normal subjects scored lower than the clinical groups. Significant differences between the clinical groups were also observed. Ferrando (1996) analysed the factorial invariance across gender for the SW items. He found evidence for strong factorial invariance as suggested by Wells' exploratory analyses. Freeman and Garety (1999) used a single item of the M-W scale (item-22) to distinguish between an anxious group and a group with persecutory delusions. Both groups reported high levels of Meta-Worry.

COMMENT: In general, the AnTI has a replicable factor structure that is relatively invariant in both sexes, and acceptable psychometric properties. Its main limitations are of two types. First, the factor structure is not a simple structure: some of the items are factorially complex and the M-W factor is possibly multidimensional (note that the M-W scale is the one with the lowest internal consistency). Second, although the AnTI was designed mainly for non-psychiatric populations, the scale scores (specially in the HW and M-W scales) tend to show low means, reduced variability and positive skewed distributions in non-clinical samples (Wells, 1994a; Ferrando, 1995).

REFERENCES:

Ferrando, P.J. (1995). *Estructura Factorial y Propiedades Psicométricas del iInventario 'AnTI'*. Unpublished manuscript.

Ferrando, P.J. (1996). Calibration of invariant item parameters in a continuous item response model using the extended Lisrel measurement submodel. *Multivariate Behavioral Research, 31*, 419-439.

Freeman, D., & Garety, P.A. (1999). Worry, worry processes and dimensions of delusions: An exploratory investigation of a role for anxiety processes in the maintenance of delusional distress. *Behavioural and Cognitive Psychotherapy, 27*, 47-62.

Wells, A. (1992). *A multidimensional measure of Worry: Development and preliminary validation of the Anxious Thoughts Inventory*. Paper presented at the World Congress of Cognitive Therapy, Toronto, June 1992.

Wells, A. (1994a). A multidimensional measure of Worry: Development and preliminary validation of the Anxious Thoughts Inventory. *Anxiety, Stress and Coping, 6*, 289-299.

Wells, A. (1994b). Attention and the control of Worry. In G.C.L. Davey and F. Tallis (eds.) *Worrying: Perspectives on Theory, Assessment and Treatment* (pp. 91-114). New York: J.Wiley.

REVIEWER: Pere J. Ferrando, Department of Psychology, 'Rovira i Virgili' University, 43007, Tarragona, Spain. E-mail: pjfp@fcep.urv.es

5.04: ARABIC CHILDREN'S DEPRESSION INVENTORY, THE.
AUTHOR: Abdel-Khalek.

VARIABLE: Childhood depression.

DESCRIPTION: Self-report scale which contains 27 brief items representing a mix of affective, cognitive, and somatic indicators. Of these, 19 of the items are positive indicators to depression (*e.g.* 'I am sad'), while 8 items are considered negative indicators (*e.g.* 'Life is rosy'). Respondents are asked about how they feel generally. They have to rate each item on a three point scale: *Rarely* (1), *Sometimes* (2), and *Often* (3). The 8 negative items are reverse scored so that possible scores on the inventory can range from 27 to 81. Higher scores on the inventory indicate a higher degree of depression. The inventory has two equivalent Arabic and English versions.

SAMPLE: Abdel-Khalek (1993) intended the scale to be used for the assessment of childhood depression in non-psychiatric school children and adolescents populations.

RELIABILITY: Internal consistency: It demonstrated between satisfactory to high levels in seven Arabic countries (the Arabic version) as well as U.S.A. (the English form) (Abdel-Khalek & Soliman, 1999). Cronbach's alpha, and split-half reliability coefficients ranged from .81 to .91. Test-retest: Abdel-Khalek (1993) reported a test-retest correlation of .85, and .89 among 69 Egyptian school-boys and girls, respectively after one week interval.

VALIDITY: Convergent: It demonstrated between satisfactory and good convergent validity with the Kovacs' Children's Depression Inventory (1992), and the Kazdin, Rodgers, & Colbus (1986) Hopelessness Scale for Children in Egyptian School Children. The correlations ranged from .64 and .75 (Abdel-Khalek, 1993). Three further studies in Kuwaiti (Abdel-Khalek, 1998, Abdullatif, 1995) and Syrian (Abdel-Khalek & Ridwan, 1999) school children gave rise to correlations ranged between .48 and .75, demonstrating good convergent validity. Factorial: The intercorrelations between the scale items were factor analyzed, separately, in seven Arabic countries as well as an American sample. There is an agreement between the following factors in the 8 countries: lack of concentration, pessimism, sleep problems, dysphoria, weakness, and loneliness.

LOCATION: Abdel-Khalek, A.M. (1993). The construction and validation of the Arabic Children's Depression Inventory. *European Journal of Psychological Assessment, 9*, 41-50.

COMMENT: The scale has been administered to over than 21,000 school children and adolescents in eight countries: Egypt, Kuwait, Saudi Arabia, Qatar, Bahrain,

Syria, Jordan in its Arabic version, and U.S.A. in its English form. The psychometric properties of the scale are quite satisfactory. However, the English form of the scale needs further research among English-speaking children other than the U.S.A.

REFERENCES:

Abdel-Khalek, A.M. (1993). The construction and validation of the Arabic Children's Depression Inventory. *European Journal of Psychological Assessment, 9,* 41-50.

Abdel-Khalek, A. M. (1996). Factorial structure of the Arabic Children's Depression Inventory among Kuwaiti subjects. *Psychological Reports, 78,* 963-967.

Abdel-Khalek, A.M. (1998). Criterion-related validity of the Arabic Children's Depression Inventory. *Psychological Reports, 82,* 930.

Abdel-Khalek, A.M. (1999a). The Arabic Children's Depression Inventory: A review of results on eight societies, *Journal of the Social Sciences,* Kuwait University, *27,* 103-123. (in Arabic).

Abdel-Khalek, A.M. (1999b). *A Jordanian results on the Children' s Depression Inventory.* Unpublished Manuscript.

Abdel-Khalek, A.M., & Ridwan, S.J. (1999). A preliminary standardization of the Arabic Children's Depression Inventory in Syrian samples. *The Educational Journal, Kuwait University, 14,* 29-58. Accepted, (in Arabic).

Abdel-Khalek, A.M., & Soliman, H.H. (1999). A cross-cultural evaluation of depression in children: Egypt, Kuwait, and United States. *Psychological Reports, 85,* 973-980.

Abdullatif, H.I. (1995). Prevalence of depression among middle-school Kuwaiti students following the Iraqi Invasion. *Psychological Reports, 77,* 643-649.

Fukhro, H.A., El-Nayal, M.A., & Torky, A.A. (1998). *Developmental and correlational study on psychological variables among Qatari school children.* Symposium on Psychology and Development in the Arabian Peninsula. The Faculty of Education, University of Qatar, in 11-13 May, 1998 (in Arabic).

Ismail, A.A. (1999). *The factorial structure of the Arabic Children's Depression Inventory among Saudi School children.* Paper presented at the conference on Social Service and Development, Kuwait University, 5-7 April, 1999 (in Arabic).

Tawfic, A.T. (1999). The factorial structure of depression in Bahraini school children. *The Educational Journal, Kuwait University, 13,* 173-200 (in Arabic).

REVIEWER: Ahmed M. Abdel-Khalek, College of Social Sciences, Kuwait University, PO Box 68168, Kaifan, Code No. 71962, Kuwait.

5.05: ARABIC OBSESSIVE COMPULSIVE SCALE, THE
AUTHOR: Abdel-Khalek.

VARIABLE: Obsessive-compulsive traits.

DESCRIPTION: Self-report scale in two equivalent Arabic and English forms. It contains 32 statements representing obsessive-compulsive traits and behavior, *i.e.* obsessive doubts, orderliness, discipline, slowness, hesitation, rumination, compulsion, meticulousness, repetition, and checking. Respondents are asked about how they feel generally and to rate each item on a *Yes/No* formats. Of the 32 items, 23 are positive indicators of obsession and compulsion, and 9 items are negative indicators. The 9 negative items on the scale are reverse scored. So, the possible scores on the scale can range between 0 and 32. Higher scores on the scale indicate a higher frequency of obsessive-compulsive traits.

SAMPLE: Abdel-Khalek (1992, 1998) intended the scale to be used for the assessment of obsessive-compulsive traits in psychiatric and non-psychiatric populations. El-Saadany (1996) used the scale in research with obsessive-compulsive disorder patients.

RELIABILITY: **Internal consistency:** Cronbach's alpha reached .80 in Egyptian subjects (Abdel-Khalek, 1992, 1998), while it was .76 and .82 in Kuwaiti and American subjects, respectively (Abdel-Khalek & Lester, 1998), and in Bahraini undergraduates it was .74 (Tawfik, 1999). In Saudi four samples, the Spearman-Brown reliabilities were ranged between .70 and .73 (Abdel-Khalek & Al-Damaty, 1995). **Test-retest:** Abdel-Khalek (1992, 1998) reported a test-retest correlation of r=.85 in 33 male and female Egyptian undergraduates after an one week interval.

VALIDITY: **Convergent:** It demonstrated from satisfactory to high criterion-related validity with the Maudsley Obsessive-Compulsive Inventory in Egyptians (Abdel-Khalek, 1992, 1998), Kuwaitis and Americans (Abdel-Khalek & Lester, 1999), and Bahrainis (Tawfic, 1999). **Discriminant:** El-Saadany (1996) demonstrated the discriminant validity of the scale among obsessive compulsive disorder patients. He also used the scale as an outcome measure in a drug trial. The scale succeeded to reflect the clinical improvement after administering clomipramine HCI, citalopram, and cognitive therapy to 3 different obsessive-compulsive groups of patients.

LOCATION: Abdel-Khalek, A.M. (1998). The development and validation of the Arabic Obsessive Compulsive Scale. *European Journal of Psychological Assessment, 14*, 146-158.

COMMENT: The Arabic Obsessive Compulsive Scale was administered to large size samples in Egypt, Kuwait, Saudi Arabia, Qatar, Bahrain, Lebanon, Syria, and Jordan in its Arabic form, while it was used with U.S.A. undergraduates in its English version (Abdel-Khalek & Lester 1998; Lester & Abdel-Khalek, 1998). There is growing evidence for the satisfactory psychometric properties of the scale in the aforementioned countries. Nevertheless, there is a need to use the scale in psychiatric populations, namely the patients of obsessive-compulsive disorder, other than El-Saadany's (1996) clinical research.

REFERENCES

Abdel-Khalek, A.M. (1992). *Manual for the Arabic Obsessive Compulsive Scale.* Alexandria (Egypt): Dar Al-Maarifa Al-Jamiiyah (in Arabic).

Abdel-Khalek, A.M. (1998). The development and validation of the Arabic Obsessive Compulsive Scale. *European Journal of Psychological Assessment, 14*, 146-158.

Abdel-Khalek, A.M., & Al-Damaty, A.A. (1995). Obsessions and compulsions: A study on Saudi samples. *Derasat Nafseyah, 5*, 1-17, (in Arabic).

Abdel-Khalek, A.M., & Lester, D. (1998). Reliability of the Arabic Obsessive-Compulsive Scale in Kuwaiti and American students. *Psychological Reports, 83*, 1470.

Abdel-Khalek, A.M., & Lester, D. (1998). Obsession Compulsion in college students in the United States and Kuwait. *Psychological Reports, 85*, 799-800.

Abdel-Khalek, A.M., & Lester, D. (1999). Criterion-related validity of the Arabic
    Obsessive-Compulsive Scale in Kuwaiti and American students.
    Psychological Reports, *85*, 1111-1112.

Abdel-Khalek, A.M., & Lester, D. (in press). Obsession-compulsion, locus of
    control, depression and helplessness in American and Kuwaiti students.
    Psychological Reports.

Abdel-Khalek, A.M., & Lester, D. (Submitted). *The factorial structure of the
    Arabic Obsessive-Compulsive Scale in Kuwaiti and American students*.

El-Saadany, M.K.E. (1996). *Epidemiological, biochemical, phenomenological
    study of obsessive compulsive disorder in Alexandria*. M.D. Thesis
    (Unpublished), Faculty of Medicine, University of Alexandria, Egypt.

Lester, D., & Abdel-Khalek, A.M. (1998). Suicidality and personality in
    American and Kuwaiti students. *International Journal of Social
    Psychiatry*, *44*, 280-283.

Tawfic, A.T. (1999). *Obsessive-compulsive disorder among Bahrain students*.
    Paper presented at the Conference on Psychological Service and
    Development. Kuwait University, 5-7 April, 1999.

REVIEWER: Ahmed M. Abdel-Khalek, College of Social Sciences, Kuwait
University, PO Box 68168, Kaifan, Code No. 71962, Kuwait.

5.06: BEHAVIOR AND SYMPTOM IDENTIFICATION SCALE (BASIS-32).
AUTHORS: Eisen, Dill, and Grob.

DESCRIPTION: Behaviour and Symptom Identification Scale (BASIS-32) is a
brief but comprehensive measure of self-reported difficulty in the major symptom
and functioning domains that lead to the need for psychiatric treatment. These

include mood disturbances, anxiety, suicidality, psychotic symptoms, self-understanding, interpersonal relations, role functioning, daily living skills, impulsivity and substance abuse. It cuts across diagnoses, acknowledging the wide range of symptoms and problems that occur across the diagnostic spectrum. BASIS-32 consists of 32 items for which respondents are asked to indicate the degree of difficulty they have been experiencing during the past week. Degree of difficulty is rated on a 5-point scale as follows: (0) *No difficulty*, (1) *A little*, (2) *Moderate*, (3) *Quite a bit* and (4) *Extreme*. Assessments can be done at intake and at specified intervals during or following completion of treatment. The 32 items are scored into one of five subscales: relation to self and others, daily living and role functioning, depression and anxiety, impulsive and addictive behavior, and psychosis. In addition, an overall summary score is computed. Subscale and overall mean scores can range from 0 to 4.

SAMPLE: The scale is intended for completion by individuals receiving any type of behavioral health treatment at all levels of care including inpatient, residential, partial hospital and outpatient (Eisen, Dill, & Grob, 1994, Eisen *et al.*, 1999; Eisen, Leff, & Schaefer, 1999).

RELIABILITY: Internal consistency: Internal consistency (Cronbach's alpha) coefficients were computed for each subscale on a sample of 387 hospitalised cases, yielding the following results: relation to self and others, $\alpha=.76$; daily living and role functioning skills, $\alpha=.80$; depression and anxiety, $\alpha=.74$; impulsive and addictive behavior, $\alpha=.71$; psychosis, $\alpha=.63$. Full scale reliability was $\alpha=.89$ (Eisen, Dill, & Grob, 1994). These results were replicated in two additional inpatient studies (Corresponding internal consistency coefficients for outpatients ranged from . 65 to .89 with a full scale reliability of .95. **Test-retest:** Test-retest reliability coefficients, computed on a separate sample of 40 cases were as follows: $r=.80$ for relation to self and others, $r=.81$ for daily living and role functioning, $r=.78$ for depression and anxiety, $r=.65$ for impulsive and addictive behavior, and $r=.76$ for psychosis.

VALIDITY: Concurrent validity was assessed by relating objective indicators of functioning at follow-up (six months post-hospital admission) with BASIS-32 follow-up scores. Two objective indicators - continued hospitalisation or rehospitalisation during the six months after admission, and employment status at follow-up - were compared with patients' subjective reports of difficulty at the follow-up point. Consistent with their hospital status, patients who were discharged to the community and had remained so during the six months reported the least difficulty, whereas patients who were hospitalised at the six-month follow-up point reported the greatest difficulty. Regarding employment status among patients identified at admission as having a paid occupation, scores on the daily living and role functioning subscale at follow-up were expected to differentiate those who were working at follow-up from those who were not. Results supported this expectation; patients who were working reported significantly less difficulty with respect to daily living and role functioning than those who were not working. Discriminant validity was assessed by analysing whether specific BASIS-32 subscales predicted corresponding diagnoses. As expected, results indicated that patients with a diagnosis of unipolar depression had significantly higher scores on the depression and anxiety subscale compared with patients with other diagnoses. Patients with a psychotic disorder had significantly higher scores on the psychosis subscale compared with patients not diagnosed with psychosis; and patients with a substance abuse disorder had significantly higher scores on the impulsive and addictive behavior subscale compared with patients without a substance abuse diagnosis.

COMMENT: BASIS-32 has also be shown to be sensitive to change. Comparison of admission scores with those obtained at a six-month follow-up point were highly significant, as were changes during the course of a hospitalisation (from admission to discharge). Improvement following 4-12 weeks of outpatient treatment was also significant. Effect sizes ranged from .53 for outpatients to .84 for inpatients (Eisen, Dill, & Grob, 1994; Eisen *et al.*, 1999; Eisen, Leff, & Schaefer, 1999; Hoffmann, Capelli, & Mastrianni, 1997; Russo *et al.*, 1997). There are several major strengths of BASIS-32. As a 'generic' measure applicable to a wide range of people receiving mental health treatment, it is not limited to a particular diagnosis or symptom pattern. Second, all of the major symptom and problem domains that bring people to inpatient treatment are included. Third, staff and respondent burden are minimal, due to its brevity and simplicity of design. Weaknesses of the instrument include relatively high correlations among three of the five subscales (.58 to .66), suggesting limited discriminant validity of these subscales. In addition, acutely psychotic, intoxicated or demented patients may be unable to respond appropriately.

LOCATION: BASIS-32 is copyrighted by McLean Hospital. The instrument, accompanying Instruction Manual and a site license are available from the first author at Department of Mental Health Services Research, McLean Hospital, 115 Mill St., Belmont, MA 02478, U.S.A.

REFERENCES:

Eisen, S.V., Dill, D.L., & Grob, M.C. (1994). Reliability and validity of a brief patient-report instrument for psychiatric outcome evaluation. *Hospital and Community Psychiatry, 45*, 242-247.

Eisen, S.V., Leff, H.S., & Schaefer, E. (1999). Implementing outcome systems: Lessons learned from a test of the BASIS-32 and the SF-36. *Journal of Behavioral Health Services and Research, 26*, 18-26.

Eisen, S.V., Wilcox, M., Leff, H.S., Schaefer, E., & Culhane, M.A. (1999). Assessing behavioral health outcomes in outpatient programs: Reliability and validity of the BASIS-32. *Journal of Behavioral Health Services and Research, 26,* 5-17.

Hoffmann, F.L., Capelli, K., & Mastrianni, X. (1997). Measuring treatment outcome for adults and adolescents: Reliability and validity of BASIS-32. *Journal of Mental Health Administration, 24,* 316-331.

Russo, J., Roy-Byrne, P., Jaffe, C., Ries, R., Dagadakis, C., Dwyer-O'Connor, J., & Reeder, D. (1997). The relationship of patient-administered outcome assessments to quality of life and physician ratings: Validity of the BASIS-32. *Journal of Mental Health Administration, 22,* 200-214.

REVIEWER: S.V. Eisen, Department of Mental Health Services Research, McLean Hospital, 115 Mill St., Belmont, MA 02478, U.S.A.

5.07: CATASTROPHIC COGNITIONS QUESTIONNAIRE-MODIFIED (CCQ-M).
AUTHORS: Khawaja, Oei, and Baglioni.

VARIABLES: Catastrophic Cognitions of Anxiety Disorders.

DESCRIPTION: The scale is based on cognitive theories of clinical anxiety. According to the cognitive models of anxiety, danger schemas are important in the development and maintenance of anxiety disorders. The scale is a self-report scale, which consists of 21 items. It is a modified version of the Catastrophic Cognitions Questionnaire (CCQ; Khawaja & Oei, 1992). The scale was designed to assess the element dangerousness associated by a person with his/her unpleasant emotions, physical changes or thinking difficulties. The scale measures catastrophic cognitions by asking the respondents to indicate, on a 5-point Likert scale, the extent to which they rate each item as dangerous to themselves. The modified scale had three-factor oblique solution. These are *Emotional Catastrophes* (factor 1), *Physical Catastrophes* (factor 2), and *Mental Catastrophes* (factor 3).

SAMPLE: Student, clinical and community samples were used to investigate the factor structure and the psychometric properties of the scale. The clinical sample consisted of out patients with a primary diagnosis of anxiety disorders.

RELIABILITY: Cronbach's alphas for the three subscales were calculated on the basis of student and clinical samples. The Cronbach's alphas ranged from .83 to .91. The test re test reliability, over an interval of 2 weeks, was estimated on the basis of clinical sample. The scale (.63) and factors 1 (.71), 2 (.58), and 3 (.67) had moderately good reliability.

VALIDITY: Concurrent validity was examined by correlating the total score and the score of the three subscales of CCQ-M with a number of anxiety scales. The correlations on the basis of student sample ranged from low (.19) to moderate (.57). However, the correlations on the basis of clinical sample ranged from moderate (.38) to moderately high (.66). Overall, the scale has acceptable discriminant validity as it differentiates between patients and non-clinical populations. All factors except the second one discriminate the patients from the non-clinical samples.

LOCATION: Khawaja, N.G., Oei, T.P.S., & Baglioni, A.J. Jr. (1994). Modification of the Catastrophic Cognitions Questionnaire (CCQ-M) for normals and patients: Exploratory and LISREL Analysis. *Journal of Psychopathology and Behavioural Assessment, 16,* 325-342.

COMMENT: CCQ-M is a useful instrument to measure catastrophic cognitions in normal and anxiety disorder cases.

REFERENCES:

Khawaja, N.G., & Oei, T.P.S. (1992). Development of the Catastrophic Cognitions Questionnaire. *Journal of Anxiety Disorders, 6,* 305-318.

Khawaja, N.G., Oei, T.P.S., & Baglioni, A.J. Jr. (1994). Modification of the Catastrophic Cognitions Questionnaire (CCQ-M) for normals and patients: Exploratory and LISREL Analysis. *Journal of Psychopathology and Behavioural Assessment, 16,* 325-342.

Khawaja, N.G., & Oei, T.P.S (1997). Catastrophic cognitions in Panic Disorder with and without Agoraphobia. *Clinical Psychology Review, 18,* 341-365.

Khawaja, N.G., & Oei, T.P.S. (1998). Catastrophic cognitions and the clinical outcome: Two case studies. *Behavioural and Cognitive Psychotherapy, 26,* 271-282.

REVIEWER: Nigar G. Khawaja, School of Psychology & Counselling, Queensland University of Technology, Brisbane, Australia.

5.08: CHART OF INTERPERSONAL REACTIONS IN CLOSED LIVING ENVIRONMENTS (CIRCLE).

AUTHORS: Blackburn and Renwick.

VARIABLES: Interpersonal styles representing the octants of the Leary interpersonal circumplex (dominant, coercive, hostile, withdrawn, submissive, compliant, nurturant and gregarious).

DESCRIPTION: A 49-item schedule of observer ratings of verbal and nonverbal interpersonal behaviours in an institutional environment. Each item is rated on a 4-point scale (*Not at all, Occasionally, Fairly often, Usually* or *frequently*) and scored 0-3. Ratings are obtained from two independent observers and summed, each item therefore having a score of 0-6. Items are assigned to one of eight scales representing octants of the interpersonal circle, and two summary scores of dominance-submission and hostility-nurturance can be derived to measure the orthogonal axes of the circle. Angular location and vector scores can be derived to represent the individual's modal interpersonal style and its intensity.

SAMPLE: CIRCLE was developed for clinical and research use with forensic psychiatric patients detained in secure hospitals, but is also appropriate for other institutions, such as prisons or psychiatric hospital wards.

RELIABILITY: Internal consistency: Blackburn and Renwick (1996) found mean alpha coefficients in two samples of .80 (range .49 to .87) and .83 (range .58 to .90). **Inter-rater:** In two samples, Blackburn and Renwick (1996) found mean intraclass correlations for two raters of .61 (range .55 to .68) and .73 (range .60 to .81). In another sample, McCartney, Collins, Park, Larkin, and Duggan (1999) found a mean intraclass correlation of .63 (range .55 to .72). **Test-retest:** Two-week retest correlations ranged from .83 to .91 (n=102), with a mean of .88 (Blackburn & Renwick, 1996).

VALIDITY: **Convergent:** Convergent validity is demonstrated by correlations of CIRCLE scales with self-reported aggression, extraversion, and avoidance (Blackburn & Fawcett, 1999), and with personality disorder measures (Blackburn, 1998a). Construct validity is further supported by the association of dominant-hostile styles with criminality in nonpsychotic offenders (Blackburn, 1998b). Unpublished research indicates that the scales have predictive utility in short-term risk assessment of hospitalised mentally disordered offenders.

LOCATION: Blackburn, R., & Renwick, S. J. (1996). Rating scales for measuring the interpersonal circle in forensic psychiatric patients. *Psychological Assessment, 8,* 76-84.

COMMENT: CIRCLE scales have satisfactory psychometric properties and meet the geometric requirements of a circumplex. They can be used for testing predictions from interpersonal theory (Blackburn, 1998c), but also provide a practical instrument for assessing social functioning in institutionalised populations that avoids the shortcomings of self-report measures. As yet, relationships with other measures of the interpersonal circumplex have not been assessed.

REFERENCES:

Blackburn, R. (1992). Criminal behaviour, personality disorder, and mental illness: The origins of confusion. *Criminal Behaviour and Mental Health, 2,* 66-77.

Blackburn, R. (1998a). Relationship of personality disorders to observer ratings of interpersonal style in forensic psychiatric patients. *Journal of Personality Disorders, 12*, 77-85.

Blackburn, R. (1998b). Criminality and the interpersonal circle in forensic psychiatric patients. *Criminal Justice and Behavior, 25*, 155-176.

Blackburn, R. (1998c). Psychopathy and personality disorder: Implications of interpersonal theory. In D. J. Cooke, A. E. Forth and R. D. Hare (Eds.). *Psychopathy: Theory, Research and Implications for Society* (pp. 269-301). Amsterdam: Kluwer.

Blackburn, R. (1999). Violence and personality: Distinguishing among violent offenders. In D. Curran and W. G. McCartney (Eds.). *Psychological Perspectives on Serious Criminal Risk.* (pp. 109-127). Leicester: British Psychological Society.

Blackburn, R., & Fawcett, D. (1999). The Antisocial Personality Questionnaire: An inventory for assessing personality deviation in offenders. *European Journal of Psychological Assessment, 15*, 14-24.

Blackburn, R., & Renwick, S. (1996). Rating scales for measuring the interpersonal circle in forensic psychiatric patients. *Psychological Assessment, 8*, 76-84.

McCartney, M., Collins, M., Park, B., Larkin, E., & Duggan, C. (1999). The assessment and meaning of the legal classification of offenders in a special hospital using observer ratings of interpersonal style. *Journal of Forensic Psychiatry, 10*, 17-33.

REVIEWER: Ron Blackburn, Department of Clinical Psychology, University of Liverpool, Liverpool L69 3GB, England, U.K.

5.09: CHILD REPORT OF POST-TRAUMATIC SYMPTOMS (CROPS).
AUTHOR: Greenwald and Rubin.

VARIABLE: Children's post-traumatic symptoms.

DESCRIPTION: The Child Report of Post-traumatic Symptoms (CROPS; Greenwald & Rubin, 1999) is a 24-item self-report covering the broad range of children's post-traumatic symptoms which have been noted in the literature (Fletcher, 1993) and which are conducive to self-reporting. Items were further selected for responsiveness to change (*e.g.* following successful treatment). Items are self-statements regarding specific symptoms over the past week, to be endorsed as *None* (0), *Some* (1), or *Lots* (2). The single full-scale score is tallied in about a minute and compared to the 'clinical concern' cut-off.

SAMPLE: The original validation studies used a community sample of children ages 8-15 (Greenwald & Rubin, 1999). Additional studies including older adolescents are underway; younger children would have trouble with the reading level but may respond orally. This instrument is intended for use as a screen for post-traumatic symptoms in post-disaster, mental health, pediatric, and educational settings, and as a treatment outcome measure.

RELIABILITY: Internal consistency: In published validation studies, coefficient alpha for the CROPS was .91, with each item-total correlation significant at the .001 level, ranging from .36 to .66 (Greenwald & Rubin, 1999). **Test-retest:** A sub-sample was re-tested after 4-6 weeks having first used paper-and-pencil, then the alternate form of telephone interview. For the total score the test-retest correlation was .80 ($p<.001$) (Greenwald & Rubin, 1999).

VALIDITY: Degree of trauma/loss exposure had a correlation of .60 ($p<.001$) with CROPS scores (Greenwald & Rubin, 1999). CROPS scores also declined following successful trauma-focused treatment as indicated by declines in other validated trauma measures and in severity of presenting problems (Greenwald, in press; Soberman, Greenwald, & Rule, in press). Additional studies are in progress.

LOCATION:

Greenwald, R., & Rubin, A. (1999). Brief assessment of children's post-traumatic symptoms: Development and preliminary validation of parent and child scales. *Research on Social Work Practice, 9,* 61-75. The test can also be found at www.childtrauma.com and www.sidran.org

COMMENT: It is essential to use trauma-specific instruments to assess post-traumatic symptoms, as anxiety and depression measures are insufficiently sensitive to this construct. When used in conjunction with the Parent Report of Post-traumatic Symptoms (PROPS), this instrument provides brief yet comprehensive coverage of children's and adolescents' post-traumatic symptoms. Further study is needed for fuller confidence in the measure.

REFERENCES:

Fletcher, K.E. (1993, October). *The spectrum of post-traumatic responses in children.* Presented at the Annual Meeting of the International Society for Traumatic Stress Studies, San Antonio.

Greenwald, R. (in press). Motivation - Adaptive Skills - Trauma Resolution (MASTR) therapy for adolescents with conduct problems: An open trial. *Journal of Aggression, Maltreatment, and Trauma.*

Greenwald, R., & Rubin, A. (1999). Brief assessment of children's post-traumatic symptoms: Development and preliminary validation of parent and child scales. *Research on Social Work Practice, 9,* 61-75.

Soberman, G.S., Greenwald, R., & Rule, D.L. (in press). A controlled study of eye
    movement desensitization and reprocessing (EMDR) for boys with
    conduct problems. *Journal of Aggression, Maltreatment, and Trauma*.

REVIEWER: Ricky Greenwald, 483 Belknap Rd., Framingham, MA 01701, U.S.A. E-mail: rickygr@childtrauma.com.

5.10: CODEPENDENCY ASSESSMENT TOOL (CODAT).
AUTHORS: Hughes-Hammer, Martsolf, and Zeller.

VARIABLE: Codependency, conceptualized as comprised of one core concept (Other Focus/Self Neglect) and four codependency subconcepts (Family of Origin Issues; Low Self-Worth; Hiding Self; and Medical Problems).

DESCRIPTION: Self-report scale which contains 25 items; 5 items represent core concept of 'Other Focus/Self Neglect' and 5 items represent each of the 4 codependency subconcepts. The scale has a five-point Likert-type format. Subjects are asked to record how often they feel in the way indicated by the item; responses range from *Rarely or never*=1 to *Most of the time*=5. One item is reversed scored. Scoring for the total CODAT is done by adding the scores on the 25 items after the score on item 20 has been reversed. Subscale scores are determined by adding the scores on the five items which comprise each of the separate subscales. Minimal codependency was defined as CODAT scores of 25-50; mild codependency was defined as CODAT scores of 51-75; moderate codependency was defined as CODAT scores of 76-100; and severe codependency was defined as CODAT scores of 101-125.

SAMPLES: The CODAT has been shown to be a reliable measure of the concept in varying populations including mental health clients, women in codependency therapy groups; depressed women; elderly men and women living in the community; and both male and female helping professionals.

RELIABILITY: Internal consistency: The CODAT has been shown to have satisfactory levels of internal reliability ranging from .76-.91 (Hughes-Hammer, Martsolf, & Zeller, 1998a; Hughes-Hammer, Martsolf, & Zeller, 1998b; Martsolf, Hughes-Hammer, Estok, & Zeller, 1999; Sedlak, Dohney, Estok, & Zeller, under review). **Test-retest:** Hughes-Hammer, Martsolf, and Zeller (1998b) reported a test-retest correlation of .91 in a sample of 32 undergraduate students in a course in psychiatric nursing after a two-week interval.

VALIDITY: Convergent: The nature and the strength of the relationship between depression measured by the Beck Depression Inventory (Beck, Steer, & Brown, 1996) and codependency as measured by the CODAT was shown to be strongly positive (r=.76, F=144.95, df=1,106, p<.001). (Hughes-Hammer, Martsolf, & Zeller, 1998a). **Construct:** Construct validity was established using known groups techniques. A 'norm' group of 38 professional women (university professor, administrators, and scientists) and a 'codependent' group of 21 women in treatment for codependency completed the CODAT. Differences between groups means on the total CODAT score and all five subscale scores were statistically significant (p<.01 (Hughes-Hammer, Martsolf, & Zeller, 1998b).

LOCATION: Hughes-Hammer, C., Martsolf, D.S., & Zeller, R.A. (1998). *Archives of Psychiatric Nursing, 12*, 264-272.

COMMENT: Codependency has been poorly defined and conceptualized in the literature and there has been a dearth of empirical evidence to support its usefulness as a concept. Therefore, its use in clinical practice has been compromised. The Hughes-Hammer, Martsolf, and Zeller conceptualization of the concept is an attempt to deal with this problem. The Hughes-Hammer *et al.* model has been tested and has been shown to have significant merit has a valid construction of the construct in differing subject populations.

REFERENCES:

Hughes-Hammer, C., Martsolf, D.S., & Zeller, R.A.(1998a). Depression and codependency in women. *Archives of Psychiatric Nursing 12*, 326-334.

Hughes-Hammer, C., Martsolf, D.S., & Zeller, R.A. (1998b). Development and testing of the codependency assessment tool. *Archives of Psychiatric Nursing, 12*, 264-272.

Martsolf, D.S., Hughes-Hammer, C., Estok, P. & Zeller, R.A. (1999). Codependency in male and female helping professionals. *Archives of Psychiatric Nursing, 13*, 97-103.

Martsolf, D.S., Sedlak, C., & Doheny, M.O. (2000). Codependency and related health variables. *Archives of Psychiatric Nursing, 14*, 150-158.

Sedlak, C., Doheny, M.O., Estok, P., & Zeller, R.A. (under review). *Alcohol use in women 65 years of age and older.*

REVIEWER: Donna S. Martsolf, 314 Henderson Hall, College of Nursing, Kent State University, Kent, OH 44242, U.S.A. E-mail: dmartsol@kent.edu

5.11: CONSTRUCTED MEANING SCALE, THE.
AUTHOR: Fife.

DEFINITION: Meaning is defined as individuals' unique perceptions of the world given the incidence of a personal crisis, and the ways that event redefines their world, their place in that world, and their self or identity.

DESCRIPTION: The most recent version of the Constructed Meaning Scale is comprised of 11 items on a 4-point Likert-type scale with the following responses: *Strongly agree, Agree, Disagree, Strongly disagree.* Scoring is on a continuum from positive to negative (11 to 44) with the highest possible score indicating the most positive construction of meaning. Negative items are reverse scored. Items pertain to the individual's identity, the relationship of the self to others, and the perception of possibilities for the future given the crisis. Instructions ask participants to respond to each item based on how they have been feeling about life during the past two weeks.

SAMPLES: This scale has been used by the author in two studies. An original version of 8 items, as reported in Fife (1995), included 422 persons diagnosed with various forms of cancer. The most recent version was incorporated in a comparison study of 76 persons with cancer and 130 persons with HIV/AIDS (Fife, under review).

RELIABILITY: Cronbach's alpha, item-total correlations, and factor analyses were used to assess reliability and validity in both of these studies. Cronbach's alpha for the total scale was .813 for the original scale as reported in the study of persons with cancer (study 1), and it was .895 for the latest version as used in the comparison study of persons with cancer and HIV/AIDS (study 2). Item-total correlations ranged from .501 to .727 in study 1 and from .351 to .714 in study 2, with all but two items having correlations of .56 or above. A factor analysis based on principal components extraction was carried out in each of these studies, and both versions of the scale were shown to be comprised of one predominant factor, which in study 1 explained 57.3% of the variance and in study 2 explained 70.8% of the variance.

VALIDITY: Construct: Construct validity, or the extent to which the scale performs in accordance with theoretical expectations, was supported in both studies by its correlations with other theoretically relevant variables.

LOCATION: Fife, B.L. (1994). The conceptualization of meaning in illness. *Social Science and Medicine, 38,* 309-316

COMMENT: There has been increased interest in the concept of meaning within the context of stress research. It has been suggested by several scholars that it is the meaning ascribed to a life-changing event which shapes individuals' responses. Therefore, further exploration of this concept within the coping process appears warranted, and this scale provides one means of reliably measuring the construct.

REFERENCES:
Fife, B.L. (1994). The conceptualization of meaning in illness. *Social Science and Medicine, 38,* 309-316

Fife, B.L. (1995). The measurement of meaning in illness. *Social Science and Medicine, 40,* 1021-1028

Fife, B.L. (Under Review). The role of constructed meaning in adaptation to the Stress of Personal Crises.

Fife B.L., Huster, G.A., Cornetta, K.G., Kennedy, V.N., Akard, L.P., & Broun E.R. (2000). Longitudinal study of adaptation to the stress of bone marrow transplantation. *Journal of Clinical Oncology, 18*, No. 7, April.

REVIEWER: B.L. Fife, Center for Nursing Research, School of Nursing, Indiana University, Indianapolis, IN 46202, U.S.A.

5.12: DEATH DEPRESSION SCALE, THE.

AUTHORS: Templer, Lavoie, Chalgujian, and Thomas-Dobson.

VARIABLE: Death Depression.

DESCRIPTION: Self-report scale contains 17-items with a true-false format (15 T, versus 2 F). Respondents are asked about how they feel generally, and to rate each item on a true (15 items) false (2 items) format. Both of the negative items are reverse scores, so that possible scores on the scale can range between 0 and 17. In the meantime, a Likert format was explored. Higher scores on the scale indicate a higher level of death depression.

SAMPLE: Templer *et al.* (1990) intended the scale to be used for the assessment of death depression in non-psychiatric populations.

RELIABILITY: Internal consistency: It demonstrated satisfactory levels of internal reliability in a U.S.A. sample by using the English version (Templer *et al.*, 1990), as well as in three Arab countries by using the Arabic version: Egypt, Lebanon, and Kuwait (Abdel-Khalek, 1997, 1998, in press).

VALIDITY: **Convergent:** It demonstrated satisfactory convergent validity with measures of death anxiety, general anxiety, and general depression. **Discriminant:** Good differentiation between death anxiety and death depression.

LOCATION: Templer, D.I., Lavoie, M., Chalgujian, H., & Thomas-Dobson, S. (1990). The measurement of death depression. *Journal of Clinical Psychology, 46,* 834-839.

COMMENT: The Death Depression Scale has good psychometric properties but less than optimal differentiation from the death anxiety. So, Templer and his colleagues (Templer, personal communication) are carrying out the Death Depression Scale Revised.

REFERENCES:

Abdel-Khalek,A.M. (1997). Death, anxiety, and depression. *Omega: Journal of Death and Dying, 35,* 219-229.

Abdel-Khalek, A.M. (in press). Death, anxiety, and depression in Kuwaiti undergraduates. *Omega: Journal of Death and Dying.*

Abdel-Khalek, A.M. (1998). Death, anxiety, and depression in Lebanese undergraduates. *Omega: Journal of Death and Dying, 37,* 289-302.

Alvarado, K.A., Templer, D.I., Bresler, C., & Thomas-Dobson, S. (1992-93). Are death anxiety and death depression distinct entities? *Omega: Journal of Death and Dying, 26,* 113-118.

Alvarado, K.A., Templer, D.I., Bresler, C., & Thomas-Dobson, S. (1995). The relationship of religious variables to death depression and death anxiety. *Journal of Clinical Psychology, 51,* 202-204.

Hintze, J., Templer, D.I., Cappelletty, G.G., & Frederick, W. (1993). Death depression and death anxiety in HIV-infected males. *Death Studies, 17,* 333-341.

Siscoe, K., Reimer, W., Yanovsky, A., Thomas-Dobson, S., & Templer, D.I. (1992). Death depression versus death anxiety: Exploration of different correlates. *Psychological Reports, 71*, 1191-1194.

Templer, D.I., Lavoie, M., Chalgujian, H., & Thomas-Dobson, S. (1990). The measurement of death depression. *Journal of Clinical Psychology, 46*, 834-839.

Triplett, G., Cohen D., Reimer, W., Rinaldi, S., Hill, C., Roshdieh, S., Stanczak, E.M., Siscoe, K., & Templer, D.I. (1995). Death discomfort differential. *Omega: Journal of Death and Dying, 31*, 295-304.

REVIEWER: Ahmed M. Abdel-Khalek, College of Social Sciences, Kuwait University, PO Box 68168, Kaifan, Code No. 71962, Kuwait.

5.13: DEATH OBSESSION SCALE, THE.
AUTHOR: Abdel-Khalek.

VARIABLE: Death obsession.

DESCRIPTION: Self-report scale in two equivalent Arabic and English versions. It contains 15 statements representing death obsession, in which three factors were disclosed: death rumination, death domination, and death idea repetition. Respondents are asked about how they feel generally and to rate each item on a five-point scale, *i.e. No* (1), *A little* (2), *A fair amount* (3), *Much* (4), and *Very much* (5). So, the possible scores on the scale can range between 15 and 75. All the items are positively scored. Higher scores on the scale indicate a high level of death obsession.

SAMPLE: Abdel-Khalek (1998) intended the scale to be used for the assessment of death obsession in non-psychiatric populations. However, Abdel-Khalek (unpublished a, b) tested psychiatric patients.

RELIABILITY: **Internal consistency:** Cronbach's alpha reliabilities of the scale were .90, .91, and .91 for males, females and the combined group respectively. **Test-retest:** Abdel-Khalek (1998) reported a test-retest correlation of r=.91, .92, and .92 for males, females, and the combined group of undergraduates respectively after an one-week interval.

VALIDITY: **Convergent:** It demonstrated satisfactory convergent validity with measures of death anxiety, death depression, general obsession, general anxiety, and general depression (Abdel-Khalek, 1998).

LOCATION: Abdel-Khalek, A.M. (1998). The structure and measurement of death obsession. *Personality and Individual Differences, 24*, 159-165.

COMMENT: There is good evidence for the satisfactory psychometric properties of the Death Obsession Scale in its Arabic version. However, there is a need to use the English form of the scale with English-speaking samples.

REFERENCES:

Abdel-Khalek, A.M. (1998). The structure and measurement of death obsession. *Personality and Individual Differences, 24*, 159-165.

Abdel-Khalek, A.M. (Unpublished a). Death obsession in normals, neurotics, psychotics, and addicts.

Abdel-Khalek, A.M. (Unpublished b). Death obsession among Egyptians, Kuwaitis, and Syrians.

REVIEWER: Ahmed M. Abdel-Khalek, College of Social Sciences, Kuwait University, PO Box 68168 Kaifan, Code No. 71962, Kuwait.

5.14: DEPRESSION ANXIETY STRESS SCALES (DASS).
AUTHORS: Lovibond and Lovibond.

VARIABLE: Depression, Anxiety, Stress/Tension.

DESCRIPTION: The DASS is a 42-item self-report scale designed to distinguish between the negative emotional states of depression, anxiety and stress. Respondents are asked to rate the extent to which they have experienced each symptom over the past week on a 4-point severity/frequency scale. Responses range from *Did not apply to me at all* (0) to *Applied to me very much, or most of the time* (3). Scores for Depression, Anxiety and Stress scales are calculated by summing the scores for the relevant 14 items. In addition to the 42-item questionnaire, a short version, the DASS21 is available with 7 items per scale. Totals for each scale on the DASS21 are doubled, so that they are comparable to those for the 42-item DASS. Note that an earlier version of the DASS was referred to as the Self-Analysis Questionnaire (SAQ).

SAMPLE: Lovibond and Lovibond (1995) carried out the initial development of the DASS with non-clinical samples. However, since the basic assumption underlying the DASS is that differences between the depression, anxiety and stress experienced by normal subjects and clinical subjects are essentially differences of degree, the DASS may also be used in clinical settings for clarifying the locus of emotional disturbance as part of a broader clinical assessment. Thus, the psychometric properties of the DASS have also been examined among clinical groups (Antony, Bieling, Cox, Enns, & Swinson, 1998).

RELIABILITY: **Internal consistency:** Demonstrated satisfactory levels in both clinical and normal samples (Lovibond & Lovibond, 1995; Brown, Korotitsch, Chorpita, & Barlow, 1997; Antony et al., 1998). Cronbach's alphas range from .91, .81 and .89 (Lovibond & Lovibond, 1995) to .97, .92 and .95 (Antony et al., 1998) respectively on the depression, anxiety and stress sub-scales. Internal consistency within diagnostic groups ranges from .88 to .96 (Brown et al., 1997). For the DASS21, Cronbach's alphas range from .81, .73 and .81 (Lovibond & Lovibond, 1995) to .94, .87 and .91 (Antony et al., 1998) respectively for the depression, anxiety and stress sub-scales. **Test-retest:** Evidence of favourable temporal stability with test-retest correlations of $r=.71$ for depression, .79 for anxiety and .81 for stress among 20 clinical subjects after a 2-week interval (Brown et al., 1997). Lovibond, (1998) reported moderate temporal stability with test-retest correlations of .29 for depression, .41 for anxiety and .39 for stress among 882 university students over a 3-8 year period. The stability of the 3 scales did not vary appreciably as a function of the duration of the follow up period.

VALIDITY: **Convergent:** Each of the respective sub-scales demonstrated satisfactory convergence with various measures including those of depression and anxiety (Lovibond & Lovibond, 1995; Brown et al., 1997; Antony et al., 1998) and worry (Brown et al., 1998). Convergence of DASS21 scales to other measures of anxiety and depression followed a similar pattern although there were some changes in magnitude (Antony et al., 1998). **Discriminant:** The validity of the DASS is also supported by its ability to differentiate between various DSM-III-R anxiety and mood groups (panic disorder, generalised anxiety disorder, social phobia, simple phobia, obsessive compulsive disorder and mood disorder) in the predicted directions (Brown *et al.*, 1997; Antony *et al.*, 1998). The DASS also successfully discriminates between the three negative emotional syndromes in non-clinical samples (Lovibond & Lovibond, 1995; Antony, 1998). Furthermore these observations appear to extend to the DASS21 (Antony, 1998).

LOCATION: Lovibond, S.H., & Lovibond, P.F. (1995). *Manual for the Depression Anxiety Stress Scales*. (2nd Ed). Sydney, Australia: The Psychology Foundation of Australia.

COMMENT: There is growing evidence for the excellent psychometric properties of the DASS. The scales not only provide measures of anxiety and depression, but both of these scales are further differentiated from the related state of tension/stress. Future work should assess the sensitivity of the DASS and DASS21 for measuring change in anxiety and depression following treatment.

REFERENCES:

Antony, M.M., Bieling, P.J., Cox, B.J., Enns, M.W., & Swinson, R.P. (1998). Psychometric properties of the 42-item and 21-item versions of the Depression Anxiety Stress Scales (DASS) in clinical groups and a community sample. *Psychological Assessment, 10*, 176-181.

Brown, T.A., Chorpita, B.F., Korotisch, W., & Barlow, D.H. (1997). Psychometric properties of the Depression Anxiety Stress Scales (DASS) in clinical samples. *Behaviour Research and Therapy, 35*, 79-89.

Lovibond, P. F. (1998). Long-term stability of depression, anxiety, and stress syndromes. *Journal of Abnormal Psychology, 107*, 520-526.

Lovibond, S.H., & Lovibond, P.F. (1995). *Manual for the Depression Anxiety Stress Scales*. (2nd Ed). Sydney, Australia: The Psychology Foundation of Australia.

Lovibond, S.H., & Lovibond, P.F. (1995). The structure of negative emotional states: Comparison of the Depression Anxiety Stress Scales (DASS) with the Beck Depression and Anxiety Inventories. *Behaviour Research and Therapy, 33*, 335-343.

REVIEWER: Caroline Hunt and Edmund Keogh, Department of Psychology, Goldsmiths College, University of London, New Cross, London, SE14 6NW, England, U.K. E-mail: psp01ch@gold.ac.uk and e.keogh@gold.ac.uk.

5.15: DEPRESSION-HAPPINESS SCALE, THE.
AUTHORS: McGreal and Joseph.

VARIABLE: Subjective well-being, Positive affect.

DESCRIPTION: The Depression-Happiness Scale (McGreal & Joseph, 1993) is a self-report scale which contains 25 items representing a mix of affective, cognitive, and bodily experiences. Of these, 12 of the items concern positive thoughts, feelings, and bodily experiences and 13 concerned negative thoughts, feelings, and bodily experiences. Respondents are asked about how they had felt in the past 7 days and to rate each item on a 4-point scale: *Never* (0), *Rarely* (1), *Sometimes* (2), and *Often* (3). The 13 negative items are reverse scored so that possible scores on the scale can range between 0 and 75. Higher scores on the scale indicate a higher frequency of positive thoughts, feelings, and bodily experiences.

SAMPLE: McGreal and Joseph (1993) intended the scale to be used for the assessment of subjective well-being in non-psychiatric populations and were concerned that the measure should be able to capture individual differences in affect without ceiling or floor effects.

RELIABILITY: **Internal consistency:** It demonstrated satisfactory levels of internal reliability (McGreal & Joseph, 1993; Cammock, Joseph, & Lewis, 1994; Lewis & Joseph, 1995; Walsh, Joseph, & Lewis, 1995; Joseph, Lewis, & Olsen, 1996; Lewis, Joseph, & McCollam, 1996; Joseph & Lewis, 1998), ranging from .85 (Lewis, Lanigan, Joseph, & de Fockert, 1997) to .93 (Joseph, Lewis, & Olsen, 1996). **Test-retest:** Lewis and Joseph (1997) reported a test-retest correlation of $r=.55$ among 14 female Northern Irish university students after a two year interval.

VALIDITY: **Convergent:** It demonstrated satisfactory convergent validity with various measures of subjective well-being, including those of depression (McGreal & Joseph, 1993; Lewis, Joseph ,& McCollam, 1996; Joseph, Lewis, & Olsen, 1996; Joseph & Lewis, 1998), happiness (Lewis & Joseph ,1995; Joseph & Lewis, 1998), locus of control (Cammock, Joseph, & Lewis, 1994), self-esteem (Cammock, Joseph, & Lewis, 1994), anxiety (Cammock, Joseph, & Lewis, 1994; Lewis, Joseph, & McCollam, 1996), general health (Walsh, Joseph, & Lewis, 1995), and satisfaction with life (Lewis & Joseph, 1995; Lewis, Lanigan, Joseph, & de Fockert, 1997).

LOCATION: McGreal, R., & Joseph, S. (1993). The Depression-Happiness Scale. *Psychological Reports, 73,* 1279-1282.

COMMENT: There is growing evidence for the satisfactory psychometric properties of the Depression-Happiness Scale. However, the assessment of negative and positive feelings using a statistically bipolar scale is a controversial issue.

REFERENCES:

Cammock, T., Joseph, S., & Lewis, C.A. (1994). Personality correlates of scores on the Depression-Happiness Scale. *Psychological Reports, 75*, 1649-1650.

Joseph, S., & Lewis, C.A. (1998). The Depression-Happiness Scale: Reliability and validity of a bipolar self-report scale. *Journal of Clinical Psychology, 54*, 537-544.

Joseph, S., Lewis, C.A., & Olsen, C. (1996). Convergent validity of the Depression-Happiness Scale with measures of depression. *Journal of Clinical Psychology, 52*, 551-554.

Lewis, C.A., & Joseph, S. (1995). Convergent validity of the Depression-Happiness Scale with measures of happiness and satisfaction with life. *Psychological Reports, 76*, 876-878.

Lewis, C.A., Joseph, S., & McCollam, P. (1996). Convergent validity of the Depression-Happiness Scale with the Crown-Crisp Experiential Index. *Psychological Reports, 78*, 497-498.

Lewis, C.A., & Joseph, S. (1997). Is the Depression-Happiness Scale a measure of a state or trait? Test-retest data over two years. *Psychological Reports, 81*, 1313-1314.

McGreal, R., & Joseph, S. (1993). The Depression-Happiness Scale. *Psychological Reports, 73*, 1279-1282.

Walsh, J., Joseph, S., & Lewis, C.A. (1995). Internal-reliability and convergent validity of the Depression-Happiness Scale with the General Health Questionnaire in an employed adult sample. *Psychological Reports*, *76*, 137-138.

REVIEWER: Christopher Alan Lewis, School of Psychology and Communication Sciences, University of Ulster at Magee College, Londonderry, BT48 7JL, Northern Ireland, U.K.

5.16: DISSOCIATION QUESTIONNAIRE (DIS-Q).

AUTHORS: Vanderlinden, Van Dyck, Vertommen, and Vandereycken.

VARIABLE: A broad spectrum of dissociative experiences.

DESCRIPTION: The **Dissociation Questionnaire** (DIS-Q) is a 63-item self-reporting scale for measurement of dissociative experiences. Factor analysis detected four subscales which together accounted for 77 % of the common variance: identity confusion (referring experiences of derealisation and depersonalisation), loss of control over behaviour, thoughts and emotions, amnesia, and absorption (referring to experiences of enhanced concentration which are supposed to play an important role in hypnosis). Five different answer categories were chosen. The subjects indicate to what extent that item is applicable to that particular subject:1 (=*Not at all*) to 5 (=*Extremely*). All scores are average scores, obtained by dividing the total score by the number of items

SAMPLE: The DIS-Q is developed to assess the prevalence of dissociative symptoms in both general and psychiatric population.

RELIABILITY: **Internal consistency:** The DIS-Q has a good internal consistency. The Cronbach's alpha coefficient was .96 for the total scale and .94, .93, .88, and .67 for the four subscales. **Test-retest:** Test-retest was measured with an interval of 3 to 4 weeks in a group of 50 subjects randomly selected from the general population (25 adolescents and 25 adults). The test-retest for the total score is .94 and respectively .92, .92, .93 and .75 for the subscales.

VALIDITY: **Convergent:** The most important findings supporting the convergent validity are the high correlation with the Dissociative Experiences Scale (r=.85) and the Somatoform Dissociation Questionnaire (r=.82). Divergent validity is supported by the low correlations between the subscale Psychoticism and Extraversion of the Eysenck Personality Questionnaire and the DISQ. **Discriminant:** The DIS-Q differentiates clearly between patients with dissociative pathology and other psychiatric categories. A history of traumatisation is linked to significantly higher DIS-Q scores. The highest DIS-Q scores are obtained in the sample reporting a history of sexual abuse.

FURTHER EMPIRICAL USES: The DIS-Q has been translated into 15 languages and can be used for diagnostic purposes and therapy evaluation.

LOCATION: Vanderlinden, J., Van Dyck, R., Vandereycken, W., Vertommen, H., & Verkes, R.J. (1993). The Dissociation Questionnaire (DIS-Q): Development and characteristics of a new self-report questionnaire. *Clinical Psychology and Psychotherapy, 1,* 21-27.

COMMENT: The critical total score between patients with dissociative disorders and non-clinical individuals was established at 2.5. With this cut-off score the sensitivity index was 91% and the specificity index was 97%.

REFERENCES:

Nijenhuis, E., Spinhoven, P., Van Dyck, R., Van der Hart, O., & Vanderlinden, J. (1998). Psychometric characteristics of the Somatoform Dissociation Questionnaire: A replication study. *Psychotherapy and Psychosomatics*, *67*, 17-23.

Vanderlinden, J. (1993). *Dissociative Experiences, Trauma and Hypnosis: Research Findings and Clinical Applications in Eating Disorders*. Delft: Eburon

Vanderlinden, J., Van Dyck, R., Vandereycken, W., Vertommen, H., & Verkes R.J. (1993). The Dissociation Questionnaire (DIS-Q): Development and characteristics of a new self-report questionnaire. *Clinical Psychology and Psychotherapy*, *1*, 21-27.

Vanderlinden, J., & Vandereycken W. (1997). *Trauma, Dissociation and Impulse Dyscontrol in Eating Disorders*. New York: Brunner/Mazel.

Vanderlinden, J., Vandereycken, W., Van Dyck, R., & Vertommen, H. (1993). Dissociative experiences and trauma in eating disorders. *International Journal of Eating Disorders*, *13*, 187-194.

REVIEWER: Michel Probst, Katholieke Universiteit Leuven, Faculty of Physical Education & Physiotherapy, Department of Rehabilitation Sciences and University Center Sint Jozef, Leuvensesteenweg 517, B-3070 Kortenberg, Belgium. E-mail: michel.probst@flok.kuleuven.ac.be

5.17: ENDLER MULTIDIMENSIONAL ANXIETY SCALES (EMAS).

AUTHORS: Endler, Edwards, and Vitelli.

VARIABLE: Four aspects of Trait anxiety (EMAS-Trait; Social Evaluation, Physical Danger, Ambiguous and Daily Routines); two aspects of State anxiety (EMAS-State; Cognitive-worry and Autonomic-emotional); and five aspects of Perception, indicating the type of anxiety evoked by a specific situation (EMAS-Perception; Social Evaluation, Physical Danger, Ambiguous, Daily Routines, and Degree of Threat evoked by the situation).

DESCRIPTION: The Endler Multidimensional Anxiety Scales (EMAS; Endler, Edwards & Vitelli, 1991). The EMAS-Trait measures predisposition to anxiety. The scale consists of 60 items, with 15 items for each of Social Evaluation trait anxiety, Physical Danger trait anxiety, Ambiguous trait anxiety, and Daily Routines trait anxiety. Responses for the EMAS-Trait measures are scored on a 5-point intensity scale ranging from (1) *Not at all* to (5) *Very much*. The EMAS-State measures current levels of anxiety. The scale consists of 20 items, with 10 items for Cognitive-worry state anxiety and 10 items for Autonomic-emotional state anxiety. Responses for the EMAS-State measures are scored on a 5-point intensity scale ranging from (1) *Not at all* to (5) *Very much*. The EMAS-Perception scales measure 5 facets of perception of stressful situations (social evaluation, physical danger, ambiguous, daily routines, and degree of threat). Responses for the EMAS-Perception measure are scored on a 5 point intensity scale ranging from not at all to very much. There are an additional 3 open ended clinical questions for the EMAS-P: (1) Please describe briefly the situation you are in right now; (2) Does anything in particular about the situation threaten you? Please specify; and (3) Is there anything else about this experience as a whole that you feel threatened by? Please specify.

SAMPLE: Normative data for the EMAS scales are provided for U.S.A. adults, undergraduate university students, psychiatry patients, military forces, Canadian adolescents and adults.

RELIABILITY: **Internal consistency:** The coefficient alpha reliabilities for the EMAS scales are provided for males and females separately. The alphas for EMAS-Trait Social Evaluation range from .87 to .94 for males and .92 to .94 for females. The alphas for EMAS-Trait Physical Danger range from .87 to .92 for males and .91 to .95 for females. The alphas for EMAS-Trait Ambiguous range from .91 to .94 for males and .90 to .94 for females. The alphas for EMAS-Trait Daily Routines range from .82 to .95 for males and .84 to .96 for females. The alphas for EMAS-State Cognitive-worry range from .82 to .91 for males and .83 to .90 for females. The alpha for EMAS-State Autonomic-emotional range from .83 to .88 for males and .78 to .90 for females. The alphas for EMAS-State Total range from .88 to .92 for males and .89 to .94 for females. The EMAS-Perception scales are one item scales, and thus no reliability coefficients can be computed for this measure. **Test-retest:** The test-retest reliabilities for EMAS-Trait were computed on one sample with a two week interval and two samples with a four week interval. For the two week interval, the test-retest reliabilities for the Social Evaluation, Physical Danger, Ambiguous, and Daily Routines facets of trait anxiety were .75, .79, .71 and .60 respectively. For the first two week interval sample, the test-retest reliabilities for the above four facets were .62, .56, .59 and .50. For the second two week interval sample they were .79, .74, .68 and .59 . No test-retest reliabilities were computed for EMAS-State or the EMAS-Perception because of the expectation that people will react differently in different situations (*e.g.*, stressful vs. non-stressful).

VALIDITY: The EMAS Scales are derived from the Multidimensional Interaction Model of Stress and Anxiety (Endler, Edwards, & Vitelli, 1991; Endler, Edwards,

Vitelli & Parker, 1989). Factor analysis of the EMAS-State and -Trait attest to the multidimensionality of these scales (and hence, construct validity) for the various samples for which normative data are provided (see section on Sample, above; Endler *et al.*, 1991; Endler, Parker, Bagby, & Cox, 1991). Results of a number of specific studies are provided which show that each of the EMAS scales have good construct, content, and criterion validity. For example, moderate to high item-remainder correlations for the EMAS-State and -Trait subscales attest to their content validity, and criterion validity was confirmed through correlating the EMAS-State and EMAS-Trait with various other measures, including the Spielberger (1983) State-Trait Anxiety Inventory, the Anxiety Sensitivity Index (Peterson & Heilbronner, 1987), and the neuroticism subscale from Eysenck and Eysenck (1968) Personality Inventory (EPI).

FURTHER EMPIRICAL USES: The EMAS can be used in research and also to assess changes in state and trait anxiety as a function of education, training, counselling and psychotherapy, in clinical and non-clinical settings (see *EMAS Manual*, Endler, Edwards, & Vitelli, 1991, for specific studies pertaining to these areas). The scales can also be used to further assess the Multidimensional Interaction Model of Stress and Anxiety (Endler, Edwards, & Vitelli, 1991; Endler, Edwards, Vitelli, & Parker, 1989).

LOCATION: Endler, N.S., Edwards, J.M., & Vitelli, R. (1991). *Endler Multidimensional Anxiety Scales (EMAS): Manual.* Los Angeles, CA: Western Psychological Services.

COMMENT: The assessment of state and trait anxiety and the perception of stressful situations are based on theory and supported by empirical research. Further research is needed to validate the EMAS scales in specific populations and for changes in state anxiety and perception of stressful situations as a result therapeutic applications. Behavioural and physiological measures of anxiety would also be useful in further validating the EMAS scales.

REFERENCES

Endler, N.S., Edwards, J.M., Vitelli, R., & Parker, J.D.A. (1989). Assessment of state and trait anxiety: Endler Multidimensional Anxiety Scales. *Anxiety Research: An International Journal, 2,* 1-14.

Endler, N.S., Parker, J.D.A., Bagby, R.M., & Cox, B. (1991). The multidimensionality of state and trait anxiety: The factor structure of the Endler Multidimensional Anxiety Scales. *Journal of Personality and Social Psychology, 60,* 919-926.

Eysenck, H.J., & Eysenck, S.B.G. (1968). *The Manual of the Eysenck Personality Inventory.* San Diego, CA: Educational and Industrial Testing Service.

Peterson, R.A., & Heilbronner, R.L. (1987). The Anxiety Sensitivity Index: Construct validity and factor analytic structure. *Journal of Anxiety Disorders, 1,* 117-121.

Spielberger, C.D. (1983). *Manual for the State-Trait Anxiety Inventory (Form V).* Palo, Alto, CA: Consulting Psychologists Press.

REVIEWER: Norman S. Endler and Sophia D. Macrodimitris, Department of Psychology, York University, 4700 Keele St., Toronto, Ontario, Canada, M3J 1P3.

5.18: FEAR OF PAIN QUESTIONNAIRE-III.
AUTHORS: McNeil and Rainwater.

VARIABLE: Fear of pain.

DESCRIPTION: The Fear of Pain Questionnaire-III (FPQ-III; McNeil & Rainwater, 1998) is a self-report measure that allows for an evaluation of fear responses to specific, environmentally-based pain situations. It consists of 30 items distributed equally onto 3 subscales designed to assess fear of minor pain (*e.g.*, biting your tongue while eating), severe pain (*e.g.*, falling down a flight of concrete stairs), and medical pain (*e.g.*, breaking your neck). The FFQ-III is structured such that painful situations are presented and respondents are asked to rate the degree to which they fear experiencing pain in each situation using a 5-point Likert scale ranging from 1 (*Not at all*) to 5 (*Extreme*). Scores range from 10 to 50 for each subscale and 30 to 150 for the total score. Higher scores indicate greater fear. Sperry-Clark, McNeil, and Ciano-Federoff (1999) report that the instrument possesses ease of readability (grade level of approximately 6.4) and, thus, is effective for a general adult audience.

SAMPLE: The FPQ-III was designed to assess situational fear of pain in healthy individuals, patients with acute and chronic pain, and patients with other medical conditions. It can be used in both clinical and research settings. To date, this measure has been applied in university students (McNeil & Rainwater, 1998; Sullivan, Bishop, & Pirik, 1995), chronic pain patients (McCracken, Gross, Aikens, & Carnrike, 1996; McNeil & Rainwater, 1998; Sperry-Clark *et al.*, 1998), general medical patients (McNeil & Rainwater, 1998), orofacial pain patients (McNeil, Au, Zvolensky, Rettig-McKee, Klineberg, & Ho, 1999), and headache sufferers (Hursey & Jacks, 1992; Kaiser, Primavera, & Schwartz, 1993; Thonsgaard, Hursey, Oliver, & McGruder, 1992).

RELIABILITY: **Internal consistency:** Internal consistency for each subscale and total score has been found to be acceptable in university students (FPQ-III minor pain: α=.88, FPQ-III severe pain: α=.87, FPQ-II medical pain: α=.87, FPQ-III total score: α=.92; McNeil & Rainwater, 1998). Additionally, acceptable test-retest reliability for each subscale and total score (test-retest interval=3 weeks) has been observed in university students (FPQ-III minor pain: r=.69, FPQ-III severe pain: r=.73, FPQ-III medical pain: r=.76, FPQ-III total score: r=.74; McNeil & Rainwater, 1998). Data from samples of headache sufferers (Hursey & Jacks, 1992; Thonsgaard *et al.*, 1992) are similar to those reported above and, as such, suggest acceptable internal consistency in medical populations.

VALIDITY: The FPQ-III has demonstrated acceptable convergent, discriminant, and construct validity. To illustrate, McNeil *et al.* (1999), studying dental patients, found the FPQ-III subscale and total scores to be significantly and positively associated with scores on a measure of fear of dental-related stimuli (convergent validity) and to be weakly associated with other general measures, depression, anxiety, and general discomfort (discriminant validity). McNeil and Rainwater (1998), studying university students, found those with high fear of pain to score higher on other measures of fear (*i.e.*, Fear Survey Schedule-III; Dental Fear Survey) and fear propensity (*i.e.*, Anxiety Sensitivity Index) and to exhibit greater avoidance/escape behaviour in a painful situation when compared to those with low fear of pain (construct validity). Data supporting favourable convergent, discriminant, and construct validity have also been reported by others (*e.g.*, Hursey & Jacks, 1992; Weaver *et al.*, 1999). To date, there has been little evaluation of the factor structure of the FPQ-III. The only published factor analysis (McNeil & Rainwater, 1998) has shown evidence of general factorial validity. Specifically, 9 of 10 items from the FPQ-III severe pain and medical pain subscales exhibited reasonably high factor loading (*i.e.*, .50 or greater) on their parent factor. However, for minor pain, only 6 of 10 items had a high factor loading on the parent factor. These results suggest that the factor structure of the FPQ-III may prove to be stable but that its simple structure might be improved. Because some items had salient cross-loadings on non-parent factors, and higher-order factor structure has not been assessed, additional research is needed before firm conclusions regarding the factorial validity of the FPQ-III can be drawn.

LOCATION: The FPQ-III can be found in McNeil, D. W., & Rainwater III, A. J. (1998), Development of the fear of pain questionnaire-III, *Journal of Behavioral Medicine, 21,* 389-410. The authors have provided permission to users to copy the instrument for research and clinical purposes. Alternatively, the FPQ-III can be obtained by writing Daniel W. McNeil, Ph.D., Department of Psychology, Anxiety, Psychophysiology, and Pain Research Laboratory and Clinic, West Virginia University, P. O. Box 6040, Morgantown, West Virginia 26506-6040, U.S.A. Fax: (304) 293-6606, E-mail dmcneil@wvu.edu.

COMMENT: The FPQ-III is in the early stages of development; however, there is evidence to suggest that it is a sound measure with which to assess fear responses to specific, environmentally-based pain situations. Its short length permits it to be administered in a time efficient manner in both clinical and research settings. Patient and non-patient norms are available in several of the above mentioned publications (*e.g.*, McNeil & Rainwater, 1998; Sperry-Clark *et al.*, 1999). Although criticised for not providing a multidimensional evaluation of fear responses (*i.e.*, an evaluation of cognitive, physiological, and behavioural components; Larsen, Taylor, & Asmundson, 1997; McCracken *et al.*, 1996), the FPQ-III may be particularly useful in research protocols and clinical/medical cases where an assessment of fear responses to specific pain situations is required. For example, the FPQ-III may be used to identify individuals who may experience complications and require psychological consultation prior to medical procedures due to fear of pain. Overall, the FPQ-III appears very promising and, as noted by

McNeil and Rainwater (1998), combined application with the Pain Anxiety Symptoms Scale (McCracken, Zayfert, & Gross, 1992, 1993) may provide the most comprehensive approach to assessing fear of pain.

REFERENCES:

Hursey, K.G., & Jacks, S.D. (1992). Fear of pain in recurrent headache sufferers. *Headache, 32,* 283-286.

Kaiser, R.S., Primavera, J.P., & Schwartz, A.L. (1993). *Perceived competence and fear of pain as contributory factors in analgesic rebound patients.* Paper presented at the annual meeting of the American Association for the study of Headache, San Francisco, CA.

Larsen, D.K., Taylor, S., & Asmundson, G.J.G.(1997). Exploratory factor analysis of the Pain Anxiety Symptom Scale in patients with chronic pain complaints. *Pain,* 69, 27-34.

McCracken, L.M., Zayfert, C., & Gross, R.T. (1992). The Pain Anxiety Symptom Scale: Development and validation of a scale to measure fear of pain. *Pain, 50,* 67-73.

McCracken, L.M., Zayfert, C., & Gross, R.T. (1993). The pain anxiety symptoms scale (PASS): A multimodal measure of pain-specific anxiety symptoms. *Behavior Therapist,* 16, 183-184.

McCracken, L.M., Gross, R.T., Aikens, J., & Carnrike Jr., C.L.M. (1996). The assessment of anxiety and fear in person's with chronic pain: A comparison of instruments. *Behavioral Research and Therapy, 34,* 927-933.

McNeil, D.W., & Rainwater III, A. J. (1998). Development of the fear of pain questionnaire-III. *Journal of Behavioral Medicine, 21,* 389-410.

McNeil, D.W., Au, A.R., Zvolensky, M.J., Rettig-McKee, D., Klineberg, I.J., & Ho, C.C.K. (1999). *Fear of pain in orofacial pain patients.* Unpublished manuscript.

Sperry-Clark, J.A., McNeil, D.W., & Ciano-Federoff, L. (1999). In L. VandeCreek & T.L., Jackson (Eds.), *Innovations in Clinical Practice: A Source Book*, Vol. 17, (pp. 293-305). Sarasota, FL: Professional Resource Press.

Sullivan, M.J.L., Bishop, S.R., & Pirik, J. (1995). The Pain and Catastrophizing Scale: Development and validation. *Psychological Assessments*, 7, 524-532.

Thornsgaard, S., Hursey, K.G., Oliver, K.C., & McGrunder, A.K. (1992). *The fear of pain questionnaire: Reliability and validity in recurrent tension headache sufferers*. Poster presented at the meeting of the Association for Advancement of Behavior Therapy, Boston, MA.

Weiver, B., McNeil, D., Graves, R., McKee, D., Zvolensky, M., Capehart, K., & Wlson, J. (1999). *Fear of pain in oral surgery patients*. Poster presented at the meeting of the International Association of Dental Research, Vancouver, B.C., Canada.

REVIEWERS: Gordon J.G. Asmundson, and Michel F. Bonin, Clinical Research and Development, Regina Health District, Saskatchewan, Canada, S4S 0A5. E-mail gasmundson@reginahealth.sk.ca

5.19: HEALTH ANXIETY QUESTIONNAIRE (HAQ), THE.

AUTHORS: Lucock and Morley.

DESCRIPTION: A self report questionnaire with 21 items describing health worry and preoccupation, fear of illness and death, reassurance seeking behaviours and the extent to which symptoms interfere with the person's life. The questionnaire is based on Kellner's Illness Attitude Scale (Kellner, Abbott, Winslow, & Pathak,

1987) and the cognitive behavioural model of health anxiety. It was developed to identify individuals with high levels of concern about their health. Respondents rate each item on a four point scale: *Never or rarely* (0), *Sometimes* (1), *Often* (2) or *Most of the time* (3).

SAMPLE: Lucock and Morley (1996) developed the HAQ with a sample of 284 adult subjects comprising: a lay group of 91 (*Mean*=8.62; SD=8.0); 83 student nurses (*Mean*=12.1; SD=6.7); 66 medical outpatients (*Mean*=17.35; SD=11.2); and 44 patients referred to an Adult Clinical Psychology service (*Mean*=22.98; SD=14.1).

STRUCTURE OF THE QUESTIONNAIRE: Cluster and factor analyses revealed four interrelated factors, health worry and preoccupation, fear of illness and death, reassurance seeking behaviours and interference with life. Despite this factor structure, the questionnaire should be used as a whole.

RELIABILITY: **Internal consistency:** It was demonstrated to be high with the total sample of 284 in the Lucock and Morley (1996) study (Cronbach's α=.92). In addition, split-half reliability was calculated with the Pearson product moment correlation using the Spearman Brown correlation formula. Split-half reliabilities were calculated for the whole group (r=.91, p<.001). **Test-retest** reliability was measured with 39 subjects in the lay group: r=.94.

VALIDITY: **Discriminant:** The HAQ significantly discriminated between the four groups using a one-way between-groups analysis of variance (F(3,280)=25.9, p<.0001). Post hoc multiple range tests (Tukey's Honesty Significant Difference) with α=.05 revealed that all the differences between the group means were significant apart from the lay and nursing groups. A discriminant function test was carried out using the 21 items as predictors of membership of the four groups.

The three disciminative functions accounted for 63.5, 21.6 and 14.6 per cent of the between group variability (combined $\chi 2=213.1$; $p=.0001$). The first function was the one the questionnaire was designed to reflect, maximally separating the lay group from the clinical psychology patients with the medical outpatients and nurses in between. **Predictive:** A study by Lucock, Morley, White and Peake (1997) showed the HAQ to be a good predictor of patient's responses to medical reassurance following a gastroscopy. The high HAQ group with scores above 14 were found to remain worried about their health up to a year after the investigation and subsequent reassurance whilst the medium (9-13) and low (0-8) HAQ groups responded well to the reassurance. This effect in the high HAQ group occurred despite a short term reduction in health anxiety after the reassurance. Lucock, White, Peake and Morley (1998) provided some preliminary evidence that high health anxiety defined by the HAQ may negatively bias the perception and recall of medical reassurance.

LOCATION: Lucock, M.P., & Morley, S. (1996). The Health Anxiety Questionnaire. *British Journal of Health Psychology, 1,* 137-150.

COMMENT: The Health Anxiety Questionnaire appears to reflect relatively enduring features consistent with the cognitive-behavioural model of health anxiety. It has been shown to identify patients with persistent health anxiety despite medical reassurance and is a promising measure to be used clinically and for research purposes.

REFERENCES

Kellner, R., Abbott, P., Winslow, W.W., & Pathak, D. (1987). Fears, beliefs and attitudes in DSM-111 hypochondriasis. *Journal of Nervous and Mental Disease, 175,* 20-25.

Lucock, M.P., & Morley, S. (1996). The Health Anxiety Questionnaire. *British Journal of Health Psychology, 1*, 137-150.

Lucock, M.P., Morley, S., White, C., & Peake, M.D. (1997). Responses of consecutive patients to reassurance after gastroscopy: Results of self administered questionnaire survey. *British Medical Journal, 315*, 572-575.

Lucock, M.P., White, C., Peake, M.D., & Morley, S. (1998). Biased perception and recall of reassurance in medical patients. *British Journal of Health Psychology, 3*, 237-243.

REVIEWER: M.P. Lucock, Adult Psychological Therapies Service, Pontefract, General Infirmary, Friarwood Lane, Pontefract, W8 1PL, England, U.K. E-mail: MikeLucock@wpch-tr.northy.nhs.uk

5.20: INCEST SURVIVORS (DSIS), A DIAGNOSTIC SCALE FOR.

AUTHORS: Pearce and Lovejoy.

VARIABLE: 20 item diagnostic scale.

DESCRIPTION: The Diagnostic Scale for Incest Survivors (DSIS; Pearce and Lovejoy, 1994) has drawn on some of the symptoms noted in post-traumatic stress disorder and borderline personality disorder as outlined in the DSM-IIIR. It has also incorporated items based on research indicating that tactile, visual and auditory hallucinations are experienced by incest survivors (Ellenson; 1985, 1989), which has also been found in clinical studies (Heins, Gray, & Tennant, 1990). Other items were developed for the scale based on observations and discussions with incest survivors. The scale used the categories *Never, Only a long time ago, Sometimes,* and *Often* to grade responses to each item.

SAMPLE: Pearce and Lovejoy (1994) intended the scale to be used during admission to drug and alcoholic rehabilitation services.

RELIABILITY: **Internal consistency:** The scale demonstrated good internal reliability with a Cronbach's alpha of .92 (Pearce and Lovejoy, 1994).

VALIDITY: A statistical comparison of group scores showed a significant difference between the two incest survivor groups and the two non-incest survivor groups (F3,81=29.7537, *p*=.0000). The Schaffe (.05) range test indicated that the mean scores for groups 3 and 4 were significantly different from the means of groups 1 and 2 at the .05 level. The validity of the scale as a clinical measure is established by this comparison, as the scale appears to be specific for incest survivors regardless of their drug and alcohol use history.

LOCATION: Pearce, E.J., & Lovejoy, F.H. (1994). The development and testing of a diagnostic scale for incest survivors. *Journal of Social Psychology, 135,* 677-681.

COMMENT: The scale is currently being re-tested using different populations of respondents.

REFERENCES:
American Psychiatric Association. (1987). *Diagnostic and Statistical Manual of Mental Disorder* (3rd Edition Revised). Washington DC: American Psychiatric Association.

Ellenson, G.S. (1985). Detecting a history of incest: A perspective syndrome. *Social Casework: The Journal of Contemporary Social Work*, November, 255 – 532.

Ellenson G.S. (1989). Horror, rage, and defences in the symptoms of female adult sexual abuse survivors. *Social Casework: The Journal of Contemporary Social Work*, December, 589-596.

Heins, T., Gray, A., & Tennant M. (1990). Persisting hallucinations following childhood sexual abuse. *Australian and New Zealand Journal of Psychiatric, 24*, 561-565.

Pearce, E.J., & Lovejoy, F.H. (1994). The development and testing of a diagnostic scale for incest survivors. *Journal of Social Psychology, 135*, 677-681.

REVIEWER: Elizabeth Pearce, 103 Bardia Parade, Holsworthy, NSW, 2173, Australia.

5.21: LANCASHIRE QUALITY OF LIFE SCALE.

AUTHOR: Oliver and Huxley.

VARIABLE: Quality of Life.

DESCRIPTION: The developers of the Lancashire Quality of Life Profile (LQoLP) aimed at an instrument that could describe the quality of life of people with mental illness and could also serve as a research tool in multidisciplinary U.K. fieldwork settings. The LQoLP is based on Lehman's Quality of Life Interview (Lehman *et al.*, 1982) and offers both objective QoL indicators and a subjective QoL estimate. For the subjective QoL estimate, the LQoLP focuses on nine specific domains: work & education, leisure & participation, religion, finances, living situation, legal & safety, family relations, social relations, and health. The evaluated time period is the past week, month or year. The questions pertaining to the subjective QoL appraisal allow patients to rate their satisfaction on a seven-point scale (*'can't be worse'* to *'can't be better'*). The sum of the nine dimension scores is the 27-item 'perceived QoL-score'. In addition, the LQoLP assesses positive and negative affect (using the Affect-Balance Scale; Bradburn, 1969), positive and negative self-esteem (using a modified version of the Self-Esteem Scale; Rosenberg, 1965) and global well-being (using a 100 mm linear analogue version of Cantril's Ladder, a Happiness Scale and an average Life Satisfaction Score; LSS score). Mean administration time is 33 minutes (SD=11 mins; Oliver *et al.*, 1997).

SAMPLE: Severely mentally ill patients in general; patients suffering from schizophrenia, schizoaffective disorder, bipolar disorder, and other psychoses.

RELIABILITY: **Internal consistency:** The Cronbach's alpha for the 'perceived QoL-score' is .84 (Oliver *et al.*, 1996). For the nine specific domains the alpha ranges between .33 and .91 with around 55% of the domains showing an alpha ≥.70 (see Oliver *et al.*, 1997). Only one test of inter-rater reliability has been conducted (using the QoL Uniscale), and a modest correlation was found (*r*=.40). The **test-retest reliability** is variable with Pearson correlations ranging from .49 to .78 (Oliver, 1991-92; Oliver *et al.*, 1996).

VALIDITY: For the LQoLP the construct validity has been explored by computing the inter-correlations between the 'perceived QoL-score' and psychological well-being measures (*e.g.* Cantril's ladder): bi-variate correlations range between .35 and .57. Criterion validity supported by hierarchical regression analysis (Oliver *et al.*, 1996).

LOCATION: Oliver, J.P.J. (1991-92). The social care directive: Development of a quality of life profile for use in the community services for the mentally ill. *Social Work and Social Sciences Review*, *3*, 5-45.

COMMENT: The LQoLP is one the most applied QoL-instruments in Europe. It is used in the U.K., Austria, Germany, the Netherlands, the Scandinavian countries and Spain. Recently, a short version has been introduced, called the Manchester Short Assessment of Quality of Life (MANSA; see Priebe *et al.*, 1999).

REFERENCES:

Oliver, J.P.J. (1991-92). The social care directive: Development of a quality of life profile for use in the community services for the mentally ill. *Social Work and Social Sciences Review 3*, 5-45.

Oliver, J.P.J., Huxley, P., Bridges, K., & Mohamad, H. (1996). *Quality of Life and Mental Health Services*. Routledge: London & New York.

Oliver, J.P.J., Huxley, P.J., Priebe, S., & Kaiser, W. (1997). Measuring the quality of life of severely mentally ill people using the Lancashire Quality of Life Profile. *Social Psychiatry and Psychiatric Epidemiology*, 32, 76-83.

Priebe, S., Oliver, J.P.J., & Kaiser, W. (1999). *Quality of Life and Mental Health Care*. Wrightson Biomedical Publishing Ltd: Petersfield, U.K. and Philadelphia, U.S.A.

REVIEWERS: Ch. van Nieuwenhuizen, TBS-kliniek De Kijvelanden, Forensic Psychiatric Hospital, Department of Psychotherapy & Research, P.O. Box 900, 3160 AC Rhoon, The Netherlands, E-mail: **chinie@kyvelandem.nl** and A.H. Schene, University of Amsterdam, Meibergdreef 9, 1105 AZ Amsterdam, The Netherlands **and** M.W.J. Koeter, Academic Medical Center, University of Amsterdam, Meibergdreef 9, 1105 AZ Amsterdam, The Netherlands.

5.22: MCGILL QUALITY OF LIFE QUESTIONNAIRE, THE

AUTHORS: Cohen and Mount

VARIABLE: Quality of life, defined as subjective well-being.

DESCRIPTION: The McGill Quality of Life Questionnaire (MQOL) is a 17-item self-report questionnaire designed to measure the quality of life of people with a life-threatening illness. MQOL contains a single item scale measuring global quality of life as well as 16 items which form the MQOL subscales and MQOL Total score. Subscales determined through principal components analysis include physical symptoms (3 items), psychological (4 items), existential well-being (6 items), and support (2 items), with a single item measuring general physical well-being. The response format is a numerical rating scale (0-10) with verbal anchors at each end. Subscale scores are the mean of the subscale items. The MQOL Total score is the mean of the subscale scores. Therefore all scores range from 0 to 10. MQOL is designed to be able to be read aloud as well as self-completed. MQOL was developed simultaneously in English and French, and has been translated into several other languages. MQOL items are based on those from several other questionnaires.

SAMPLE: MQOL is designed for use with people with a life-threatening illness. The brevity and format were selected to allow completion even by those who are very weak physically.

RELIABILITY: **Internal consistency**: Internal consistency was determined to be good in three separate populations: people living with HIV/AIDS (Cohen et al., 1996b); oncology outpatients (Cohen et al., 1996a); people followed by palliative care services (Cohen et al., 1997). The range of Cronbach's alphas in the three studies is .83 to .89 for the MQOL Total score, .77 to .84 for the Psychological subscale; .79 to .87 for the Existential Well-being subscale, and .74 to .84 for the Support Subscale. The Physical Symptoms subscale had acceptable reliability in HIV/AIDS (.84) and oncology outpatient (.85) studies but was low in the palliative care study (.62), despite the fact that all three items are identical (the participant lists the three most problematic symptoms and rates them). Test-retest: Test-retest reliability was tested over a period of two days with oncology outpatients and palliative care patients. Because of the unstable condition of this population, data were retained only for those cases where the participant indicated that quality of life had not changed during this time. The intraclass correlation co-efficient for the MQOL Total score was .75 (Cohen & Mount 1996c).

VALIDITY: Convergent and divergent validity of MQOL Total and subscale scores was demonstrated with the MQOL single–item scale measuring global quality of life, with the self-administered version of the Spitzer Quality of Life Index (Spitzer *et al.*, 1981), as well as with a measure of physical symptoms (Cohen *et al.*, 1996a, b; 1997). The MQOL Physical Well-being item and Physical Symptom subscale scores discriminate amongst groups differing in disease status (Cohen *et al.*, 1996a, b). In addition, the MQOL scores are significantly different on days the participants consider to be *Good, Average*, and *Bad* days (Cohen & Mount, 1996c).

LOCATION:

Original:

Cohen, S.R., Mount, B.M., Strobel, M.G., & Bui, F. (1995). The McGill Quality of Life Questionnaire: A measure of Quality of Life appropriate for people with advanced disease. A Preliminary Study of Validity and Acceptability, *Palliative Medicine, 9*, 207-219.

Revised:

Cohen, S.R., Mount, B.M., Tomas, J., & Mount, L. (1996). Existential well-being is an important determinant of Quality of Life: Evidence from the McGill Quality of Life Questionnaire, *Cancer, 77*, 576-586.

Cohen, S.R., Hassan, S.A., Lapointe, B.M., & Mount, B.M. (1996). HIV disease and AIDS: Increasing importance of the existential domain in determining Quality of Life as T4 Cell counts decrease. *AIDS, 10*, 1421-1427.

Cohen, S.R., Mount, B.M., Bruera, E., Provost, M., Rowe, J., & Tong, K. (1997). validity of the McGill Quality of Life Questionnaire in the palliative Care setting. A multi-center Canadian study demonstrating the importance of the existential domain. *Palliative Medicine, 11*, 3-20.

COMMENT: To date, MQOL appears to have acceptable psychometric properties when used to measure the quality of life of people with a life-threatening illness. It has demonstrated acceptability to even a physically frail population. More testing is, however, needed. MQOL measures subjective well-being and is not intended to measure specific physical symptoms, which are also of great importance for this population. MQOL has been translated into several languages by investigators other than the authors of the instrument but the validity in different cultures has not yet been studied. Since content validity was based on a literature review and clinical experience, it remains to be demonstrated whether the instrument is sufficiently comprehensive to include all domains relevant to the quality of life of this population.

REFERENCES:

Cohen, S.R., Hassan, S.A., Lapointe, B.M., & Mount, B.M. (1996b). HIV disease and AIDS: Increasing importance of the existential domain in determining Quality of Life as T4 Cell counts decrease. *AIDS, 10*, 1421-1427.

Cohen, S.R., & Mount, B.M. (1996c). Good days, Bad days. Quantitative and qualitative differences for Oncology patients. *Journal of Palliative Care, 12*, 582.

Cohen, S.R., Mount, B.M., Strobel, M.G., & Bui, F. (1995). The McGill Quality of Life Questionnaire: A measure of Quality of Life appropriate for people with advanced disease. A preliminary study of validity and acceptability. *Palliative Medicine, 9*, 207-219.

Cohen, S.R., Mount, B.M., Tomas, J., & Mount, L. (1996a). Existential well-being is an important determinant of Quality of Life: Evidence from the McGill Quality of Life Questionnaire. *Cancer, 77*, 576-586.

Cohen, S.R., Mount, B.M., Bruera, E., Provost, M., Rowe, J., & Tong, K. (1997). Validity of the McGill Quality of Life Questionnaire in the palliative care setting. A Multi-center Canadian Study demonstrating the importance of the existential domain. *Palliative Medicine, 11*, 3-20.

Spitzer, W.O., Dobson, A.J., Hall, J., Chesterman, E., Levi, J., Shepherd, R. *et al.* (1981). Measuring the quality of life of cancer patients. *Journal of Chronic Diseases, 34,* 585-97.

REVIEWER: S. Robin Cohen, Division of Palliative Care, Dept. Oncology, McGill University, 687 Pine Avenue West, Montreal, QC, H3A 1A1, Canada. E-mail: mcob@musica.mcgill.ca

5.23: MANIC-DEPRESSIVENESS SCALE, THE.

AUTHORS: Thalbourne, Delin and Bassett.

VARIABLE: Manic and depressive tendencies.

DESCRIPTION: The Manic-Depressiveness Scale is an 18-item self-report scale, with 9 items to assess depressive-experience and 9 items to measure manic-experience. Each item is answered true versus false. The 9 depression items are all keyed positively (a *true* answer indicates depression), where 7 of the mania items are keyed positively and two are keyed negatively. Higher scores on both scales indicate stronger depressive tendencies and stronger manic tendencies. Thalbourne *et al.* have also explored the use of the combined score from the two subscales.

SAMPLE: The scales were devised using 241 Australian college students and 86 manic-depressive patients.

RELIABILITY: **Internal consistency:** Cronbach's alphas were .63 for the depression scale, .56 for the mania scale and .71 for the combined scale

(Thalbourne *et al.*, 1994). On a sample of 612 American college students, Cronbach's alphas were .59 for depression scores, .31 for manic scores and .58 for the combined scores (Lester, 1999). The Pearson correlation between the two scales for 239 Australian students was .39 (Thalbourne *et al.*, 1994). For 612 American college students, the correlation was .26 (Lester, 1999). For the American sample, depression and mania scores were not significantly correlated with age; depression scores, but not mania scores were higher for the women (point-biserial *r*'s=-.24 and -.02, respectively) (Lester, 1999). A Principal Components factor analysis with a varimax rotation identified 5 factors, two with depression items, two with mania items and one mixed factor (Lester, 1999). **Test-retest:** The test-retest Pearson correlations for 29 students after 11 months were .79 for depression scores, .48 for mania scores, and .67 for the combined scale (Thalbourne *et al.*, 1994).

VALIDITY: Concurrent: Correlations between scores on the MMPI Hypomania Scale and the Manic Depressiveness Scale were .31 for depression scores, .50 for mania scores and .47 for the combined score (Thalbourne *et al.*, 1994). Manic-depressive patients scored higher on all three measures than the students (Thalbourne *et al.*, 1994). The severity of the manic-depressive disorder for the patient sample, as measured by the number of different medications, was positively associated with the scores, but not length of time since the last psychiatric episode nor the total number of psychiatric hospitalizations. Bipolar patients obtained higher mania scores than unipolar patients (Thalbourne & Bassett, 1998) but did not differ on depression scores. For the bipolar patients, mania scores were associated with a higher number of affective disorder-relevant medications being taken while depression scores were associated with a higher number of hospitalizations. **Correlates:** Both depression and mania scores were correlated with measures of magical ideation, schizotypal personality, neuroticism and psychoticism, and mania scores were also associated with creative personality

(Thalbourne, Keogh, & Crawley, 1999). Depression scores were also associated with low self esteem, while both depression and mania scores were associated with negative attitudes toward others (Andrews, Haas, & Lester, 1994). Depression and mania scores were positively associated with measures of eating disorder (Williams & Lester, 1996) and negatively associated with scores on a measure of optimism (Meelheim & Lester, 1999). Depression but not mania scores were associated with having half and step-siblings rather than full-siblings (Bergman, Carmel, & Lester, 1997). Two items on the depression scale measure prior suicidal ideation and attempts; responses to these items were associated with the depression scores (minus the score for the suicide items) but not with mania scores (Kaplan & Lester, 1994; Lester & Rife, 1998). Depression and mania scores were not associated with belief in paranormal phenomena, extraversion scores or mystical experience (Thalbourne, Keogh, & Crawley, 1999), religiosity (Rife & Lester, 1997), belief in life after death (Andrews & Lester, 1998), birth order or number of siblings (Bergman, Carmel, & Lester, 1997).

LOCATION: Thalbourne, M. A., Delin, P. S., & Bassett, D. L. (1994). An attempt to construct short scales measuring manic-depressive-like experience and behaviour. *British Journal of Clinical Psychology, 33*, 205-207.

COMMENT: This scale is quite new, and reliability and validity studies are ongoing by those who devised the scale. The scale appears to have reasonable reliability for a brief scale, but little research has appeared on its validity. For example, scores on the depression scale have not been compared with scores on the major self-report measures of depression. The availability of a mania scale is a welcome innovation, for other self-report measures of depression do not assess this trait.

REFERENCES:

Andrews, L., Haas, D., & Lester, D. (1994). Manic-depressive tendencies and acceptance of self and others. *Psychological Reports, 74*, 1382.

Andrews, L., & Lester, D. (1998). Manic-depressive tendencies and belief in life after death. *Psychological Reports, 82*, 1114.

Bergman, K.J., Carmel, L.H., & Lester, D. (1997). Birth order, suicidal preoccupation, and scores suggesting manic-depressive tendencies. *Psychological Reports, 80*, 442.

Kaplan, S., & Lester, D. (1994). Depression, mania and suicidal preoccupation. *Psychological Reports, 74*, 974.

Lester, D. (1999). Unpublished data.

Lester, D., & Rife, J. (1998). Predicting suicidality. *Perceptual & Motor Skills, 87*, 498.

Meelheim, L.G., & Lester, D. (1999). Optimism and manic-depressive tendencies. *Psychological Reports, 84*, 1122.

Rife, J., & Lester, D. (1997). Religiosity and psychological disturbance. *Psychological Reports, 81*, 978.

Thalbourne, M.A., Keogh, E., & Crawley, S.E. (1999). Manic-depressiveness and its correlates. *Psychological Reports, 85*, 45-53.

Thalbourne, M.A., & Bassett, D. L. (1998). The Manic Depressiveness Scale: A preliminary effort at replication and extension. *Psychological Reports, 83*, 75-80.

Thalbourne, M.A., Delin, P.S., & Bassett, D. L. (1994). An attempt to construct short scales measuring manic-depressive-like experience and behaviour. *British Journal of Clinical Psychology, 33*, 205-207.

Williams, D., & Lester, D. (1996). Eating disorder and manic-depressive tendencies. *Psychological Reports*, *78*, 794.

REVIEWER: David Lester, Psychology Program, The Richard Stockton College of New Jersey, Pomona, New Jersey 08240, U.S.A.

5.24: MICRO/MACRO WORRIES SCALE, THE

AUTHORS: Boehnke, Schwartz, Stromberg, and Sagiv.

VARIABLES: Micro and macro worries

DESCRIPTION: The self-report Micro/Macro Worries Scale consists of 33 items. While some of the items are based on the already established Goldring-Doctor scale (1986), additional items were newly developed to adequately represent the postulated conceptualization of worries. The scale distinguishes between two aspects of worries: (1) 2 objects of worries (micro/macro) and (2) 7 domains of life the worry refers to. Micro worries include worries about the self (11 items) and the in-group (5 items). Macro worries include worries about the society (10 items) and the world (5 items). In addition, there are two mixed object items in each group, that is, self/in-group (1 micro item) and society/world (1 macro item). The items are further distinguished to represent 7 domains of life micro and macro worries may pertain to. These domains represent: health (5 items), environment (3 items), social relations (5 items), meaning (2 items), achievement (work) (3 items), economics (4 items), and safety (6 items). Five items pertain to two domains each: Health/Safety (1 item), Meaning/Society (1 item), Safety/Environment (1 item), Meaning/Achievement (1 item), and Economics/Environment (1 item). There is also one nonspecific item about worries about the future. This item was treated as a micro indicator in later analyses because high the micro factor loadings. All items are ordered randomly with two items of the same domain never being adjacent to another. Respondents are asked to answer each item on a 5-point scale indicating whether the respondent was *Not at all worried* (0) about a given item or *Extremely worried* (4) about a given item.

SAMPLE: The sample consists of a total of n=583 students in the social sciences, education and economics in Israel (n=183), West-Germany (n=195), and East-Germany (n=205).

RELIABILITY: **Internal consistency:** The internal consistency of the two subscales (micro and macro worries) was high in all three sub-samples (Boehnke, Schwartz, Stromberg & Sagiv, 1998). For the micro scale Cronbach's alphas were .87 (Israel), .81 (West-Germany), and .87 (East-Germany). For the macro scale Cronbach's alphas were .84 (Israel, .84 (West-Germany), and .88 (East-Germany). **Test-retest:** The test-retest reliability was estimated using a subsample of 123 East and West German students in a four-week interval. The correlations were .84 for micro worries and .73 for macro worries.

VALIDITY: **Convergent:** As predicted by the authors, the micro worry items correlated positively with scores on scales of trait anxiety, negative affect, and negatively with scores on scales of satisfaction with life, positive affect, and general mental health in all three samples. Macro worries were either unrelated or relate positively to well being. However, these associations were weak for all three samples.

LOCATION: Boehnke, K., Schwartz, S., Stromberg, C., & Sagiv, L. (1998). The structure and dynamics of worry: Theory, measurement, and cross-national replications. *Journal of Personality, 66,* 745-782.

COMMENT: The scale captures some important differentiating aspects of the content and structure of worries. The proposed conceptualization of worries having distinct objects (micro/macro) and pertaining to different domains of life (*i.e.,* health, environment, social relations, meaning, achievement (work), economics, and safety) is further confirmed by the scale. Open question remain concerning the links between micro- and macro-worries and the seven domains and their relation to mental health and psychological well-being. More research is needed to further test the robustness and cross-cultural applications of the scale.

REFERENCES:

Boehnke, K., Fuß, D., & Rupf, M. (1999). Values and well-being: The mediating role of worries. In P. Schmuck (Ed.), *Life Goals and Well-Being.* Lengerich: Pabst Science Publishers, in press.

Boehnke, K., Regmi, M.P., Richmond, B.O., Chandra, S., & Stromberg, C. (1996). Worries, values and well-being: A comparison of East and West German, Nepalese and Fijian undergraduates. In H. Grad, A. Blanco & J. Georgas (Eds.), *Key Issues in Cross-cultural Psychology* (pp. 227-239). Lisse: Swets & Zeitlinger.

Boehnke, K., & Schwartz, S.H. (1997). Fear of war: Relations to values, gender, and mental health in Germany and Israel. *Peace and Conflict: Journal of Peace Psychology, 3,* 149-165.

Boehnke, K., Schwartz, S., Stromberg, C., & Sagiv, L. (1998). The structure and dynamics of worry: Theory, measurement, and cross-national replications. *Journal of Personality, 66,* 745-782.

Boehnke, K., Stromberg, C., Regmi, M.P., Richmond, B.O., & Chandra, S. (1998). Reflecting the world 'out there': A cross-cultural perspective on worries, values and well-being. *Journal of Social and Clinical Psychology, 17,* 227-247.

Goldenring, J., & Doctor, R. (1986). Teenage worry about nuclear war: North American and European questionnaire studies. *International Journal of Mental Health, 15,* 72-92.

Schwartz, S.H., Sagiv, L., & Boehnke, K. (1999). Worries and values. *Journal of Personality,* in press.

REVIEWER: Angela Ittel, Chemnitz University of Technology, Chemnitz, Germany.

5.25: MOOD AND ANXIETY SYMPTOM QUESTIONNAIRE (MASQ).
AUTHORS: Watson and Clark.

VARIABLES: General Distress; Anhedonic Depression; Anxious Arousal.

DESCRIPTION: The Mood and Anxiety Symptom Questionnaire (MASQ) is a 90-item scale that was developed to measure both the common and specific symptoms associated with anxiety and depression. Respondents are required to indicate on a 5-point scale how much they have experienced each symptom during the past week, including the day of testing. Items were constructed from the criteria for mood and anxiety disorders as outlined in the DSM-III-R, and categorised into three scales. The general distress (GD) scale consists of 38 items that are common to both mood and anxiety disorders. Although originally split into three subscales, recent factor analyses suggest that GD is best viewed as one factor (Keogh & Reidy, 2000; Watson, Clark, Weber, Assenheimer, Strauss, & McCormick, 1995). The anxiety-specific scale is called Anxious Arousal (AA) and consists of 17 items that appear in one or more anxiety disorder. AA items related to somatic tension and hyperarousal. The depression-specific scale is called Anhedonic Depression (AD) and consists of 22 items that appear in one or more mood disorder. Within the AD scale 14 items are reversed-keyed items relating to Positive Affect and 8 are related to loss of interest. The remaining items are fillers.

SAMPLE: The MASQ was developed to measure the common and specific symptoms associated with anxiety and depression in both clinical and non-clinical adult groups. In the original development of the MASQ, Watson *et al.* (1995) validated the measure on five adult samples: three student (*n*=516; *n*=381; *n*=522), an adult (*n*=329), and a clinical group (*n*=470).

RELIABILITY: Internal consistency: The MASQ demonstrates good internal consistency for all the scales. Alpha coefficients for the GD scale ranges from .78 to .92, for the AA scale alpha ranges .86 to .90, and for the AD scale alpha ranges .90 to .93 (Watson, Weber, Assenheimer, Clark, Strauss, & McCormick, 1995).

VALIDITY: Convergent: The specific scales of the MASQ have demonstrated satisfactory convergent validity with various measures of anxiety and depression, including the Profile of Mood States (Anxiety and Depression scales), Beck Anxiety Inventory, Beck Depression Inventory (Watson, Weber *et al.*, 1995) and the Hospital Anxiety and Depression Scale (Reidy & Keogh, 1997). Discriminant: Similarly, the specific scales of the MASQ exhibit good discriminant validity with the measures mentioned above. Furthermore, the correlation coefficients between the specific scales of the MASQ are typically much lower than those usually found for measures of anxiety and depression.

Indeed, Watson, Weber *et al.* (1995) report that the correlations between AA and AD range from .25 to .49.

LOCATION: **Original 90-item version**: Watson, D., Clark, L. A., Weber, K., Assenheimer, J. S., Strauss, M. E., & McCormick, R. A. (1995). Testing a tripartite model: II. Exploring the symptom structure of anxiety and depression in student, adult and patient samples. *Journal of Abnormal Psychology, 104,* 15-25. **Revised 60-item version**: Keogh, E., & Reidy, J. (2000). Exploring the factor structure of the Mood and Anxiety Symptom Questionnaire (MASQ). *Journal of Personality Assessment, 74,* 106-125.

COMMENT: Based on the tripartite model of anxiety and depression, the MASQ has excellent potential for discriminating between anxiety and depression. Factor analytical studies have consistently revealed that the three-factor solution provides the best solution (Keogh & Reidy, in press; Watson, Clark *et al.*, 1995). More recently, Keogh & Reidy (in press) have suggested removing some of the less reliable items from the MASQ, reducing the total number of items from 90 to 60. The two specific factors were renamed Positive Affect and Somatic Anxiety. Reliability analysis (Cronbach's alpha) for the revised version of the MASQ revealed that for the 21-item General Distress scale, alpha was .95, for the 23-item Positive Affect Scale alpha was .95, and finally for the 16-item Somatic Anxiety scale alpha was .88. Future research should aim to use confirmatory factor analysis to determine further reliability of the factor structure of the MASQ.

REFERENCES :
Keogh, E., & Reidy, J. (2000). Exploring the factor structure of the Mood and Anxiety Symptom Questionnaire (MASQ). *Journal of Personality Assessment, 74,* 106-125.

Reidy, J., & Keogh, E. (1997). Testing the discriminant and convergent validity of the Mood and Anxiety Symptoms Questionnaire using a British sample. *Personality and Individual Differences, 23*, 337-344.

Watson, D., Clark, L.A., Weber, K., Assenheimer, J.S., Strauss, M.E., & McCormick, R.A. (1995). Testing a tripartite model: II. Exploring the symptom structure of anxiety and depression in student, adult and patient samples. *Journal of Abnormal Psychology, 104*, 15-25.

Watson, D., Weber, K., Assenheimer, J.S., Clark, L.A., Strauss, M.E., & McCormick, R.A. (1995). Testing a tripartite model: I. Evaluating the convergent and discriminant validity of anxiety and depression symptom scales. *Journal of Abnormal Psychology, 104*, 3-14.

REVIEWER: Edmund Keogh, Department of Psychology, Goldsmiths College, University of London, New Cross, London, SE14 6NW, England, U.K. E-mail: e.keogh@gold.ac.uk

5.26: NEECHAM CONFUSION SCALE, THE.
AUTHORS: Neelon and Champagne.

VARIABLE: Acute confusion, delirium.

DESCRIPTION: The NEEHCAM Confusion Scale (NEECHAM) was developed for rapid and unobtrusive bedside assessment of cognitive function and for documentation of acute confusional behavior or delirium like syndromes. Because the NEECHAM places a minimal response burden on the patient, NEECHAM ratings can be repeated at frequent intervals to monitor changes in the patient's status and response to treatment. The NEECHAM has 9 scaled items organized into 3 subscales of assessment.

SAMPLES: The validity and reliability of the NEECHAM has been evaluated in 3 samples of elderly patients hospitalized for acute medical illnesses (n=158, 168, 258) (Neelon, Champagne, McConnell, Carlson, & Funk, 1992; Neelon, Champagne, Carlson, & Funk, 1996) and in a sample of stable elderly nursing home residents (n=14) (Champagne, Neelon, McConnell, & Funk, 1987). Psychometric testing of a Swedish version of the scale was done among patients with hip fracture (Johansson, Hamrin, & Larsson, in press).

RELIABILITY: Internal consistency: The total score was high for all samples (Cronbach's α=.90). Structural analysis showed that there were not multiple independent dimensions and demonstrated stability across samples. The interrater reliability was good between researchers (r=.96) and between trained staff nurses (r=.91). Test-retest: In stable elderly nursing home residents was strong (r=.98).

VALIDITY: NEECHAM scores were correlated with other cognitive and clinical health status variables: High positive correlation with the Mini Mental State Exam (MMSE) (Folstein, Folstein, & McHugh, 1975) (r=.87) and a high negative correlation with the sum of DSM-III-R (American Psychiatric Association, 1987) positive items (r= -.91) (Neelon et al., 1996). NEECHAM scores were moderately correlated with functional status. Correlations with illness severity, age, and education were weaker.

LOCATION:
English: Matteson, M.A., McConnell, E.S., & Linton, A.D. (1996). *Gerontological Nursing* (2nd Edition). Philadelphia:W.B. Saunders.

Miller, J., Neelon, V., Champagne, M., Bailey, M., Ngandu, N., Belyea, M., Jarrell, E., & Montoya, L. (1997). The assessment of confusion as part of nursing care. *Applied Nursing Research, 10,* 143-151.

Swedish: Johansson, I., Hamrin, E., & Larsson, G. (submitted). Psychometric testing of the NEECHAM Confusion Scale among patients with hip fracture. *Research in Nursing and Health.*

COMMENT: The findings support the validity of the NEECHAM as a reliable instrument for assessing acute confusion or delirium in hospitalized elderly patients, particularly in the early stages. The scale can be rapidly scored with data derived during routine clinical assessments. Accurate scoring of the NEECHAM requires an awareness of physical disabilities that may affect the patient's mode of responding. Internal consistency for the full scale was high.

REFERENCES:

American Psychiatric Association. (1987). *Diagnostic and Statistical Manual of Mental Disorders* (3rd Edition Revised). Washinton, DC: American Psychiatric Association.

Champagne, M.T., Neelon, V. J., McConnell, E. S., & Funk, S. (1987). The NEECHAM Scale: Assessment of acute confusion in the hospitalized elderly. *The Gerontologist, 27,* (October Special), 4A.

Csokasy J. (1999). Assessment of acute confusion: Use of the NEECHAM Confusion Scale. *Applied Nursing Research, 12,* 51-5.

Folstein, M.F., Folstein, S.E., & McHugh, P.R. (1975). Mini-Mental State: A practical method for grading the cognitive state of patients for clinicians. *Journal of Psychiatric Research, 12,* 189-198.

Johansson, I., Hamrin, E., & Larsson, G. (submitted). Psychometric testing of the NEECHAM Confusion Scale among patients with hip fracture. *Research in Nursing and Health.*

Matteson M.A., McConnell E.S., & Linton A.D. (1996). *Gerontological Nursing* (2nd Edition). Philadelphia: W.B. Saunders.

Miller, J., Neelon, V., Champagne, M., Bailey, M., Ngandu, N., Belyea, M., Jarrell, E., & Montoya, L.. (1997). The assessment of confusion as part of nursing care. *Applied Nursing Research, 10,* 143-151.

Neelon, V.J., Champagne, M.T., Carlson, J.R., & Funk, S.G. (1996). The NEECHAM Confusion Scale: Construction, validation, and clinical testing. *Nursing Research, 45,* 324-330.

Neelon, V.J., Champagne, M.T., McConnell, E. *et al.* (1992). Use of the NEECHAM Confusion Scale to assess acute confusional states of hospitalized older patients. In S. Funk, E. Tornquist, M. Champagne, & R. Wiese, (Eds.), *Key Aspects of Elder Care: Managing Falls, Incontinence, and Cognitive Impairment* (pp. 278-289). New York: Springer.

REVIEWER: Virginia J. Neelon, School of Nursing, CB #7460, University of North Carolina at Chapel Hill, Chapel Hill, NC 27799, U.S.A. E-mail: vneelon@email.unc.edu

5.27: PAIN ANXIETY SYMPTOMS SCALE .

AUTHOR: McCracken, Zayfert, and Gross.

VARIABLE: Fear of pain.

DESCRIPTION: The Pain Anxiety Symptoms Scale (PASS; McCracken, Zayfert, & Gross, 1992, 1993) is a self-report instrument developed to measure fear of pain. The original PASS (McCracken, Zayfert, & Gross, 1992) comprised 62 rationally-derived items but was later shortened to 40 items distributed equally on four subscales (McCracken, Zayfert, & Gross, 1993). The four 10-item subscales are designed to measure different dimensions of fear of pain and correspond closely to multiple response modalities identified in the three-system model of fear (Lang, 1968; Hugdahl, 1981): (1) fearful appraisals of pain (*e.g.*, "Pain sensations are terrifying"); (2) cognitive anxiety/interference related to pain (*e.g.*, "I find it hard to concentrate when I hurt"); (3) physiological symptoms arising from pain (*e.g.*, "Pain seems to cause my heart to pound or race"); and, (4) escape/avoidance behaviour in response to activities that are associated with pain (*e.g.*, I try to avoid activities that cause pain"). Respondents are asked to indicate, on a 6-point scale anchored from 0 (*Never*) to 5 (*Always*), the extent to which they engage in the thoughts and activities represented by the items when they experience pain. Five items (*i.e.*, items 2, 8, 16, 31, and 40) are reverse scored. The PASS subscale scores can range between 0 and 50 and are calculated by adding together the 10 items for each subscale. The PASS total score can range between 0 and 200 and is calculated by adding together the subscale scores (*i.e.*, all items). Higher scores indicate greater fear of pain.

SAMPLES: The PASS was originally designed to assess fear of pain in individuals who have chronic or recurrent pain disorders. It has been used primarily in samples of patients with a primary complaint of chronic back pain but has recently been used in studies of patients with recurrent headache (Asmundson, Norton, & Veloso, in press) and cancer pain (Turk *et al.*, 1998). The measure has also been used to assess fear of pain in a community sample (Osman, Barrios, Osman, Schneekloth, & Troutman, 1994).

RELIABILITY: The PASS has acceptable **internal consistency** with coefficient alpha for the subscale and total scores exceeding .80 and .90, respectively, in most cases. **Test-retest** reliability correlations have been reported to be greater than .85

for all PASS subscale scores, except escape/avoidance at .74, and for the PASS total score over a test-retest interval ranging from 4 to 44 days (McCracken, Gross, Hexum, & Semenchuk, 1993). Reliability data are reviewed in detail by McCracken and Gross (1995).

VALIDITY: The PASS has performed well on tests of convergent, discriminant, known-groups, concurrent, and incremental validity. For example, PASS subscale and total scores are significantly and positively correlated with other measures of anxiety and fear (convergent validity) (Asmundson & Norton, 1995; McCracken *et al.*, 1992; Osman *et al.*, 1994); PASS subscale and total scores have higher correlations with a measure of affective pain compared to a measure of sensory pain (discriminant validity) (McCracken *et al.*, 1992); PASS subscale (Asmundson, Norton, & Allerdings, 1997) and total (McCracken, Spertus, Janeck, Sinclair, & Wetzel, 1999) scores are higher in globally dysfunctional compared to interpersonally distressed and adaptively coping pain patients (known-groups validity); and, the PASS predicts self-reported and observed (*e.g.*, passive straight leg raise test) disability and interference with activities of daily living after controlling for variables such as pain severity, depression, and trait anxiety (incremental validity) (McCracken *et al.*, 1992; McCracken, Gross, Sorg, & Edmands, 1993). Several of the validity studies are reviewed in detail by McCracken and Gross (1995). To date, the factorial validity of the PASS has been the subject of two exploratory (Larsen, Taylor, & Asmundson, 1997; McCracken, Gross, Hexum, & Semenchuk, 1993) and one confirmatory (Osman *et al.*, 1994) factor analytic studies. The results of these studies suggest that the proposed four-factor structure of the PASS is reasonably stable. However, Larsen *et al.* (1997) did suggest that the PASS may be best conceptualised as comprising five factors, with the cognitive anxiety/interference factor breaking into distinct factors for cognitive interference and coping strategies.

LOCATION: The PASS can be obtained by writing to Lance M. McCracken, University of Chicago, Psychiatry (MC3077), 5841 S Maryland Avenue, Chicago, IL 60637-1470, U.S.A. E-mail lmccracken@yoda.bsd.uchicago.edu

COMMENT: There is growing evidence to indicate that the psychometric properties of the PASS are good and that it is a reasonably sound measure that allows detailed clinical and/or research based assessment of fear of pain. A notable strength of the PASS is that it is the only published fear of pain measure to consider the multiple (*i.e.*, cognitive, physiological, and behavioural) modalities of the fear response. Although not readily available, patient and community norms can be gleaned through several of the publications noted above. Based on earlier work that raised questions regarding the factorial validity of the PASS (Larsen *et al.*, 1997), McWilliams and Asmundson (1998) have recently expanded and revised the PASS to provide a more comprehensive assessment of the relevant domains of fear of pain in nonclinical samples. As well, McCracken (personal communication, June 1999) has recently developed a short 20-item version of the PASS. Although promising, further psychometric evaluation of these revisions of the PASS are needed.

REFERENCES:

Asmundson, G.J.G., & Norton, G. R. (1995). Anxiety sensitivity in patients with physically unexplained chronic back pain: A preliminary report. *Behaviour Research and Therapy, 33,* 771-777.

Asmundson, G.J.G., Norton, G.R., & Allerdings, M.D. (1997). Fear and avoidance in dysfunctional chronic back pain patients. *Pain, 69,* 231-236.

Asmundson, G.J.G., Norton, P.J., & Veloso, F. (1999). Anxiety sensitivity and fear of pain in patients with recurring headaches. *Behaviour Research and Therapy, 37,* 703-713.

Hugdahl, K. (1981). The three-system model of fear and emotion: A critical examination. Behaviour Research and Therapy, *19*, 75-85.

Lang, P.J. (1968). Fear reduction and fear behavior: Problems in treating a construct. In J. M. Shilen (Ed.), *Research in Psychotherapy*, Vol. 3, (pp. 90-103). Washington, DC: American Psychological Association.

Larsen, D.K., Taylor, S., & Asmundson, G.J.G. Exploratory factor analysis of the Pain Anxiety Symptoms Scale in patients with chronic pain complaints. *Pain, 69*, 27-34.

McCracken, L.M., & Gross, R.T. (1995). The Pain Anxiety Symptoms Scale (PASS) and the assessment of emotional responses to pain. In L. VandeCreek, S. Knapp, and T.L. Jackson (Eds.), *Innovations in Clinical Practice: A Sourcebook*, Vol. 14, (pp. 309-321). Sarasota, FL: Professional Resource Press.

McCracken, L.M., Gross, R.T., Hexum, C.L., & Semenchuk, E.M. (1993, March). *Factor structure and temporal stability of the Pain Anxiety Symptoms Scale.* Paper presented at the annual convention of the Society of Behavioural Medicine, San Francisco, CA.

McCracken, L. M., Gross, R. T., Sorg, P. J., & Edmands, T. A. (1993). Prediction of pain in patients with chronic low back pain: Effects of inaccurate prediction and pain-related anxiety. *Behaviour Research and Therapy, 31*, 647-652.

McCracken, L.M., Spertus, I.L., Janeck, A.S., Sinclair, D., & Wetzel, F.T. (1999). Behavioral dimensions of adjustment in persons with chronic pain: Pain-related anxiety and acceptance. *Pain, 80*, 283-289.

McCracken, L.M., Zayfert, C., & Gross, R.T. (1992). The pain anxiety symptoms scale: Development and validation of a scale to measure fear of pain. *Pain, 50*, 67-73.

McCracken, L.M., Zayfert, C., & Gross, R.T. (1993). The pain anxiety symptoms scale (PASS): A multimodal measure of pain-specific anxiety symptoms. *Behavior Therapist, 16*, 183-184.

McWilliams, L., & Asmundson, G.J.G. (1998). Factor structure and validity of a revised Pain Anxiety Symptoms Scale. *International Journal of Rehabilitation and Health, 4,* 95-109.

Osman, A., Barrios, F.X., Osman, J.R., Schneekloth, R., & Troutman, J.A. (1994). The Pain Anxiety Symptoms Scale: Psychometric properties in a community sample. *Journal of Behavioral Medicine, 17,* 511-522.

Turk, D.C., Sist, T.C., Okifuji, A., Miner, M.F., Florio, G., Harrison, P., Massey, J., Lema, M.L., & Zevon, M.A. (1998). Adaptation to metastatic cancer pain, regional/local cancer pain and non-cancer pain: Role of psychological and behavioral factors. *Pain, 74,* 247-256.

REVIEWERS: Gordon J.G. Asmundson, and Derrick K. Larsen, Clinical Research and Development, Regina Health District and University of Regina, Regina, Saskatchewan, Canada, S4S 0A5. E-mail gasmundson@reginahealth.sk.ca

5.28: PAIN CATASTROPHIZING SCALE, THE.
AUTHORS: Sullivan, Bishop, and Pivik.

VARIABLE: Pain Catastrophizing.

DESCRIPTION: The Pain Catastrophizing Scale (PCS; Sullivan *et al.*, 1995) is a 13 item self-report measure of catastrophic thinking associated with pain. The PCS instructions ask participants to reflect on past painful experiences, and to indicate the degree to which they experienced each of 13 thoughts or feelings when experiencing pain, on 5-point scales with the end points (0) *Not at all* and (4) *All the time.* Items were constructed based on examples of catastrophic thinking provided by Spanos and his colleagues (Spanos, Radtke-Bodorik, Ferguson, &

Jones, 1979; Spanos, Brown, Jones, & Horner, 1981) and Chaves and Brown (1987). Five items from the catastrophizing subscale of the Coping Strategies Questionnaire (CSQ; Rosenstiel & Keefe, 1983) are included in the PCS.

SAMPLES: The PCS yields a total score and three subscale scores assessing rumination "I keep thinking about how much it hurts", magnification "I become afraid that the pain may get worse" and helplessness "There is nothing I can do to reduce the intensity of the pain". Scale items and psychometric properties are described in Sullivan et al. (1995).

RELIABILITY: The factor structure of the PCS has been replicated in a clinical population (Osman, Barrios, Copper, Hauptman, Jones, & O'Neill, 1997) and a sport population (Sullivan, Tripp, Rodgers, & Stanish, 2000). **Internal consistency:** The PCS subscales have been shown to have adequate to high internal consistency (coefficient alphas: total PCS=.87, rumination=.87, magnification=.66, and helplessness=.78; Sullivan et al., 1995). **Test-retest:** PCS total scores have been shown to be stable over a 10 week period (test-retest r=.70) (Sullivan et al., 1995).

VALIDITY: The PCS has been shown to predict pain intensity ratings in several populations including chronic pain patients (Sullivan, Stanish, Waite, Sullivan, & Tripp, 1998), patients undergoing aversive diagnostic procedures (Sullivan et al., 1995, Study 3), dental patients (Sullivan & Neish, 1998), sport participants (Sullivan et al. in press) and undergraduates participating in experimental pain procedures (Sullivan et al., 1995, Study 4). The PCS has also been shown to predict emotional distress (Sullivan et al., 1995, Study 2) and pain behaviour (Sullivan, Tripp, & Santor, 2000) in response to aversive stimulation. **Convergent:** The PCS has been shown to correlate with interview-based methods of assessing pain-related catastrophic thinking (Sullivan et al. Studies 2 and 3,

1995). **Discriminant:** The PCS has been shown to be distinct from related cognitive and emotional variables such as depression, anxiety, and fear of pain (Sullivan *et al.*, 1995, 1998).

LOCATION: Sullivan, M.J.L., Bishop, S., & Pivik, J. (1995). The Pain Catastrophizing Scale: Development and validation. *Psychological Assessment, 7,* 524-532.

COMMENT: Research conducted to date suggests that attentional factors may be the primary mechanisms by which catastrophizing exerts its effects on pain experience. Catastrophizers, compared to noncatastrophizers, show greater attentional interference to a pain warning signal (Crombez, Eccleston, Baeyens, & Eelen, 1998), they experience more thought intrusions when attempting to suppress thoughts about pain (Sullivan, Rouse, Johnston, & Bishop, 1997), and benefit more from disclosure manipulations (Sullivan & Neish, 1999). The rumination subscale of the PCS was shown to be the best predictor of pain in a sample of dental patients (Sullivan & Neish, 1998), and the best predictor of disability in a sample of chronic pain patients (Sullivan *et al.*, 1998).

REFERENCES:

Chaves, J.F., & Brown, J.M. (1987). Spontaneous coping strategies for the control of clinical pain and stress. *Journal of Behavioural Medicine, 10,* 263-276.

Crombez, G., Eccleston, C., Baeyens, F., & Eelen, P. (1998). When somatic information threatens, catastrophic thinking enhances attentional interference. *Pain, 75,* 187-198.

Osman, A., Barrios, F., Copper, B., Hauptmann, W., Jones, J., & O'Neill, E. (1997). Factor structure, reliability, and validity of the Pain Catastrophizing Scale. *Journal of Behavioral Medicine, 20,* 589-605.

Rosenstiel, A.K., & Keefe, F.J. (1983). The use of coping strategies in chronic low back patients: Relationship to patient characteristics and current adjustment. *Pain, 17*, 33-44.

Spanos, N.P., Brown, J.M., Jones, B., & Horner, D. (1981). Cognitive activity and suggestions for analgesia in the reduction of reported pain. *Journal of Abnormal Psychology, 90*, 554-561.

Spanos, N.P., Radtke-Bodorik, H.L., Ferguson, J.D., & Jones, B. (1979). The effects of hypnotic susceptibility, suggestions for analgesia, and utilization of cognitive strategies on the reduction of pain. *Journal of Abnormal Psychology, 88*, 282-292.

Sullivan, M.J.L., Bishop, S., & Pivik, J. (1995). The Pain Catastrophizing Scale: Development and validation. *Psychological Assessment, 7*, 524-532.

Sullivan, M.J.L., & Neish, N. (1998). Catastrophizing, anxiety and pain during dental hygiene treatment. *Community Dentistry and Oral Epidemiology, 26*, 344-349.

Sullivan, M.J.L., & Neish, N. (1999). The effects of disclosure on pain during dental hygiene treatment: the moderating role of catastrophizing. *Pain, 79*, 155-163.

Sullivan, M.J.L., Rouse, D., Johnston, S., & Bishop, S. (1997). Thought suppression, catastrophizing and pain. *Cognitive Therapy and Research, 21*, 555-568.

Sullivan, M.J.L., Stanish, W., Waite, H, Sullivan, M.E., & Tripp, D. (1998). Catastrophizing, pain, and disability in patients with soft tissue injuries. *Pain, 77*, 253-260.

Sullivan, M.J.L., Tripp, D.A., Rodgers, W.M., & Stanish, W. (2000). Catastrophizing and pain perception in sports participants. *Journal of Applied Sport Psychology*.

Sullivan, M.J.L., Tripp, D.A., & Santor, D. (2000). Gender differences in pain
and pain behaviour: The role of catastrophizing. *Cognitive Therapy and
Research, 24,* 121-134.

REVIEWER: Michael J.L. Sullivan, Department of Psychology, Life Sciences
Building, Dalhousie University, Halifax, Nova Scotia, B3H 4J1, Canada. E-mail:
sully@is.dal.ca

5.29: PANIC DISORDER SEVERITY SCALE

AUTHORS: Shear, Brown, Barlow, Money, Sholomskas, Woods, Gorman, and
Papp.

VARIABLE: Panic disorder severity.

DESCRIPTION: The Panic Disorder Severity Scale (PDSS; Shear, Brown, Barlow,
Money, Sholomskas, Woods, Gorman, & Papp, 1997) is an interview-based
instrument for assessing the severity of panic disorder and associated symptoms in
the past month. The scale comprises seven dimensions: (1) frequency of panic
attacks, (2) distress during panic attacks, (3) anticipatory anxiety, (4) phobic
avoidance of situations, (5) phobic avoidance of sensations, (6) impairment or
interference with work functioning, and (7) impairment or interference with social
functioning. On the basis of the individual's responses to a scripted interview, the
interviewer rates the severity of each dimension on a 0 to 4 scale (higher ratings
reflect greater degrees of symptom severity). Each dimension is measured by a
single item. The composite score is the mean of the seven items. The PDSS is
modelled after the Yale-Brown Obsessive Compulsive Scale (Goodman, Price,

Rasmussen, Mazure, Fleischmann *et al.*, 1989; Goodman, Price, Rasmussen, Mazure, Delgado *et al.*, 1989).

SAMPLE: Shear *et al.* (1997) intended the scale to be used among individuals who have been diagnosed with panic disorder.

RELIABILITY: Internal consistency: Internal consistency was investigated among 186 participants who had received a DSM-III-R diagnosis of panic disorder with no or mild agoraphobia (Shear *et al.*, 1997). Correlations between each item and the total score were modest for some items (coefficients varying between .28 and .45), reflecting a possible lack of unidimensionality. The Cronbach's alpha for the entire scale was .65. A two-factor model suggested a better fit. Panic frequency and panic distress formed the first factor and the remaining items formed the second one. The two factors were moderately correlated (r=.55). **Interrater:** Ten experienced clinicians who underwent extensive training in use of this scale rated independently 24 audiotaped PDSS assessments. Interrater Reliability on individual scale items ranged from .74 to .87, and the intraclass correlation coefficient was .87 (Shear *et al.*, 1997).

VALIDITY: Convergent: The correlation between the PDSS total score and the clinical severity rating of panic disorder on the Anxiety Disorder Interview Schedule, Revised (ADIS-R; Di Nardo & Barlow, 1988) was .55 (Shear *et al.*, 1997). Overall, individual items showed good convergent validity with the ADIS-R or other questionnaires measuring a similar or overlapping domain (*i.e.*, panic frequency, agoraphobic avoidance).

COMMENTS: The Panic Disorder Severity Scale allows monitoring of panic disorder severity in individuals for whom a diagnosis has been established. It benefits from the sensitivity of clinician's rated instrument, but it lacks the flexibility of self-report measures. Based on comparisons of treatment responders and nonresponders, the PDSS was associated with favourable levels of sensitivity to change following a short-term treatment (Shear *et al.*, 1997). Given the nature of the study sample (*i.e.*, enrolment in a randomised controlled trial involving medication regimens), Shear *et al.* (1997) pointed out that psychometric results should be regarded as somewhat tentative. They further proposed that the two-factor model obtained for this scale was reflective of the multidimensionality structure of panic disorder. However, no explanations were offered as to the nature of these two factors. Finally, the PDSS has been used in treatment trials of panic disorder that have investigated medication treatment outcome among adults (Pollack, Otto, Worthington, Manfro, & Wolkow, 1998) and rate of improvement during a cognitive-behavioral group treatment (Penava, Otto, Maki, & Pollack, 1998).

LOCATION: Shear, M.K., Brown, T.A., Barlow, D.H., Money, R., Sholomskas, D. E., Woods, S.W., Gorman, J.M., & Papp, L.A. (1997). Multicenter collaborative panic disorder severity scale. *American Journal of Psychiatry*, *154*, 1571-1575.

REFERENCES:

Di Nardo, P. A, & Barlow, D. H. (1988). *Anxiety Disorders Interview Schedule, Revised (ADIS-R)*. Albany, NY: Graywind Publications.

Goodman, W.K., Price, L.H., Rasmussen, S.A., Mazure, C., Fleischmann, R.L., Hill, C.L., Heninger, G.R., & Charney, D.S. (1989). The Yale-Brown Obsessive Compulsive Scale, I: Development, use, and reliability. *Archives of General Psychiatry*, *46*, 1006-1011.

Goodman, W.K., Price, L.H., Rasmussen, S.A., Mazure, C., Delgado, P., Heninger, G.R., & Charney, D.S. (1989). The Yale-Brown Obsessive Compulsive Scale, II: Validity. *Archives of General Psychiatry*, *46*, 1012-1016.

Penava, S.J., Otto, M.W., Maki, K.M., & Pollack, M.H. (1998). Rate of improvement during cognitive-behavioral group treatment for panic disorder. *Behaviour Research and Therapy, 36,* 665-673.

Pollack, M.H., Otto, M.W., Worthington, J.J., Manfro, G.G., & Wolkow, R. (1998). Sertraline in the treatment of panic disorder: A flexible-dose multicenter trial. *Archives of General Psychiatry, 55,* 1010-1016.

Shear, M.K., Brown, T.A., Barlow, D.H., Money, R., Sholomskas, D.E., Woods, S.W., Gorman, J.M., & Papp, L.A. (1997). Multicenter collaborative panic disorder severity scale. *American Journal of Psychiatry, 154,* 1571-1575.

REVIEWERS: Marie-Claude Laplante School of Psychology, University of Ottawa, Ottawa, Ontario, Canada, K1N 6N5 and Stéphane Bouchard Département de Psychoéducation, Université du Québec à Hull, Hull, Québec, J8X 3X7, Canada.

5.30: PARANOIA/SUSPICIOUSNESS QUESTIONNAIRE (PSQ), THE.
AUTHORS: Rawlings and Freeman.

VARIABLE: Paranoid ideation and behaviour; suspiciousness.

DESCRIPTION: Self-report questionnaire including 47 questions (three reverse-scored) requiring a *yes* or *no* answer, developed mostly using modified items from established scales. Five moderately inter-correlated sub-scales are labelled Interpersonal Suspiciousness/Hostility (IS), Negative Mood/Withdrawal (NM), Anger/Impulsiveness (AI), Mistrust/Wariness (MW) and Perceived Hardship/Resentment (PH). A 7-item short form of the questionnaire devised by Freeman (1997) includes questions 5, 6, 20, 21, 22, 33 and 42 of the original.

SAMPLE: Rawlings and Freeman (1996) developed the questionnaire for use with non-psychiatric populations.

RELIABILITY: Internal consistency: The original article reports alpha-coefficients in two separate studies of .87 and .89 for the full scale, employing samples of over 200 student subjects. Sub-scale reliabilities were also satisfactory: .77 for IS, .66 for NM, .71 for AI, .65 for MW and .74 for PH. Freeman (1997) reported two separate studies in which the reliability of the short form was estimated at .78 and .79 respectively, using the weighted composite structural equation modelling method described by Raykov (1997). **Test-retest:** The original article reports a test-retest reliability coefficient of .82 over a period of three months in a sample of 74 subjects for the full scale PSQ. Test-retest coefficients for the sub-scales were .82 for IS, .68 for NM, .59 for AI, .64 for MW and .79 for PH.

VALIDITY: The PSQ was developed as a measure of 'schizotypy' - the appearance of minor signs of schizophrenia/psychosis in otherwise normal people. Rawlings and Freeman (1997) report that the scale shows both moderate correlations with, and clear differentiation from, the scales of the Oxford-Liverpool Inventory of Feelings and Experiences (O-Life) - a multi-dimensional measure of schizotypy. They also note that the questionnaire is associated in predictable ways with the scales of the Eysenck Personality Questionnaire-Revised and the NEO Personality Inventory-Revised. Specifically, it is positively correlated with Neuroticism and negatively correlated with Agreeableness. Freeman (1997) found the short form of the scale was correlated positively with a measure of schizotypy (the Rust Inventory of Schizotypic Cognitions) and an alternative measure of paranoia (the P scale from the Millon Clinical Multiaxial Inventory), while high scorers showed a paranoid attributional style of the type often found in clinically paranoid individuals.

LOCATION: Rawlings, D., & Freeman, J.L. (1996). A questionnaire for the measurement of paranoia/suspiciousness. *British Journal of Clinical Psychology*, *35*, 451-461.

COMMENT: The limited research so far conducted appears promising. More research using the long and short versions of the questionnaire with different samples and in various research contexts is needed to establish the usefulness of the instrument.

REFERENCES:

Freeman, J.L. (1997). *Paranoia, schizotypy and normal personality*. Unpublished Ph.D thesis, University of Melbourne.

Rawlings, D., & Freeman, J.L. (1996). A questionnaire for the measurement of paranoia/suspiciousness. *British Journal of Clinical Psychology*, *35*, 451-461.

Rawlings, D., & Freeman, J.L. (1997). Measuring paranoia/suspiciousness. In G. Claridge (Ed.), *Schizotypy: Implications for Illness and Health* (pp. 38-60). Oxford: Oxford University Press.

REVIEWERS: David Rawlings, Department of Psychology, University of Melbourne, Parkville, Victoria 3052, Australia, E-mail: d.rawlings@psych.unimelb.edu.au and Justin L. Freeman, Anti-Cancer Council of Victoria, 1 Rathdowne Street, Carlton South, Victoria 3053, Australia. E-mail: justin.freeman@accv.org.au

5.31: PARENT REPORT OF POST-TRAUMATIC SYMPTOMS (PROPS).

AUTHORS: Greenwald and Rubin.

VARIABLE: Children's post-traumatic symptoms.

DESCRIPTION: The Parent Report of Post-traumatic Symptoms (PROPS; Greenwald and Rubin, 1999) is a 30-item parent report covering the broad range of children's post-traumatic symptoms which have been noted in the literature (Fletcher, 1993) and which are conducive to reporting on the basis of observation. Items were further selected for responsiveness to change (*e.g.* following successful treatment). Items are specific symptoms over the past week, to be endorsed as *Never* (0), *Sometimes* (1), or *Often* (2). The single full-scale score is tallied in about a minute and compared to the 'clinical concern' cut-off.

SAMPLE: The original validation studies used a community sample of children ages 8-15 (Greenwald & Rubin, 1999). Additional studies including older adolescents are underway; it has also been used in clinical settings re younger children. This can also be completed by other knowledgeable adults such as a staff member in a residential setting. This instrument is intended for use as a screen for post-traumatic symptoms in post-disaster, mental health, pediatric, and educational settings, and as a treatment outcome measure.

RELIABILITY: Internal consistency: In published validation studies, coefficient alpha for the PROPS was .93, with each item-total correlation significant at the .001 level, ranging from .43 to .65 (Greenwald & Rubin, 1999). **Test-retest:** A sub-sample was re-tested after 4-6 weeks having first used paper-and-pencil, then the alternate form of telephone interview. For the total score the test-retest correlation was .79 (*p*<.001) (Greenwald & Rubin, 1999).

VALIDITY: Degree of trauma/loss exposure had a correlation of .56 ($p<.001$) with PROPS scores (Greenwald & Rubin, 1999). PROPS scores also declined following successful trauma-focused treatment as indicated by declines in other validated trauma measures and in severity of presenting problems (Greenwald, in press; Soberman, Greenwald, & Rule, in press). Additional studies are in progress.

LOCATION: Greenwald, R. & Rubin, A. (1999). Brief assessment of children's post-traumatic symptoms: Development and preliminary validation of parent and child scales. *Research on Social Work Practice, 9*, 61-75. The test can also be found at www.childtrauma.com. and www.sidran.org.

COMMENT: It is essential to use trauma-specific instruments to assess post-traumatic symptoms, as anxiety and depression measures are insufficiently sensitive to this construct. It is also essential to obtain the parent's viewpoint as self-report will not provide complete information. When used in conjunction with the Child Report of Post-traumatic Symptoms (CROPS), this instrument provides brief yet comprehensive coverage of children's and adolescents' post-traumatic symptoms. Further study is needed for fuller confidence in the measure.

REFERENCES:

Fletcher, K. E. (1993, October). *The spectrum of post-traumatic responses in children*. Presented at the Annual Meeting of the International Society for Traumatic Stress Studies, San Antonio.

Greenwald, R. (in press). Motivation - Adaptive Skills - Trauma Resolution (MASTR) therapy for adolescents with conduct problems: An open trial. *Journal of Aggression, Maltreatment, and Trauma.*

Greenwald, R. & Rubin, A. (1999). Brief assessment of children's post-traumatic symptoms: Development and preliminary validation of parent and child scales. *Research on Social Work Practice, 9*, 61-75.

Soberman, G.S., Greenwald, R., & Rule, D.L. (in press). A controlled study of eye movement desensitization and reprocessing (EMDR) for boys with conduct problems. *Journal of Aggression, Maltreatment, and Trauma.*

REVIEWER: Ricky Greenwald, 483 Belknap Rd., Framingham, MA 01701, U.S.A., rickygr@childtrauma.com.

5.32: PENN STATE WORRY QUESTIONNAIRE (PSWQ).
AUTHORS: Meyer, Miller, Metzger, and Borkovec.

VARIABLE: Pathological worry.

DESCRIPTION: With the advent of the DSM-III-R (American Psychiatric Association, 1987), generalized anxiety disorder (GAD) was established as an independent diagnosis within the canon of the anxiety disorders. The cardinal criterion for a diagnosis of GAD is pathological worry, that is chronic, excessive, and uncontrollable worry, more days than not, over a period of at least six months. The Penn State Worry Questionnaire (PSWQ) is a self-report scale of pathological worry. It contains 16 items that cover excessiveness, duration, uncontrollability and associated distress of worry as experienced by clients diagnosed with GAD (*e.g.*, "Many situations make me worry"; "I find it easy to dismiss worrisome thoughts", reverse-scored). Of the 16 items, 5 are reverse-scored. With a 5-point answer scale from *Not at all typical of me* (1) to *Very typical of me* (5), the potential range of PSWQ total scores is 16-80. Reference values for nonclinical, analog, and clinical groups can be found in Molina and Borkvoc (1994; see also Gillis, Haaga, & Ford, 1995). There are two adaptations of the PSWQ, one for the assessment of pathological worry in children and adolescents (Chorpita, Tracey,

Brown, Collica, & Barlow, 1997) and one for weekly assessment of pathological worry to monitor changes during therapy (Stöber & Bittencourt, 1998).

SAMPLES: The PSWQ is intended to be used in nonclinical and clinical adult samples.

RELIABILITY: Internal consistency: The PSWQ has demonstrated high levels of internal consistency. On average, Cronbach's alphas are above .90 (*cf.* Molina & Borkovec, 1994; Stöber, 1998). Test-retest: Across intervals from two to ten weeks, the PSWQ has shown test-retest correlations between .75 and .93 (*cf.* Molina & Borkovec, 1994; Stöber, 1998).

VALIDITY: Convergent: The PSWQ has demonstrated substantial convergent correlations with other measures of worry (*e.g.*, Davey, 1993; Stöber, 1995) and a self-report GAD questionnaire (Roemer, Borkovec, Posa, & Borkovec, 1995). Moreover, it has shown high correlations with measures of anxiety (*e.g.*, Meyer, Miller, Metzger, & Borkovec, 1990; Molina & Borkovec, 1994). Finally, it has shown substantial correlations with various measures related to poor mental health such as maladaptive coping styles (Davey, 1993), intolerance of uncertainty (Freeston, Rhéaume, Letarte, Dugas, & Ladouceur, 1994), procrastination (Flett, Blankstein, & Martin, 1995), obsessive-compulsive symptoms (Wells & Papageorgiou, 1998), and perfectionism (Stöber & Joormann, in press). Discriminant: Brown, Antony, and Barlow (1992) investigated the psychometric properties of the PSWQ in an anxiety disorders sample and found only moderate correlations with depression. Also in nonclinical samples, the PSWQ has shown moderate correlations with depression (Molina & Borkovec, 1994). However, some studies have found correlations above .50 with depression (*e.g.*, Stöber & Joormann, in press). Still, PSWQ correlations with measures of worry and anxiety are usually higher than correlations with measures of depression.

LOCATION:

Meyer, T.J., Miller, M.L., Metzger, R.L., & Borkovec, T.D. (1990). Development and validation of the Penn State Worry Questionnaire. *Behaviour Research and Therapy, 28*, 487-495.

Chorpita, B.F., Tracey, S.A., Brown, T.A., Collica, T.J., & Barlow, D.H. (1997). Assessment of worry in children and adolescents: An adaptation of the Penn State Worry Questionnaire. *Behaviour Research and Therapy, 35*, 569-581.

Stöber, J., & Bittencourt, J. (1998). Weekly assessment of worry: An adaptation of the Penn State Worry Questionnaire for monitoring changes during treatment. *Behaviour Research and Therapy, 36*, 645-656.

COMMENT: The PSWQ is a reliable and valid measure of individual differences in pathological worry. Since its publication in 1990, it has become the 'gold standard' for the assessment of chronic, excessive, and uncontrollable worry. Critical comments are few and concern the factorial structure of the PSWQ (*i.e.*, whether it is one- or two-factorial; *e.g.*, Stöber, 1995), the overlap with depression symptoms (*e.g.*, Starcevic, 1995), and the sometimes low specificity when compared to measures of nonpathological worry and trait anxiety (*e.g.*, Davey, 1993; Stöber & Joormann, in press).

REFERENCES:

American Psychiatric Association (Ed.). (1987). *Diagnostic and Statistical Manual of Mental Disorders*. (3rd Edition. Revised). Washington, DC: American Psychiatric Association.

Brown, T.A., Antony, M.M., & Barlow, D.H. (1992). Psychometric properties of the Penn State Worry Questionnaire in a clinical anxiety disorders sample. *Behaviour Research and Therapy, 30*, 33-37.

Chorpita, B.F., Tracey, S.A., Brown, T.A., Collica, T.J., & Barlow, D.H. (1997).

Assessment of worry in children and adolescents: An adaptation of the Penn State Worry Questionnaire. *Behaviour Research and Therapy, 35,* 569-581.

Davey, G.C.L. (1993). A comparison of three worry questionnaires. *Behaviour Research and Therapy, 31,* 51-56.

Flett, G.L., Blankstein, K.R., & Martin, T.R. (1995). Procrastination, negative self-evaluation, and stress in depression and anxiety: A review and preliminary model. In J. R. Ferrari, J. L. Johnson, & W. G. McCown (Eds.), *Procrastination and Task Avoidance: Theory, Research, and Measurement* (pp. 137-167). New York: Plenum.

Freeston, M.H., Rhéaume, J., Letarte, H., Dugas, M., & Ladouceur, R. (1994). Why do people worry? *Personality and Individual Differences, 17,* 791-802.

Gillis, M.M., Haaga, D.A.F., & Ford, G.T. (1995). Normative values for the Beck Anxiety Inventory, Fear Questionnaire, Penn State Worry Questionnaire, and Social Phobia and Anxiety Inventory. *Psychological Assessment, 7,* 450-455.

Meyer, T.J., Miller, M.L., Metzger, R.L., & Borkovec, T.D. (1990). Development and validation of the Penn State Worry Questionnaire. *Behaviour Research and Therapy, 28,* 487-495.

Molina, S., & Borkovec, T.D. (1994). The Penn State Worry Questionnaire: Psychometric properties and associated characteristics. In G.C.L. Davey & F. Tallis (Eds.), *Worrying: Perspectives on Theory, Assessment, and Treatment* (pp. 265-283). New York: Wiley.

Roemer, L., Borkovec, M., Posa, S., & Borkovec, T.D. (1995). A self-report diagnostic measure of generalized anxiety disorder. *Journal of Behavior Therapy and Experimental Psychiatry, 26,* 345-350.

Starcevic, V. (1995). Pathological worry and major depression: A preliminary report. *Behaviour Research and Therapy, 33,* 55-56.

Stöber, J. (1995). Besorgnis: Ein Vergleich dreier Inventare zur Erfassung allgemeiner Sorgen. (Worry: A comparison of three inventories for the assessment of general worries). *Zeitschrift für Differentielle und Diagnostische Psychologie, 16*, 50-63.

Stöber, J. (1998). Reliability and validity of two widely-used worry questionnaires: Self-report and self-peer convergence. *Personality and Individual Differences, 24*, 887-890.

Stöber, J., & Bittencourt, J. (1998). Weekly assessment of worry: An adaptation of the Penn State Worry Questionnaire for monitoring changes during treatment. *Behaviour Research and Therapy, 36*, 645-656.

Stöber, J., & Joormann, J. (in press). Worry, procrastination, and perfectionism: Differentiating amount of worry, pathological worry, anxiety, and depression. *Cognitive Therapy and Research.*

Wells, A., & Papageorgiou, C. (1998). Relationships between worry, obsessive-compulsive symptoms, and meta-cognitive beliefs. *Behaviour Research and Therapy, 36*, 899-913.

REVIEWER: Joachim Stöber, Martin Luther University of Halle-Wittenberg, Department of Educational Psychology, Franckesche Stiftungen, Haus 5, D-06099 Halle (Saale), Germany. E-mail: stoeber@paedagogik.uni-halle.de

5.33: PERSONAL DISTURBANCE SCALE (DSSI/sAD).

AUTHOR: Bedford and Foulds.

VARIABLES: States of anxious and depressed mood.

DESCRIPTION: A self-report scale of seven items each for anxious and depressed mood states. After deciding whether true or false the respondent (if true) indicates which of three possibilities reflects the degree of psychological upset recently experienced. Each scale, therefore, has a range of possible scores 0-21.

SAMPLE: Originally intended for use with British psychiatric patients, or as a screening measure with general populations, in practice had much wider application *e.g.* additionally, the elderly in the community, acquired hearing loss, childbirth disorders, gambling, parental bereavement, genetic twin studies, psychosomatic groups, etc. Lyketsos *et al.* (1979) produced norms for Greek men and women, whilst in Australia similar reports include Henderson (1981) and Kendler *et al.* (1986) where *n*=3,798 pairs of adult twins. The latter includes means and standard deviations for each item by sex.

RELIABILITY: Internal consistency: A study of 480 psychiatric patients involving principal axis, principal component and confirmatory factor analyses by Bedford and Deary (1997), claimed that the item structure may legitimately be interpreted conceptually as: (1) general psychological distress; or (2) clinical states of anxiety and depression; or (3) 'normal' mood dimensions of hedonic tone and tense arousal. This view was confirmed by Bedford *et al.* (1999) with 132 subjects undergoing psychological therapy. These authors also presented factorially purer orthogonal short-forms of anxiety (four items) and depression (five items) with Cronbach's alpha coefficients of .73 and .86 respectively. Epidemiological genetic studies using the sAD items, and involving factor analyses, included Kendler *et al.* (1987) (*n*=1,978 subjects). Bedford and Deary (1997) also carried out a successful confirmatory factor analysis using Bentler's EQS structural equation modelling (SEM) programme. Similarly, Christensen *et al.* (1999), with 2,622 people drawn from the electoral roll, in an SEM analysis concluded that the best fit for the 14 sAD items was a two-factor model of anxiety and depression. Cronbach's alpha coefficients of .80 and .86 had also been established by them for the anxiety and depression scales respectively. Jorm *et al.* (1989) with 386 normal adults calculated a Cronbach's of .88 for the 14 items. **Test-retest:** When 68 acute psychiatric in-patients were tested on admission and re-tested after a one month interval their mean sAD scores were initially 12.7 (SD=9.1), whilst at re-test the mean was 6.4 (SD=8.3), $p<.00005$ (Bedford & Foulds, 1978). In a placebo controlled double-blind trial of 40 obese females a significant improvement in mood was shown at 12 week retest (Abell *et al.*1986). Examining the re-test artefact Jorm *et al.* (1989) reported total sAD score correlations at 4, 11, 21 and 34 weeks as being .77, .51, .56 and .59 respectively. The means and standard deviations of 3.92 (4.88) and 3.24 (4.52) differed significantly ($p<.01$) between test and first retest.

VALIDITY: **Convergent:** Item content was validated against the judgements of experienced clinical psychologists and senior psychiatrists with a very high degree of concordance. Similarly, the psychiatrists' ratings of their in-patients were statistically significantly related to the patients' scores on anxiety, depression and sAD total with $p<.05$, .001 and .01 respectively (Bedford & Foulds, 1978; Bedford *et al.*, 1976). Henderson (1981) in wave 3 of an epidemiological study (*n*=243) obtained significant correlations between sAD anxiety and the GHQ (.54), the Zung SDS (.62) and his own 4NS (.50), and for sAD depression .58, .61 and .51 respectively. Bedford and McIver (1978) confirmed in patient and normal groups, that the sAD related to a 'general instability' scale comprising Cattell's 16PF factors C (emotionally unstable), O (apprehensive) and Q4 (tense), but not to the 'psychopathy' scale made up of G (expedient), plus L (suspicious) and Q3 (undisciplined self-conflict). Bedford *et al.* (submitted for publication), found correlations for 132 psychiatric out-patients, between the sAD and the Hospital Anxiety and Depression Scale, of .67 for the anxiety scales and .64 for the depression scales, both $p=.000$. The four-point ratings of the consultant correlated .43 for sAD anxiety and .45 for sAD depression, both $p=.000$. When forty-three of these patients were retested at their next appointment these correlations were .77, .67, .49 (all $p=.0000$) and .29 ($p=.06$, N.S.). Psychophysiological characteristics were significantly associated with puerperal mental state (Little *et al.*, 1981). Among the research programmes finding sAD associations in a series of studies are *e.g.* Morgan *et al.* (1991) re the elderly in the community ($n=1,042$); Vance *et al.* (1995) re: parental bereavement ($n=697$); Angelopoulos *et al.* (1996) re: psychosomatic and other conditions; Mellors *et al.* (1994) re: hypertension ($n=7,616$); Mackinnon *et al.* (1990) re: genetic studies ($n=462$ twin pairs), and Benson *et al.* (1987) re: psychiatric disorders of childbirth. **Discriminant:** Psychiatric patients ($n=480$) had a Mean of 7.1 (SD=4.7) for anxiety and 7.5 (SD=5.5) for depression. By contrast, non-patient subjects ($n=200$) had a Mean of .9 (S.D.=1.3) and .6, (SD=1.5) respectively (Bedford & Foulds, 1978).

LOCATION (all contain the test items)

Bedford, A., & Deary, I.J. (1997). The personal disturbance scale (DSSI/sAD): Development, use and structure. *Personality and Individual Differences, 22,* 493-510.

Bedford, A., & Foulds, G.A. (1978). *Manual of the Personal Disturbance Scale* (DSSI/sAD). Windsor: NFER-Nelson.

Bedford, A., Foulds, G.A., & Sheffield, B.F. (1976). A new Personal Disturbance Scale. *British Journal of Social and Clinical Psychology, 15,* 387-394.

Bedford, A., Grant, E., de Pauw, K., & Deary, I.J. (1999). The personal disturbance scale (DSSI/sAD): Structural cross-validation and proposed short forms. *Personality and Individual Differences, 27,* 251-261.

Foulds, G.A. (1976). *The Hierarchical Nature of Personal Illness.* London: Academic Press.

COMMENT: The breadth of studies involving associations with other assessments including psychometric ones, interviews, clinical judgements and demographic factors, has added considerably to knowledge of the utility, reliability, validity and structure of the sAD scales. Besides further clinical investigations, particularly monitoring treatments/therapies, it would be useful to see more theoretical research where the sAD was used in conjunction with 'normal' mood scales in experimental studies of mood structure and mood change.

REFERENCES:

Abell, C.A., Farquhar, D.L., Galloway, S. McL, Steven, F., Philip, A.E., & Munro, J.F. (1986). Placebo controlled double-bind trial of fluvoxamine maleate in the obese. *Journal of Psychosomatic Research, 30,* 143-146.

Angelopoulos, N.V., Mantas, C., Dalekos, G.N., Vasalos, K., & Tsianos, E.V. (1996). Psychiatric factors in patients with ulcerated colitis according to disease entity. *European Journal of Psychiatry, 10,* 87-99.

Bedford, A., de Pauw, K., Grant, E., & Deary, I.J. (Submitted for publication). *A comparison of two self-report anxiety-depression questionnaires (DSSI/sAD and HAD): Construction, content, structure and clinical rating.*

Bedford, A., & McIver, D. (1978). Foulds' "general instability" and "psychopathy" 16PF scales and their relationship to psychiatric mood state. *Journal of Clinical Psychology, 34,* 417-418.

Benson, P., Little, B.C., Talbert, G.D., Dewhurst, J., & Priest, R.G. (1987). Foetal heart rate and maternal emotional state. *British Journal of Medical Psychology, 60,* 151-154.

Christensen, H., Jorm, A.F., Mackinnon, A.J., Korten, A.E., Jacomb, P.A., Henderson, A.S., & Rodgers, B. (1999). Age differences in depression and anxiety symptoms: A structural equation modelling analysis of data from a general population sample. *Psychological Medicine, 29,* 325-339.

Henderson, A.S. with Byrne, D.G., & Duncan-Jones, P. (1981). *Neurosis and the Social Environment.* London: Academic Press.

Jorm, A.F., Duncan-Jones, P., & Scott, R. (1989). An analysis of the re-test artefact in longitudinal studies of psychiatric symptoms and personality. *Psychological Medicine, 19,* 487-493.

Kendler, K.S., Heath, A., Martin, N.G., & Eaves, L.J. (1986). Symptoms of anxiety and depression in a volunteer twin population. *Archives of General Psychiatry, 43,* 213-221.

Kendler, K.S., Heath, A.C., Martin, N.G., & Eaves, L.J. (1987). Symptoms of anxiety and symptoms of depression: Same genes, different environments? *Archives of General Psychiatry, 44,* 451-457.

Little, B.C., Hayworth, J., Bonham Carter, S.M., Dewhurst, J., Raptopoulos, P., Sandler, M., & Priest, R.G. (1981). Personal and psychophysiological characteristics associated with puerperal mental state. *Journal of Psychosomatic Research, 25,* 385-393.

Lyketsos, G.C., Blackburn, I.M., & Mouzaki, D. (1979). Personality variables and dysthymic symptoms: A comparison between a Greek and a British sample. *Psychological Medicine, 9,* 753-758.

Mackinnon, A.J., Henderson, A.S., & Andrews, G. (1990). Genetic and environmental determinants of the lability of trait neuroticism and the symptoms of anxiety and depression. *Psychological Medicine, 20,* 581-590.

Mellors, V., Boyle, G.J., & Roberts, L. (1994). Effects of personality, stress and lifestyle on hypertension: An Australian twin study. *Personality and Individual Differences, 16,* 967-974.

Morgan, K., Dallosso, H., Bassey, E.J., Ebrahim, S., Fentem, P.H., & Arie, T.H.D. (1991). Customary physical activity, psychological well-being and successful Aging. *Ageing and Society, 11,* 399-415.

Vance, J.C., Boyle, F.M., Najman, J.M., & Thearle, M.J. (1995). Gender differences in parental psychological distress following perinatal death or sudden infant death syndrome. *British Journal of Psychiatry, 167,* 806-811.

REVIEWER: Alan Bedford, York Clinical Psychology Services, The Old Chapel, Bootham Park, York, YO30 7BY and Department of Psychology, University of York, Heslington, York YO10 5DD, England, U.K.

5.34: PERSONAL FEELINGS QUESTIONNAIRE-2.
AUTHORS: Harder and Zalma.

VARIABLE: Shame and guilt proneness.

DESCRIPTION: Self-report scale which is a revision of an earlier instrument (Harder & Lewis, 1987). Ten items mention emotional reactions associated with shame (*e.g.*, "embarrassment," "feeling ridiculous," and "self-consciousness"). Six more record guilt ("mild guilt," "worry about hurting or injuring someone," and "remorse"). Responses vary along a five-point scale indicating the frequency with which feelings are experienced: *You experience the feeling continuously or* *almost continuously* (4), *Frequently but not continuously* (3), *Some of the time* (2), *Rarely* (1), or *Never* (0). Higher scores indicate greater shame and guilt proneness.

SAMPLE: Harder and Zalma (1990) developed these two scales for use with non-psychiatric populations.

RELIABILITY: **Internal consistency:** Acceptable internal reliabilities have been demonstrated in a number of investigations (Harder & Zalma, 1990; Quiles & Bybee, 1997; Watson, Morris, Ramsey, Hickman, & Waddell, 1996; Watson, Hickman, & Morris, 1996). **Test-retest:** Across a two-week interval, the test-retest reliability for the shame scale was .93, and for the guilt measure, it was .85 (Harder & Zalma, 1990).

VALIDITY: **Convergent:** Evidence of convergent validity for one or both measures has been documented in expected relationships with depression (Harder & Zalma, 1990; Harder, Cutler, & Rockart, 1992; Tangney, Burggraf, & Wagner, 1995), state and trait anxiety (Tangney, Burggraf, & Wagner, 1995) empathy (Tangney, Burggraf, & Wagner, 1995), self-derogation (Harder & Zalma, 1990; Harder, *et al.*, 1992; Harder, *et al.*, 1994), public and private self-consciousness (Harder & Zalma, 1990; Watson, Morris, Ramsey, Hickman, & Waddell, 1996), self-instability (Harder, *et al.*, 1994), shyness (Harder, *et al.*, 1992; Harder, Rockart, & Cutler, 1994), social anxiety (Harder, *et al.*, 1992; Harder, *et al.*, 1994; Watson, Morris, Ramsey, Hickman, & Waddell, 1996), various psychiatric symptoms (Harder, Cutler, & Rockart, 1992; Tangney, Burggraf, & Wagner, 1995), self-monitoring (Watson, Morris, Ramsey, Hickman, & Waddell, 1996); narcissism (Watson, Hickman, & Morris, 1997), self-esteem (Tangney, Burggraf, & Wagner, 1995; Watson, Hickman, & Morris, 1997), splitting (Tangney, Burggraf, & Wagner, 1995), and fear of negative evaluation (Tangney, Burggraf, & Wagner, 1995). **Discriminant:** The discriminant validity of both scales was

636   Psychological Well Being

formally established by demonstrating that neither measure predicts Machiavellianism (Harder & Zalma, 1990).

LOCATION: Harder, D.W., & Zalma, A. (1990). Two promising shame and guilt scales: A construct validity comparison. *Journal of Personality Assessment, 55,* 729-745.

COMMENT: Personal Feelings Questionnaire-2 (PFQ2) shame and guilt scales have clear face validity and require less sophisticated reading skills than some other instruments (Harder, 1995; Tangney, 1996). Direct comparisons with other shame and guilt scales sometimes (Harder & Zalma, 1990; Harder, Cutler, & Rockart, 1992), though not invariably (Tangney, Burggraf, & Wagner, 1995) reveal the PFQ2 to be as valid as other available self-report measures. PFQ2 data apparently are not influenced by social desirability factors (Harder & Zalma, 1990; Harder, Cutler, & Rockart, 1992). The two scales do display a fairly robust direct relationship, and the PFQ2 has been criticized because it presupposes an ability to differentiate between the experiences of guilt and shame that respondents simply may not have. Especially with the guilt scale, high scores my reflect "a generalized tendency to experience negative self-directed affect (*e.g.,* both shame and guilt)" (Tangney, 1996, p. 747). Empirical support for this possibility has been obtained (Quiles & Bybee, 1997). Partial correlations can be used to examine shame after controlling for guilt and vice versa (*e.g.,* Tangney, Burggraf, & Wagner, 1995), and this procedure seems to be useful, but is not without liabilities (Harder, 1995, p. 387). A confirmatory factor analysis nevertheless has demonstrated that the Shame Scale does define a latent shame factor whereas the Guilt Scale can do the same with regard to a latent guilt factor (Ferguson & Crowley, 1997).

REFERENCES:

Ferguson, T. J., & Crowley, S. L. (1997). Measure for measure: A multitrait-multimethod analysis of guilt and shame. *Journal of Personality Assessment, 69,* 425-441.

Harder, D. W. (1995). Shame and guilt assessment, and relationships of shame- and guilt-proneness to psychopathology. In J.P. Tangney & K.W. Fischer (Eds.), *Self-conscious emotions: The Psychology of Shame, Guilt, Embarrassment, and Pride* (pp. 368-392). New York: Guilford.

Harder, D.W., Cutler, L., & Rockart, L. (1992). Assessment of shame and guilt and their relationships to psychopathology. *Journal of Personality Assessment, 59,* 584-604.

Harder, D.W., & Lewis, S.J. (1987). The assessment of shame and guilt. In J. N. Butcher & C. D. Spielberger (Eds.), *Advances in Personality Assessment,* Vol. 6, (pp. 89-114). Hillsdale, NJ: Erlbaum.

Harder, D.W., Rockart, L., & Cutler, L. (1993). Additional validity evidence for the Harder Personal Feelings Questionnaire-2 (PFQ2): A measure of shame and guilt proneness. *Journal of Clinical Psychology, 49,* 345-348.

Harder, D.W., & Zalma, A. (1990). Two promising shame and guilt scales: A construct validity comparison. *Journal of Personality Assessment, 55,* 729-745.

Quiles, Z.N., & Bybee, J.B. (1997). Chronic and predispositional guilt: Relations to mental health, prosocial behavior and religiosity. *Journal of Personality Assessment, 69,* 104-126.

Tangney, J.P. (1996). Conceptual and methodological issues in the assessment of shame and guilt. *Behavior Research and Therapy, 34,* 741-754.

Tangney, J.P., Burggraf, S.A., & Wagner, P.E. (1995). Shame-proneness, guilt-proneness, and psychological symptoms. In J. P. Tangney & K. W. Fischer (Eds.), *Self-conscious Emotions: The Psychology of Shame, Guilt, Embarrassment, and Pride* (pp. 343-367). New York: Guilford.

Watson, P.J., Hickman, S.E., & Morris, R.J. (1996). Self-reported narcissism and shame: Testing the defensive self-esteem and continuum hypotheses. *Personality and Individual Differences, 21*, 253-259.

Watson, P.J., Morris, R.J., Ramsey, A., Hickman, S.E., & Waddell, M.G. (1996). Further contrasts between self-reflectiveness and internal state awareness factors of private self-consciousness. *Journal of Psychology, 130*, 183-192.

REVIEWER: P.J. Watson, Psychology/Department #2803, 350 Holt Hall - 615 McCallie Avenue, University of Tennessee at Chattanooga, Chattanooga, TN. 37403, U.S.A. E-mail: paul-watson@utc.edu

5.35: PSYCHOLOGICAL DISTRESS MANIFESTATION SCALE (PDMS).

AUTHOR: Massé, Poulin, Dassa, Lambert, Bélair, and Battaglini.

VARIABLE: Psychological distress.

DESCRIPTION: Self-report scale containing 23-items representing a mix of affective, behavioral and cognitive distress manifestations. These items are grouped into four oblique factors (self-depreciation, 7 items ; irritability/agressivity, 5 items ; anxiety/depression, 5 items ; social disengagement, 6 items). Respondents are asked how they have felt in the past month and rate each item on a 5-point scale; *never* (1), *rarely* (2), *half the time* (3), *frequently* (4), and *almost always* (5). Higher scores on the scale indicate a higher prevalence and frequency of occurrence of psychological distress manifestations.

SAMPLE: Massé, Poulin, Dassa, Lambert *et al.* (1998) intended the scale to be used for the assessment of psychological distress in non-psychiatric populations and to be sensitive to social differences.

RELIABILITY: Internal consistency: It demonstrated a high level of internal reliability for the entire scale (α=.93) as well as for the subscales based on exploratory and confirmatory factor analysis (between .81 and .89) (Massé *et al.*, 1998a) as well as in confirmatory factor analysis (Massé *et al.*, 1998b). **Test-retest:** Only items showing a high Kappa coefficient have been kept : based on a random sub-sample of 120 respondents retested after 5-8 days.

VALIDITY: Convergent: It has shown a .81 correlation with the Psychological Distress Index, a french adaptation (Préville *et al.*, 1995) of the Psychiatric Symptom Index (Ilfeld, 1976) (unpublished data from the Québec General Health Survey of 1998) and a .65 correlation with the Well-Being Manifestations Measure Scale (Massé *et al.*, 1998b). **Criterion:** High scores on PDMS are strongly associated with alcohol and drugs consumption, visits to health professionals, and unsatisfaction toward life in general. (Massé *et al.*, 1998a). **Content:** The 23 items originate from an initial pool of 73 items submitted to construct validity analysis. These 73 items themselves come from a corpora of more than 2000 distress manifestations reported by 195 French Canadian adults who were asked to describe, in details, the manifestations experienced in a significant lived episode of mental distress, in the past weeks or months.

LOCATION: Massé, R., Poulin, C., Dassa, C., Lambert, J., Bélair, S., & Battaglini, A. (1998a). Élaboration et validation d'un outil de mesure de la détresse psychologique dans une population non clinique de Québécois francophones, *Canadian Review of Public Health*, *89*, 183-189. Originally in French. English version comes from a translation/back translation exercise (Massé *et al.*, 1997) and a pre-test of the English version by the Center for Health and Social Surveys of Québec (Canada) (unpublished).

COMMENT: PDMS has been used recently in the Québec General Health Survey with 20 773 respondents (Santé Québec and Center of Health and Social Surveys of Québec, to be published in summer 2000). Psychometric properties of this scale as well as discriminant validy have been demonstrated. However, a high level of psychological distress does not mean automatically a low level of subjective well-being (Massé et al., 1998b). It is suggested that epidemiological assessment of general population mental health should use concomitant measures of positive and negative manifestations.

REFERENCES:

Ilfeld, F.W. (1976). Further validation of a psychiatric symptom index in a normal population, *Psychological Reports, 39*, 1215-1228.

Massé, R., Poulin, C., Dassa C., Lambert, J. Bélair, S., & Battaglini, A. (1997). *Élaboration et validation d'un Outil de Mesure de la Santé Mentale des Montréalais Francophones*. Rapport de recherche, Direction de la Santé Publique de Montréal, Écologie Humaine et Sociale.

Massé, R., Poulin, C., Dassa, C., Lambert, J., Bélair, S. & Battaglini, A. (1998a). Élaboration et validation d'un outil de mesure de la détresse psychologique dans une population non clinique de Québécois francophones. *Canadian Review of Public Health, 89*, 183-189.

Massé, R. Poulin, C., Dassa C., Lambert, J., Bélair, S., & Battaglini A. (1998b). The structure of Mental Health: Higher-order confirmatory factor analysis of psychological distress and well-being measures. *Social Indicators Research, 45*, 475-504.

Préville, M., Potvin, L., & Boyer, R. (1995). The structure of psychological distress. *Psychological Reports, 77*, 275-293.

REVIEWER: Massé Raymond. Department of Anthropology, Laval University, Québec, Canada G1K 7P4. E-mail: raymond.masse@ant.ulaval.ca

5.36: QUALITY OF LIFE IN DEPRESSION SCALE.

AUTHORS: Tuynman-Qua, Jonghe, McKenna, and Hunt.

VARIABLE: Health-Related Quality of Life.

DESCRIPTION: The Quality of Life in Depression Scale (QLDS) was developed to deal adequately with a situation in which a counselor and a client disagree about the results of a particular medical treatment. According to the developers, a person's quality of life depends on whether or not his or her individual needs are satisfied. Several self-report rating scales were used for the construction, such as the Beck Depression Scale, the Zung Depression Rating Scale and the Hospital Anxiety and Depression Scale. The QLDS assesses 'overall quality of life'. Thirty-four items are scored on a dichotomised scale (*yes/no* or *true/false*). The evaluated time period is the previous few days. No information is available on the time necessary to complete the scale.

SAMPLE: Patients suffering from depression.

RELIABILITY: The reliability and scale homogeneity of the QLDS are good; alpha ranges from .92 to .95; reported test-retest reliability between .78 and .94.

VALIDITY: For the QLDS, the construct validity is acceptable. The correlations between the instrument and other health-related QoL-instruments has been explored, *i.e.*: Sickness Impact Profile (r=.71) and the General Well-Being Index (r=.79).

LOCATION: Tuynman-Qua, H., De Jonghe, F., McKenna, A., & Hunt, S. (1992). *Schaal voor de meting van de kwaliteit van het leven bij depressie.* Houten: Ibero Publikaties.

COMMENT: Because of its symptom-specific design, the question is whether this instrument is also useful for other patients with severe mental illness. Moreover, the correlation between the QLDS and depression scales is substantial: r=.61 with the Hamilton Depression rating Scale and r=.86 with the Hospital Anxiety and Depression Scale.

REFERENCES:

Tuynman-Qua, H., De Jonghe, F., McKenna, A., & Hunt, S. (1992). *Schaal voor de meting van de kwaliteit van het leven bij depressie.* Houten: Ibero Publikaties.

REVIEWERS: Ch. van Nieuwenhuizen, TBS-kliniek De Kijvelanden, Forensic Psychiatric Hospital, Department of Psychotherapy & Research, P.O. Box 900, 3160 AC Rhoon, The Netherlands, **and** A.H. Schene, Academic Medical Center, University of Amsterdam Meibergdreef 9, 1105 AZ Amsterdam, The Netherlands, **and** M.W.J. Koeter, Academic Medical Center, University of Amsterdam Meibergdreef 9, 1105 AZ Amsterdam, The Netherlands.

5.37: QUALITY OF LIFE IN MENTAL HEALTH INDEX.
AUTHOR: Becker, Diamond and Sainfort.

VARIABLE: Quality of Life.

DESCRIPTION: In developing the Quality of Life Mental Health Index, the researchers have tried to address the major limitations of existing instruments such as lack of careful attention to principles of test construction, scoring systems that do not take into account the fact that individuals may differ in how important various domains are, and relying on the person as a single source of information. The QLI-MH is as far as possible adopted from scales already in use with known psychometric properties and reliability. The QLI-MH assesses nine domains: satisfaction level for objective QoL indicators, occupational activities, psychological well-being, physical health, social relations, economics, activities of daily living, symptoms, goal attainment. The evaluated time period is the past week, fortnight, or month. Depending on the version (family, provider or client) 28, 42 or 68 items are scored on variable scales. The administration time for the provider version is 10 to 20 minutes; for the client version the administration time is 20 to 30 minutes.

SAMPLE: Patients suffering from schizophrenia.

RELIABILITY: There are only data available about the test-retest reliability of the QLI-MH which ranges from $r=.82$ to .87.

VALIDITY: The criterion validity is supported by the correlation between the QLI-MH with other quality of life instruments. For the patient version the correlations are .91 with QL-Index, $r=.68$ with Uniscale, $r=.60$ with QL-Index Provider, and

r=.50 with Uniscale Provider. For the provider version the correlation is .77 with QL-Index Provider and .80 with Uniscale Provider.

LOCATION: Becker, M, Diamond, R., & Sainfort, F. (1993). A new patient focused index for measuring quality of life in patients with severe and persistent mental illness. *Quality of Life Research*, 2, 239-251.

RESULTS AND COMMENT: The QLI-MH is the first instrument which can be used for proxy measurement.

REFERENCES:

Becker, M, Diamond, R., & Sainfort, F. (1993). A new patient focused index for measuring quality of life in patients with severe and persistent mental illness. *Quality of Life Research*, 2, 239-251.

Sainfort, F., Becker, M., & Diamond, R. (1996). Judgments of quality of life of individuals with severe mental disorders: Patient self-report versus provider perspectives. *American Journal of Psychiatry*, *153*, 497-502.

Diamond, R., & Becker, M. (1999). The Wisconsin Quality of Life Index: A multidimensional model for measuring Quality of Life. *Journal of Clinical Psychiatry*, *60*, 29-31.

REVIEWERS: Ch. van Nieuwenhuizen, TBS-kliniek De Kijvelanden, Forensic Psychiatric Hospital, Department of Psychotherapy & Research, P.O. Box 900, 3160 AC Rhoon, The Netherlands, Email: chinie@kÿvelanden.nl **and** A.H. Schene, Academic Medical Center, University of Amsterdam, Meibergdreef 9, 1105 AZ Amsterdam, The Netherlands, **and** M.W.J. Koeter, Academic Medical Center, University of Amsterdam, Meibergdreef 9, 1105 AZ Amsterdam, The Netherlands.

5.38: QUALITY OF LIFE SELF-ASSESSMENT INVENTORY.
AUTHOR: Skantze.

VARIABLE: Quality of Life.

DESCRIPTION: The starting-point of the Quality of Life Self-Assessment Inventory (QLS-100) was that people appraise life differently, as a consequence of which a person's quality of life and values can only be assessed subjectively. The QLS-100 has its origins in the Quality of Life Checklist (Malm *et al.*, 1981) and assesses 14 different life domains or classes: housing, environment, knowledge and education, contacts, dependence, inner experience, mental health, physical health, leisure, work, religion. One hundred items are scored by circling the items that are unsatisfactory ones. The evaluated time period is 'now'. Administration time is 10 minutes plus 40 to 50 to complete the interview.

SAMPLE: Patients suffering from schizophrenia.

RELIABILITY: The test-retest reliability is acceptable: test-rest reliability $r=.88$. The QLS-100 total score seems to represent overall quality of life with intercorrelations between this score and each subclass ranging from $r=.48$ to .87 (Skantze, 1993).

VALIDITY: The validity of the QLS-100 was explored by one-way ANOVA between the QLS-100 total score and demographic variables. Results shows that older patients report greater dissatisfaction with life than their younger counterparts and employed patients a higher satisfaction with life compared to unemployed patients.

646   Psychological Well Being

LOCATION: Skantze, K. (1993). *Defining subjective quality of life goals in schizophrenia: The Quality of Life Self-Assessment Inventory, QLS-100, a new approach to successful alliance and service development*. Sweden: Department of Psychiatry, Sahlgrenska Hospital, University of Gothenburg, Gothenburg.

RESULTS AND COMMENT: The QLS-100 shows its empirical basis in the appealing items questioned, but is not sufficiently comprehensive in its present form in terms of the general characteristics of people with psychiatric disability.

REFERENCES:

Malm, K., May, P.R.A., & Dencker, S.J. (1981). Evaluation of the quality of life of the schizophrenic outpatient: A checklist. *Schizophrenia Bulletin, 7*, 477-486.

Skantze, K., Malm, U., Dencker, S.J., & Philip, R.A. (1990). Quality of life in schizophrenia. *The Nordic Journal of Psychiatry, 44*, 71-75.

Skantze, K., Malm, U., Dencker, S.J., May, P.R.A., & Corrigan, P. (1992). Comparison of quality of life with standard of living in schizophrenic outpatients. *British Journal of Psychiatry, 161*, 797-801.

Skantze, K. (1993). *Defining subjective quality of life goals in schizophrenia: The Quality of Life Self-Assessment Inventory, QLS-100, a new approach to successful alliance and service development*. Sweden: Department of Psychiatry, Sahlgrenska Hospital, University of Gothenburg, Gothenburg.

REVIEWERS: Ch. van Nieuwenhuizen, TBS-kliniek De Kijvelanden, Forensic Psychiatric Hospital, Department of Psychotherapy & Research, P.O. Box 900, 3160 AC Rhoon, The Netherlands **and** A.H. Schene, Academic Medical Center, University of Amsterdam, Meibergdreef 9, 1105 AZ Amsterdam, The

Netherlands, **and** M.W.J. Koeter, Academic Medical Center, University of Amsterdam, Meibergdreef 9, 1105 AZ Amsterdam, The Netherlands.

5.39: ROLE FUNCTIONING SCALE (RFS).

AUTHOR: McPheeters.

VARIABLE: Five items, covering four specific areas of role functioning and one global personal distress domain.

DESCRIPTION: The RFS consists of four subscales, each with an anchor statement that summarises one of seven ordered levels of functional status. The four subscales (Working Productivity, Independent Living/Self-Care, Immediate Social Network Relationships, Extended Social Network Relationships) are summed to create a Global Role Functioning score, which can range from 4 to 28. The values on each of the four subscales range from one, which represents a very minimal level of role functioning, to seven, the hypothetically optimal level of role functioning. A fifth subscale (the Global Personal Distress Scale) is included as an estimate of a patient's subjective feelings of personal dissatisfaction with themselves. This quality was hypothesized to be independent of the level of role functioning, yet an important factor for use in evaluating the effectiveness of mental health programs. Ratings range from one (constant and pervasive awareness of painful symptoms) to seven (no apparent or reported personal distress).

SAMPLE: McPheeters (1984) intended the scale to be used in psychiatric populations.

RELIABILITY: **Internal consistency:** Goodman *et al.* (1993) computed the inter-item reliability on 112 subjects to test whether subscale scores covaried together within subjects and between scales in producing the Global RFS summary score. Results indicated that each subscale score is composed of the same general factors across subjects based on the final score computed (between measures $F(3,333)=13.01$, $p<.001$; Cronbach's $\alpha=.918$). **Test-retest:** Goodman *et al.* (1993) reported test-retest correlations for the four subscales and the Global RFS summary score ranging from .85 to .92, and a correlation of .68 for the Global Personal Distress subscale. **Interrater:** Goodman *et al.* (1993) reported intraclass correlation coefficients for the four subscales and the Global RFS summary score ranging from .64 to .82, and an intraclass correlation coefficient of .21 for the Global Personal Distress subscale.

VALIDITY: **Convergent:** Correlational analysis of the data (n=112) from Goodman *et al.* (1993) found that as Global RFS summary scores increases, there was a corresponding increases in higher self-esteem (r=.40, $p<.001$), and a decrease in severity of psychiatric disturbance (r=.84, $p<.001$). **Discriminant:** Global RFS summary scores for well women versus depressed or schizophrenic women (n=112) were submitted to a oneway ANOVA. Results showed well women scored significantly higher than those with psychiatric disorders ($F(1,110)=58.44$, $p<.001$). In addition, discriminant function analysis using the four RFS subscale scores as predictors and diagnostic status (well or disturbed) as outcomes showed an average prediction accuracy of 78.8% (72.8% for disturbed; 93.1% for well). Discriminant analysis of the Global RFS summary score alone on the same outcomes yielded an average hit rate of 77.9% (73.2% for disturbed, 89.7% for well).

LOCATION: Wieduwilt, K.M., & Jerrell, J.M. (1998). Measuring the sensitivity to change of the Role Functioning Scale through the utilization of the RC_{ID} index . *International Journal of Methods in Psychiatric Research, 7*, 163-170.

COMMENT: The psychometric properties of the RFS have been well-documented. Previous studies have reported on both the reliability and validity of the RFS (Goodman, Sewell, Cooley, & Leavitt, 1993), as well as its sensitivity to detecting clinical change (Wieduwilt & Jerrell, 1999) and the generalisability and superiority of the RFS, with respect to similar brief psychosocial rating scales, in monitoring the effectiveness of programs that serve persons with severe and persistent mental illness (Green & Gracely, 1987; Green & Jerrell, 1994). Additionally, the RFS is generally used in conjunction with the SAS-SMI as a brief psychosocial rating scale by providing a global assessment for each subject in each of the various functional areas covered in the SAS-SMI.

REFERENCES:

Green, R.S., & Gracely, E.J. (1987). Selecting a rating scale for evaluating services to the chronically mentally ill. *Community Mental Health Journal, 23*, 91-102.

Green, R.S., & Jerrell, J.M. (1994). The generalizability of brief ratings of psychosocial functioning. *Evaluation and Program Planning, 17*, 141-151.

Goodman, S.H., Sewell, D.R., Cooley, E.L., & Leavitt, N. (1993). Assessing levels of adaptive functioning: The Role Functioning Scale. *Community Mental Health Journal, 29*, 119-131.

McPheeters, H.L. (1984). Statewide mental health outcome evaluation: A perspective of two southern states. *Community Mental Health Journal, 20*, 44-55.

Wieduwilt, K.M., & Jerrell, J.M. (1998). Measuring the sensitivity to change of the Role Functioning Scale through the utilization of the RC_{ID} index. *International Journal of Methods in Psychiatric Research, 7,* 163-170.

REVIEWER: Kristin M. Wieduwilt and Jeanette M. Jerrell, Department of Neuropsychiatry and Behavioral Sciences, University of South Carolina School of Medicine, Clinical Education Building, 3555 Harden Street Extension, Columbia, SC 29203, U.S.A. E-mail:kwieduwilt@sc.edu

5.40: SELF-DESCRIPTION QUESTIONNAIRE-II.
AUTHOR: Marsh.

VARIABLE: Self-concept, 11 specific aspects of self-concept.

DESCRIPTION: 102-item self-report scale based on theoretical model of Shavelson, Hubner, and Stanton (1976). Suitable for group or individual administration. Respondents are asked to select from one of six options: *false, mostly false, more false than true, more true than false, mostly true,* and *true.* Special training is not required to administer the SDQ-II. Administration time is usually less than 20 minutes.

SAMPLE: Marsh intended the scale to be used with secondary level students in grades 7- 12. Specific purposes are not made explicit in the manual. SDQ-II was normed on 5494 students from Australia.

RELIABILITY: **Test-retest:** Marsh and Peart (1988) reported 7-week coefficients for the 11 domains ranging from .72 to .88 for 137 high school females. Gilman,

Laughlin, and Huebner (in press) reported 4 week test-retest coefficients ranging from .68 to .83 for the 11 domains and .83 for the Total score for 700 US middle school students (males and females).

VALIDITY: Results of exploratory factor analyses support the dimensionality of the SDQ-II across age and gender. Questions remain regarding the hierarchical nature of SDQ-II responses, however. Meaningful relationships have been found between SDQ-II scales and demographic variables, academic competence, masculinity, femininity, androgyny, and therapeutic interventions.

LOCATION: Marsh, H. W (1990). *Self-Description Ouestionnaire-II Manual.* Campbelltown, NSW, Australia: University of Western Sydney.

COMMENT: The SDQ-II has been developed from a strong theoretical orientation. Existing data support its reliability and validity. However, some issues with respect to discriminant validity have been identified with a US sample (Gilman, Laughlin, & Huebner, in press), which suggest the need for additional cross-cultural research. An estimate of its readability level would also be useful (Keith & Bracken, 1996).

REFERENCES:

Gilman, R., Laughlin, J., & Huebner, E.S. (in press). Validation of the Self-Description Questionnaire-II with an American sample. *School Psychology International.*

Keith, L., & Bracken, B.A. (1996). Self-concept instrumentation: A historical and evaluative review. In B.A. Bracken (Ed.), *Handbook of Self-concept: Developmental, Social-and Clinical Considerations* (pp. 38-90). New York: John Wiley and Sons.

Marsh, H.W. (1990). *Self-Description Ouestionnaire-II Manual.* Campbelltown,

NSW, Australia: University of Western Sydney.

Marsh, H.W., & Peart, N.D. (1988). Competitive and cooperative physical fitness training programs for girls: Effects of physical fitness on multidimensional self-concepts. *Journal of Sports Psychology*, *10*, 390-407.

Shavelson, R., Hubner, J.J., & Stanton, G.C. (1976). Validation of construct interpretations. *Review of Educational Research. 46*, 407-441.

REVIEWER: Scott Huebner, Department of Psychology, University of South Carolina, Columbia, SC 29208.

5.41: SELF-ESTEEM WORKSHEET.

AUTHOR: Overholser.

VARIABLE: An Idiographic Assessment of Self-Esteem.

DESCRIPTION: The Self-Esteem Worksheet is a one-page measure that examines the person's self-esteem from each person's unique vantage point. Three steps are used to complete the Self-Esteem Worksheet. First, subjects are asked to identify several different areas of their life that play an important role in their self-esteem. These areas can include a diverse range of topics, from general qualities (*e.g.*, "my personality") to specific traits (*e.g.*, "my sense of humor"). Subjects are encouraged to identify 3-15 areas of their lives that play a central role in their self-esteem. During the second step, subjects are asked to rate the importance of each area in terms of personal estimates of relative importance. This is framed in terms of percentage points, so that the different life areas should total to 100 percent. During the third step, subjects are asked to rate their self-perceived success in each area. Each success rating is done separately, so that each area can be rated anywhere from 0 to 100 percent success. When these three steps are completed, the Self-Esteem Worksheet can be scored to produce a total self-esteem score that can range from 0 to 100 possible points. Also, the Self-Esteem Worksheet allows for a unique assessment from each subject. All subjects are encouraged to fill out the Self-Esteem Worksheet in a manner that captures their own personality, life style and aspirations.

SAMPLE: The Self-Esteem Worksheet was developed on 376 college students. However, it has been used in clinical practice with adult psychiatric outpatients. Also, the original idea for the development of the scale came from outpatient psychotherapy sessions that focused on the assessment and treatment of self-esteem deficits in adult clients.

RELIABILITY: Test-retest: Over a ten-week interval, scores from the Self-Esteem Worksheet were reasonably stable, $r(240)=.61$, $p<.0001$. Scores from male subjects were more stable than for female subjects, males $r(115)=.73$, $p<.0001$; females $r(123)=.54$, $p<.0001$. Because of the design of the Self-Esteem Worksheet, internal consistency estimates are not appropriate for this measure.

VALIDITY: Concurrent: The Self-Esteem Worksheet correlates with several other measures of self-esteem, including the widely used Rosenberg Self-Esteem Scale ($r=.36$, $p<.0001$), as well as two other published measures. Also, lower scores on the Self-Esteem Worksheet have been associated with higher levels of depression on the Beck Depression Inventory ($r=-.25$, $p<.0001$), higher levels of loneliness on the UCLA Loneliness Scale ($r=-.03$, $p<.0001$), and tendencies for self-criticism on the Depressive Experiences Questionnaire ($r=-.29$, $p<.0001$). Also, when scores from the Self-Esteem Worksheet were dichotomised into high self-esteem (total score>75) and low self-esteem (total score<75), significant differences were observed on other measures. The high self-esteem subjects scored significantly higher on three other measures of self-esteem. Furthermore, these elevations were maintained 10-weeks later.

LOCATION: Overholser, J.C. (1993). Idiographic, quantitative assessment of self-esteem. *Personality and Individual Differences, 14*, 639-646.

COMMENT: The Self-Esteem Worksheet has shown preliminary evidence of reliability and validity. It appears useful in both research and clinical settings. However, additional studies are needed to continue to evaluate the psychometric properties of this measure. Also, because of the different method used, the Self-Esteem Worksheet shares less method variance than seen when all questionnaires are used in data collection. This different method may reduce the correlations between measures, but may enhance the ability of investigators to assess self-esteem as it relates to different individuals.

REFERENCES:

Overholser, J.C. (1993). Idiographic, quantitative assessment of self-esteem. *Personality and Individual Differences, 14*, 639-646.

REVIEWER: James C. Overholser, Department of Psychology, Case Western Reserve University, 10900 Euclid Avenue, Cleveland, Ohio, U.S.A. 44106-7123. E-mail: jxo5@po.cwru.edu

5.42: SELF-HARM INVENTORY (SHI), THE.

AUTHORS: Sansone, Wiederman, and Sansone.

VARIABLE: History of specific self-harm behaviors.

DESCRIPTION: The Self-Harm Inventory (SHI) is a one-page, 22-item, yes/no questionnaire that explores respondents' history of self-harm behaviors. Items are preceded by the statement, "Have you ever on intentionally, or on purpose ..." and include "overdosed, cut yourself on purpose, burned yourself on purpose, hit yourself, attempted suicide, prevented wounds from healing," and "driven recklessly." Each endorsement is considered pathological. Some items inquire about the number of times a given behavior has occurred as well as the last or most recent time of occurrence. The final item in the questionnaire explores the presence of "any other self-destructive behaviors that were not asked about in this inventory," with a space for write-in responses. However, frequencies and additional self-harm behaviors are not used in the scoring. An overall score is generated by summing the number of the 22 items endorsed so that possible scores range from 0 to 22. Higher scores indicate a history of engaging in a greater range of self-harm behaviors.

SAMPLE: The SHI was intended for use in both psychiatric (Sansone, Fine, & Nunn, 1994; Sansone, Gage, & Wiederman, 1998; Sansone, Sansone, & Morris, 1996) and non-psychiatric (Sansone, Sansone, & Fine, 1995; Sansone, Sansone, & Wiederman, 1995; Sansone, Sansone, & Wiederman, 1996; Sansone, Wiederman, & Sansone, 1996; Sansone, Wiederman, & Sansone, 1998; Sansone, Wiederman, Sansone, & Touchet, 1998; Wiederman, Sansone, & Sansone, 1998) populations.

RELIABILITY: Internal consistency: As the items are dichotomous and were written to sample a range of self-harm behaviors, internal consistency coefficients are not applicable.

VALIDITY: In the initial validation of the SHI, using a cut-off score of 5 or greater resulted in accurately classifying 84% of respondents as to the presence of borderline personality disorder, using the Diagnostic Interview for Borderlines (DIB; Kolb & Gunderson, 1980) as the criterion. Subsequent research has shown satisfactory convergent validity with self-report measures of borderline personality (Sansone, Gage, & Wiederman, 1998), depression (Sansone, Wiederman, Sansone, & Touchet, 1998), and history of childhood abuse (Sansone, Sansone, & Wiederman, 1996; Sansone, Wiederman, & Sansone, 1996; Sansone, Wiederman, & Sansone, 1998).

LOCATION: Sansone, R.A., Wiederman, M.W., & Sansone, L.A. (1998). The Self-Harm Inventory (SHI): Development of a scale for identifying self-destructive behaviors and borderline personality disorder. *Journal of Clinical Psychology, 54,* 973-983.

COMMENT: By no means does the SHI inquire about all possible forms of self-harm behavior. However, the items were selected from a larger initial pool based on their frequency of endorsement, their relationship to established measures for borderline personality disorder, and their judged clinical relevance. The SHI represents an improvement over other self-report measures for borderline personality symptomatology in that the items inquire about concrete behavioral experiences. The SHI may be useful as a brief screening measure for borderline personality symptomatology.

REFERENCES:

Kolb, J.E., & Gunderson, J.G. (1980). Diagnosing borderline patients with a semistructured interview. *Archives of General Psychiatry, 37,* 37-41.

Sansone, R.A., Fine, M.A., & Nunn, J.L. (1994). A comparison of borderline personality symptomatology and self-destructive behavior in women with eating, substance abuse, and both eating and substance abuse disorders. *Journal of Personality Disorders, 8,* 219-228.

Sansone, R.A., Gage, M.D., & Wiederman, M.W. (1998). Investigation of borderline personality disorder among non-psychotic, involuntarily hospitalized clients. *Journal of Mental Health Counseling, 20,* 133-140.

Sansone, R.A., Sansone, L.A., & Fine, M.A. (1995). The relationship of obesity to borderline personality, self-harm behaviors, and sexual abuse in female subjects in a primary-care medical setting. *Journal of Personality Disorder, 9,* 254-265.

Sansone, R.A., Sansone, L.A., & Morris, D. (1996). Prevalence of borderline personality symptoms in two groups of obese subjects. *American Journal of Psychiatry, 153,* 117-118.

Sansone, R.A., Sansone, L.A., & Wiederman, M.W. (1995). The prevalence of trauma and its relationship to borderline personality symptoms and self-destructive behaviors in a primary-care setting. *Archives of Family Medicine, 4,* 439-442.

Sansone, R.A., Sansone, L.A., & Wiederman, M.W. (1996). Borderline personality symptomatology and health care utilization in a primary care setting. *Southern Medical Journal, 89,* 1162-1165.

Sansone, R.A., Wiederman, M.W., & Sansone, L.A. (1996). The relationship between borderline personality symptomatology and healthcare utilization among women in an HMO setting. *Journal of Managed Care, 2,* 515-518.

Sansone, R.A., Wiederman, M.W., & Sansone, L.A. (1998). Borderline personality symptomatology, experience of multiple types of traumas, and health care utilization among women in a primary care setting. *Journal of Clinical Psychiatry, 59*, 108-111.

Sansone, R.A., Wiederman, M.W., Sansone, L.A., & Touchet, B. (1998). An investigation of primary care patients on extended treatment with SSRI's. *American Journal of Managed Care, 4*, 1721-1723.

Wiederman, M.W., Sansone, R.A., & Sansone, L.A. (1998). History of trauma and attempted suicide among women in a primary care setting. *Violence and Victims, 13*, 3-9.

REVIEWERS: Randy A. Sansone, Department of Psychiatry, Wright State University School of Medicine, P.O. Box 927, Dayton, Ohio, 45401-0927, U.S.A. and Michael W. Wiederman, Department of Human Relations, Columbia College, Columbia, SC, 29203, U.S.A.

5.43: SOCIAL ADJUSTMENT SCALE FOR THE SEVERELY MENTALLY ILL (SAS-SMI).
AUTHORS: Wieduwilt and Jerrell.

VARIABLE: 24 items, covering 7 main content areas.

DESCRIPTION: The Social Adjustment Scale for the Severely Mentally Ill (SAS-SMI) was originally developed as an abbreviated version of the Social Adjustment Scale-II (Schooler, Hogarty, & Weissman, 1979; Weissman, Sholomskas, & John, 1981) for use in randomised clinical trials to assess changes in subjective and objective psychosocial functioning of severely mentally ill clients receiving services from a public mental health service system. The SAS-SMI follows a semi-structured interview format and was developed to be administered by trained clinical interviewers. The scale consists of 24 items, covering 7 main content areas: Social, Family, Work Performance, Work Affect, Romantic Activity, Residential Stability, and Personal Well-Being.

SAMPLE: Wieduwilt and Jerrell (1999) intended the scale to be used in psychiatric populations.

RELIABILITY: Internal consistency: Cronbach's alpha coefficients were computed to assess the internal consistency of the 24 items on each of the seven content areas or scales identified. In all but one case (Personal Well-Being), the alpha coefficient was well above the minimum acceptable level of .60 Items on four of the seven scales, Residential Stability, General Social, Romantic Activity, and General Family, demonstrated the highest internal consistency, with r=.86 to .91. Test-retest: The test-retest reliability (r_{tt}) of the seven subscales was examined in sample of 207 subjects. Overall, reliability coefficients were fair to excellent, ranging from .45 to .84. The affective measures (*i.e.*, Work Affect, Romantic Interest) tended to fall in the fair to moderate range, while the more concrete scales (*i.e.*, Work Performance, Residential Stability) yielded test-retest reliabilities in the good to excellent range. Interrater Reliability: Interrater reliability across trained interviewers was assessed via intraclass correlation coefficients for each scale using a random sample of 82 cases, with each case rated by the same four randomly selected raters. Across the 24 items measured, intraclass correlations ranged from .49 to .99, with only one item (Physical Health & Care) achieving a correlation of less than .60.

VALIDITY: Convergent: Concurrent validity correlations between the seven SAS-SMI subscales and related constructs were calculated using self-reported life satisfaction, subjective and objective measures of social functioning, and demographic and diagnostic indicators. Greater convergent validity was found for the Work scales (Performance and Affect), in that all correlations exceeded .32, the equivalent of sharing 10 percent of their variance. Two of three convergent validity correlations exceeded .32 for Personal Well-Being. Half of all related convergent validity correlations exceeded .32 for Residential Stability, Romantic Activity, General Social, and General Family. **Discriminant:** Discriminant validity was examined by identifying correlations between related variables and SAS-SMI subscales that were at least 20 percent lower than the convergent validity correlation in the same row. Two-thirds of the correlations for six of the seven scales met this criteria. The discriminant validity correlations were poor, with only one of the four related measures demonstrating that two-thirds of the correlations were at least 20 percent lower than the convergent validity correlation in the same row.

LOCATION: Wieduwilt, K.M., & Jerrell, J.M. (1999). The reliability and validity of the SAS-SMI. *Journal of Psychiatric Research, 33,* 105-112.

COMMENT: Overall, results of the psychometric analyses for the SAS-SMI point to factor structures similar to the SAS-II from which it was derived, fair to excellent internal consistency and interrater reliability, and support for convergent and divergent validity for the majority of its subscales. The psychometric performance of the SAS-SMI can be seen as comparable to the SAS-II employed in previous investigations but takes less time to administer and can be used efficiently within a battery of other instruments assessing symptomatology and satisfaction with services. Additionally, SAS-SMI is typically used in conjunction with the Role Functioning Scale (McPheeters, 1984), a brief psychosocial rating scale which provides global scores for each of the various functional areas covered in the SAS-SMI. Results indicate that the SAS-SMI is a potentially useful instrument in investigations of outcomes of care for severely and persistently mentally ill adults.

REFERENCES:

Schooler, N., Hogarty, G., & Weissman, M. (1979). Social adjustment scale II (SAS-II). In W.A. Hargreaves, C.C. Attkisson, and J.E. Sorenson (Eds.) *Resource Materials for Community Mental Health Program Evaluators* (pp. 290-303). Rockville, MD: United States Department of Health, Education, and Welfare.

Weissman, M.M., Sholomskas, D., & John, K. (1981). The assessment of social adjustment: An update. *Archives of General Psychiatry, 38,* 1250-1258.

Schooler, N.R., & Severe, J.B. (1982). Social adjustment in relation to measures of psychopathology and self-report in schizophrenic outpatients. In R Turner (Chair), *Outcome Measurement in Community Mental Health.* Symposium conducted at the meeting of the Eastern Psychological Association, Baltimore, MD.

Weissman, M.M., & Sholomskas, D. (1982). The assessment of social adjustment by the clinician, the patient, and the family. In E.I. Burdock, A. Sudilovsky, & S. Gershon (Eds.), *The Behavior of Psychiatric Patients: Quantitative Techniques for Evaluation.* New York: Marcel Dekker.

Toupin, J., Cyr, M., Lesage, A., & Valiquette, C. (1993). Validation d'un questionnaire d'évaluation du fonctionnement social des personnes ayant des troubles mentaux chroniques. *Canadian Journal of Community Mental Health, 12,* 143-156.

Wieduwilt, K.M., & Jerrell, J.M. (1999). The reliability and validity of the SAS-SMI. *Journal of Psychiatric Research, 33,* 105-112.

REVIEWER: Kristin M. Wieduwilt and Jeanette M. Jerrell, Department of Neuropsychiatry and Behavioral Sciences, University of South Carolina School of Medicine, Clinical Education Building, 3555 Harden Street Extension, Columbia, SC 29203, U.S.A. E-mail: kweiduwilt@sc.edu

5.44: SOCIAL PHOBIA AND ANXIETY INVENTORY FOR CHILDREN.

AUTHORS: Beidel, Turner, and Morris.

VARIABLE: Social fears and social phobia.

DESCRIPTION: The Social Phobia and Anxiety Inventory for Children (SPAI-C; Beidel *et al.*, 1995) is an empirically derived self-report measure that assesses the somatic, cognitive, and behavioral aspects of social phobia in children ages 8 through 14. The 26-items, some of which require multiple responses, are rated on a 3-point scale as to the frequency with which each symptom is experienced: *Never or hardly ever* (0), *Sometimes* (1), *Most of the time or always* (2). Scores range from 0 to 52, with higher scores reflecting higher anxiety in social settings.

SAMPLE: Beidel and her colleagues (1995; Beidel, Turner, & Fink, 1996; Beidel, Turner, & Morris, 1998) intended the SPAI-C to serve as a screening measure for social anxiety and phobia in diverse settings (*e.g.*, schools, outpatient clinics, inpatient units, etc.), and both a clinical and research tool for improving clinical assessment and documenting treatment outcome.

RELIABILITY: Internal consistency: Internal consistency reliabilities for the SPAI-C have ranged from .92 to .95 (Beidel *et al.*, 1995; 1996). **Test-retest:** Two-week test-retest reliability has been demonstrated (r=.86), and the stability over a 10-month interval was r=.63 (Beidel *et al.*, 1995).

VALIDITY: Convergent: The SPAI-C has demonstrated good convergent validity with various measures of children's self-reported anxiety and fears (Beidel *et al.*, 1995), measures of children's self-reported social anxiety in both community and clinical samples (Epkins, 2000; Morris & Masia, 1998), daily diary ratings of social distress (Beidel *et al.*, 1996), and behavioral assessment measures of skill and anxiety (Beidel *et al.*, 1998). Children's scores on the SPAI-C are also related to parents' ratings of children's social anxiety-related behaviors (Beidel *et al.*, 1995; 1998; Epkins, 2000). **Discriminant:** The SPAI-C has been found to differentiate (1) children with social phobia from both children with externalising disorders and those with no disorder (Beidel *et al.*, 1996); and (2) children with social phobia from children with other anxiety disorders (Beidel *et al.*, 1998).

FURTHER EMPIRICAL USES: Preliminary data find the SPAI-C is sensitive to improvement following treatment, and may be a useful measure of treatment outcome (Beidel *et al.*, 1996).

LOCATION:

Beidel, D.C., Turner, S.M., & Morris, T.L. (1995). A new inventory to assess childhood social anxiety and phobia: The Social Phobia and Anxiety Inventory for Children. *Psychological Assessment, 7,* 73-79.

Beidel, D.C., Turner, S.M., & Morris, T.L. (1998). *Social Phobia and Anxiety Inventory for Children (SPAI-C) Manual.* North Tonawanda, NY: Multi-Health Systems Inc.

COMMENT: Initial studies support the reliability and validity of the SPAI-C. The SPAI-C is a promising measure that can be used as a screening tool in school settings, an assessment measure in clinical settings, and an instrument to gauge treatment effects. Additional research is needed to establish norms for different clinical and nonclinical groups, to determine whether separate cut-offs based on gender and/or racial/ethnic groups should be developed, and to document the ability of the SPAI-C to reflect treatment outcome.

REFERENCES:

Beidel, D.C., Turner, S.M., & Fink, C.M. (1996). Assessment of childhood social phobia: Construct, convergent, and discriminative validity of the Social Phobia and Anxiety Inventory for Children (SPAI-C). *Psychological Assessment, 8*, 235-240.

Beidel, D.C., Turner, S.M., & Morris, T.L. (1995). A new inventory to assess childhood social anxiety and phobia: The Social Phobia and Anxiety Inventory for Children. *Psychological Assessment, 7*, 73-79.

Beidel, D.C., Turner, S.M., & Morris, T.L. (1998). *Social Phobia and Anxiety Inventory for Children (SPAI-C) Manual.* North Tonawanda, NY: Multi-Health Systems Inc.

Epkins, C.C. (2000). *Agreement between measures and informants in the assessment of children's social anxiety in clinic and community samples.* Manuscript submitted for publication.

Morris, T.L., & Masia, C.L. (1998). Psychometric evaluation of the Social Phobia and Anxiety Inventory for Children: Concurrent validity and normative data. *Journal of Clinical Child Psychology, 27*, 452-458.

REVIEWER: Catherine C. Epkins, Department of Psychology, Texas Tech University, Box 42051, Lubbock, Texas 79409-2051, U.S.A.   E-mail: DJCCE@ttacs.ttu.edu

5.45: WELL-BEING MANIFESTATIONS MEASURE SCALE.

AUTHORS: Massé, Poulin, Dassa, Lambert, Bélair, and Battaglini.

VARIABLE: Mental well-being.

DESCRIPTION: Self-report scale containing 25-items representing a mix of affective, behavioral and cognitive signs of mental health. These items are grouped into six oblique factors (self-esteem, 4 items ; social involvement, 4 items ; mental balance, 4 items ; Sociability, 4 items, control of self and Events, 4 items ; happiness, 5 items.). Respondents are asked how they have felt in the past month and rate each item on a 5-point scale ; *never* (1), *rarely* (2), *half the time* (3), *frequently* (4), and *almost always* (5). Higher scores on the scale indicate a higher prevalence and frequency of occurrence of mental well-being manifestations.

SAMPLE: Massé, Poulin, Dassa, Lambert *et al.*, 1998 intended the scale to be used for the assessment of mental well-being in non-psychiatric populations and to be sensitive to social differences.

RELIABILITY: Internal consistency: It demonstrated a high level of internal reliability for the entire scale (α=.93) as well as for the subscales based on exploratory and confirmatory factor analyses (between .71 and .85) (Massé *et al.*, 1998a ; Massé *et al.*, 1998b). **Test-retest:** Only items showing a high Kappa coefficient have been kept ; based on a random sub-sample of 120 respondents retested after 5-8 days.

VALIDITY: Convergent: It has shown a -.65 correlation with the Psychological Distress Manifestation Scale (Massé *et al.*, 1998b). **Criterion:** Low scores on PDMS are strongly associated with alcohol and drugs consumption, visits to health professionals, and dissatisfaction toward life in general. (Massé *et al.*, 1998a). **Content**: The 25 items originate from an initial pool of 76 items submitted to construct validity analysis. These 76 items themselves come from a corpora of more than 2000 signs of mental well-being reported by 195 French Canadian adults who were asked to describe, in details, the manifestations experienced in a significant lived episode of good mental health, in the past weeks or months.

LOCATION: Massé, R. Poulin, C., Dassa C., Lambert, J., Bélair, S., & Battaglini A. (1998a). Élaboration et validation d'un outil de mesure du bien-être psychologique: l'ÉMMBEP. *Canadian Review of Public Health, 89*, 352-357. Originally in French. English version comes from a translation exercise (Massé *et al.*, 1997).

COMMENT: Psychometric properties of this scale as well as discriminant validity have been demonstrated in two studies to be published in 2000-2001. However, a high level of mental well-being does not mean automatically a low level of psychological distress (Massé *et al.*, 1998b). It is suggested that epidemiological assessment of general population mental health should use concomitant measures of positive and negative manifestations of mental health.

REFERENCES

Massé, R., Poulin, C., Dassa C., Lambert, J. Bélair, S., & Battaglini, A. (1997). *Élaboration et validation d'un Outil de Mesure de la Santé Mentale des Montréalais Francophones*. Rapport de recherche, Direction de la Santé Publique de Montréal, Écologie Humaine et Sociale.

Massé, R. Poulin, C., Dassa C., Lambert, J., Bélair, S., & Battaglini A. (1998a). Élaboration et validation d'un outil de mesure du bien-être psychologique: l'ÉMMBEP. *Canadian Review of Public Health, 89,* 352-357.

Massé, R. Poulin, C., Dassa C., Lambert, J., Bélair, S., & Battaglini A. (1998b). The structure of mental health: Higher-order confirmatory factor analysis of psychological distress and well-being measures. *Social Indicators Research, 45,* 475-504.

REVIEWER: Massé Raymond. Department of Anthropology, Laval University, Québec, Canada G1K 7P4. E-mail: raymond.masse@ant.ulaval.ca

5.46: WORRY AND ANXIETY QUESTIONNAIRE (WAQ), THE.

AUTHORS: Dugas, Freeston, Lachance, Provencher, and Ladouceur.

VARIABLE: DSM-IV diagnostic criteria for generalized anxiety disorder.

DESCRIPTION: The Worry and Anxiety Questionnaire (WAQ; Dugas, Freeston, Lachance, Provencher, & Ladouceur, 1995) is an 11-item self report scale that assesses DSM-IV diagnostic criteria for generalized anxiety disorder (GAD). Of the WAQ's eleven items, the first asks the respondent to list up to six of the subjects they worry about most often (worry themes). All the other items on the questionnaire are rated on 9-point Likert-type scales. The second item on the WAQ asks the respondent to rate the excessiveness of their worry (ranging from 0=*Not at all excessive*, to 8=*Totally excessive*); the third asks them to rate the frequency of their worry over the past 6 months (ranging from 0=*Never*, to 8=*Every day*). The fourth item asks the respondent to rate the difficulty they have controlling their worry (ranging from 0=*No difficulty*, to 8=*Extreme difficulty*), while the last item asks them to rate how much worry interferes with their life (ranging from 0=*Not at all*, to 8=*Very severely*). The remaining 6 items of the WAQ make up a subscale which measures the somatic symptoms characteristic of GAD: restlessness, fatigue, difficulty concentrating, muscle tension, irritability, and sleep disturbance. The items of this somatic subscale are also rated on a 9-point Likert-type scale, ranging from 0 (*Not at all*) to 8 (*Very severely*).

SAMPLE: Dugas and colleagues (1995) constructed the WAQ primarily for the purpose of screening for GAD symptoms according to DSM-IV criteria. Therefore, the WAQ was tested in both clinical and non-clinical populations. The WAQ has been shown to be equally effective in both populations, as well as accurately differentiating between them (Dugas *et al*., 1995).

RELIABILITY: The WAQ shows good test-retest reliability after a four week time lapse (r=.76; Beaudoin *et al*., 1997). In addition, 75% of subjects who met GAD criteria according to the WAQ during initial testing met the same criteria at a 2 1/2 month retest, while 82% of those who did not initially meet this GAD criteria also did not meet the criteria at retest (Dugas *et al*., 1995). The WAQ has also been tested in an adolescent population and demonstrates good psychometric properties (Fournier, 1997).

VALIDITY: **Construct:** The WAQ accurately discriminated between a sample of clinical GAD patients and a group of matched controls, with 89.5% of the GAD group meeting diagnostic criteria according to the WAQ, and only 5.3% of the control group meeting this criteria (Dugas *et al*., 1995). Furthermore, all subjects who scored in the fourth quartile on a measure of the tendency to worry, the Penn State Worry Questionnaire (PSWQ; M=59.8), met GAD criteria according to the WAQ, whereas no subjects scoring in the first quartile on the PSWQ (M=33.2) met GAD criteria according to the WAQ (Dugas *et al*., 1995).

SENSITIVITY TO CHANGE OVER TREATMENT: The WAQ somatic subscale has been shown to be sensitive to change over treatment. Ladouceur and colleagues (in press) found that scores on the WAQ somatic subscale significantly decreased following cognitive-behavioral therapy for GAD whereas they remained unchanged in a wait-list control condition. For treated patients, scores on the somatic subscale of the WAQ significantly decreased in concordance with a decrease in ratings on the Anxiety Disorders Interview Schedule for the DSM-IV (ADIS-IV) Severity Scale.

LOCATION: Dugas, M., Freeston, M.H., Lachance, S., Provencher, M., & Ladouceur, R. (1995). *The Worry and Anxiety Questionnaire: Initial validation in non-clinical and clinical samples*. Poster presented at the World Congress of Behavioural and Cognitive Therapies, Copenhagen, Denmark.

COMMENT: The WAQ provides quick and accurate screening for GAD symptoms according to DSM-IV criteria, in both clinical and non-clinical populations. A study by Beaudoin *et al.* (1997) showed that 53% of non-clinical subjects who met GAD criteria according to the WAQ also met diagnostic requirements for GAD according to the ADIS-IV. Moreover, 93% of the subjects who did not meet criteria for GAD according to the WAQ also did not meet GAD criteria according to the ADIS-IV. In other words, the WAQ is an ideal preliminary screening measure, in that it is over-inclusive, but rarely fails to detect features of GAD when they are present (more false positives than false negatives). The WAQ also shows sensitivity to treatment gains following treatment for GAD (Ladouceur *et al.* in press). Thus, the WAQ is a concise and sensitive measure, which can be applied to both psychological research and clinical practice.

REFERENCES:

Dugas, M., Freeston, M.H., Lachance, S., Provencher, M., & Ladouceur, R. (1995). *The Worry and Anxiety Questionnaire: Initial validation in non-clinical and clinical samples.* Poster session presented at the World Congress of Behavioural and Cognitive Therapies, Copenhagen, Denmark.

Beaudoin, S., Tremblay, M., Carbonneau, C., Dugas, M. J., Provencher, M., & Ladouceur, R. (1997, October). *Validation d'un instrument diagnostique pour le trouble d'anxiété généralisée* (Validation of a diagnostic measure for generalized anxiety disorder). Poster session presented at the annual meeting of the Société québecoise pour la recherche en psychologie, Sherbrooke, Quebec, Canada.

Fournier, S. (1997). *Worry themes and tendency to worry among a teenage sample.* Non-published Master's thesis, Laval University, Quebec City, Quebec, Canada.

Ladouceur, R., Dugas, M.J., Freeston, M.H., Léger, E., Gagnon, F., & Thibodeau, N. (In press). Efficacy of a new cognitive-behavioral treatment for Generalized Anxiety Disorder: Evaluation in a controlled clinical trial. *Journal of Consulting and Clinical Psychology.*

REVIEWERS: Michel J. Dugas and Kylie Francis, Department of Psychology, Concordia University, 7141 Sherbrooke St. West, Montréal, Québec, Canada, H4B 1R6

5.47: WORRY DOMAINS QUESTIONNAIRE (WDQ).
AUTHOR: Tallis, Eysenck, and Mathews.

VARIABLE: Non-pathological worry.

DESCRIPTION: The Worry Domains Questionnaire (WDQ) is a self-report scale that was developed by Tallis *et al.* (1992) for the measurement of non-pathological worry. It covers a wide range of everyday worries. A list of 25 worries is presented (*e.g.*, "I worry that I will lose close friends"). For each item, respondents are asked to indicate how much they worry on a five-point scale from *Not at all* (0) to *Extremely* (4). The list covers five worry domains: Relationships, Lack of Confidence, Aimless Future, Work Incompetence, and Financial. The questionnaire thus consists of five subscales. Possible scores on the WDQ can range between 0 and 100. The total WDQ score is supposed to give a general indication of amount of worry (*cf.* Stöber & Joormann, in press) while the subscales provide information with respect to specific worry contents.

SAMPLES: The WDQ is intended to be used in nonclinical and analogue adult samples. Using the WDQ as a clinical instrument is questionable, as elevated scores might reflect, at least in part, problem-focused coping (Tallis, Davey, & Bond, 1994).

RELIABILITY: Internal consistency: The WDQ has demonstrated high levels of internal consistency. On average, Cronbach's alphas are above .90 and in the range of .71 to .86 for the subscales (Davey, 1993; Joormann & Stöber, 1997; Stöber, 1998). **Test-retest:** Test-retest correlations in the range of .79 (.46 to .86 for the WDQ-subscales; Tallis, Davey, & Bond, 1994) and .85 (.71 to .86 for the subscales; Stöber, 1998) have been reported across an interval of four weeks.

VALIDITY: **Convergent:** The WDQ has demonstrated substantial convergent correlations with other measures of worry (*e.g.*, Davey, 1993; Stöber, 1995). Correlations with the Penn State Worry Questionnaire (PSWQ; Meyer *et al.*, 1990) are above .60 (Stöber & Joormann, in press; Stöber, 1998). Stöber (1998) reports correlations of self-peer ratings of .49. **Discriminant:** The discriminant validity of the WDQ has been questioned. Correlations with anxiety scores ranging from .52 (Stöber & Joormann, in press) to .71 (Davey, 1993) and with depression scores of .59 have been found. Stöber and Joormann (in press) report associations with procrastination and perfectionism scores independent of anxiety and depression. Davey (1993) reports correlations with active cognitive coping (.26) and avoidance coping (.30) that are independent of trait anxiety. A correlation of WDQ scores with social desirability scores of -.35 was reported by Stöber (1998).

FURTHER EMPIRICAL USES: Stöber and Bittencourt (1998) employed a modified version of the WDQ to monitor weekly changes in general amount of worry during therapy. In addition, WDQ items have been used to identify participants' current topics of worry for subsequent inductions of worry (East & Watts, 1994) or problem elaborations (Stöber *et al.* in press).

LOCATION: Tallis, F., Eysenck, M.W., & Mathews, A. (1992). A questionnaire for the measurement of non-pathological worry. *Personality and Individual Differences, 13*, 161-168.

COMMENT: The WDQ is a reliable and valid measure of individual differences in non-pathological worry. Critical comments are few and concern the factorial structure of the WDQ (Joormann & Stöber, 1997), the high overlap with depression measures (Stöber & Joormann, in press), and the sometimes low specificity when compared to measures of trait anxiety (*e.g.*, Davey, 1993; Stöber & Joormann, in press).

REFERENCES:

Davey, G.C.L. (1993). A comparison of three worry questionnaires. *Behaviour Research and Therapy, 31,* 51-56.

East, M.P., & Watts, F.N. (1994). Worry and the suppression of imagery. *Behaviour Research and Therapy, 32,* 851-855.

Joormann, J., & Stöber, J. (1997). Measuring facets of worry: A LISREL analysis of the Worry Domains Questionnaire. *Personality and Individual Differences, 23,* 827-837.

Meyer, T., Miller, M., Metzger, R., & Borkovec, T.D. (1990). Development and validation of the Penn State Worry Questionnaire. *Behaviour Research and Therapy, 28,* 487-495.

Stöber, J. (1995). Besorgnis: Ein Vergleich dreier Inventare zur Erfassung allgemeiner Sorgen (Worry: A comparison of three inventories for the assessment of general worries). *Zeitschrift für Differentielle und Diagnostische Psychologie, 16,* 50-63.

Stöber, J. (1998). Reliability and validity of two widely-used worry questionnaires: Self-report and self-peer convergence. *Personality and Individual Differences, 24,* 887-890.

Stöber, J., & Bittencourt, J. (1998). Weekly assessment of worry: An adaptation of the Penn State Worry Questionnaire for monitoring changes during treatment. *Behaviour Research and Therapy, 36,* 645-656.

Stöber, J., & Joormann, J. (in press). Worry, procrastination, and perfectionism: Differentiating amount of worry, pathological worry, anxiety, and depression. *Cognitive Therapy and Research.*

Stöber, J., Tepperwien, S., & Staak, M. (in press). Worrying leads to reduced concreteness of problem elaborations: Evidence for the avoidance theory of worry. *Anxiety, Stress, and Coping.*

Tallis, F., Davey, G.C.L., & Bond, A. (1994). The Worry Domains Questionnaire. In G. C. L. Davey & F. Tallis (Eds.), *Worrying: Perspectives on Theory, Assessment, and Treatment* (pp. 285-297). New York: Wiley.

Tallis, F., Eysenck, M.W., & Mathews, A. (1992). A questionnaire for the measurement of nonpathological worry. *Personality and Individual Differences, 13,* 161-168.

REVIEWER: Jutta Joormann, Freie Universität Berlin, Department of Psychology II (WE 08), Habelschwerdter Allee 45, 14195 Berlin, Germany. E-mail: joormann@zedat.fu-berlin.de

CHAPTER 6

DEVELOPMENTAL PSYCHOLOGY:
CHILDHOOD, FAMILIES, ADULTHOOD AND AGING

6.01: ADOLESCENT BEHAVIOR CHECKLIST (ABC), THE.

AUTHORS: Adams, Kelley, and McCarthy.

VARIABLE: ADHD symptomatology and adjustment difficulties.

DESCRIPTION: A 44-item, adolescent self-report measure comprised of 6 factors: Conduct Problems, Impulsivity/Hyperactivity, Poor Work Habits, Inattention, Emotional Lability, and Social Problems. Respondents are asked to indicate the degree to which they exhibited each behavior problem over the last 6 months, on the following 4-point Likert-type scale: *Not at all, Just a little, Pretty much,* or *Very much.* Item scores are totaled for each factor and the overall measure. These scores, in turn, are compared to those in the normative sample.

SAMPLE: The ABC is intended for use with adolescents between 11 and 17 years of age who are exhibiting behavior problems associated with ADHD. Adams, Kelley, and McCarthy (1997) examined the psychometric properties of the measure using a sample of 909 adolescents between the ages of 11 and 17 years living in southern Louisiana. Eighty-two percent of the sample was Caucasian, 15% was African American, and 3% was adolescents of other ethnic minorities. The average socioeconomic level was middle class; however, the sample represented a broad range of socioeconomic levels.

RELIABILITY: Internal consistency: For the entire measure, the Cronbach's alpha coefficients was excellent (.94), and within the individual factors, internal consistency was low-moderate to good (.60 to .85) (Adams, Kelley, & McCarthy, 1997). Test-retest: Adams *et al.* (1997) reported a test-retest correlation coefficient of .79 ($p<.001$) among 81 adolescents after a two week interval. Coefficient scores for the factors indicated moderate to highly satisfactory levels of test score stability across the two-week interval (.62 to .81).

VALIDITY: Convergent and Divergent: To examine convergent validity, factor scores on the ABC were correlated with subscale scores on the Child Behavior Checklist (Achenbach & Edelbrock, 1991a), the Youth Self Report (YSR; Achenbach & Edelbrock, 1991b), and the Conners Parent Rating Scale (CPRS-48; Conners, 1989). Using the standardization sample, highest correlation coefficients were obtained with the ABC factor scores and similar criterion subscales; the lowest correlation coefficients were obtained between ABC factors and dissimilar criterion subscales (Adams *et al.*, 1997). Similar results were obtained in a later study by Adams, Reynolds, Perez, Powers and Kelley (1998). **Discriminant:** Results using 15 adolescents diagnosed with ADHD were suggestive of the discriminant validity of ABC scores (Adams *et al.*, 1997). Among the clinical group, the total score and the scores on each individual factor (except Conduct Problems) was significantly higher than that of the normative sample. Adams *et al.* (1998) evaluated the discriminant validity scores from 120 adolescents ranging in age from 11 to17 years. Participants consisted of adolescents diagnosed with

ADHD, a psychiatric control group, and a non-clinical control group. Using the ABC, significant differences were found between these groups, indicating the measure has adequate discriminant validity. Compared to the YSR (Achenbach & Edelbrock, 1991a), the ABC was found to be somewhat better in classifying when used in a multi-informant, discriminant analysis.

LOCATION: Adams, C.D., Kelley, M.L., & McCarthy, M. (1997). The adolescent behavior checklist: Development and initial psychometric properties of a self-report measure for adolescents with ADHD. *Journal of Clinical Child Psychology*, *26*, 77-86.

The questionnaire, scoring instructions, and normative data can be obtained by contacting Chrisina Adams, West Virginia University, Department of Psychology, Box 6040, Morgantown, WV 26506-6040, U.S.A. E-mail: cadams4@wvu.edu.

COMMENT: Research conducted by Adams *et al.* (1998) demonstrates that the ABC is a reliable and valid measure. An advantage of the ABC over other measures is ease of administration and brevity. Furthermore, the ABC is a self-report measure that was constructed to aid in assessing adolescents with ADHD, based on accepted diagnostic criteria and empirical findings regarding associated problems.

REFERENCES:

Achenbach, T.M., & Edelbrock, C. (1991a). *Manual for the Child Behavior Checklist/4-18*. Burlington: University of Vermont, Department of Psychiatry.

Achenbach, T.M., & Edelbrock, C. (1991b). *Manual for the Youth Self-Report*. Burlington: University of Vermont, Department of Psychiatry.

Adams, C.D., Kelley, M.L., & McCarthy, M. (1997). The adolescent behavior checklist: Development and initial psychometric properties of a self-report measure for adolescents with ADHD. *Journal of Clinical Child Psychology, 26,* 77-86.

Adams, C.D., Reynolds, L.K., Perez, R.A., Powers, D., & Kelley, M.L. (1998). The Adolescent Behavior Checklist: Validation using structured diagnostic interviews. *Journal of Psychopathology and Behavioral Assessment, 20,* 103-125.

Conners, C.K. (1989). *Conners' Rating Scales Manual: Conners' Teacher Rating Scales, Conners' Parent Rating Scales.* North Tonawanda, New York: Multi-Health Systems, Inc.

REVIEWER: Ethan S. Long, Vicki A. Lumley, and Christina D. Adams, West Virginia University, Department of Psychology, Box 6040, Morgantown, WV 26506-6040, U.S.A.

6.02: ADOLESCENT HOME SITUATIONS QUESTIONNAIRE-PARENT REPORT (AHSC-PR); ADOLESCENT HOME SITUATIONS QUESTIONNAIRE-SELF REPORT (AHSC-SR); AND ADOLESCENT SCHOOL SITUATIONS QUESTIONNAIRE-SELF REPORT (ASSQ-SR).
AUTHORS: Adams, McCarthy, and Kelley.

VARIABLE: Adolescent situational behavior problems.

DESCRIPTION: **Home Situations Questionnaires:** The parent-report and self-report version each consist of 15 items or situations that occur at home. The respondent first indicates whether each behavior listed is present. For items marked *yes* the respondent then rates the severity of each behavior problem on a 9-point, Likert type scale ranging from 1 (*Mild*) to 9 (*Severe*). The measures yield two scores: Problem Score (the total number of yes responses) and the Mean Severity Score (the total of severity ratings divided by the problem score). **School Situation Questionnaire:** The measure consists of 14 situations that occur at school, and the adolescent indicates whether he or she experiences attention problems during those situations. As with the HSQ, for items marked *yes* the respondent rates the severity of each behavior problem on a 9-point, Likert type scale. The measure also yields a Problem Score and a Mean Severity Score.

SAMPLE: The measures are intended for use with adolescents who may potentially meet criteria for ADHD. The measures were validated on 943 adolescents between the ages of 11 and 17 years from southern Louisiana. Eighty-one percent of the sample were Caucasian, 16% were African American, and 3% were adolescents of other ethnic minorities. A normal distribution of socioeconomic status (SES) was represented, with the average being middle class.

RELIABILITY: Internal consistency: Satisfactory internal consistency levels were obtained for all forms and for all age categories. For the item severity scores, Cronbach's alpha was .82 for the AHSQ-pr, .80 for the AHSQ-sr, and .84 for the ASSQ-sr. **Inter-Rater:** Pearson product-moment correlations were conducted on item severity data for the AHSQ-pr and AHSQ-sr. Correlations between identical sets of 15 items ranged from .09 to .37. **Test-retest:** Adams *et al.* (1995) evaluated the stability of test scores over a two-week period using a sample of 81 adolescents. The authors found test-retest correlations of .64 for the Problem Score and .65 for the mean severity score for the AHSQ-sr. For the ASSQ-sr, the correlation for the problem score was .72 and the correlation for the Mean Severity Score was .84.

VALIDITY: Convergent: To examine convergent validity, the Pearson product-moment correlation coefficient was conducted between the Mean Severity Score of each questionnaire and the Child Behavior Checklist (CBCL; Achenbach & Edelbrock, 1991a) Externalizing Behavior scale and Attention Problems subscale, the Youth Self-Report (YSR; Achenbach & Edelbrock, 1991b) Externalizing Behavior scale and Attention Problems subscale, and the Conners' Parent Rating Scale (CPRS-48; Conners, 1989) Conduct Problems subscale, Impulsive-Hyperactive subscale, and the Hyperactivity Index. To examine **divergent validity,** correlations were conducted between the Mean Severity Score of each questionnaire and the Internalizing Behavior scale of the YSR and CBCL. For all 3 measures, same-informant correlations for externalizing behavior scales and attention problems subscales were high. For additional similar criterion measures, correlations were modest, and were low for dissimilar measures.

LOCATION: Adams, C.D., McCarthy, M., & Kelley, M.L. (1995). Adolescent version of the home and school situations questionnaires: Initial psychometric properties. *Journal of Clinical Child Psychology, 24,* 377-385.

The questionnaire, scoring instructions, and normative data can be obtained by contacting Christina Adams, West Virginia University, Department of Psychology, Box 6040, Morgantown, WV 26506-6040, U.S.A; E-mail: cadams4@wvu.edu

COMMENT: The self-report versions of the AHSQ and ASSQ provide unique information with respect to an adolescent's perception of his or her behavior as a function of home and school situations. Initial reliability and validity data suggest the utility of these questionnaires in the assessment of ADHD in adolescents.

REFERENCES:

Achenbach, T. M., & Edelbrock, C. (1991a). *Manual for the Child Behavior Checklist/4-18.* Burlington: University of Vermont, Department of Psychiatry.

Achenbach, T. M., & Edelbrock, C. (1991b). *Manual for the Youth Self-Report.* Burlington: University of Vermont, Department of Psychiatry.

Adams, C.D., McCarthy, M., & Kelley, M.L. (1995). Adolescent version of the home and school situations questionnaires: Initial psychometric properties. *Journal of Clinical Child Psychology, 24,* 377-385.

Conners, C. K. (1989). *Conners' Rating Scales Manual: Conners' Teacher Rating Scales, Conners' Parent Rating Scales.* North Tonawanda, New York: Multi-Health Systems, Inc.

REVIEWERS: Vicki A. Lumley, Ethan S. Long, and Christina D. Adams, West Virginia University, Department of Psychology, Box 6040, Morgantown, WV 26506-6040, U.S.A.

6.03: ADULT ATTACHMENT INTERVIEW (AAI), THE.

AUTHORS: Interview: George, Kaplan and Main; **Scoring and classification system:** Main and Goldwyn.

VARIABLE: Current state of mind with respect to attachment.

DESCRIPTION: The AAI is a semi structured interview consisting of 18 questions and lasting approximately one hour (ranging from 45 to 100 minutes). Subjects are probed on their childhood relationships with their parents, on experiences of being hurt, upset and ill, on experiences of loss, rejection and separation, on their current relationships with their parents and on their understanding of the effects that their attachment relationships have had on their current personality. Interviews are transcribed verbatim from audio recordings, and written transcripts are rated according to the classification system developed by Main and Goldwyn (1998). The subject's relationship with each parent is rated on five nine-point scales: Love, Rejection, Role-Reversal, Pressure to Achieve and Neglect. The subject's state of mind with regard to the experiences is rated next on 11 scales: Idealization, Lack of recall, Anger, Derogation, Metacognitive monitoring, Passivity, Fear of loss of own child, Unresolved loss, Unresolved trauma and Coherence of transcript and of mind. Finally, the score pattern of these scales as well as the overall pattern of the interview are used to classify subjects according to the following attachment categories: autonomous (F), preoccupied (E), dismissing (Ds), unresolved (U) or cannot classify (CC), and according to 12 sub-categories (F1-5; E1-3; Ds1-4). The U category pertains to discussion of a particular experience of loss or abuse, and is always assigned in conjunction with an alternative best-fitting category (F, Ds, E or CC). The F category is considered secure, while Ds, E, U and CC are insecure attachment categories.

SAMPLE: The AAI was first intended to be used with adult mothers, and then with fathers. Its use has since been extended to non-parent adults, elderly people, adolescents, preadolescents, psychiatric populations and criminal offenders. The AAI is being used in English, French, German, Italian, Hebrew, Dutch, and American Sign Language.

RELIABILITY: The identity of the interviewer (Bakermans-Kranenburg & Van IJzendoorn, 1993) and the fact that an interviewer also rates the interviews (Sagi et al., 1994) have no bearing on the classifications. The test-retest reliability of the AAI is excellent, with stability of the main category ranging from 77% (Steele & Steele, 1994) to 90% (Benoit & Parker, 1994, Sagi et al., 1994) over periods of one month to one year.

VALIDITY: **Discriminant:** Social desirability, SES, reasoning quality, IQ, level of education, verbal expression, general discourse style, cognitive style, cognitive complexity and ability to recall experiences unrelated to attachment do not influence the AAI classification (Bakermans-Kranenburg & Van IJzendoorn, 1993, Crowell *et al.*, 1996; Sagi *et al.*, 1994). The AAI also taps different constructs than those assessed by self-report measures (Crowell, Fraley & Shaver, 1999). **Convergent:** The AAI classification is related, among others, to parental sensitivity, loneliness, anxiety, ego resiliency, psychopathology, ways of coping, responsiveness to psychotherapy, romantic and family functioning, subject's infant attachment to them, interactions with own children, and subject's children's personal adjustment and psychopathology (see Hesse, 1999, for a review).

LOCATION: Hesse, E. (1999). The Adult Attachment Interview: Historical and current perspectives. In J. Cassidy & P.R. Shaver (Eds.), *Handbook of Attachment: Theory, Research and Clinical Applications* (pp. 395-433). New York: Guilford.

SPECIAL COMMENT: Conducting and coding the AAI requires a 2-week training period with Mary Main or with her colleagues. The training is followed by a reliability check, in which the candidate must demonstrate 80% inter-rater agreement with Mary Main and Erik Hesse on a sequence of 30 consecutive transcripts.

REFERENCES:
Bakermans-Kranenburg, M.J., & Van IJzendoorn, M.H. (1993). A psychometric study of the Adult Attachment Interview: Reliability and discriminant validity. *Developmental Psychology, 29*, 870-879.

Benoit, D., & Parker, K.C.H. (1994). Stability and transmission of attachment across three generations. *Child Development, 65*, 1444-1456.

Crowell, J. A., Fraley, R.C., & Shaver, P.R. (1999). Measurement of individual differences in adolescent and adult attachment. In J. Cassidy & P.R. Shaver (Eds), *Handbook of Attachment: Theory Research and Clinical Applications* (pp. 434-465). New York: Guilford.

Crowell, J. A. & Waters, E., Treboux, D., O'Connor, E., Colon-Downs, C., Fetter, O., Golby, B., & Posada, G. (1996). Discriminant validity of the Adult Attachment Interview. *Child Development, 67*, 2584-2599.

George, C., Kaplan, N., & Main, M. (1996). *Adult Attachment Interview Protocol* (3rd Edition). Unpublished manuscript, University of California at Berkeley.

Hesse, E. (1999). The Adult Attachment Interview: Historical and current perspectives. In J. Cassidy & P.R. Shaver (Eds), *Handbook of Attachment: Theory, Research and Clinical Applications* (pp. 395-433). New York: Guilford.

Main, M., & Goldwyn, R. (1998). *Adult Attachment classification system draft 6.2.* Unpublished manuscript, University of California at Berkeley.

Sagi, A., van IJzendoorn, M. H., Scharf, M., Koren-Karie, N., Joels, T., & Mayseless, O. (1994). Stability and discriminant validity of the Adult Attachment Interview: A psychometric study in young Israeli adults. *Developmental Psychology, 30*, 771-777.

Steele, H., & Steele, M. (1994). Intergenerational patterns of attachment. In D. Perlman, & K. Bartholomew (Eds), *Advances in Personal Relationships, vol. 5.* London: Kinsley.

REVIEWER: Annie Bernier, Ecole de psychologie, Universite Laval, Quebec, QC, GlK 7P4. Canada. E-mail: annie.bernier@umit.maine.edu

6.04: ATTACHMENT STYLE QUESTIONNAIRE (ASQ).
AUTHORS: Feeney, Noller, and Hanrahan.

VARIABLE: Five dimensions of adult attachment: (1) Confidence; (2) Discomfort with Closeness; (3) Need for Approval; (4) Preoccupation; (5) Relationships as Secondary.

DESCRIPTION: The Attachment Style Questionnaire contains 40 items, which are answered on a 6-point scale from 1=*Totally disagree* to 6=*Totally agree*, covering the major features described in both three- and four-styles of adult attachment. The items are based on four constructs: (1) positive view of self and positive view of other (self-esteem - comfort with closeness - trust - healthy dependence); (2) positive view of self and negative view of other (avoidance of intimacy - lack of trust - value on independence - compulsive self-reliance - emphasis on achievement); (3) negative view of self and positive view of other (overdependence - interpersonal anxiety - aloneness - desire for approval - lack of confidence - preoccupation with relationships); and (4) negative view of self and negative view of other (low self-esteem - lack of trust - interpersonal anxiety - desire for contact and intimacy - need for approval - aloneness - anger/hostility). The final version of the questionnaire contains five subscales: (1) Confidence (in self and others)=8 items: (2) Discomfort with Closeness=10 items; (3) Need for Approval=7 items; (4) Preoccupation with Relationships=8 items; (5) Relationships as Secondary=7 items. (Feeney *et al.*, 1994, have tested a three-factor solution. All information about this solution are presented in their chapter in Sperling & Berman's, 1994 book).

SAMPLE: Feeney *et al.* (1994) intended the scale to be used in populations with little or no experience of romantic relationships (ex. young adolescents).

RELIABILITY: **Internal consistency:** Cronbach's alphas were calculated for the five subscales. For the factors of Confidence, Discomfort with Closeness, Need for Approval, Preoccupation, and Relationships as Secondary, coefficient alphas were .80, .84, .79, .76, and .76, respectively (Feeney *et al.*, 1994). **Test-retest:** Reliability coefficients for the five scales over a period of approximately 10 weeks were . 74 (both Confidence and Discomfort with Closeness), .78 (Need for Approval), .72 (Preoccupation), and .67 (Relationships as Secondary) (Feeney *et al.*, 1994).

VALIDITY: **Construct:** Factor analyses were carried out to test a three- and a five-factor solution. The three-factor solution accounted for 35.7% of the total variance, and yielded three factors: Security - Avoidance - Anxiety, which are in line with Hazan and Shaver's (1987) conceptualization of adult attachment. The five-factor solution accounted for 43.3% of the total variance, and yield five factors: Confidence - Discomfort with Closeness - Need for Approval - Preoccupation - Relationships as Secondary (to achievement). These results indicate that the constructs central to Hazan and Shaver's (1987) and to Bartholomew and Horowitz's (1991) conceptualizations of attachment are present in the five-factor solution (Feeney *et al.*, 1994). **Convergent Validity:** The five attachment scales of the ASQ were correlated with the Likert ratings derived from Hazan and Shaver's forced-choice measure. Secure attachment was positively correlated with Confidence, and negatively correlated with the four other scales. Avoidant attachment was strongly correlated with Discomfort with Closeness, and moderately correlated with Relationships as Secondary. And Anxious/Ambivalent attachment was strongly correlated with Preoccupation and Need for Approval. These correlations support the validity of the new scales in assessing the constructs proposed by Hazan and Shaver (1987) (Feeney *et al.*, 1994). Moreover, Feeney and collaborators carried out analyses of variance, in which subjects were divided into Secure, Avoidant, and Anxious/Ambivalent groups, and were compared on the five factors of the ASQ. Secure subjects scored significantly higher than the other groups on the Confidence scale, and significantly lower than the other groups on Discomfort with Closeness. Anxious/Ambivalent subjects scored significantly higher than the other groups on the Preoccupation with Relationships scale, and on the Need for Approval scale. Avoidant subjects scored significantly higher that secure subjects on the Relationships as Secondary scale.

LOCATION: Feeney, J.A., Noller, P., & Hanrahan, M. (1994). Assessing Adult Attachment. In M.B. Sperling & W.H. Berman (Eds.), *Attachment in Adults*: *Clinical and Developmental Perspectives* (pp. 128-152). New York: Guilford Press.

COMMENT: The results of Feeney *et al.*'s (1994) analyses indicate that the ASQ represents a new measure of attachment style that could be used to clarify issues concerning adult attachment and the number of styles needed to define essential individual differences. It is also a measure suitable for young adolescents, and for those with little or no experience of romantic relationships.

REFERENCES:

Bartholomew, K., & Horowitz, L.M. (1991). Attachment styles among young adults: A test of a four-category model. *Journal of Personality and Social Psychology*, *61*, 226-244.

Feeney, J.A., Noller, P., & Hanrahan, M. (1994). Assessing Adult Attachment. In M.B. Sperling & W.H. Berman (Eds.), *Attachment in Adults*: *Clinical and Developmental Perspectives* (pp. 128-152). New York: Guilford Press.

Hazan, P., & Shaver, C. (1987). Romantic love conceptualized as an attachment process. *Journal of Personality and Social Psychology*, *52*, 511-524.

Sperling, M. B., & Berman, W. H. (Eds.). (1994). *Attachment in Adults: Clinical and Developmental Perspectives.* New York: Guilford Press.

REVIEWER: Nathalie Soucy, Faculté des sciences de l'éducation, Département d'études sur l'enseignement et l'apprentissage, Université Laval, Québec (Québec), G1K 7P4, Canada. E-mail: acc303@agora.ulaval.ca

6.05: ATTACHMENT AND OBJECT RELATIONS INVENTORY (AORI), THE.
AUTHORS: Buelow, McClain, and McIntosh.

VARIABLE: Important factors in attachment and object relations.

DESCRIPTION: The Attachment and Object Relations Inventory (AORI; Buelow, McClain, & McIntosh, 1996), a dimensional measure based on factor structure, was developed in response to the psychometric problems typical to attachment style measures which are categorical in nature and that do not ascertain attachment objects. The AORI consists of both attachment and object relations dimensions. Each dimension contains three subscales of ten items each that are reported on a Likert-type 5-point scale ranging from (1) *Strongly disagree* to (5) *Strongly agree*. The attachment dimension measures levels of closeness, security, and independence. The object relations dimension measures interdependence with parents, peers, and romantic partners or significant-others.

SAMPLE: The scale was piloted and normed on late adolescent/early adult samples. A MANOVA comparing men and women in the samples found that women saw themselves as wanting, and capable of having, significantly closer relationships than men. A MANOVA based on ethnicity was not significant. The scale is intended for both research and clinical/diagnostic purposes, and may be used among normative or clinical populations.

RELIABILITY: **Internal consistency:** Internal consistency on a further sample of 165 students (Buelow, Schreiber, & Range, In Press) was .91. **Test-retest:** Reliability on the original 75 items was .92 over a 6-week interval using a pilot sample of 26 undergraduate students; internal consistency for the pilot sample (Cronbach's alpha) was .95. Internal consistency for the selected final 60 items in the standardization sample of 296 students was .93. **Factor analysis:** Factor analysis of the original pool of AORI items confirmed the existence of at least 6 factors and 60 retained items explained approximately 50% of the item variance.

VALIDITY: The validity and structural integrity of the AORI is supported by factor analysis. Social desirability correlations (Crowne & Marlowe, 1960) were not significant. Factor analysis supported the existence of at least 6 factors with Eigenvalues of over 1.0 that were made up of items that centered on two dimensions, including views of others as accessible and responsive (peers, parents, and partners or spouses). Factors representing views of self as responsive to others included independent versus dependent, close versus distant, and secure versus insecure. Item factor loadings ranged from .36 to .90, and factors yielded by the final oblique rotation were minimally intercorrelated, averaging .15. Convergent validity was supported by significant positive correlations between AORI subscales and appropriate subscales of the 16PF, including, reserved, toughminded, and secure, for example (Cattell, 1989; IPAT, 1979), Bell Object Relations and Reality Testing Inventory (Bell, Billington, & Becker, 1986; Bell, 1994), and the Adult Attachment Measure (Bartholomew & Horowitz, 1991). Discriminant validity was supported by significant negative correlations between the AORI and the Beck Depression Inventory (BDI; Beck & Steer, 1987) and the State Trait Anxiety Inventory (STAI; Spielberger, et al., 1983). Further, the attachment subscales have been examined in relationship to subjects' ability to relate in a secure way with persons with disabilities (Jandry, 1998). Finally, the AORI is currently being used in a variety of psychological research projects that will provide further reliability and validity data.

FURTHER EMPIRICAL USES: Continuing research using the AORI (Buelow, Shreiber, & Range, in press) has shown that young adults with lowered attachment had higher levels of suicidal ideation (Suicide Behavior Questionnaire; Linehan & Nielsen, 1981) and lowered reasons for living (College Student Reasons for Living Inventory; Westefeld, Cardin, & Deaton, 1992). The authors believe that the AORI may be useful in clinical practice to better understand attachment and object relations concerns, to help judge the ability of clients (or therapists in training) to form a therapeutic alliance, and to assess clients' specific attachment difficulties that may act to lower their attachment to living.

LOCATION: Buelow, G.D., McClain, M., & McIntosh, I. (1996). A new measure for an important construct: The Attachment and Object Relations Inventory. *Journal of Personality Assessment, 66,* 604-623.

REFERENCES:

Bartholomew, K., & Horowitz, L.M. (1991). Attachment styles among young adults: A test of a four-category model. *Journal of Personality and Social Psychology, 61,* 226-244.

Beck, A.T., & Steer, R.A. (1987). *Beck Depression Inventory Manual.* San Antonio: The Psychological Corporation.

Bell, M.D. (1994). *Construct validity of the Bell object relations and reality testing inventory.* Paper presented at the Society for Personality Assessment, Chicago, Illinois.

Bell, M.D., Billington, R.J., & Becker, B. (1986). A scale for the assessment of Object Relations: Reliability, validity, and factorial invariance. *Journal of Clinical Psychology, 42*, 733-741.

Buelow, G.D., McClain, M., & McIntosh, I. (1996). A new measure for an important construct: The Attachment and Object Relations Inventory. *Journal of Personality Assessment, 66*, 604-623.

Buelow, G.D., Schreiber, R., & Range, L. (in press). Attachment pattern, reasons for living and suicide risk among college students. *Journal of College Student Counseling.*

Cattell, H.B. (1989). *The 16PF: Personality in Depth.* Champaign, IL: Institute for Personality and Ability Testing, Inc.

Cattell, R.B., & Gibbons, B.D. (1968). Personality factor structure of the combined Guilford and Cattell personality questionnaires. *Journal of Personality and Social Psychology, 9*, 107-120.

Crowne, D.P., & Marlowe, D. (1960). A new scale of social desirability independent of psychopathology. *Journal of Counseling Psychology, 24*, 349-354.

IPAT Staff. (1979). *Administrator's Manual for the 16PF.* Champaign, IL: Institute for Personality and Ability Testing, Inc.

Linehan, M.M., & Nielsen, S.L. (1981). Assessment of suicide ideation and parasuicide: Hopelessness and social desirability. *Journal of Consulting and Clinical Psychology, 49*, 773-775.

Spielberger, C.D., Gorsuch, R.L., Lushene, R., Vagg, P.R., & Jacobs, G.A. (1983). *Manual for the State-Trait Anxiety Inventory.* Palo Alto, CA: Consulting Psychologists Press.

Westefeld, J.S., Cardin, L.D., & Deaton, W.L. (1992). Development of the College Student Reasons for Living Inventory. *Suicide and Life-Threatening Behavior*, 22,442-452.

REVIEWER: George Buelow, Psychology Department, Box 5025, University of Southern Mississippi, Hattiesburg, MS 39406-5025, U.S.A.

6.06: AYCLIFFE INVENTORY OF DELINQUENT ATTITUDES.
AUTHOR: Porteous.

VARIABLES: Self-Image, Victimisation, Aggressiveness, Behaviour problems, Home experiences and Anti social attitudes.

DESCRIPTION: The Aycliffe Inventory of Delinquent Attitudes is a self-administered True-False 88-item inventory for use with adolescents. It gives percentile scores on the above 6 factors.

SAMPLE: Children in Full time residential care in England. Normative data are from a sample of 600 children who were in the 'social care' system of English Local Authorities and who were sent for assessment to a residential assessment centre

RELIABILITY: Internal consistency: for each subscale is separately, in excess of .75. Test-retest: One sample $r=>.75$ for overall composite rating

VALIDITY: Three validation studies have been reported illustrating some correlates and applications of the inventory. One looks at how Aycliffe Inventory of Delinquent Attitudes relates to allocation policy of adolescent offenders to residential provision. This shows that scores on this inventory were correlated with residential treatment decisions. The second study shows, in a 'normal' school context, the relationships between AIDA scores and self-reported adolescent problems, derived from the Porteous Checklist. The third study showed the relationships between AIDA, Sensation Seeking and unrecorded delinquency.

FURTHER EMPIRICAL USES: For use in delinquency assessment or research with disturbed and troublesome adolescents. Appropriate for counselling settings.

LOCATION: Available from M.A. Porteous, Applied Psychology Department, University College Cork, Cork, Ireland.

REFERENCES:

Porteous, M.A. *Some Correlates Of The Aycliffe Inventory Of Delinquent Attitudes*, ("*AIDA*"). Paper presented at European Association for study of Personality, University of Surrey, July 1998.

REVIEWER: M.A.Porteous, Applied Psychology Department, University College Cork, Cork, Ireland. E-mail: STAY8012@ucc.ie

6.07: CHILD BEHAVIOR SCALE, THE.
AUTHORS: Ladd and Profilet.

VARIABLES: Children's Aggressive, Withdrawn, and Prosocial Behavior with Peers.

DESCRIPTION: The CBS is a teacher-rating instrument containing 59 items, 35 of which are used to create subscales representing 6 dimensions of young children's behavior in peer contexts, such as classrooms. The 6 subscales (number of items) are labelled: aggressive with peers (7), prosocial with peers (7), excluded by peers (7), asocial with peers (6), hyperactive-distractible (4), and anxious-fearful (4). Respondents are asked to rate the behavior described in each item in terms of how characteristic or 'applicable' it is for the targeted child, using scale points labelled (defined) as: 1=*Doesn't apply* (child seldom displays the behavior); 2=*Applies sometimes* (child occasionally displays the behavior); and 3=*Certainly applies* (child often displays the behavior). Subscale scores are created by averaging children's scores across the items included in each subscale, and higher scores imply that children more frequently exhibit behaviors that correspond to the rated construct.

SAMPLE: The CBS was designed to provide reliable and valid data on young children's (ages 4-6) behavior in peer contexts, such as classrooms. Collectively, the subscales provide measures of several behaviors that can be considered indicators of interpersonal 'risk' and 'competence' in young children. The scale has also been evaluated with children from diverse socioeconomic and ethnic backgrounds, and older age levels (*e.g.*, middle childhood), and found to possess favourable psychometric properties with these samples.

RELIABILITY: Each of the six CBS subscales yielded scores that were internally consistent (ranged from .77 to .96), distinct from other subscales, and relatively stable over time (r's ranged from .54 to .83 over 4 months). Moreover, homogeneity, dimensionality, and stability were examined for the CBS over time for the same sample (invariance), and across samples (cross validation). The obtained psychometric properties were highly similar (replicated) across time and samples.

VALIDITY: The validation paradigm employed in this study produced a network of correlations that was, overall, consistent with the hypothesized conceptual structure of the CBS. The construct validity of the CBS was examined by correlating subscale scores with observational, teacher-report, and peer-report measures of children's behavior. In general, subscale scores yielded higher correlations with measures of the same or closely-related behaviors (convergent validity) than with measures of different or less-related behaviors (discriminant validity). These findings also replicated across samples (cross validation). These results lent support to the conclusion that the six CBS subscales tap the constructs that they were intended to measure.

LOCATION: Ladd, G.W., & Profilet, S.M. (1996). The Child Behavior Scale: A teacher-report measure of young children's aggressive, withdrawn, and prosocial behaviors. *Developmental Psychology, 32,* 1008-1024.

COMMENT: A number of investigators have used the CBS to measure the targeted aspects of young children's peer-related behavior with samples containing children from a range of ethnic groups and socioeconomic strata. Thus far, these researchers have found that the scale yields psychometric properties that are similar to those reported in our original publication.

REFERENCES:

Birch, S.H., & Ladd, G.W. (1998). Children's interpersonal behaviors and the teacher-child relationship. *Developmental Psychology, 34*, 934-946.

Kochenderfer, B.J., & Ladd, G.W. (1996). Peer victimization: Manifestations and relations to school adjustment. *Journal of School Psychology, 34*, 267-284.

Kochenderfer, B.J., & Ladd, G.W. (1997). Victimized children's responses to peers' aggression: Behaviors associated with reduced versus continued victimization. *Development and Psychopathology, 9*, 59-73.

Ladd, G.W., & Burgess, K.B. (1999). Charting the relationship trajectories of aggressive, withdrawn, and aggressive/withdrawn children during early grade school. *Child Development, 70*, 910-929.

Ladd, G.W., & Kochenderfer, B.J. (1998). Parenting behaviors and the parent-child relationship: Correlates of peer victimization in kindergarten? *Developmental Psychology, 34*, 1450-1458.

Ladd, G.W., & Profilet, S.M. (1996). The Child Behavior Scale: A teacher-report measure of young children's aggressive, withdrawn, and prosocial behaviors. *Developmental Psychology, 32*, 1008-1024.

Ladd, G.W., Birch, S.H., & Buhs, E. (in press). Children's social and scholastic lives in Kindergarten: Related spheres of influence? *Child Development.*

REVIEWER: Gary Ladd, Childrens Research Center 183, University of Illinois, Illinois, IL 61820, U.S.A.

6.08 CHILDREN'S INTERVIEW FOR PSYCHIATRIC SYNDROMES (CHILD AND PARENT FORMS, ChIPS AND P-CHIPS).

AUTHORS: Weller, Weller, Rooney and Fristad.

VARIABLES: DSM-IV behavior, anxiety, mood and other disorders; psychosocial stressors; general functioning.

DESCRIPTION: Structured interviews (child and parent forms) that cover 20 clinical disorders (attention deficit hyperactivity disorder, oppositional defiant disorder, conduct disorder, substance abuse, specific phobia, social phobia, separation anxiety disorder, generalized anxiety disorder, obsessive-compulsive disorder, acute stress disorder, post-traumatic stress disorder, anorexia, bulimia, major depressive disorder, dysthymic disorder, mania, hypomania, enuresis, encopresis, schizophrenia/psychosis), as well as questions about the child's presenting problem, general functioning at home, school/work and with peers, and prior treatment, including medication. There are also sections assessing psychosocial stressors in general and abuse in particular.

SAMPLE: Weller, Weller, Rooney and Teare (1999a, 1999b) intended the instrument to be used with child and adolescent inpatients, outpatients, and community based samples.

RELIABILITY: Test-retest: Fitzpatrick and Fristad (in submission) report six month test-retest correlation coefficients of $r=.50$ and $r=.62$, respectively, for child and parent ratings of behavior disorders, and $r=.30$ and $r=.48$, respectively, for child and parent ratings of anxiety disorders.

VALIDITY: Concurrent: A series of five studies have demonstrated overall adequate kappa coefficients when results from ChIPS are compared to those obtained from another structured interview (Fristad *et al.*, 1998a, 1998b; Teare *et al.*, 1998a, 1998b) and when P-ChIPS results are compared to clinicians' diagnoses (average kappa=.49; Fristad *et al.*, 1998c). **Convergent:** Fitzpatrick and Fristad (in submission) demonstrate moderate to strong convergent validity for the ChIPS mood scales when compared to various clinical rating scales for depression and mania (r=.41 to .89).

FURTHER ANALYSES: **Sensitivity:** ChIPS' overall sensitivity (based on five published psychometric studies) is .66 (range=.44 to .79) while P-ChIPS overall sensitivity is .83 (Weller *et al.* 2000). **Specificity:** ChIPS' overall specificity (based on five published psychometric studies) is .88 (range=.77 to .995). P-ChIPS overall specificity is .78 (Weller *et al.* 2000). **Parent-child agreement:** Moderate levels of parent-child agreement are reported (average kappa=.41: Fristad *et al.*, 1998c). **Administration time:** A series of studies have indicated administration time is less for ChIPS than for a comparison structured interview (Fristad *et al.*, 1998a, 1998b; Teare *et al.*, 1998b)

LOCATION:

Rooney, M.T., Fristad, M.A., Weller, E.B., & Weller, R.A. (1999). *Children's Interview for Psychiatric Syndromes: Administration Manual.* American Psychiatric Press, Inc.

Weller, E.B. Weller, R.A., Rooney M.T., & Fristad, M.A. (1999a). *Children's Interview for Psychiatric Syndromes (ChIPS).* American Psychiatric Press, Inc.

Weller, E.B. Weller, R.A., Rooney, M.T., & Fristad, M.A. (1999b). *Parent Form - Children's Interview for Psychiatric Syndromes (P-ChIPS).* American Psychiatric Press, Inc.

COMMENT: Structured interviews are considered essential when conducting assessments in research settings, but they are not routinely used in clinical settings. This is quite possibly due to the pragmatic and psychometric limitations inherent in first generation interviews. As a 'second generation' interview, ChIPS was designed to build upon the strength of the original instruments while attempting to improve upon their drawbacks. ChIPS relies heavily on branching procedures that results in brief administration times. Interviewers read questions from a reusable interview booklet and score responses on a succinct record booklet that greatly minimizes storage needs. A comprehensive administration manual provides detailed administration guidelines and training requirements. ChIPS appears to be a psychometrically sound instrument. However, further testing with a variety of investigators and settings is advised.

REFERENCES:

Fitzpatrick, K.K., & Fristad, M.A. (in submission). *Test-retest reliability and convergent validity for the Children's Interview for Psychiatric Syndromes* (*ChIPS*). Manuscript under submission.

Fristad, M.A. (1999). A new diagnostic tool: The Children's Interview for Psychiatric Syndromes. *Child and Adolescent Psychopharmacology News*, *4*, 10-12.

Fristad, M.A., Cummins, J., Verducci, J.S., Rooney, M. Teare, Weller, E.B., & Weller, R.A. (1998a). Part IV: Children's Interview for Psychiatric Syndromes (ChIPS): Revised psychometrics for DSM-IV. *Journal of Child and Adolescent Psychopharmacology, 8*, 225-234.

Fristad, M.A., Glickman, A.R., Verducci, J.S., Rooney, M. Teare, Weller, E.B., & Weller, R.A. (1998b). Part V: Children's Interview for Psychiatric Syndromes (ChIPS): Psychometrics in nonclinical samples. *Journal of Child & Adolescent Psychopharmacology, 8*, 235-243.

Fristad, M.A., Rooney M. Teare, Weller, E.B., Weller, R.A., & Salmon, P. (1998c) Part III: Development and psychometric properties of the parent version of the Children's Interview for Psychiatric Syndromes (P-ChIPS). *Journal of Child and Adolescent Psychopharmacology*, *8*, 219-224.

Teare, M., Fristad, M.A., Weller, R.A., Weller, E.B., & Salmon, P. (1998a). Part I: Development and psychometric properties of the Children's Interview for Psychiatric Syndromes (ChIPS). *Journal of Child and Adolescent Psychopharmacology*, *8*, 203-209.

Teare, M., Fristad, M.A., Weller, R.A., Weller, E.B., & Salmon, P. (1998b). Part II: Reliability & validity of the DSM-III-R Children's Interview for Psychiatric Syndromes (ChIPS). *Journal of Child & Adolescent Psychopharmacology*, *8*, 211-217.

Weller, E.B., Weller, R.A., Fristad, M.A., Rooney, M.T., & Schecter, J. (2000). Children's Interview for Psychiatric Disorders (ChIPS). *Journal of American Academy Child Adolescent Psychiatry*, *39*, 76-84.

REVIEWER: Mary A. Fristad, , Division of Child & Adolescent Psychiatry, The Ohio State University, 1670 Upham Drive Suite 460G, Columbus, OH 43210-1250, U.S.A. E-mail: fristad.1@osu.edu

6.09: CHILDREN'S EATING ATTITUDES TEST (ChEAT), THE.

AUTHORS: Maloney, McGuire, Daniels and Specker.

VARIABLE: Self-report instrument for eating attitudes and dieting behaviors in children and adolescents.

DESCRIPTION: The Children's Eating Attitudes Test (ChEAT; Maloney *et al.*, 1989) is a child/adolescent version of the Eating Attitudes Test (EAT, Garner and Garfinkel, 1979). The ChEAT is a 26-item, 3-subscale self-report instrument in which each item is scored on a 6-point Likert scale (*Never* through to *Always*). The response reflecting the most disturbed eating attitude is scored 3, the adjacent response 2, and the next response 1. Remaining three responses are not scored. Higher scores are indicative of more disturbed eating attitudes. This accords with the procedure described by Garner and Garfinkel (1979). EAT scores above 20 have been suggested to be a cut-off for developing clinical eating disorders (Garner, Olmsted, Bohr & Garfinkel, 1982). The suggested cut-off of $\geq$ 20 for the ChEAT has not been validated. The three subscales are Dieting (13 items), Bulimia and Food Preoccupation (6 items) and Oral Control (7 items).

SAMPLES: The ChEAT is intended to be used for the assessment of self-reported dieting behaviours, food preoccupation, bulimia and concerns about being overweight among children and adolescents.

RELIABILITY: Internal consistency: Satisfactory internal consistency comparable to the EAT has been demonstrated (Edlund, Hallqvist & Sjödén, 1994; Edlund, Halvarsson & Sjödén, 1996; Edlund, Halvarsson, Gebre-Mehdin, & Sjödén, 1999; Maloney, McGuire, & Daniels, 1988; Mukai & McCloskey, 1996; Smolak & Levine, 1994; Veron-Guidry, Williamson, & Netmeyer, 1997) with alpha values ranging between .76 and .87 in samples ages 7 through 16. There are indications that internal consistency improves if items 19 (Edlund *et al.*, 1999; Maloney *et al.*, 1988; Smolak & Levine, 1994), 25 (Edlund, *et al.*, 1999; Smolak & Levine, 1994) and 23 (Smolak & Levine, 1994) are excluded. **Test-retest:** A test-retest correlation of .81 (.75 to .88 for different age groups; Maloney *et al.*, 1988) has been reported among children in Grades 3-6 (*n*=68) after a three- week interval.

VALIDITY: **Convergent:** Convergent Validity has been demonstrated by significant correlations between the ChEAT and measures of weight management behavior and body dissatisfaction (Smolak & Levine, 1994), as well as between the ChEAT and the Dutch Eating Behavior Questionnaire (DEBQ; Halvarsson & Sjödén, 1998). In the latter study, the highest correlations were demonstrated between the ChEAT Dieting scale and the DEBQ Restrained Eating scale (.75; Halvarsson & Sjödén, 1998) suggesting adequate concurrent validity. **Discriminant:** In a number of studies, significant differences in ChEAT scores have been demonstrated between children/adolescents who report dieting behavior and those who do not (Edlund *et al.*, 1994, 1996, 1999; Maloney *et al.*, 1989; Halvarsson, Lunner, & Sjödén, in press), which suggests adequate discriminant Validity. Similar results have been demonstrated in a 3-year longitudinal study (Halvarsson, Lunner, Westerberg, & Sjödén, under submission). **Factor structure:** Two 4-factor structures have been suggested. The first by Smolak and Levine (1994), including dimensions dieting, restricting and purging, food preoccupation and oral control, and by Kelly, Ricciardelli, and Clarke (1999), including; global problems, dieting vs. purging, dieting and food preoccupation, and emotional eating.

LOCATION: **Original version:** Maloney, M.J., McGuire, J., Daniels, S.R., & Specker, B. (1989). Dieting behavior and eating attitudes in children. *Pediatrics*, *84*, 482-489. **Japanese Version:** Mukai, T., & McCloskey, L.A. (1996). Eating

Attitudes among Japanese and American elementary school girls. *Journal of Cross-Cultural Psychology*, 27, 424-435. **Swedish version:** Edlund, B., Hallqvist, G., & Sjödén, P-O. (1994). Attitudes to food, eating and dieting behaviour in 11 and 14-year-old Swedish children. *Acta Pædiatrica*, *83*, 572-577.

COMMENTS: The ChEAT seems to be a promising instrument for the assessment of eating attitudes and dieting behaviors in children and adolescents. It appears stable across cultures (Edlund *et al.*, 1994, 1996, 1999; Halvarsson *et al.*, 1998, in press; Mukai & McCloskey, 1996; Sasson, Lewin, & Roth, 1995) and over time (Halvarsson *et al.*, under submission). However, the assessment of children ages 7-8 should be conducted with care since there are indications that some questions may be too difficult to comprehend for this age group (Halvarsson, *et al.*, in press; Veron-Guidry & Williamson, 1996). The usefulness of the ChEAT for predicting eating disturbances and treatment outcome needs to be investigated.

REFERENCES:

Edlund, B., Hallqvist, G., & Sjödén, P-O. (1994). Attitudes to food, eating and dieting behaviour in 11 and 14-year-old Swedish children. *Acta Pædiatrica*, *83*, 572-577.

Edlund, B., Halvarsson, K., & Sjödén, P-O. (1996). Eating behaviours and attitudes to eating, dieting and body image in 7-year-old Swedish girls. *European Eating Disorders Review*, *4*, 40-53.

Edlund, B., Halvarsson, K., Gebre-Medhin, M., & Sjödén, P-O. (1999). Psychological correlates of dieting in Swedish adolescents: A cross-sectional study. *European Eating Disorders Review*, *7*, 47-61.

Garner, D.M., & Garfinkel, P.E. (1979). Eating Attitudes Test: An index of the symptoms of anorexia nervosa. *Psychological Medicine*, *9*, 273-279.

704   Developmental Psychology

Garner, D.M., Olmsted, M.P., Bohr, Y., & Garfinkel, P.E. (1982). The Eating attitudes test: Psychomatric features and clinical correlates. *Psychological Medicine, 12,* 871-878.

Halvarsson, K., & Sjödén, P-O. (1998). Psychometric properties of the Dutch Eating Behavior Questionnaire (DEBQ) among 9-10-year-old Swedish girls. *European Eating Disorders Review, 6,* 115-125.

Halvarsson, K., Lunner, K., & Sjödén, P-O. (in press). Assessment of eating and attitudes to eating, dieting and body in pre-adolescent Swedish: A one-year follow. *Acta Paediatrica.*

Halvarsson, K., Lunner, K., Westerberg, J., & Sjödén, P-O. (under submission). Dieting, Eating Attitudes and Coping in Swedish adolescent girls: changes over 3 years.

Kelly, C., Ricciardelli, L.A., & Clarke, J.D. (1999). Problem eating attitudes and behaviors in young children. *International Journal of Eating Disorders, 25,* 281-6.

Maloney, M., McGuire, J., & Daniels, S. (1988). Reliability testing of a children's version of the Eating Attitudes Test. *Journal of the American Academy of Child and Adolescent Psychiatry, 5,* 541-543.

Maloney, M.J., McGuire, J., Daniels, S.R., & Specker, B. (1989). Dieting behavior and eating attitudes in children. *Pediatrics, 84,* 482-489.

Mukai, T., & McCloskey, L.A. (1996). Eating attitudes among Japanese and American elementary school girls. *Journal of Cross-Cultural Psychology, 27,* 424-435.

Sasson, A., Lewin, C., & Roth, D. (1995). Dieting behavior and eating attitudes in Israeli children. *International Journal of Eating Disorders, 17,* 67-72.

Smolak, L., & Levine, M.P. (1994). Psychometric properties of the Children's Eating Attitudes Test. *International Journal of Eating Disorders, 16,* 275-282.

Veron-Guidry, S., & Williamson, D.A. (1996). Development of a body image assessment for children and preadolescents. *International Journal of Eating Disorders, 20*, 287-293.

Veron-Guidry, S., Williamson, D.A., & Netemeyer, R.G. (1997). Structural modeling analysis of body dysphoria and eating disorders symptoms in preadolescent girls. *Eating Disorders: The Journal of Treatment and Prevention, 5*, 15-27.

REVIEWERS: Klara Halvarsson, and Per-Olow Sjödén, Uppsala University, Department of Public Health and Caring Sciences/ Section of Caring Sciences, Uppsala Science Park, SE-751 83 Uppsala, Sweden. E-mail: Klara.Halvarsson@ccs.uu.se.

6.10: CHILD PSYCHOTHERAPY PROCESS SCALES (CPPS).
AUTHOR: Estrada and Russell.

VARIABLE: Child and therapist psychotherapy process; positive and negative child behaviours in child therapy; positive and negative therapist behaviours in child therapy.

DESCRIPTION: The Child Psychotherapy Process Scales (CPPS) are designed to assess both positive and negative aspects of child and therapist behaviors and attitudes as displayed within whole therapy sessions or segments of therapy. The instrument consists of 33 items, including 15 child and 18 therapist items. Most of the child and therapist items are rated on a 5-point Likert-type scale indicating the extent to which the characteristic is present: *Not at all* (1), *Some* (2), *Fair amount* (3), *Pretty much* (4), and *A great deal* (5). Two of the child and therapist items relate to more global impressions of the productivity of therapy and the quality of the therapeutic relationship and are rated on a five point Likert-type scale: (1) *Very poor*, (2) P*oor*, (3) *Fair*, (4) *Good*, and (5) *Excellent*.

SAMPLE: Estrada and Russell (1999) developed the scale to evaluate children's verbal and play therapy across a broad spectrum of theoretical orientations and techniques with both non-psychiatric and psychiatric populations. The CPPS items were selected for their likely impact in facilitating or impeding progress in child therapy, focus on single therapy processes, and requirement for minimal levels of inference to allow for use among graduate student raters with limited clinical experience.

RELIABILITY: **Inter-rater:** Estrada and Russell (1999) reported adequate levels of inter-rater reliability across 35 child therapy sessions which were conducted with school aged children with a range of externalizing disorders. These sessions were divided into thirds, providing 105 segments for evaluation. Agreements between coders averaged above .77 ($.59< r <.94$) for the child and therapist items with over 90% of paired ratings falling within one scale point of each other. **Internal consistency:** Estrada and Russell (1999) conducted principal component analyses which revealed three child factors, Therapeutic Relationship, Child Therapeutic Work, and Child Readiness. Additionally, three therapist factors were found including Therapist Technical Work, Therapeutic Relationship, and Technical Lapse. Adequate levels of internal consistency (ranging from .73 to .88) were found for two of the child and therapist scales. Lower levels found for Child Readiness (.68) and Therapist Technical Lapse (.49), which were each comprised of three items.

VALIDITY: **Discriminant:** Russell, Bryant, and Estrada (1996, 1999) compared child and therapist discourse in sessions rated as high or low in quality on the

CPPS. Confirmatory P-technique analyses revealed that the structure of therapist and child in-session discourse differed significantly across high and low CPPS-scored sessions, providing strong evidence for the discriminant validity of the CPPS (see Russell, Bryant & Estrada, 1996, 1999 for details).

LOCATION: Estrada, A.U. & Russell, R. (1999). The development of the child psychotherapy process scales. *Psychotherapy Research, 9*, 153-165.

COMMENT: The child and therapist factors of the CPPS describe clinically significant and valid processes of child therapy. These factors mirror processes derived from clinical theory and research using other instruments and methods of therapy analysis, contributing to the validity of the CPPS.

REFERENCES:

Russell, R.L., Bryant, F., & Estrada, A.U. (1996). Confirmatory P-technique analyses of therapist discourse: High versus low quality child therapy sessions. *Journal of Consulting and Clinical Psychology. 64*, 1366-1376.

Russell, R.L., Bryant, F., & Estrada, A.U. (Under review). *Updating P-technique of child therapy processes: Bootstrapping, confirmatory and discriminant analyses.*

REVIEWER: Ana Ulloa Estrada, Department of Family Resources and Human Development, Arizona State University, Tempe, AZ 85287-2502, U.S.A. E-mail: aestrada@asu.edu

6.11: CORE BEREAVEMENT ITEMS (CBI).

AUTHORS: Burnett, Middleton, Raphael, & Martinek.

VARIABLE: Frequently experienced phenomena in the bereaved.

DESCRIPTION: The Core Bereavement Items (CBI; Burnett, Middleton, Raphael, & Martinek, 1997) contains 17-items which measure the frequency of commonly occurring responses to the loss of a loved one. Images and thoughts about the lossed person is measured by 7 items, acute separation is assessed using 5 items whilst grief is measured by 5 items. Each item is responded to using a 4-point scale: (4) *A lot of the time/continuously/always*; (3) *Quite a bit of the time*; (2) *A little bit of the time*; and (1) *Never*.

SAMPLE: Burnett *et al.* (1997) developed the scale using a sample of 158 recently bereaved subjects living in a metropolitan area in Australia. Subjects were recruited into three groups: bereaved spouses under the age of 70, adult children who had lost a parent and parents who had lost a child between the ages of 1 and 18. The number of bereaved spouses was 53 (mean age 53 years, 74% female), adult children numbered 52 (mean age 40 years, 63% female) and there were 53 bereaved parents (mean age 40 years, 57% female) with 57%, 57% and 48% participation rates respectively.

RELIABILITY: The 17-item Core Bereavement Items (CBI) Scale has an alpha reliability coefficient of .91 (Burnett *et al.*, 1997). The alpha coefficients for each of the three subscales are Images and Thoughts, .74; Acute Separation, .77; and Grief, .86 (Middleton, 1996).

VALIDITY: A number of indicators suggest that the CBI is a valid measure. The discriminant validity of the CBI was assessed by comparing the three different groups of bereaved. Those who on theoretical grounds were expected to score highly, did so, and those who were expected to produce lower scores did so providing evidence for discriminant validity. In examining the face validity of the CBI, there do not appear to be any items that are not central to the construct of grief in the way it is generally conceptualised in Western culture. The CBI appears to have good face validity with respect to the grief related dimensions of the bereavement process.

LOCATION: Burnett, P.C, Middleton, W., Raphael, B., & Martinek, N. (1997). Measuring bereavement phenomena. *Psychological Medicine, 27,* 49-57.

REFERENCES:

Burnett, P.C, Middleton, W., Raphael, B., & Martinek, N. (1997). Measuring bereavement phenomena. *Psychological Medicine, 27,* 49-57.

Middleton, W. (1996). *The phenomenology of bereavement and the processes of resolution.* MD thesis, University of Queensland.

Middleton, W., Burnett, P.C. Raphael, B., & Martinek, N. (1996). The bereavement response: A cluster analysis. *British Journal of Psychiatry, 169,* 167-171.

Middleton, W., Raphael, B., Burnett, P.C., & Martinek, N. (1997). Psychological distress and bereavement. *Journal of Nervous and Mental Diseases, 185,* 447-453.

Middleton, W., Raphael, B., Burnett, P.C., & Martinek, N. (1998). A longitudinal study comparing bereavement phenomena in recently bereaved spouses, adult children and parents. *Australian and New Zealand Journal of Psychiatry, 32,* 235-241.

REVIEWER: Paul C Burnett, Head, School of Teacher Education, Charles Sturt University, Bathurst NSW 2795, Australia.

6.12: DEFINING ISSUES TEST (DIT), THE.
AUTHOR: Rest.

VARIABLE: Moral judgement development.

DESCRIPTION: The measure includes 6 stories that describe a moral dilemma. Following each story are 12 items. Of these, the majority are written to reflect Kohlberg's moral judgment stages. The remaining items are reliability checks designed to identify participants who attend to the complexity of the statements rather than their meaning. Participants are asked to consider the protagonist's position in the story and select a course of action (*i.e.*, pro, con or can't decide). Following the decision choice, participants first rate each of the 12 items in terms of the item's importance in reaching a decision (assessed on a five-point scale) and then rank their top four items. Higher scores on the two major indices (P and N2 scores) represent an increased reliance on post-conventional reasoning. Scoring of the DIT includes two reliability checks: the meaningless item ratings mentioned above and a rate-rank inconsistency check. Subjects failing either check are flagged for possible elimination from the sample.

SAMPLE: The DIT is intended for participants with reading skills typically found in early secondary education populations in the US (*i.e.*, 9th grade), (Rest, 1987). As such, the measure is most sensitive to the shift from conventional to postconventional moral reasoning in Kohlberg's model.

RELIABILITY: Internal consistency: Satisfactory levels of internal reliability have been presented in the literature ranging from .76 to .83. in large heterogeneous samples (Rest, 1979). Similar levels have been noted in the most recent revision of the measure (Rest, Thoma, Narvaez & Bebeau, 1997). **Test-**

retest: Davison (in Rest, 1979) summarised 4 samples and found a range of test-retest correlations from .71 to .86.

VALIDITY: DIT researchers present 6 criteria to support the measure: 1) sensitivity to educational interventions; 2) differentiating known groups; 3) longitudinal trends; 4) correlations with measures of moral comprehension; 5) links to behavior; and 6) links to Civil Libertarian attitudes. These criteria blend classical measurement issues such as discriminate and convergent validity, with concerns specific to a developmental measure. Each of the 6 criteria includes multiple studies and samples collected from over 20 years of DIT research. Recent summaries of these data are found in Rest, Thoma, and Edwards (1997); Rest, Thoma, Narvaez, and Bebeau (1997); and in Rest, Narvaez, Bebeau, and Thoma (1999).

LOCATION: The DIT can be obtained from the Center for the Study of Ethical Development, 206 Burton Hall, 178 Pillsbury Drive SE; University of Minnesota, Minneapolis, MN 55455, U.S.A. Descriptions of the measure are also provided in Rest (1979, 1986) and Rest *et al.*, (1999).

COMMENT: The DIT is by far the most widely used and scrutinised measure of moral judgment development in the Kohlberg tradition (approximately 700 studies have used the DIT since the late 1970s). From this extensive database, one can reasonably conclude that the DIT is a successful group-based measure of moral judgment development for adolescent and adult populations. Recent attention to the underlying construct as well as the development of new experimental indices should only increase the utility of the measure (*i.e.*, Rest, Narvaez, Bebeau, & Thoma, 1999; Thoma & Rest, 1999).

REFERENCES:

Rest, J. (1979). *Development in Judging Moral Issues*. Minneapolis: University of Minnesota Press.

Rest, J. (1986). *Moral Development: Advances in Research and Theory*. New York: Praeger.

Rest, J. (1987). *Guide for the Defining Issues Test*. Unpublished manuscript, the University of Minnesota, Minneapolis.

Rest, J., Narvaez, D., Bebeau, M., & Thoma, S. (1999). *Postconventional moral thinking: A neo-Kohlbergian approach*.   Mahwah, NJ: Lawrence Erlbaum Associates.

Rest, J., Thoma, S. J., & Edwards, L. (1997). Devising and validating a measure of moral judgment: Stage preference and stage consistency approaches. *Journal of Educational Psychology, 89*, 5-28.

Rest, J., Thoma, S.J., Narvaez, D., & Bebeau, M. J. (1997). Alchemy and beyond: Indexing the Defining Issues Test. *Journal of Educational Psychology, 89*, 498-507.

Thoma, S.J., & Rest, J. The relationship between decision making, and patterns of consolidation and transition in moral judgment development. *Developmental Psychology, 35*, 323-334.

REVIEWER: Stephen J. Thoma.   205 Child Development Center, University of Alabama, Tuscaloosa, AL 35487-0158 U.S.A

6.13: DOMINIC-R: A PICTORIAL YOUNG CHILD MENTAL HEALTH QUESTIONNAIRE .

AUTHOR: Valla.

VARIABLE: Most frequent mental disorders of young children.

DESCRIPTION: The DOMINIC-R is a paper-based cartoon-like self-report questionnaire to evaluate the following seven mental disorders of children aged 6 to 11 years: Separation Anxiety (SAD) - 13 items, Oppositional Defiant Disorder (ODD) - 13 items, Overanxious Disorder (OAD) - 11 items, Simple Phobia (SPh) - 10 items, Conduct Disorder (CD) - 12 items, Major Depressive Disorder (MDD) - 19 items and Attention-deficit Hyperactivity Disorder (ADHD) - 16 items. A child named Dominic is depicted, either alone, or interacting with peers or adults facing situations based on both the daily life of children and DSM-III-R criteria. Every item includes one question offering an auditory symptom description and one to three images. Contrary to projective tests, the DOMINIC-R illustrates precise situations allowing for little if any interpretation. For each of the seven disorders the number of positive answers represents a symptom scale score. Since the cognitive limitations of the 6 to 11 year-old children do not allow for time-related measurements, no attempt was made to incorporate follow-up questions pertaining to frequency, duration or age of onset.

SAMPLE: Valla (1996a) intended the instrument to be used for systematic screening, epidemiological population studies, clinical work and detection of children with symptoms at the subclinical level.

RELIABILITY: Internal consistency: Cronbach's alpha ranges from .64 to .83 depending on the symptom scale; and .89 when grouping the internalising (SPh, SAD, OAD, MDD) and externalising items (ADHD, ODD, CD) (Valla, Bergeron,

Bidault-Russell, St-Georges, & Gaudet, 1997). Cronbach's alpha ranges from .78 to .90 for the TERRY – African-American version (Bidaut-Russell, Valla, Thomas, Bergeron, & Lawson, 1998), and .48 to .82 for the TONI-R – Austrian version (Ederer & Buchmann, 1998) depending on the symptom scale (Buchmann, 2000; Buchmann & Ederer, 1999; Ederer, 1999). **Test-retest:** 7 to 12 days test-retest-correlations ranging from .71 to .81 depending on the symptom scale, whereby older children are more reliable than younger children; .20 to .60 or more depending on the symptom, whereby low kappas are associated with low base-rates; and .44 to .69 for the cut-off points on the various symptom scales (Valla, Bergeron, Bidault-Russell, St-Georges, & Gaudet, 1997). Moreover, 3 to 25 days test-retest correlations ranging from .77 to .88 for the symptom scales and from .70 to .75 for the diagnoses using the TERRY – African-American version (Bidaut-Russell, Valla, Thomas, Bergeron & Lawson, 1998). In addition, 5 to 15 days test-retest correlations for the INTERACTIVE DOMINIC (Valla & co-workers, 2000) ranging from .59 to .80 depending on the symptom scale; and .45 to .50 depending on the symptom (Valla & co-workers, in preparation).

VALIDITY: Results concerning **criterion-related validity** were published only for the initially purely picture-based DOMINIC questionnaire (Valla, Bergeron, Berube, Gaudet, & St-Georges, 1994), no validity data were reported for the DOMINIC-R (Valla, 1996a; Valla, Bergeron, Bidault-Russell, St-Georges, & Gaudet, 1997) and for the INTERACTIVE DOMINIC (Valla & co-workers, In prep). **Convergent:** Buchmann (2000), Buchmann and Ederer (1999) and Ederer (1999) report significant correlations between those symptom scale scores of the TONI-R – Austrian version (Ederer & Buchmann, 1998) and subscale scores of the DTK (Depression Test for Children; Rossmann, 1993) which should correlate highly with each other. **Discriminant:** Buchmann (2000); Buchmann & Ederer, 1999 and Ederer (1999) obtain no significant correlations between those symptom scale scores of the TONI-R – Austrian version (Ederer & Buchmann, 1998) and subscale scores of the DTK (Depression Test for Children; Rossmann, 1993) which should correlate poorly with each other.

LOCATION (including translations / modifications):

Valla, J.P. (1996a). *DOMINIC-R: Booklet 1 and Booklet 2* (6th Version). Unpublished Test, Riviere-des-Prairies Hospital, Research Unit, 7070, Perras Blvd., Montreal, Qc H1E 1A4, Canada.

Valla, J.P. (1996b). *TONI-R: Heft 1 und Heft 2. Deutschsprachige Version des DOMINIC-R* (6. Auflage). Nicht publizierter Test, Riviere-des-Prairies Hospital, Research Unit, 7070, Perras Blvd., Montreal, Qc H1E 1A4, Canada.

Ederer, E.M., & Buchmann, C. (1998). *TONI-R – Austrian version: Revision der Übersetzung des TONI-R und des INTERAKTIVEN TONI von Valla in Hinblick auf die Übereistimmung der Fragenformulierungen mit der deutschen Bearbeitung des DSM-III-R bzw. DSM-IV und Adaptation des TONI-R für die Verwendung bei österreichischen Kindern.* Paper, Karl-Franzens-Universität Graz, Österreich.

Valla, J.P. & co-workers (2000). *DOMINIC INTERACTIVE 1.1. Digital interactive multimedia assessment tool.* Riviere-des-Prairies Hospital, Research Unit, 7070, Perras Blvd., Montreal, Qc H1E 1A4, Canada.

Valla, J.P. & co-workers (in preperation). *INTERACTIVE DOMINIC for English speaking Caucasian children and interactive DOMINIC versions based on DSM-IV criteria for female and male children: for German speaking Caucasian children (INTERACTIVE TONI), for African-American children (INTERACTIVE TERRY), for Asian children (INTERACTIVE MING) and for Latino-Hispanic children (INTERACTIVE GABI and INTERACTIVE LUPE).* Riviere-des-Prairies Hospital, Research Unit, 7070, Perras Blvd., Montreal, Qc H1E 1A4, Canada.

COMMENT: By avoiding time-related components and increasing young children's understanding of questions using a combination of visual and auditory signals as an improvement of the initially purely picture-based DOMINIC questionnaire (Valla, Bergeron, Berube, Gaudet, & St-Georges, 1994), the DOMINIC-R questionnaire allows reliable standardised assessment of children as young as 6 years. With its original format and robust psychometric properties, this instrument brings the structured interview of young child informants in line with standard clinical practice. However, since the DOMINIC-R questionnaire only approximates DSM-III-R criteria it does not allow for DSM-III-R diagnoses. The good psychometric data obtained with the DOMINIC-R as paper questionnaire and the desire to produce an instrument to be used in different cultural/linguistic settings, combined with contemporary technological advance, led to the development of different computerised cultural/linguistic versions, the Interactive DOMINIC versions for female and male children based on DSM-IV criteria (Valla, In prep; Valla 2000; Valla, Bergeron, & Smolla, 2000).

REFERENCES:

Bidaut-Russell, M., Valla, J.P., Thomas, J.M., Bergeron, L., & Lawson, E. (1998). Reliability of the Terry: A mental health cartoon-like screener for Afrikan-American children. *Child Psychiatry and Human Development, 28,* 249-263.

Buchmann, C. (2000). *Emotionale Befindlichkeit und Verhaltensauffälligkeiten im frühen Schulalter aus der Perspektive von Kindern und ihren LehrerInnen: Erprobung eines Bildverfahrens.* Diplomarbeit an der Geisteswissenschaftlichen Fakultät der Karl-Franzens-Universität Graz.

Buchmann, C., & Ederer, E.M. (1999). *Emotionale Befindlichkeit und Verhaltensstörungen im frühen Schulalter aus der Perspektive von Kindern und ihren LehrerInnen.* Beitrag auf der wissenschaftlichen Tagung der Österreichischen Gesellschaft für Psychologie (ÖGP),

Aktuelle Ergebnisse psychologischer Forschung in Österreich, 3-4. Dezember 1999, Graz, Österreich.

Ederer, E.M. (1999, July). *Screening for mental health problems in young school children: Self- and teacher-reports.* Paper presented at the Sixth European Congress of Psychology, Rome, Italy.

Rossmann, P. (1993). *Depressionstest für Kinder (DTK).* Bern: Huber.

Valla, J.P., Bergeron, L., Berube, H., Gaudet, N., & St-Georges, M. (1994). A structured pictorial questionnaire to assess DSM-III-R-based diagnoses in children (6-11 years): Development, validity and reliability. *Journal of Abnormal Child Psychology, 22,* 403-423.

Valla, J.P., Bergeron, L., Bidault-Russell, M., St-Georges, M., & Gaudet, N. (1997). Reliability of the DOMINIC-R: A young child mental health questionnaire combining visual and auditory stimuli. *Journal of Child Psychology and Psychiatry and Allied Disciplines, 38,* 717-724.

Valla, J.P., Bergeron, L., & Smolla, N. (2000). The Dominic-R: A Pictorial Interview for 6- to 11-year-old Children. *Journal of the American Academy of Child and Adolescent Psychiatry, 39,* 85-93.

REVIEWER: Elfriede Maria Ederer, Department of Educational Psychology, University of Graz, Merangasse 70/2, A-8010 Graz, Austria, E-mail: elfriede.ederer@kfunigraz.ac.at

6.14: EDINBURGH FAMILY SCALE, THE.

AUTHOR: Blair.

VARIABLE: Family functioning.

DESCRIPTION: A self report scale of 27 items with three subscales: Enmeshment, Rigidity and Conflict devised to operationalise dimensions of Minuchin's model of the psychosomatic family. Respondents are asked to endorse statements about life in their family on a 4-point Likert scale from *Strongly agree* to *Strongly disagree*. The raw scores are summed and converted to standardised scores (T scores). There are transformation tables for adolescents (13+) and adults. It takes 10-15 minutes to complete.

SAMPLE: Suitable for use in community and clinic samples of households with an adolescent member.

RELIABILITY: **Internal Reliability:** In a community sample of 189 adults and 192 adolescents internal consistency (Cronbach's alpha) for each subscale ranged from .60 to .76 (Blair, 1996).

VALIDITY: The scale was developed through principal components analysis (orthogonal varimax rotation) with a 3 factor solution corresponding to the 3 hypothesised 'psychosomatic' dimensions. Correlation of subscales with the Family Assessment Measure (Skinner *et al.*, 1983) ranged from .50 to .75 and with the Family Assessment Device (Epstein *et al.*, 1983) from .50 to .65 (Blair, 1996). In a study of family functioning in anorexia nervosa, cystic fibrosis and well adolescents there were statistically significant correlations between Expressed Emotion (EE) emotional over-involvment and the EFS but not between EFS conflict and EE criticism (Blair *et al.*, 1995).

LOCATION: Blair, C. (1996). The Edinburgh Family Scale: A new measure of family functioning. *International Journal of Methods in Psychiatric Research, 6,* 15-22.

COMMENT: The scale has the advantage that it is derived from a theoretical model of family functioning, has fairly robust psychometric properties and has been developed through factor analysis on a large sample. Work needs to be done on discriminant validity: For example a comparison of the families of bulimia nervosa sufferers and anorexia nervosa sufferers or a comparison between families of conduct disordered or ADHD adolescents and the families of young people with emotional disorders.

REFERENCES:

Blair, C. (1996). The Edinburgh Family Scale: A new measure of family functioning. *International Journal of Methods in Psychiatric Research, 6,* 15-22.

Blair, C., Freeman, C., & Cull, A. (1995). The families of anorexia nervosa and cystic fibrosis patients. *Psychological Medicine, 25,* 985-993.

Epstein, N.B., Baldwin, A., & Bishop, D.S. (1983). The McMaster Family Assessment Device. *Journal of Marital and Family Therapy, 9,* 171-180.

Skinner, H., Steinhauser, P., & Santa- Barbara, J. (1983). The Family Assessment Measure *Canadian Journal of Community Mental Health, 2,* 91-105.

REVIEWER: Caroline Blair, Young Peoples Unit, Lothian Primary Care NHS Trust, Tipperlinn Road, Edinburgh, EH10 5HF, Scotland, U.K.

6.15: FAMILY ATTITUDE QUESTIONNAIRE (FAS), THE.

AUTHORS: Kavanagh, O'Halloran, Manicavasagar, Clark, Piatkowska, Tennant and Rosen.

DESCRIPTION: The Family Attitude Scale (FAS; Kavanagh, O'Halloran, Manicavasagar, Clark, Piatkowska, Tennant and Rosen, 1997) is a 30-item self-report measure of attitudes and behaviour towards another person. Items are rated on a 5-point scale from *Never* (0) to *Every day* (4). The FAS derives a single score based on a total of item ratings, with 10 items being reverse-scored. Higher scores reflect more negativity in the relationship. The items are reproduced in Kavanagh *et al.* (1993).

SAMPLE: The scale was originally designed for use with families who had a member with schizophrenia, but its content is applicable to any relationship, whether other person has a disorder or not, and regardless of whether they are in the same family. Normative and reliability data from the families of undergraduate students are available.

RELIABILITY: Internal consistency: The scale has demonstrated internal consistency by coefficient alpha of .94-.97, and a single-factor structure best fits the items. **Inter-rater:** Four items refer to specific behaviours (*e.g.* "I shout at him"). These items allow for a comparison of reports by the respondent and by the other person in the dyad. In a student sample, reports by the student and their mother on these items correlated .57, and student reports correlated .42 with the fathers.

VALIDITY: In families of people with schizophrenia (Kavanagh *et al.*, 1997) the FAS total score correlated significantly with Camberwell Family Interview (CFI) Criticism (Mothers: r=.66; Fathers: r=.38), Hostility (Mothers: r=.39; Fathers:

r=.31) and lack of Warmth (Mothers: r=-.42; Fathers: r=-.36). It was not significantly associated with Emotional Over-Involvement on the CFI. Total FAS scores do not provide a direct measure of the frequency of arguments in the family, since these are likely to be multiply determined. Correlations between parental FAS scores and student reports of family arguments were significant, but accounted for a relatively small proportion of the variance (e. g. argument frequency: 5.3% for mothers, 3.2% for fathers; argument duration: 11.6% for mothers, 3.2% for fathers). FAS scores of parents were significantly related to scores of their student children, indicating higher levels of anger, anger expression and (to a lesser extent) anxiety. Responses on the FAS also show substantial reciprocity (i. e. a negative view of one person in the dyad is reciprocated by the other). A student's rating of their mother correlated .49 with the mother's view of them, and their view of their father correlated .43 with the reciprocated rating.

FURTHER EMPIRICAL USES: The scale is currently being tested in studies on people with psychosis, to test its utility as a predictor of outcomes. It has been translated into German and Chinese, but these versions are still under trial and have not yet been published. The nature of the items is such that the scale may prove useful outside a clinical context. However (apart from the initial validation sample) no data on applications to populations such as families in conflict are available as yet.

LOCATION: Kavanagh, D.J., O'Halloran, P., Manicavasagar, V., Clark, D., Piatkowska, O., Tennant, C., & Rosen, A. (1997). The Family Attitude Scale: Reliability and validity of a new scale for measuring the emotional climate of families. *Psychiatry Research, 70,* 185-195.

COMMENT: This scale has potential as a measure of the negativity of relationships, particularly relating to anger, hostility and a sense of burden. If reciprocal ratings are used, a measure of relationship quality might be obtained, although there are no studies at present that assess the relationship of the FAS with other standard measures of dyadic relationships (such as the Dyadic Adjustment Scale). There are also indications that the FAS may prove useful as a predictor of psychological distress in the other person in the dyad. However there are no published data at present on its utility as a predictor of psychopathological outcomes (analogous to a prediction from expressed emotion). We must await replications of initial development studies before the utility of the FAS can be clearly established.

REFERENCES

Kavanagh, D.J., O'Halloran, P., Manicavasagar, V., Clark, D., Piatkowska, O., Tennant, C., & Rosen, A. (1997). The Family Attitude Scale: Reliability and validity of a new scale for measuring the emotional climate of families. *Psychiatry Research, 70*, 185-195.

REVIEWER: D.J. Kavanagh, Department of Psychiatry, Mental Health Center, Royal Brisbane Hospital, University of Queensland, Herston, QLD 4064, Australia.

6.16: FAMILY SATISFACTION SCALE.

AUTHORS: Carver and Jones.

VARIABLE: Satisfaction with family of origin (*i.e.*, the family in which one "grew up").

DESCRIPTION: A 20-item self-report measure of the degree to which respondent is satisfied with the family of origin (*i.e.*, the family in which one was raised). Respondents are asked to indicate degree of agreement with each statement on a 5- point Likert-type response format (*i.e.*, *Strongly agree, Agree, Undecided, Disagree, Strongly disagree*). Scores can range from 20 to 100 with higher scores indicating greater satisfaction and happiness.

SAMPLE: The scale has been used with college students and non-college adults with comparable psychometric performance.

RELIABILITY: Internal consistency: High internal consistency as indicated by coefficient alpha of .95 in a sample of 120 college students and .95 in a sample of 168 non-college adults. **Test-retest:** The temporal stability of the scale was .88 over a two month time period among 143 college students.

VALIDITY: Convergent: Several procedures demonstrated the convergent validity of the Scale as follows: (a) significant correlations (rs varied from .33 to .64) between the Family Satisfaction Scale and several of the subscales of the Family Assessment Measure (Skinner, Steinhauer & Santa-Barbara, 1984) especially denial (inversely) task acceptance, and communication; significant correlationships between the scale and subscales of the Family Environment Scale (Moos & Moos, 1974), most notably cohesion (r=.73) and expressiveness (r=.60); (b) significant correlations with selected measures of relationship satisfaction and relationship effectiveness including, for example, loneliness (r=-.28, p.<.05), marital satisfaction and commitment (rs=.37, .33, p.<.01), and both quantitative and qualitative indices of social support (rs from .31 to .71) and (c) psychological characteristics (*e.g.*, similarity, reciprocity, love, etc.) of the family network. **Discriminant:** In the above analyses, Family Satisfaction Scores were more strongly related to social support from family than to social support from friends or work/school relationships as would be expected; and scale scores were more strongly related to psychological characteristics of the family network than to the structural characteristics assessed (*e.g.*, number of members, proportion of males/females, proportion of step-siblings, if any, etc.)

LOCATION: Carver, M.D., & Jones, W.H. (1992). The Family Satisfaction Scale. *Social Behavior and Personality, 20*, 71-84.

COMMENT: The Family Satisfaction Scale has the advantages of being brief, robust, and easy to use and score. Its prinicipal limitation is that it does not partition family influence into components and it may not asses certain factors including organisation and adaptability.

REFERENCES:

Carver, M.D., & Jones, W.H. (1992). The Family Satisfaction Scale. *Social Behavior and Personality, 20*, 71-84.

Couch, L.L., Adams, J.M., & Jones, W.H. (1996). The assessment of trust orientation. *Journal of Personality Assessment, 67*, 305-323.

REVIEWER: Warren H. Jones, Department of Psychology, University of Tennessee, Knoxville, Knoxville, TN 37996 U.S.A. E-mail: wjones@utk.edu

6.17: FAMILY EMPOWERMENT SCALE.

AUTHORS: Koren, DeChillo, and Friesen.

VARIABLE: Empowerment in families.

DESCRIPTION: The Family Empowerment Scale is a 34-item rating scale designed to measure a family's empowerment status across two dimensions: levels of empowerment and the way empowerment is expressed. Each item is rated on a 5-point Likert-type scale (1=*Not true at all* to 5=*Very true*). Higher scores on each subscale indicate greater empowerment. Empowerment scores can be derived for Family, Service System, and Community/Political subscales. The scale can also be scored on the 4 factors derived by Singh, Curtis, Ellis, Nicholson, Villani, and Wechsler (1995), viz., System Advocacy, Knowledge, Competence, and Self-Efficacy.

SAMPLE: Koren, DeChillo, and Friesen (1992) intended the scale to be used for the assessment of empowerment in parents and other family caretakers whose children have emotional and behavioral disorders.

RELIABILITY: Internal consistency: It demonstrated substantial levels of internal consistency, ranging from .88 to .89 (Koren, DeChillo, & Friesen, 1992). Singh, Curtis, Ellis, Nicholson, Villani, and Wechsler (1995) reported a .93 split-half estimate of reliability, and alpha coefficients ranging from .78 to .89 for the four factors. **Test-retest:** Test-retest correlations of $r=.83$ for Family subscale, $r=.77$ for Service System subscale, and $r=.85$ for Community/Political subscale were reported based on responses from 107 family members who completed the scale after a three- to four-week interval (Koren, DeChillo, & Friesen, 1992).

VALIDITY: Three types of validity have been reported. The agreement among raters in classifying the items of the scale was .83 for Family, .70 for Service System, and .77 for the Community/Political subscale, with an overall coefficient of .77. The agreement among multiple raters on the classification scheme of the conceptual framework of the scale ranged from .47 to 1.00, with an overall average of .83. These data provide support for the correspondence of the scale item content to the constructs underlying the instrument and its subscales. In addition, the scale was able to differentiate between those parents who participated in activities indicative of empowerment and those who did not. Curtis and Singh (1966) reported that the Competence and Self-Efficacy factors of the Family Empowerment Scale correlated with the Treatment factor of the Family Involvement Scale, suggesting a relationship between parental perceptions of family empowerment at the personal level and their perception of involvement in their child's treatment.

LOCATION: Koren, P.E., DeChillo, N., & Friesen, B.J. (1992). Measuring empowerment in families whose children have emotional disabilities: A brief questionnaire. *Rehabilitation Psychology, 37*, 305-321.

COMMENT: The Family Empowerment Scale has good psychometric properties and there is increasing evidence of its usefulness in research on families (Elliott, Koroloff, Koren, & Friesen, 1998). Significant correlations have been reported between family empowerment as measured on this scale and membership in a parent support group, mental health status of the child, gender of the respondent, and respondent education (Singh, Curtis, Ellis, Wechsler, Best, & Cohen, 1997).

REFERENCES:

Curtis, W.J., & Singh, N.N. (1996). Family involvement and empowerment in mental health service provision for children with emotional and behavioral disorders. *Journal of Child and Family Studies, 5*, 503-517.

Elliott, D.J., Koroloff, N.M., Koren, P.E., & Friesen, B.J. (1998). Improving access to children's mental health services: The family associate approach. In M.H. Epstein, K. Kutash, & A. Duchnowski (Eds.), *Outcomes for Children and Youth with Behavioral and Emotional Disorders and their Families: Programs and Evaluation Best Practices* (pp. 581-609). Austin, TX: Pro-Ed.

Koren, P.E., DeChillo, N., & Friesen, B.J. (1992). Measuring empowerment in families whose children have emotional disabilities: A brief questionnaire. *Rehabilitation Psychology, 37*, 305-321.

Singh, N.N., Curtis, W.J., Ellis, C.R., Nicholson, M.W., Villani, T.M., & Wechsler, H.A. (1995). Psychometric analysis of the Family Empowerment Scale. *Journal of Emotional and Behavioral Disorders, 3*, 85-91.

Singh, N.N., Curtis, W.J., Ellis, C.R., Wechsler, H.A., Best, A.L., & Cohen, R. (1997). Empowerment status of families whose children have serious emotional disturbance and Attention Deficit/Hyperactivity Disorder. *Journal of Emotional and Behavioral Disorders, 5*, 223-229.

REVIEWERS: Nirbhay N. Singh and Subhashni D. Singh, Department of Psychiatry, Medical College of Virginia, Virginia Commonwealth University, P.O. Box 980489, Richmond, Virginia 23298-0489, U.S.A.

6.18: FACILITATING OPEN COUPLE COMMUNICATION, UNDERSTANDING, AND STUDY (FOCCUS).

AUTHORS: Markey and Micheletto.

VARIABLES: Comprehensive premarital assessment of individual and couple traits predictive of marital satisfaction.

DESCRIPTION: FOCCUS is a 156-item self-report instrument which measures a variety of premarital factors shown to predict a couples' future marital satisfaction. It is published by the Archdiocese of Omaha, Nebraska, U.S.A. and is widely used by Catholic and Protestant churches, as well as non-denominational counseling services. It is available in several languages, including Spanish, Vietnamese, Italian, Polish, Braille, and in an alternate edition for persons with limited ability to read or those who speak or read English as a second language. It is also available on audio tape for non-readers. It was designed to reflect the values and ideals of marriage as sacred including issues of permanency, fidelity, openness to children, forgiveness, shared faith in God, and unconditional love (Williams & Jurich, 1995). The non-denominational edition of the questionnaire contains the same items but with specific references to the Catholic church omitted. FOCCUS assesses most (89%) of the premarital predictors of marital satisfaction (Larson & Holman, 1994). The four content areas contain 19 scales grouped as couple match (*e.g.* similarities), skills (*e.g.* communication), bonders (*e.g.* attitudes toward sex, religion, finances, dual careers, etc.) and special concern areas (*e.g.* interchurch marriages, second marriages, and cohabitation). A computer printout of results is sent to the counselor to use with the couple. It lists the scores on all scales and all the statements for each of the 19 scales and shows on which items the partners agreed both with each other and with the 'preferred responses' (an ideal or optimum response that reflects healthy individual or couple functioning). A manual is available with counselor interpretation guidelines.

SAMPLE: Developed for use with normal populations of single adults preparing for marriage or remarriage.

RELIABILITY: **Internal consistency** ranges from .86-.98 for the 19 scales (Williams & Jurich, 1995).

VALIDITY: Content, construct, and predictive validity are reported (Williams & Jurich, 1995).

LOCATION: A manual and questionnaires are available from the Family Life Office, Archdiocese of Omaha, 3214 N. 60th St., Omaha, NE, U.S.A. 68104.

COMMENT: FOCCUS strengths include the availability of several versions for couples who do not speak English or have reading problems. Key problem areas are conveniently listed on one scale. Patterns for couple study and counselor aids on especially important individual items are very helpful in interpreting the results. Remarriage, cohabitation, and interfaith items are included. Supplemental materials are available. FOCCUS does not measure three factors that predict marital quality: parental mental illness, similarity of intelligence, and overall similarity. Objective evidence for the validity of preferred responses is missing. Interpretation is moderately difficult.

REFERENCES:
Larson, J.H., & Holman, T.B. (1994). Premarital predictors of marital quality and stability. *Family Relations*, *43*, 228-237.

Markey, B., & Micheletto, M. (1997). *Facilitating Open Couple Communication, Understanding and Study Facilitator Manual.* Omaha: Archdiocese of Omaha.

Williams, L.M., & Jurich, J., (1995). Predicting marital success after five years: Assessing the predictive validity of FOCCUS. *Journal of Marital and Family Therapy, 21,* 141-154.

REVIEWER: Jeffry H. Larson, Marriage and Family Therapy Program, School of Family Life, Brigham Young University, Provo, UT, 84602, U.S.A.

6.19: FRIENDSHIP FEATURES INTERVIEW FOR YOUNG CHILDREN (FFIYC).
AUTHORS: Ladd, Kochenderfer, and Coleman.

VARIABLE: Children's perceptions of friendship processes (validation, aid, disclosure, exclusivity, conflict) and satisfaction (contentment with friend and affect when with friend).

DESCRIPTION: Friendship Features Interview for Young Children (FFIYC; Ladd, Kochenderfer, & Coleman, 1996) is a self-report measure that taps five friendship processes and two indices of friendship satisfaction. The 24-item measure was empirically-derived from an initial set of 30 questions. Children are asked to respond to each question on a scale ranging from *no* (scored as 0), *sometimes* (scored as 1), to *yes* (scored as 2). Principal Axis Factor Analysis with oblique rotation resulted in seven distinct interpretable factors (number of items) labelled as: Validation (3 items), Aid (4), Disclosing Negative Affect (2 items), Conflict (4), Exclusivity (4), Satisfaction (4), and Affective Climate (3 items). Subscale scores are created by averaging children's scores across the items included in each subscale; higher scores indicate that the corresponding construct is perceived to be more characteristic of the child's friendship.

SAMPLE: The FFIYC was designed by Ladd, Kochenderfer, and Coleman (1996) to provide a reliable and valid instrument to assess young (ages 4 to 6 years old) children's perceptions of their friendships.

RELIABILITY: Internal consistency: Each of the empirically-derived subscales evidenced satisfactory internal consistency. Cronbach's reliability coefficients are as follows: Validation, α=.80; Aid, α=.81; Conflict, α=.65; Exclusivity, α=.67; Disclosure, α=.63; Satisfaction, α=.81; Affective Climate, α=.51).

VALIDITY: Criterion: All five of the friendship processes subscales have been demonstrated to correlate significantly with children's satisfaction with their friendships: validation (r=.39, p<.01), aid (r=.24, p<.05), disclosure of negative affect (r=.30, p<.01), exclusivity (r=.45, p<.01), conflict (r=.-34, p<.01). Discriminant: Additionally, discriminant analyses using each of the five processes produced a significant discriminant function, $x^2(5)$=36.30, p<.001, and correctly classified 84.15% of the children into either stable or unstable friendships. Perceived validation (.72) and low levels of conflict (-.63) received the highest loadings on this function.

LOCATION: Ladd, G.W., Kochenderfer, B.J., & Coleman, C.C. (1996). Friendship quality as a predictor of young children's early school adjustment. *Child Development, 67,* 1103-1118.

COMMENT: Findings for the FFIYC indicate that young children are capable of distinguishing among key friendship process and do so reliably. Moreover, data indicate that the psychological benefits or costs (*e.g.,* provisions) tapped by the

FFIYC can be used to predict children's psychoemotional and school adjustment. For example, validation and aid forecasted gains in perceived support from classmates, and aid also predicted improvements in children's school attitudes. Also, for boys, conflict in friendships was associated with higher levels of loneliness and avoidance and lower levels of school liking and engagement.

REFERENCES:

Ladd, G.W., Kochenderfer, B.J., & Coleman, C.C. (1996). Friendship quality as a predictor of young children's early school adjustment. *Child Development, 67*, 1103-1118.

REVIEWER: Becky Kochenderfer-Ladd, Department of Psychology, Illinois State University, Normal, IL 61790, U.S.A.

6.20: INTERPERSONAL COMPETENCE SCALE (ICS), THE.

AUTHORS: Cairns, Leung, Gest, and Cairns.

VARIABLE: Assesses the social and academic competence of children and adolescents.

DESCRIPTION: The Interpersonal Competence Scale (ICS; Cairns, Leung, Gest, & Cairns, 1995) is a concise set of 18 rating scales to be completed by teachers and other significant adults, such as parents and caregivers. Each item is given as a 7-point bipolar scale, with higher scores denoting more descriptive characteristics. The ICS-T comprises three primary factors: AGG (argues, trouble at school, fights), POP (popular with boys, popular with girls, lots of friends), and ACA (spelling, math), as well as three secondary factors: AFF (smile, friendly), OLY (appearance, sports, wins) and INT (shyness, sad, worry). The third factor, INT, was added to create a revised version of the ICS in 1988 and consequently, there is less psychometric data for this sub-scale.

SAMPLES: The ICS-T has primarily been used to measure the interpersonal competence of participants included in the Carolina Longitudinal Study (CLS; Cairns, Leung et al., 1995). A total of 695 young people from this study, aged 10- to 20- years from seven public schools in two cohorts have been assessed using the ICS-T. This sample represents a considerable demographic range: gender, age, socioeconomic status and ethnicity were all accounted for. The scale was originally designed for this population, and the resulting profiles were factor analyzed to create the present ICS-T. In addition to the substantial sample of children and adolescents involved in the CLS, the scale has been used in a number of diverse settings. These include investigations of the social networks and perceptions of Chinese children (Leung, 1996), the development of social behavior in Taiwanese school children (Sun, 1992), and the relation between aggression and self-destructive behavior in high school students (Sussman, 1991; reported in Cairns et al., 1995). The scale has also been employed to examine female social groups during summer camp (Edwards, 1995) and the social behavior of antisocial adolescents (Clarke, 1993; reported in Cairns et al., 1995).

RELIABILITY: Internal consistency: According to Cairns et al. (1995) Cronbach's (alpha) coefficients are .82 for the ICS-T AGG factor, .81 for the ICS-T POP factor, .71 for the ICS-T ACA factor, .71 for the ICS-T AFF factor, and .67 for the ICS-T OLY factor (Cairns et al., 1995). Internal consistency data are unavailable for the INT sub-scale. The coefficient for the SC, or summed interpersonal competence score, was found to be .84 (Cairns et al., 1995). These results would suggest acceptable levels of internal consistency. Test-retest: Reports of both short-term reliability and long-term stability are available for the

ICS-T. Reliability measured at three weeks was found to be quite strong: a correlation of $r=.91$ for the summed SC factor score has been reported (Cairns et al., 1995). Analyses of long-term test-retest reliability coefficients range from .20 to .50 over a 5-yr and 8-yr period (Cairns et al., 1995). Only the AFF factor was non-significant over time.

VALIDITY: Convergent: Reports have demonstrated acceptable levels of convergent validity as measured by adjustment at maturity. Included is high school dropout (Cairns, Cairns & Neckerman, 1989; Mahoney & Cairns, 1997), teenage parenthood, imprisonment, attempted suicide and mortality (Cairns & Cairns, 1994), as well as membership in a social network (Cairns et al., 1988). Overall, the AGG factor was found to have the strongest predictive power. Discriminant: Children identified by the ICS-T as being at risk of extreme aggression were found to exhibit significantly more negative, hostile and aggressive behavior (as measured by re-administering the ICS and peer nominations) than children not at any apparent risk for such behavior (Cairns et al., 1995; Cairns & Cairns, 1994).

LOCATION: Cairns, R.B., Leung, M., Gest, S., & Cairns, B.D. (1995). A brief method for assessing social development: Structure, reliability, stability and developmental validity of the Interpersonal Competence Scale. Behavioral Research and Therapy, 33, 725-736.

COMMENT: The Interpersonal Competence Scale appears to be an effective measure of social development, compromised by neither its brevity nor the possibility of multiple teachers, or raters, over time. However, it would appear that the AGG sub-scale holds the most significance, in terms of both reliability and validity. A self-report form of the ICS has been devised for students to describe themselves. Although the scale is similar to the teacher/parent form, there are a number of considerable differences, particularly those involving psychometric and predictive properties (Cairns et al., 1995). Projected academic competence has, in particular, been found to significantly differ when assessed using the self-report and teacher reports of the scale (Xie, Mahoney, & Cairns, 1999).

REFERENCES:

Cairns, R.B., Cairns, B.D., Neckerman, H.J., Gest, S., & Gariepy, J.L. (1988). Social networks and aggressive behavior: Peer support or peer rejection? *Developmental Psychology, 25,* 320-330.

Cairns, R. B., Cairns, B. D., & Neckerman, H.J. (1989). Early school dropout: Configurations and determinants. *Child Development, 60,* 1437-1452.

Cairns, R.B., & Cairns, B.D. (1994). *Lifelines and Risks: Pathways of Youth in our Time.* London: Harvester Wheatsheaf.

Cairns, R.B., Leung, M.C., Gest, S.D., & Cairns, B.D. (1995). A brief method for assessing social development: Structure, reliability, stability and developmental validity of the Interpersonal Competence Scale. *Behavioral Research and Therapy, 33,* 725-736.

Edwards, C.A. (1995). Leadership in groups of school-age girls. *Developmental Psychology, 30,* 920-927.

Leung, M.C. (1996). Social networks and self enhancement in Chinese children: A comparison of self reports and peer reports of group membership. *Social Development, 5,* 146-157.

Mahoney, J.L., & Cairns, R.B. (1997). Do extracurricular activities protect against early school dropout? *Developmental Psychology, 33,* 241-253.

Sun, S.L. (1992, March). *Social relationships of children and adolescents in Taiwan.* Poster presented at meeting of Society of Research in Adolescence, Washington, D.C.

Xie, H., Mahoney, J.L., & Cairns, R.B. (1999). Through a looking glass or a hall of mirrors? Self-ratings and teacher-ratings of academic competence over development. *International Journal of Behavioral Development, 23*, 163-183.

REVIEWERS: Subhadra White and Thomas Keenan, Department of Psychology, University of Canterbury, Christchurch, New Zealand. E-mail: t.keenan@psych.canterbury.ac.nz

6.21: MARITAL SATISFACTION AND COMMITMENT SCALES.
AUTHORS: Jones, Adams, Monroe, and Berry.

VARIABLES: Marital Satisfaction and Marital Commitment.

DESCRIPTION: A 30-item self-report inventory designed to assess marital satisfaction (MS) and marital commitment (MC) to one's marital relationship (Jones, Adams, Monroe, & Berry, 1995). Each scale contains 15 items for which responses are rendered on a five point Likert-type response format as follows: 1=*Strongly disagree*, 2=*Disagree*; 3=*Undecided*; 4=*Agree*; and 5=*Strongly agree*. Nine items across the two scales are reversed for scoring purposes. Scores on both scales may vary from 15 to 75.

SAMPLE: The scale was developed primarily to assess satisfaction and commitment among currently married individuals and has been administered to several samples of married individuals with the total number of participants exceeding 2,000 (Jones, Adams, Monroe, & Berry, 1995). In addition, with minor rewording of items the scale has been used also to measure satisfaction and commitment among divorced individuals with respect to their former spouse and among heterosexual dating couples (Rostosky, Welsh, Kawaguchi, & Galliher, 1999).

RELIABILITY: Internal consistency: Coefficient alpha was .96 for MS and .89 for MC among a sample of over 900 married participants with mean interitem correlations of .65 and .46, respectively (Jones *et al.*, 1995). **Test-retest:** Sixty-one respondents completed the scales twice separated by a period of two months. As would be expected, MC scores showed greater stability over time ($r=.68$) than did MS scores ($r=.51$).

VALIDITY: Convergent: Validity of scale interpretations was supported by the fact that MS and MC scores were significantly related in expected directions with alternative measures of similar constructs such as Marital Adjustment, Attitudes Toward Love, Constraint Commitment, and Personal Dedication as well as biographic characteristics such as relationship length, number of times married, number of children, and church attendance. Also, MS and MC scores of a small sample of husbands and wives were significantly correlated with one another thereby further supporting the validity of these measures. **Discriminant:** A factor analysis of item responses indicated that all MS items loaded on the first of two factors and the factor that appeared to connote happiness with one's marriage; the second factor which appeared to indicate an intention to maintain one's marriage showed higher loadings for 4 of the MC items. However, the remaining MC items loaded more highly on the first factor.

LOCATION: Jones, W.H., Adams, J.M., Monroe, P.R., & Berry, J.O. (1995). A psychometric exploration of marital satisfaction and commitment. *Journal of Social Behavior and Personality, 10,* 923-932.

COMMENT: The Marital Satisfaction and Commitment Scales show good internal and temporal reliability and an interpretable pattern of concurrent and construct validity correlates. However, questions remain with respect to the Discriminant validity of the MC scale and the independence of the satisfaction and commitment constructs.

REFERENCES:

Adams, J.M., & Jones, W.H. (1997). The conceptualization of marital commitment: An integrative analysis. *Journal of Personality and Social Psychology, 72*, 1177-1196.

Jones, W.H., Adams, J.M., Monroe, P.R., & Berry, J.O. (1995). A psychometric exploration of marital satisfaction and commitment. *Journal of Social Behavior and Personality, 10*, 923-932.

Rostosky, S.S., Welsh, D.P. Kawaguchi, M.C., & Galliher, R.V. (1999). Commitment and sexual behaviors in adolescent dating relationships. In J. M. Adams, & W. H. Jones (Eds.). *Handbook of Interpersonal Commitment and Relationship Stability.* (pp 323-338). New York: Kluwer Academic/Plenum.

REVIEWER: Warren H. Jones, Department of Psychology, University of Tennessee, Knoxville, Knoxville, TN 37996, U.S.A. E-mail: wjones@utk.edu

6.22: MARITAL INTIMACY QUESTIONNAIRE (MIQ).
AUTHORS: Van den Broucke, Vertommen, and Vandereycken.

DESCRIPTION: Self-report questionnaire measuring 5 dimensions of marital intimacy: Intimacy problems, Consensus, Openness, Affection, Commitment.

Key words include marital intimacy, relationship state, self-report, multidimensional measure. There are 56 items on a 5-point Likert-type and include: *intimacy problems* - My partner and I don't always know what we can expect from each other; *consensus* - My partner and I completely understand each other, *openness* - I can entrust the most intimate things to my partner, *affection* - My partner and I like to do things together, *Commitment* - My partner and I remain faithful to each other. Per subscale the item scores (0-4) must be summed. For the negatively keyed items, the item scores must first be reversed (0=4, 1=3).

SAMPLE: Samples include: 93 married/cohabiting couples in Dutch-speaking Belgium (all Caucasian; men 22-40 years; women 21-38 years; 0 to 4 children; lower to upper middle class); 101 married/cohabiting couples in Dutch-speaking Belgium (all Caucasian; men 21-54 years; women 21-50 years; 12% childless; lower to upper middle class); 21 maritally distressed couples in Dutch-speaking Belgium (all Caucasian; mean age 33.6 for men and 31.9 for women; average of 1.6 children; lower to upper middle class); 21 couples with the female partner diagnosed as anorexic or bulimic (all Caucasian; mean age 31.2 for men and 28.9 for women; average of .7 children; lower to upper middle class).

RELIABILITY: Internal consistencies (α's): .86 for intimacy problems, .86 for consensus, .83 for openness, .82 for affection and .70 for commitment.

VALIDITY: Construct: Positive correlations (r=.21 to .47) of the consensus, openness, affection and commitment scales, and negative correlations (r=-.30 and r=-.45) of the intimacy problems subscale with measures of perceived global intimacy and communication intimacy; Negative correlations (r=-.13 to -.64) of the consensus, openness, affection and commitment scales, and positive correlations (r=.32 to .60) of the intimacy problems subscale with the marital, sexual and general life dissatisfaction scales of the Maudsley Marital

Questionnaire (MMQ). **Discriminant:** Significant discrimination ($p<.001$) between maritally distressed and nondistressed couples by all five the subscales.

LOCATION: Van den Broucke, S., Vertommen, H., & Vandereycken, W. (1995). Construction and validation of a marital intimacy questionnaire. *Family Relations*, *44*, 285-290.

REFERENCES:

Van den Broucke, S., Vandereycken, W., & Vertommen, H. (1995). Marital intimacy in patients with an eating disorder: A controlled self-report study. *British Journal of Cinical Psychology, 34*, 67-78.

Van den Broucke, S., Vertommen, H., & Vandereycken, W. (1995). Construction and validation of a marital intimacy questionnaire. *Family Relations, 44*, 285-290.

REVIEWER: S. Van den Broucke, Department of Psychology, Catholic University of Leuven, Tiensestraat, 102, 3000, Leuven, Belgium

6.23: MATERNAL ANTENATAL ATTACHMENT SCALE AND PATERNAL ANTENATAL ATTACHMENT SCALE
AUTHOR: Condon.

VARIABLE: Intensity and quality of maternal (or paternal) emotional attachment to the foetus.

DESCRIPTION: The Maternal Scale (Condon, 1993) comprises 19 self-report items and the paternal scale comprises 16 items. The items concern the expectant parent's thoughts, feelings and behaviours towards the unborn baby. Both positive and negative aspects are covered. Respondents are requested to answer each item in terms of their experiences over the previous two weeks. Each item is rated on a five-point scale. The instrument has two sub-scales, viz: 'Quality' of attachment (comprising closeness/distance, tenderness/irritation, positive/negative thoughts etc) and 'Intensity' of attachment which is concerned with the amount of time which the expectant parent spends preoccupied with his/her foetus. Scores on these two dimensions of attachment enable the respondent to be categorised into a typology of attachment involving four quadrants, corresponding to high or low scores on each of the two sub-scales. The original properties of the instrument were examined on a sample of 150 women attending a routine antenatal clinic at an Australian teaching hospital. In a subsequent study, the instrument was administered to a further 238 woman in the third trimester of pregnancy.

RELIABILITY: **Internal consistency:** Global scores on the instruments have an alpha value in excess of .8 (Condon, 1993).

VALIDITY: Factor analytic studies have been published supporting the construct validity of the instrument (Condon, 1993), and further evidence is contained in an exploration of the correlates of antenatal attachment (Condon & Corkindale, 1997).

LOCATION: Copies of the instrument are available from the author on request at no charge.

COMMENT: The instrument has been translated into several languages and is being utilised in a number of investigations of the psychology of pregnancy and pregnancy loss.

742   Developmental Psychology

Condon, J.T. (1985). The parental-foetal relationship : A comparison of male and
female expectant parents. *Journal of Psychosomatic Obstetrics and
Gynaecology*, 4, 277 -284.

Condon, J.T. (1993). The assessment of antenatal emotional attachment:
development of a questionnaire instrument. *British Journal of Medical
Psychology*, 66, 167-183.

Condon, J.T., & Corkindale, C. (1997). The correlates of antenatal attachment in
pregnant women. *British Journal of Medical Psychology*, 70, 359-372.

REVIEWER: John Condon, Department of Psychiatry, Repatriation General
Hospital Daw Park, South Australia 5041, Australia.

6.24: MATERNAL PARENT-TO-INFANT ATTACHMENT SCALE AND PATERNAL
PARENT-TO-INFANT ATTACHMENT SCALE
AUTHORS: Condon and Corkindale.

VARIABLES: The intensity and quality of the attachment between the parent and
infant under the age of 1 year.

DESCRIPTION: Both the maternal and paternal instruments comprise 19 self-report
items. The items include thoughts, feelings and behaviours towards the infant
when the infant is present and absent. Higher scores indicate higher
quality/intensity of attachment. Three sub scales can be derived from the
instrument and comprised *Quality of Attachment*, *Absence of hostility*, and
Pleasure in interaction.

SAMPLE: The maternal instrument was derived, and its properties explored, on a sample of approximately 200 women assessed at 4 weeks, 4 months and 8 months postnatally. The paternal instrument was designed on the basis of a sample of 65 men in the first postnatal year.

RELIABILITY: Reliability data is only available for the maternal instrument and has been calculated at .8 at each of the three postnatal assessment points. Test re-test reliability has been calculated as in excess of .8, with an intraclass correlation coefficient of .7.

VALIDITY: The instrument has not been assessed against behavioural measures of maternal-infant attachment. Evidence for construct validity is derived from the published factor analytic analysis.

LOCATION: The instrument is available from the author on request at no charge.

COMMENT: Both instruments should be regarded as still in their developmental stage. However, they do provide a measure of parent-infant attachment which can be obtained rapidly and at minimal costs as compared to the more widely used measures based on behavioural observation.

REFERENCES:

Condon J.T., & Corkindale C.J. (1998). The assessment of parent-to-infant attachment: Development of a self-report questionnaire instrument. *Journal of Reproductive and Infant Psychology* , *16*, 57-76.

REVIEWER: John Condon, Department Of Psychiatry, Repatriation General Hospital, Daw Park, South Australia 5041, Australia

6.25: MATERNAL SERUM SCREENING KNOWLEDGE QUESTIONNAIRE (MSSKQ).
AUTHORS: Goel, Glazier, Holzapfel, Pugh, and Summers.

VARIABLE: Knowledge of maternal serum screening.

DESCRIPTION: The Maternal Serum Screening Knowledge Questionnaire (MSSKQ; Goel, Glazier, Holzapfel, Pugh, & Summers, 1996) is a 14-item scale designed to assess women's knowledge about the Maternal Serum Screening prenatal test. The test items were derived from a review of educational materials, the literature and expert opinion. The scale has four domains: test characteristics, indications and timing, ancillary tests and target conditions. Responses are scored on a 5-point scale.

SAMPLE: The scale is intended for use in populations of pregnant women.

RELIABILITY: Internal consistency: Internal consistency was assessed with Cronbach's alpha as .74. **Test-retest:** Test-retest correlation was .76 with a 1-2 week interval.

VALIDITY: Convergent: Scores were related to income and education, with higher socio-economic women demonstrating higher knowledge levels. Higher scores were achieved by those who had heard of the test, had discussed it with their health care providers and who had received written materials (Goel *et al.*, 1996). In a randomised trial of an educational intervention for pregnant women the MSSKQ discriminated between those who received a pamphlet on Maternal Serum Screening compare with those who received a general prenatal pamphlet (Glazier *et al.*, 1997). **Discriminant:** MSSKQ was not independently associated with medical history or other clinical factors not expected to be related to knowledge (Goel *et al.*, 1998).

LOCATION: Goel, V., Glazier, R., Holzapfel, S., Pugh, P., & Summers, A. (1996). Evaluating Patient's Knowledge of Maternal Serum Screening. *Prenatal Diagnosis, 16*, 425-430.

COMMENT: The scale has been used to assess knowledge in a population-based sample (Goel *et al.*, 1998) and in a prospective randomised trial (Glazier *et al.*, 1997). It has also been applied in program evaluation in a variety of countries. The instrument can be a valuable adjunct in assessing the implementation of prenatal screening programs.

REFERENCES:

Glazier, R., Goel, V., Holzapfel, S., Summers, A., Pugh, P., & Yeung, M. (1997). Written patient information about triple-marker screening: A randomized, controlled trial. *Obstetrics and Gynecology. 90*, 769-74.

Goel, V., Glazier, R., Holzapfel, S., Pugh, P., & Summers, A. (1996). Evaluating Patient's Knowledge of Maternal Serum Screening. *Prenatal Diagnosis, 16*, 425-430.

Goel, V., Glazier, R., Summers, A., & Holzapfel, S. (1998). Psychological outcomes following maternal serum screening: A cohort study. *Canadian Medical Association Journal 159*, 651-6.

REVIEWER:Vivek Goel, Department of Health Administration, University of Toronto, ON M4N 3MS, Canada.

6.26: MORAL AUTHORITY SCALE (MAS-R), THE REVISED
AUTHOR: White.

VARIABLE: Attributed level of influence to five sources of moral authority

DESCRIPTION: The revised Moral Authority Scale (White, 1997) is derived from Henry's (1983) content reformulation of Kohlberg's (1987) formalistic notions of moral judgement development. The revised MAS-R consists of six moral issues, each of which requires an open-ended moral decision followed by the rating of five statements, each designed to exemplify a source of moral authority: Self Interest, Family, Educators, Society's Welfare and Equality. Subjects are required to rate on a ten-point scale, the level of influence each of the five statements has on their moral decision. A total score for the level of influence is determined for each source.

SAMPLE: White (1996b, 1997) intended the scale to be used for the assessment of the attributed level of influence of sources of moral authority in adolescent and adult populations.

RELIABILITY: Internal consistency: Demonstrated satisfactory levels of internal reliability (White, 1997) for each of the five source subscales: Self Interest (.88), Family (.93), Educators (.93), Society's Welfare (.75), and Equality (.82) among 364 participants aged 14-60 years. **Item-Total correlation:** White (1997) reported significant and substantial item-total correlations for each of the five source subscales with an average correlation coefficient=.80 among 364 participants aged 14-60 years. **Test-retest:** White (1997) reported test-retest correlations for each of the five source subscales: Self Interest (.96), Family (.98), Educators (.97), Society's Welfare (.95), and Equality (.92) among 285 participants aged 14-60 years after a four week interval.

VALIDITY: **Convergent:** White (1997) demonstrated satisfactory convergent validity with various measures of moral judgement, including moral reasoning as measured by the Defining Issues Test (Rest, 1979) and attitudes to prosocial behaviour as measured by the Visions of Morality Scale (Shelton & Me Adams, 1990) among 364 participants aged 14-60 years. **Discriminant:** White (1997) demonstrated that the MAS-R discriminated significantly between respondents with different political and religious affiliations among 364 participants aged 14-60 years. **Demographics:** White (in press) reported significant gender differences among 159 female and 60 male adolescents on Family and Equality sources of moral authority. With females attributing significantly greater influence to each of these sources in their moral decision making when compared to males.

FURTHER EMPIRICAL USES: Recent applications of the MAS-R within the family context have found that family members' perceptions of family cohesion, adaptability and communication are significantly associated with different levels of attributed influence to different sources of moral authority as measured by the MAS-R (White, 2000).

LOCATION: White, F.A. (1997). Measuring the content of moral judgement development: The revised Moral Authority Scale (MAS-R). *Social Behaviour and Personality, 24*, 321-334.

COMMENT: There is growing evidence for the more than satisfactory psychometric properties of the revised Moral Authority Scale (MAS-R). Particularly, the MAS-R has the potential to answer some important empirical questions regarding the socialisation of moral thought (White, 1996a; 2000).

REFERENCES:

Henry, R. (1983). *The Psychodynamic Foundations of Morality.* New York: Basel.

Kohlberg, L. (1987). *The Measurement of Moral-Judgement.* Cambridge: Cambridge University Press.

Rest, J.R. (1979). *Development in Judging Moral Issues.* Minneapolis, Minnesota: University of Minnesota Press.

Shelton, C.M., & Me Adams, D.P. (1990). In search of an everyday morality: the development of a measure. *Adolescence, 25,* 923-943.

White, F.A. (1996a). Family processes as predictors of adolescent's preferences for ascribed sources of moral authority. *Adolescence, 31,* 133-144.

White, F.A. (1996b). Sources of influence in moral thought: The new Moral Authority Scale (MAS). *Journal of Moral Education,* 25, 421-439.

White, F.A. (1997). Measuring the content of moral judgement development: The revised Moral Authority Scale (MAS-R). *Social Behaviour and Personality, 24,* 321-3 34.

White, F.A. (2000). Relationship of family socialisation processes to adolescent moral thought. *Journal of Social Psychology, 140,* 75-93.

White, F.A. (in press). Family processes involved in the transmission of moral thought between adolescents and their parents. *Australian Journal of Psychology.*

REVIEWER: Fiona A. White, Department of Psychology, University of Western Sydney, Macarthur, PO Box 555, Campbelltown NSW 2560, Australia. E-mail: f.white@uws.edu.au

6.27: PARENT-CHILD CONFLICT QUESTIONNAIRE.
AUTHOR: Frankel.

VARIABLE: Parental knowledge of parenting skills.

DESCRIPTION: The Parent-Child Conflict Questionnaire (Frankel, 1993) is a criterion-referenced test geared to prominent behaviorally oriented child compliance training where the parent is the agent of change for problematic child behavior. The scale contains 10 multiple choice questions which describe vignettes covering effective commands, praising appropriate behavior, ignoring and setting limits on inappropriate behavior and providing appropriate structure to children, ages 4 to 10 years old. Respondents are asked to pick the alternative they should do in each situation. Higher scores on the scale indicate a better knowledge of what should be done.

SAMPLE: Clinic sample was 60 mothers and 19 fathers of children referred to two different outpatient parenting clinics (mean age was 34.8 years, 72.3% were Caucasian). Nonclinic sample was 43 mothers and 2 fathers (95.2% were Caucasian) coming to hear community-based lectures on parenting.

RELIABILITY: Average Spearman-Brown corrected split-half reliability was .68. Coefficient alpha was .68.

VALIDITY: Discriminant: Number of correct items was submitted to a Group (Clinic vs. Nonclinic) X Educational Level (High school vs. College) X Number of Children Reared (1 vs. 2 vs. 3 or more). Results showed that the Nonclinic group had significantly more correct than the Nonclinic group.

LOCATION: Frankel, F. (1993). A brief test of parental behavioral skills. *Journal of Behavior Therapy and Experimental Psychiatry, 24,* 227-231.

COMMENT: One of the most interesting findings was a statistically significant Group X Number of Children interaction. While Nonclinic parents who reared more children scored higher on this test, Clinic parents did not. It has been a frequent clinical observation that Clinic parents are 'stuck' in ineffective modes of parenting while Nonclinic parents tend to change parenting practices based upon the effects upon their children. The present results suggest that this may be a knowledge as opposed to performance deficit.

REFERENCES:

Frankel, F. (1993). A brief test of parental behavioral skills. *Journal of Behavior Therapy and Experimental Psychiatry, 24,* 227-231.

REVIEWER: Fred Frankel, Department of Psychiatry & Biobehavioral Sciences, University of California at Los Angeles, Los Angeles, California 90095-6967, U.S.A.

6.28: PARENT SATISFACTION QUESTIONNAIRE, THE.
AUTHOR: Stallard.

VARIABLE: Parental satisfaction with a community child and adolescent mental health services.

DESCRIPTION: Postal satisfaction questionnaire consisting of 15 fixed choice and 4 open questions. The questionnaire assesses satisfaction with pre-appointment wait and provision of information, place of appointment in terms of location, physical environment and accessibility, the meetings with the psychologist and who was involved, the length, duration and timing of appointments, and outcome both in terms of change and overall satisfaction. Fixed choice items are scored on a 4-point scale with the lowest score 1 being attributed to the most positive dimension and the highest to the most negative.

SAMPLE: Stallard (1996) intends the scale to be used to assess parental satisfaction with community child and adolescent mental health services.

RELIABILITY: Internal reliability: Analysis of responses to 57 questionnaires revealed good internal consistency with a coefficient of .82 (Stallard, 1996a). Test-retest: A group of 32 parents completed the questionnaire on two separate occasions, an average of 41 days apart. Overall reliability of the questionnaire was good (r=.82) with similar coefficients for the pre-appointment (r=.82) and outcome sections (r=.80) with lower although significant coefficients for the sections concerned with meeting the therapist (r=.66) and appointments (r=.42). (Stallard, 1996a). Factor analysis: The questionnaire provides a three-factor structure relating to the outcome of contact, appointments, and the timing and amount of contact. (Stallard, 1996a).

VALIDITY: Construct: Assessed by examining the relationship between individual questionnaire items. Feeling understood by the psychologist and overall satisfaction (r=.73) and length of wait and satisfaction with the wait (r=.67) demonstrated good correlations (Stallard, 1996a). Concurrent: Assessed by examining family and psychologist ratings of outcome. Analysis of 57 paired ratings produced a correlation of r=.36 (Stallard, 1996a).

LOCATION: Stallard, P. (1996). Validity and reliability of the Parent Satisfaction Questionnaire. *British Journal of Clinical Psychology, 35*, 311-318.

COMMENT: Satisfaction with health services is increasingly seen as a useful way of evaluating outcomes and monitoring service quality (Donabedian, 1992; Fitzpatrick, 1991). Methodological shortfalls severely limit the conclusions of many studies which seldom consider the psychometric properties of the satisfaction scales they develop (Stallard, 1996b).

REFERENCES:

Donabedian, A. (1992). Quality assurance in health care: Consumer's role. *Quality in Health Care, 1,* 247-251.

Fitzpatrick, R. (1991). Surveys of patient satisfaction: 1. Important general considerations. *British Medical Journal, 302,* 887-889.

Stallard, P. (1995). Parental satisfaction with intervention: Differences between respondents and non-respondents to a postal questionnaire. *British Journal of Clinical Psychology, 34,* 397-405.

Stallard, P. (1996a). Validity and reliability of the Parent Satisfaction Questionnaire. *British Journal of Clinical Psychology, 35,* 311-318.

Stallard, P. (1996b). The role and use of consumer satisfaction surveys in mental health services. *Journal of Mental Health, 5,* 333-348.

Stallard, P., Hudson, J., & Davis, B. (1992). Consumer evaluation in practice. *Journal of Community and Applied Social Psychology, 2,* 291-295.

REVIEWER: Paul Stallard, Department of Child & Family Psychiatry, Royal United Hospital, Combe Park, Bath, BA1 3NG, England, U.K.

6.29: PARENTAL STRESS SCALE, THE.

AUTHORS: Berry and Jones.

VARIABLE: Stress associated with raising children.

DESCRIPTION: This is a self-report scale which contains 18 items representing pleasure or positive themes of parenthood (emotional benefits, self-enrichment, personal development) and negative components (demands on resources, opportunity costs and restrictions). Respondents were asked to agree or disagree with items in terms of their typical relationship with their child or children and to rate each item on a 5-point scale: *Strongly disagree* (1), *Disagree* (2), *Undecided* (3), *Agree* (4), and *Strongly agree* (5). The 8 positive items are reverse scored so that possible scores on the scale can range between 18-90. Higher scores on the scale indicate greater stress.

SAMPLE: Berry and Jones (1995) intended the scale to be used for the assessment of parental stress for both mothers and fathers and for parents of children with and without clinical problems.

RELIABILITY: Internal consistency: This scale demonstrated satisfactory levels of internal reliability (.83) (Berry & Jones, 1995; Berry & Rao, 1997). **Test-retest:** Berry and Jones (1995) reported a test-retest correlation of $r=.81$ for 61 parents over a 6 week interval .

VALIDITY: Convergent: This scale demonstrated satisfactory convergent validity with various measures of stress, emotion, and role satisfaction, including perceived stress (Berry & Jones, 1995; Berry & Rao, 1997), work/family stress (Berry & Rao, 1997), loneliness, anxiety, guilt, marital satisfaction, marital commitment, job satisfaction, and social support (Berry & Jones, 1995).

Discriminant: Discriminant analyses demonstrated the ability of the scale to discriminate between parents of typically developing children and parents of children with both developmental and behavioral problems (Berry & Jones, 1995).

LOCATION: Berry, J.O., & Jones, W.H. (1995). The Parental Stress Scale: Initial psychometric evidence. *Journal of Social and Personal Relationships*, *12*, 463-472.

COMMENT: The Parental Stress Scale is specific to the construct of interest, is appropriate for both mothers and fathers and for parents of children with and without clinical problems, and is brief and easy to administer and score. Additional data are needed to assess the covariation between the scale and other measures of interpersonal functioning, attitudes and emotions and to determine if the scale is an appropriate measure for broader socioeconomic and ethnic groups, for single parents, and for various clinical populations.

REFERENCES:
Berry, J.O., & Jones, W.H. (1995). The Parental Stress Scale: Initial psychometric evidence. *Journal of Social and Personal Relationships*, *12*, 463-472.
Berry, J.O., & Rao, J.M. (1997). Balancing employment and fatherhood: A systems perspective. *Journal of Family Issues*, *18*, 386-402.

REVIEWER: Judy O. Berry, Department of Psychology, The University of Tulsa, 600 S. College, Tulsa, OK 74104-3189, U.S.A. E-mail: judy-berry@utulsa.edu

6.30: PREMARITAL PERSONAL AND RELATIONSHIP EVALUATION (PREPARE).

AUTHORS: Olson, Fournier, and Druckman.

VARIABLES: Comprehensive premarital assessment of individual and couple traits

DESCRIPTION: PREPARE (Olson *et al.*, 1996), published by Life Innovations, Inc., is a 195-item self-report inventory designed to measure premarital *relationship strengths* and *work areas* in 11 categories. In addition to the standard form, the PREPARE-MC (Marriage with Children) version is available for use when one or both of the premarital partners have children. The 11 relationship areas assessed by PREPARE include 89% of the premarital factors that predict marital satisfaction (Larson & Holman, 1994). They include: marriage expectations, personality issues, communication, conflict resolution, financial management, leisure activities, sexual relationship, children and parenting, family and friends, role relationship, and spiritual beliefs. Factors missing include presence of parental mental illness, similarity of intelligence, and overall similarity. A separate Idealistic Distortion scale serves as a correction score for idealism or the tendency to answer items in socially acceptable ways. Four additional scales on PREPARE assess cohesion and adaptability in the current couple relationship and each individual's family of origin. PREPARE also assesses four personality traits: Assertiveness, self-confidence, avoidance ('a person's tendency to minimise issues and reluctance to deal with issues directly') and partner dominance. The counselor receives a computerised report to share with the couple. A counselor's manual contains detailed information on how to organise feedback to the couple.

SAMPLE: Designed for use with normal populations of single adults preparing for marriage or remarriage.

RELIABILITY: **Internal consistency** reliabilities of .73 to .85 for the 11 scales are reported (Olson, Fournier, & Druckman, 1996). Mean **test-retest** reliability is .80.

VALIDITY: Olson, Fournier, and Druckman (1996) report content, construct, and concurrent validity. Larson and Olson (1989) and Fowers and Olson (1986) report predictive validity.

LOCATION: PREPARE questionnaires and manuals can be ordered from Life Innovations, Box 190, Minneapolis, MN 55440-0190, U.S.A.

COMMENT: PREPARE's strengths include its relatively short length, comprehensiveness, and ease of administration. Excellent supplemental counseling materials are available. There are English and Spanish versions and a version for couples who are remarrying. PREPARE is the most expensive of the three major premarital assessment instruments reviewed. It is relatively more difficult to interpret the results to couples. Counselors must complete an instructor training workshop or video tape self-study before using PREPARE.

REFERENCES

Fowers, B.J., & Olson, D.H. (1986). Predicting marital success with PREPARE: A predictive validity study. *Journal of Marital and Family Therapy, 12,* 403-413.

Fowers, B.J., Montel, K.H., & Olson, D.H. (1996). Predicting marital success for premarital couple types based on PREPARE. *Journal of Marital and Family Therapy, 22,* 103-119.

Larson, A.S., & Olson, D.H. (1989). Predicting marital satisfaction using PREPARE: A replication study. *Journal of Marital and Family Therapy, 15,* 311-322.

Olson, D.H. (1996). *PREPARE/ENRICH Counselor's Manual*. Minneapolis, MN: Life Innovations.

Olson, D.H., Fournier, D., & Druckman, J. (1996). *PREPARE*. Minneapolis: Life Innovations.

REVIEWER: Jeffry H. Larson, Marriage and Family Therapy Program, School of Family Life, Brigham Young University, Provo, UT 84602, U.S.A.

6.31: PRESCHOOL PLAY BEHAVIOR SCALE, THE.

AUTHORS: Coplan and Rubin.

VARIABLES: Different forms of children's social and nonsocial play behaviors.

DESCRIPTION: The Preschool Play Behavior Scale (PPBS) is an 18-item questionnaire designed to assess a number of specific free play behaviors. Teachers rate items on a 5-point Likert scale, denoting frequency of occurrence (1=*Never*, 2=*Hardly ever*, 3=*Sometimes*, 4=*Often*, 5=*Very often*). The first three sub-scales assess three distinct forms of nonsocial play behaviors. This includes *reticent* behavior (unoccupied and onlooker behaviors), *solitary-passive* behavior (solitary-constructive and -exploratory behaviors), and *solitary-active* behavior (solitary -dramatic and -functional behaviors). The final two sub-scales assess *social* play (group play and peer conversation), and *rough*-play.

SAMPLE: The scale was intended for use with preschool-aged children.

RELIABILITY: Internal consistency: The factor structure of the PPBS was established in a sample of 337 preschoolers. Item factor loadings for all subscales were above .63, with no items cross-loading on any other factors. An identical pattern of results was observed when the factor analysis was repeated separately for males and females. Measures of internal consistency for the five sub-scales were quite high, ranging from $\alpha=.76$ to $\alpha=96$ (Coplan & Rubin, 1998). **Test-retest:** Six month test-retest reliability correlation coefficients for all sub-scales were moderate to high, ranging from .39 to .66 (Coplan & Rubin, 1998) **Inter-rater:** Inter-rater reliability coefficients were assessed between five pairs of teachers who rated the same samples of children. Moderate to high inter-teacher reliability correlations were observed for the reticent, solitary-passive, social play, and rough play sub-scales, with coefficients ranging from .61 to .89. Thus, teachers tended to agree in terms of their ratings of the children's behaviors. The solitary-active behavior sub-scale demonstrated somewhat lower reliability, with a wider range of coefficients from .10 to .83 (Coplan & Rubin, 1998).

VALIDITY: Convergent: Sub-scale scores for the *PPBS* were correlated with a number of theoretically relevant variables, as assessed by more well-established measures. Among the results, teacher-rated reticent behavior was significantly and positively associated with parent-rated temperamental shyness and emotionality and strongly related to child internalising problems (teacher-rated). Solitary-active behavior was positively associated with temperamental activity level and negatively associated with shyness. Solitary-passive behavior was not significantly associated with any of the parent-rated child temperament characteristics or teacher-rated behavior problems. Social play was positively correlated with temperamental sociability. Finally, rough play was positively related to activity level and externalizing problems, and negatively associated with attention-span (Coplan & Rubin, 1998). In another sample of $n=39$ preschoolers, *PPBS* ratings nonsocial behaviors (*i.e.*, reticent, solitary-passive, solitary-active), social play, and rough-play were generally significantly associated with observed indices of the same behaviors. Thus, for example, for three separate teachers, ratings of children's reticent behavior were significantly correlated with researchers' observations of the same behavior ($r=.50$, $r=.46$, and $r=.54$, all p's<.05) (Coplan & Rubin, 1998). **Discriminant:** In this same sample, there was an overall lack of significant inter-correlations among teacher-rated and observed *non-corresponding* forms of nonsocial behaviors.   In other words, teacher ratings of reticent behavior were only associated with observations of reticent behavior, and were *not* associated with observations of solitary-passive or solitary-active behaviors.

LOCATION: Coplan, R.J., & Rubin, K.H. (1998).   Exploring and assessing non-social play in the preschool: The development and validation of the Preschool Play Behavior Scale. *Social Development*, 7, 72-91.

COMMENT: These initial findings suggest that the PPBS can provide a reliable and valid outside source assessment measure of nonsocial play in early childhood. A multi-method approach to the study of behaviors is typically beneficial - different informants can contribute different types of information that may help to better define a behavioral construct. As such, the PPBS can provide an additional 'informant source' in the study of behavioral solitude.

REFERENCES:

Coplan, R.J. (in press). Assessing nonsocial play in early childhood: Conceptual and methodological approaches. In C.E. Schaefer, K. Gitlin, & A. Sandgrund (Eds.), *Play Diagnosis and Assessment*. (2nd Edition). New York, Wiley.

Coplan, R.J., & Rubin, K.H. (1998). Exploring and assessing non-social play in
the preschool: The development and validation of the Preschool Play
Behavior Scale. *Social Development*, 7, 72-91.

REVIEWER: Robert J. Coplan, Department of Psychology, Carleton University,
1125 Colonel By Drive, Ottawa, Ontario, K1S 5B6, Canada.

6.32: RELATIONSHIP EVALUATION (RELATE).
AUTHORS: Holman, Busby, Doxey, Klein, and Loyer-Carlson.

VARIABLES: Comprehensive premarital and marital assessment of individual and
couple traits predictive of marital satisfaction.

DESCRIPTION: RELATE is a 271-item self-report instrument published by the
Family Studies Center at Brigham Young University. There are currently
nondenominational English and Spanish versions of the questionnaire. An
Internet version will be available June 1, 2000. A unique characteristic of
RELATE is its use with nondating individuals (*e.g.*, friends or strangers), as well
as dating, engaged, cohabiting, and married couples and its adaptability for use in
the classroom. Nondating individuals can complete the test by skipping sections
that refer only to serious dating or engaged couples. Before taking the test, a
nondating person is encouraged to pair off with a partner in the class or outside of
the class whose responses to the items he or she can compare with his or her own.
RELATE items measure factors in four broad areas: (a) personality characteristics
(*e.g.* self esteem, depression, impulsivity); (b) values (*e.g.* money, sex, finances);
(c) family-of-origin functioning; and (d) relationship experiences (*e.g.*
communication skills and acquaintanceship). RELATE assesses 96% of the

premarital factors predicting later marital quality (Larson & Holman, 1994). The only factor missing is the couple's overall similarity. The results may be used with premarital couples or married couples. RELATE results are sent to the counselor or educator in the form of a 19-page computer printout that is self-interpretative. The printout can also be sent directly to a couple.

SAMPLE: Designed for use with normal populations of both single and married adults.

RELIABILITY: Internal consistency reliability of .70 or higher for all major scales is reported (Holman, Larson, & Harmer, 1994).

VALIDITY: Content, construct, and predictive validity are reported (Holman, Larson, & Harmer, 1994).

LOCATION: Copies of RELATE and a counselor/educator's manual are available from the RELATE office, 380 SWKT, Brigham Young University, Provo, UT 84602, U.S.A.

COMMENT: RELATE is unique in that it requires no assistance from the counselor in interpreting the results to a couple. Of the three major comprehensive premarital instruments available, RELATE is the easiest instrument to interpret, and the easiest to use in large groups and teaching settings. RELATE is also the most comprehensive and least expensive of the three major instruments available. It can be used in a variety of settings and with the individuals in a number of non-marital statuses. It's availability on the Internet should make it most easily accessible. There are currently no remarriage items, although a remarriage supplement will be available in June, 2000. Only English and Spanish language versions are currently available.

REFERENCES:

Holman, T.B., Busby, D.M., Doxey, C., Klein, D.M., & Loyer-Carlson, V. (1997). *RELATionship Evaluation.* Provo, UT. Brigham Young University, Family Studies Center.

Holman, T.B., Larson, J.H., & Harmer, S.L. (1994). The development and predictive validity of a new premarital assessment instrument: The Preparation for Marriage Questionnaire. *Family Relations, 43,* 46-52.

REVIEWER: Jeffry H. Larson, Marriage and Family Therapy Program, School of Family Life, Brigham Young University, Provo, UT, 84602, U.S.A.

6.33: REPUTATION ENHANCEMENT SCALE.

AUTHORS: Carroll, Houghton, Hattie, and Durkin.

VARIABLES: Sociability, Social Desirability, Self-perception, Ideal Public Self, Self-description, Ideal Private Self, Communication of Events.

DESCRIPTION: The Reputation Enhancement Scale is a self-report scale clustered into seven dimensions containing 127 items. The first dimension, *Friendliness*, contains one factor with 10 items that measure sociability and value placed on friendships and group membership. Items are scored on a 6-point Likert scale ranging from (1) *Strongly disagree* to (6) *Strongly agree*. The second dimension, *Admiration*, can be divided into two factors – Admiration of Law-breaking Activities and Admiration of Law-abiding Activities. Admiration of Law-breaking Activities contains 18 items that measure approval of and regard for delinquent-type activities. Admiration of Law-abiding Activities contains 12 items that measure approval of and regard for activities that are socially approved. Items are scored on a 6-point scale: *Not at all* (1), *Very little* (2), *Somewhat* (3), *Quite a bit* (4), *Very much* (5), and *Completely* (6). The third dimension, *Self-perception*, asks the question "What do other people think of you?" and can be divided into three factors. Non-conforming Self-perception contains 7 items that measure how participants perceive their peers to view them in terms of their non-conforming behaviour. Conforming Self-perception contains 4 items that measure how participants perceive their peers to view them in terms of their conforming behaviour. Reputational Self-perception contains 4 items that measure how participants perceive their peers to view them in terms of their reputational status. The fourth dimension, *Ideal Public Self*, contains identical items and factors to the Self-perception dimension, however, the question asked is "What would you like your friends to think of you?" The three factors are called Non-conforming Ideal Public Self, Conforming Ideal Public Self, and Reputational Ideal Public Self and measure how participants would ideally like to be viewed in terms of their non-conforming behaviour, conforming behaviour and reputational status respectively. Items are measured on a 6-point scale: *Never* (1), *Hardly ever* (2), *Occasionally* (3), *Sometimes* (4), *Often* (5), and *Always* (6). The fifth dimension, *Self-description*, provides the statement "I describe myself to be ..." and can be divided into two factors, Activity Self-description and Power-Evaluation Self-Description. Activity Self-description contains 3 items that measure how participants describe themselves in terms of activity attributes. Power/evaluation Self-description contains 9 items that measure how participants describe themselves in terms of power attributes. The sixth dimension, *Ideal Private Self*, contains identical items and factors to the Self-description dimension, however, the statement says "I would really like to be ...". The two factors are called Activity Ideal Private Self and Power/Evaluation Ideal Private Self and measure how participants would ideally like to be viewed in terms of activity attributes and power attributes, respectively. Items are scored on a 6-point Likert scale using sematic differentials.

Four of the 12 items are reverse scored. The final dimension, *Communication of Events*, can be divided into two factors - Adult Communication and Peer Communication. Adult Communication contains 18 items that measure patterns of communication of events to adults by adolescents while Peer Communication contains 18 items that measure patterns of communication of events to peers by adolescents. Using a 4-point response format, namely friends, parents, other adults, and nobody, participants indicate to which group of people they would disclose information concerning the nine different events.

SAMPLES: Carroll *et al.* (1999) intended the scale to be used by educators, developmental social psychologists, and allied professionals for the assessment of social processes among children and adolescents, including self-concepts and interpersonal and intergroup relations, and by applied social psychologists studying delinquent and related problem behaviours.

RELIABILITY: **Internal consistency:** The factor structure of the scale has been examined by Carroll *et al.* (1999), and Carroll, Houghton, and Baglioni (2000). Satisfactory levels of internal reliability have been found for the various factors of the scale ranging from .64 to .92. indicating that the factors are dependable across different samples. The coefficients of congruence were sufficiently high to investigate meaningful group differences.

VALIDITY: **Convergent:** The scale has demonstrated satisfactory convergent validity with various measures of self-reported delinquency (Carroll, Durkin, Houghton, & Hattie, 1996), self-concept (Caroll, Hattie, Houghton, & Durkin, under review), and goal setting (Carroll, Durkin, Hattie, & Houghton, 1997). **Discriminant:** The validity of the Reputation Enhancement Scale is supported by its discriminatory power in distinguishing between high school students and incarcerated youths (Carroll *et al.*, 1999) and in distinguishing between at-risk and not at-risk primary school students (Carroll, Baglioni, Houghton, & Bramston, 1999). The scale has also found to be able to discriminate between young children and adolescents with varying attitudes to substance using behaviours (Houghton, Carroll, Odgers, & Allsop, 1998; Houghton, Odgers, & Carroll, 1998). The scale's properties have been examined in relationship to gender, age and culture (Houghton & Carroll, 1996; Houghton, Carroll, & Shier, 1996).

LOCATION: Carroll, A., Houghton, S., Hattie, J., & Durkin, K., (1999). Adolescent reputation enhancement: Differentiating delinquent and nondelinquent youths. *Journal of Child Psychology and Psychiatry and Allied Disciplines, 40*, 593-606. The scale has also been translated into Spanish.

COMMENT: Until recently (Carroll *et al.*, 1999), there was no empirical measure of reputation enhancement, despite a growing body of qualitative and quantitative research that exists on the importance of reputations to adolescents. The present instrument, the Reputation Enhancement Scale, provides a psychometrically tested empirical instrument to measure the reputational profiles of different groups of adolescents. There is growing evidence of the satisfactory psychometric properties of the Scale.

REFERENCES:

Carroll, A., Baglioni, A.J., Houghton, S., & Bramston, P. (1999). At-risk and not at-risk primary school children: An examination of goal orientations and social reputations. *British Journal of Educational Psychology, 69*, 377-392.

Carroll, A., Hattie, J., Houghton, S., & Durkin, K. (under review). Unpublished data.

Carroll, A., Houghton, S., Hattie, J., & Durkin, K., (1999). Adolescent reputation enhancement: Differentiating delinquent and nondelinquent youths. *Journal of Child Psychology and Psychiatry and Allied Disciplines, 40*, 593-606.

Carroll, A., Houghton, S., & Baglioni, A.J. (2000). Goals and reputations amongst young children: The validation of the Importance of Goals and Reputation Enhancement Scales. *School Psychology International, 21*, 115-135.

Houghton, S., & Carroll, A. (1996). Enhancing reputations: The effective use of behavior management strategies by high school adolescent males. *Scientia Pedagogica Experimentalis, 33*, 227-244.

Houghton, S., Carroll, A., Odgers, P., & Allsop, S. (1998). Young children, adolescents and alcohol Part II: Reputation enhancement and self-concept. *Journal of Child and Adolescent Substance Abuse, 7*, 31-56.

Houghton, S., Carroll, A., & Shier, J. (1996). A preliminary study of a wilderness type programme with young offenders: Goals, attitudes, and image. *Journal of Offender Rehabilitation, 24*, 183-202.

Houghton, S., Odgers, P., & Carroll, A. (1998). Reputations, self-concepts and coping strategies of volatile solvent users (Abstract). *Alcohol Research, 3*, 168-169.

Houghton, S., Odgers, P., & Carroll, A. (1998). Reputations, self-concepts and coping strategies of volatile solvent users. *Journal of Drug Education, 28* 199-210.

REVIEWER: Annemaree Carroll, Schonell Special Education Research Centre, The University of Queensland, Brisbane Q4072, Australia, E-mail a.carroll@mailbox.uq.edu.au.

6.34: SOCIAL BEHAVIOR QUESTIONNAIRE – SBQ.

AUTHORS: Tremblay, *et al.*

VARIABLES: Physical aggression, Hyperactivity, Inattention, Opposition, Anxiety and Prosociality.

DESCRIPTION: The SBQ is a combined form of the Preschool Behavior Questionnaire (Behar & Stringfield, 1974) and the Prosocial Behavior Questionnaire (Weir & Duveen, 1981). It contains 38 items measuring physical aggression, opposition, hyperactivity, inattention, anxiety, and prosociality. The first three of these scales (physical aggression, opposition, and hyperactivity) can be combined to obtain a disruptiveness score. Each item is scored by the parent or teacher on a 0 (*Does not apply*), 1 (*Applies sometimes*) and 2 (*Often applies*) scale. The SBQ has been used to assess children's behaviors from early childhood to adolescence.

SAMPLE: Psychometric properties of the SBQ were assessed with a longitudinal study of 3,017 French-Canadian children assessed by their mothers and teachers at the end of the school year from 6 to 12 years of age.

RELIABILITY: Internal consistency: Cronbach's alphas were computed for each scale from 6 to 12 years of age. The alpha coefficients ranged from .81 to .88 for physical aggression; from .85 to .89 for hyperactivity; from .85 to .89 for inattention; from .79 to .83 for opposition; from .72 to .77 for anxiety; and from .90 to .91 for prosociality. **Test-retest:** Test-retest reliability within a two-month period was assessed using a random subsample of 7- to 8- year-old boys (n=87). Correlation coefficients indicated relatively high test-retest reliability for teachers' ratings of physical aggression (r=.74), hyperactivity (r=.62) anxiety (r=.65), inattention (r=.77), opposition (r=.73) and prosociality (r=.55) (Tremblay *et al.*,

1991). Test-retest reliability over one year periods (differential stability) between 6 and 12 years of age was assessed with a longitudinal study of 3,017 French-Canadian children assessed by their mothers and teachers at the end of the school year (Pagani, Boulerice, & Tremblay, 1997; Tremblay, Mâsse, Pagani, & Vitaro, 1996). Mean correlation coefficients were the following: $r=.42$ (min=.32; max=.51) for physical aggression; $r=.45$ (min=.32; max=.51) for opposition; $r=.37$ (min=.23; max=.46) for hyperactivity; $r=.46$ (min=.35; max=.62) for inattention; $r=.28$ (min=.20; max=.45) for anxiety; $r=.18$ (min=.12; max=.24) for prosociality.

VALIDITY: Convergent: Convergent validity for different scales was demonstrated comparing assessment by teachers, mothers, peers and self-reports (Gagnon, Vitaro, & Tremblay, 1992; Tremblay Vitaro, Gagnon, Royer, & Piché, 1992; Vitaro, Tremblay, & Gagnon, 1991). Predictive: Low prosocial ratings in kindergarten for boys predicted stable peer rejection from kindergarten to grade 1 (Vitaro, Gagnon, & Tremblay, 1990). Tremblay et al. (1991), Haapasalo & Tremblay (1994), as well as Nagin & Tremblay (in press) showed the stability of physical aggression, opposition and hyperactivity from 6 to 15 years of age, and their prediction of different forms of delinquency up to 17 years of age. Disruptive behavior at age 6 was related to peer-rated aggressiveness between 10 and 12 years (Tremblay, Mâsse, Vitaro, & Dobkin, 1995). Teacher rating of boys high on hyperactivity, low on anxiety, and low on prosociality at age 6 was predictive of higher scores on self-reported delinquency at age 13 (Tremblay, Pihl, Vitaro, & Dobkin, 1994). Finally, teacher report of the combination of opposition, physical aggression and hyperactivity at age 6 was shown to lead to disruptiveness at the end of elementary school, which subsequently lead to substance abuse prior to 14 years old (Dobkin, Tremblay, Mâsse, & Vitaro, 1995).

COMMENT: The SBQ has proven to be suitable for longitudinal, experimental, and cross-cultural studies of social competencies from preschool to high school (Broidy, Nagin, & Tremblay, 1999; Nagin & Tremblay, in press; Pulkinnen & Tremblay, 1992; Tremblay & al., 1995; Tremblay *et al.*, 1994).

REFERENCES:

Behar, L.B., & Stringfield, S. (1974). A behavior rating scale for the preschool child. *Developmental Psychology, 10*, 601-610.

Broidy, L., Nagin, D., & Tremblay, R. E. (1999). *The linkage of trajectories of childhood externalizing behaviors to later violent and nonviolent delinquency.* Paper presented at the Biennial Meeting of the Society for Research in Child Development, Albuquerque, NM.

Dobkin, P.L., Tremblay, R.E ., Mâsse, L.C., & Vitaro, F. (1995). Individual and peer characteristics in predicting boys' early onset of substance abuse : A seven-year longitudinal study. *Child Development, 66*, 1198-1214.

Gagnon, C., Vitaro, F., & Tremblay, R.E. (1992). Parent-teacher agreement on kindergarteners' behavior problems: A research note. *Journal of Child Psychology and Psychiatry, 33*, 1255-1261.

Haapasalo, J., & Tremblay, R.E. (1994). Physically aggressive boys from ages 6 to 12: Family background, parenting behavior, and prediction of delinquency. *Journal of Consulting and Clinical Psychology, 62*, 1044-1052.

Nagin, D., & Tremblay, R.E. (in press). Trajectories of boys' physical aggression, opposition, and hyperactivity on the path to physically violent and non violent juvenile delinquency. *Child Development.*

Pagani, L., Boulerice, B., & Tremblay, R.E. (1997). The influence of poverty upon children's classroom placement and behavior problems during elementary school: A change model approach. In G. Duncan & J.

Brooks-Gunn (Eds.), *Consequences of Growing Up Poor* (pp. 311-339). New York: Sage.

Pulkkinen, L., & Tremblay, R.E. (1992). Patterns of boys' social adjustment in two cultures and at different ages: A longitudinal perspective. *International Journal of Behavioural Development, 15*, 527-553.

Tremblay, R.E., Loeber, R., Gagnon, C., Charlebois, P., Larivée, S., & LeBlanc, M. (1991). Disruptive boys with stable and unstable high fighting behavior patterns during junior elementary school. *Journal of Abnormal Child Psychology, 19*, 285-300.

Tremblay, R. E., Mâsse, L. C., Pagani, L., & Vitaro, F. (1996). From childhood physical aggression to adolescent maladjustment: The Montréal Prevention Experiment. In R. D. Peters & R. J. McMahon (Eds.), *Preventing Childhood Disorders, Substance Abuse and Delinquency* (pp. 268-298). Thousand Oaks, CA: Sage.

Tremblay, R.E., Mâsse, L. C., Vitaro, F., & Dobkin, P. L. (1995). The impact of friends'deviant behavior on early of delinquency: Longitudinal data from6 to 13 years of age. *Development and Psychopathology, 7*, 649-667.

Tremblay, R.E., Pihl, R. O., Vitaro, F., & Dobkin, P. L. (1994). Predicting early onset of male antisocial behavior from preschool behavior. *Archives of General Psychiatry, 51*, 732-738.

Tremblay, R.E., Vitaro, F., Gagnon, C., Royer, N., & Piché, C. (1992). A prosocial scale for the Preschool Behaviour Questionnaire: Concurrent and predictive correlates. *International Journal of Behavioural Development, 15*, 227-245.

Vitaro, F., Gagnon, C., & Tremblay, R.E. (1991). Teachers' and mothers' assessment of children's behaviors from kindergarten to grade two: Stability and change within and across informants. *Journal of Psychopathology and Behavioral Assessment, 13*, 325-343.

Vitaro, F., Gagnon, C., & Tremblay, R.E. (1990). Predicting stable peer rejection from kindergarten to grade one. *Journal of Consulting Child Psychology*, *19*, 257-264.

Weir, K., & Duveen, G. (1981). Further development and validation of the prosocial behaviour questionnaire for use by teachers. *Journal of Child Psychology and Psychiatry*, *22*, 357-374.

REVIEWER: R.E. Tremblay, University of Montreal, Montreal, PQ H3T 1J7, Canada.

6.35: SOCIAL COMPETENCE INVENTORY, THE.

AUTHORS: Rydell, Hagekull and Bohlin.

VARIABLES: Social competence, prosocial orientation and social initiative.

DESCRIPTION: The SCI is a 25-item questionnaire for parents and teachers that measures children's social competence in terms of social skills and behaviour, mostly with peers. The questionnaire has two scales identified in factor analyses on several samples, Prosocial Orientation (17 items) and Social Initiative (8 items). Responses are scored on 5-step scales (1=*Does not apply* through to 5=*Applies very well to child*). Scales are constructed as means of number of items. Six items are reversed before scale construction.

SAMPLE: The SCI is intended to describe social competence in children 5-12 years old, and can be used in clinic as well as non clinic samples.

RELIABILITY: Internal: Internal consistencies have been tested in four samples of children seven to ten years old (n=75-121). For the Prosocial Orientation Scale, Cronbach's α was between .87 and .94 for mother, father and teacher ratings and for the Social Initiative Scale, the range of α-values was .75 to .92. Generally, the highest values applied to teacher ratings (Rydell *et al.*, 1997). **Test-retest:** For mothers, test-retest across one year was r=.77/r=.79 for prosocial orientation and social initiative, and for teachers, the corresponding coefficients were r=.59/r=.81 (Rydell *et al.*, 1997).

VALIDITY: Convergent: *Inter rater agreement.* Mother-father agreement was r(74)=.42/r=.44 for prosocial orientation and social initiative. Mother-teacher correspondence in two samples (n=92-93) amounted to r=.17/.29 and r=.45/47 for prosocial orientation and social initiative, respectively (Rydell *et al.*, 1997). Teacher-teacher agreement in one sample (n=62) was r=.66 for prosocial orientation and r=.76 for social initiative (unpublished data). *Observations of peer behaviour.* Both scales were related to observations in the school setting of positive peer behaviour (r(91)=.29), and the two scales discriminated between observed prosocial and observed initiative behaviours (Rydell *et al.*, 1997). **Discriminant:** Both scales discriminated between children that were sociometrically rejected and popular (Rydell *et al.*, 1997), and both scales discriminated between children in special schools for problem children and children in main stream schools (unpublished data). **Predictive:** Attachment security in infancy predicted social competence in school age (Andersson, 1999, Bohlin, Hagekull, & Rydell, 2000), and social inhibition at 4 years predicted social competence in school age (Andersson, 1999).

LOCATION: Rydell, A-M., Hagekull, B., & Bohlin, G. (1997) Measurement of two social competence aspects in middle childhood. *Developmental Psychology*, *33*, 824-833.

COMMENT: The SCI has shown good reliability and validity in several middle childhood samples, and seems to meet the need for short, easily administered parent and teacher inventories of children's social competence.

REFERENCES

Andersson, K. (1999). *Reactions to novelties. Developmental aspects.* Acta Universitas Upsaliensis. Comprehensive Summaries of Uppsala Dissertations from the Faculty of Social Sciences, nr 81.

Bohlin, G, Hagekull, B., & Rydell, A-M. (2000). Attachment and social functioning: A longitudinal study from infancy to middle childhood. *Social Development, 9,* 24-39.

Rydell, A-M., Hagekull, B., & Bohlin, G. (1997) Measurement of two social competence aspects in middle childhood. *Developmental Psychology, 33,* 824-833.

REVIEWER: Ann-Margret Rydell, Department of Psychology, Uppsala University, PO Box 1225, Uppsala S-751 42 Sweden. E-mail: annmargret.rydell@psyk.uu.se

6.36: TEMPERAMENT OF NEWBORN CHILDREN, QUESTIONNAIRE EVALUATING THE.

AUTHORS: Sulcova, and Kozeny.

VARIABLES: temperament of newborns, types.

DESCRIPTION: The aim of the authors (Sulcova & Kozeny, 1994) was to develop an objective measure to evaluate the temperament of newborn children. The rationale being that "Even from an early age, temperament is understood as a psychological construct that can be observed in newborn children in the form of precursors at psychobiological level of behaviour in other patterns of behaviour than in adults" (Sulcova & Kozeny 1994). The theoretical background is located within the theories of temperament as proposed by Galen, Kant, Wundt and Eysenck. As such, four classical types of temperament, or tendencies are proposed: Sanguine-extraverted-stable,   Melancholic-introverted-unstable, Phlegmatic-introverted-stable,   and   Choleric-extraverted-unstable.   For   the development of the scale nine theoretical approaches were utilised to obtain 17-items, including; Interactionist approach (Thomas & Chess, 1963, 1968, 1977; Carey, 1970; Carey & McDewitt, 1978a, b), Gene theories (Buss & Plomin 1975, 1984), Psychobiological theory (Rothbarth & Derryberry, 1981), Two factor temperament models (Rothbarth & Derryberry, 1981; Bornstein, Gaugham, & Homel, 1986), Behaviourally Genetic model (Goldsmith & Campos, 1982; Plomin & Rowe, 1979), Tomkins hypothesis (Tomkins, 1963; Bornstein, Gaughran, & Homel, 1986; Bates, 1987), Campos´ hypothesis (Campos, Barrett, & Lamb, 1983; Derryberry & Rotharth, 1984) and Behavioural and by Early Age Limited theory (Goldsmith & Campos 1982). All items are provided in Sulcova and Kozeny (1994). Sample items include: reactivity to objects, playthings (item-7); mood after awakening (item-14). The description of item-writing and selection that is provided is unfortunately vague. The items are scored on a verbalised 5-point Likert response, however the authors do not provide the scoring anchors.

SAMPLE: The pilot study comprised of 120 newborns, and a second sample of 180 newborns was employed for purposes of validation. Socio-demographic and health characteristics were also obtained including type of childbirth, gender and Apgar scores (Apgar, 1966). In addition information about the mothers was also obtained including, age, education, previous pregnancy. Only healthy newborns were included in the study.

VALIDITY: Using exploratory factor analysis, two factors were identified, which was subsequently supported by confirmatory factor analysis. Factor 1 was labelled as reactivity to the world (spontaneous activity reached in the world) and Factor 2 was labelled as self-regulation (ability to maintain homeostasis in biological plain). Factor 1 is perceived as a precursor of dimension Extroversion-Introversion and Factor 2 as a precursor of dimension Stability-Unstability. Convergent: In addition to the scale being administrated to the mothers, observations of the authors, analysis of video and the analysis of breast-feeding were also obtained. However no comparisons with the objective measures and scale scores are reported.

LOCATION: Sulcova, E., & Kozeny, J. (1994). Vyvoj dotazniku pro hodnoceni temperamentu novorozencu, (Development of a questionnaire to evaluate temperament in newborn children). *Ceskoslovenska Psychologie, 38*, 400-407.

COMMENT: The present work is part of an ongoing research programme and therefore further verification of the measure continues. The work of Sulcova and Kozeny (1994) provides some preliminary evidence for the early signs of Extroversion-Introversion, and Stability-Unstability among newborn children. Future work may provide more comprehensive information about the psychometric qualities of the measure, that are presently not available. Moreover, its relationship with more established measures of infant temperament: psychological (Novosad, Freudigman, & Thoman, 1999; Martin, Noyes, Wisenbaker, & Huttunen, 1999) and physiological (Stifter & Fox, 1990; Bornstein, Gaugham, & Homel, 1986). Notwithstanding this, the brief description of aspects of the methodology employed may undermine the potential for the use of the measure among prospective authors.

776   Developmental Psychology

REFERENCES:

Apgar, V. (1966). The newborn (Apgar) scoring system. Reflections and advice. *Pediatric Clinics of North America, 13*, 645-50.

Bates, J.E. (1987). Temperament in infancy. In Osofsky, J.D. (Ed.), *Handbook of Infant Development* (pp. 1101-1149). New York: Wiley Interscience.

Bornstein, M.H., Gaughran, J.M., & Homel, P. (1986). Infant temperament: Theory, tradition, critique and new assessment. In Izard, C.E., & Read, P.B. (Eds.), *Measuring Emotions in Infants and Children*, Vol. II, (pp 172-199). Cambridge: Cambridge University Press.

Buss, A.H., & Plomin, R. (1975). *A Temperament Theory of Personality Development*. New York: Wiley.

Buss, A.H., & Plomin, R. (1984). *Temperament: Early Developing Personality Traits*. NJ Hillsdale: Erlbaum.

Campos, J.J., Barrett, K.C., & Lamb, M.E. (1983). Socioemotional development. In Mussen, P.H., & Carmichael, L. (Eds.), *Handbook of Child Psychology, Vol. 2*, (pp. 783-915). New York: Wiley,

Carey, W.B., & McDevitt, S.C. (1978a). Revision of the Infant Temperament Questionnaire. *Pediatrics, 61*, 735-739.

Carey, W.B., & McDewitt, S.C. (1978b). Stability and change in individual temperamental diagnoses from infancy to early childhood. *Journal of the American Academy of Child Psychiatry, 17*, 331-337.

Derryberry, D., & Rothbart, M. K. (1984). Emotion, attention and temperament. In Izard, C.E., Kagan, J., & Zajonc, R.B. (Eds.), *Emotions, Cognitions, and Behavior* (pp. 132-166). New York: Cambridge University Press.

Goldsmith, H.H., & Campos, J.J. (1982). Toward a theory of infant temperament. In Emde, R.N., & Harmon, R.J. (Eds.), *The Development of Attachement and Affiliative systems*. New York: Plenum.

Martin, R.P., Noyes, J., Wisenbaker, J., & Huttunen, M.O. (1999). Prediction of early childhood negative emotionality and inhibition from maternal distress during pregnancy. *Merrill-Palmer Quarterly, 45,* 370-391.

Novosad, C., Freudigman, K., & Thoman, E. (1999). Sleep patterns in newborns and temperament at eight months: A preliminary study. *Journal of Developmental and Behavioral Pediatrics, 20,* 99-105.

Plomin, R., & Rowe, D.C. (1979). Genetic and environmental etiology of social behavior in infancy. *Developmental Psychology, 15,* 62-72.

Rothbart, M.K., & Derryberry, P. (1981). Development of individual differences in temperament. In: Lamb, M.E., & Brown, A.L. (Eds.): *Advances in Developmental Psychology, Vol. 1,* (pp. 37-86). NJ, Hillsdale: Erlbaum.

Stifter, C.A., Fox, N.A. (1990). Infant reactivity: Physiological correlates of newborn and 5-month temperament. *Developmental Psychology, 26,* 582-588.

Sulcova, E., & Kozeny, J. (1994). Vyvoj dotazniku pro hodnoceni temperamentu novorozencu, (Development of a questionnaire to evaluate temperament in newborn children). *Ceskoslovenska Psychologie, 38,* 400-407.

Thomas, A. (1963). *Behavioral Individuality in Early Childhood.* New York: University Press.

Thomas, A., Chess, S., & Birch, H. (1968). *Temperament and Behavioural Disorders in Children.* New York: University Press.

Thomas, A., & Chess, S. (1977). *Temperament and Development.* New York: Brunner-Mazel.

Tomkins, S. (1963). *Affect, Imagery, Consciousness, Vol. II, The Negative Affects.* New York: Springer.

REVIEWERS: Marek Navratil, Czech Academy of Science, Department of Psychology, Veveri 97, 602 00 Brno, Czech Republic. E-mail: navrc@iach.cz **and** Christopher Alan Lewis, School of Psychology and Communication, University of Ulster at Magee College, Londonderry, Northern Ireland, BT48 7JL, UK. E-mail: CA.Lewis@Ulst.ac.uk

6.37: WING SUBGROUPS QUESTIONNAIRE.

AUTHORS: Castelloe and Dawson.

VARIABLE: Subclassification of children with autism.

DESCRIPTION: The questionnaire classifies children with autism into one of Wing's three hypothesised subtypes: aloof, passive or active-but-odd (Wing & Attwood, 1987; Wing & Gould, 1979). The Wing Subgroups Questionnaire (WSQ; Castelloe & Dawson, 1993) is composed of 13 groups of 3 or 4 different descriptions that cover several behavioural domains. The total number of items is 50. Each of the descriptions corresponds to one or two of Wing's subtypes or to normal development (typical subtype). For each group of items, parents or teacher rate how frequently the child's behaviour fits each of the descriptions (0=*never*; 6=*always*). The ratings of all items are added together to derive a summary score for each of the four subtypes. Each child is assigned to the subtype for which he or she has the highest summary score.

SAMPLE: Castelloe and Dawson (1993) intended the scale to be used in children with autism or a related pervasive developmental disorder.

RELIABILITY: Internal consistency: Moderate to good levels of internal consistency were demonstrated (Castelloe & Dawson, 1993; O'Brien, 1996) for the four subtype scales with Cronbach's alpha ranging from .54 to .85. **Interrater Reliability**: O'Brien (1996) reported intraclass correlations between teachers' and assistants' summary scores for 19 subjects that ranged from .60 to .81. The percentage of agreement with regard to subtype diagnosis was 63.1 %.

VALIDITY: Correlations between summary scales scores of the three Wing subtypes were reported to be low or negative (Castelloe & Dawson, 1993; O'Brien, 1986) which suggests that the scales are measuring distinct constructs. Castelloe and Dawson (1993) found the clinicians' diagnosis of subtype in 40 subjects to be significantly related to the subgroup assignment based on the parent-completed WSQ (Spearman rank r=.73). The clinicians' diagnosis was also found to be the best predictor of WSQ diagnosis among a number of relevant variables.   Consistent with Wing's descriptions of the subtypes, significant differences in the expected direction were found among WSQ-diagnosed subtypes on measures of communication (Castelloe & Dawson, 1993; O'Brien, 1996) and social interaction (O'Brien, 1996).

LOCATION: Castelloe, P., & Dawson, G. (1993). Subclassification of children with autism and pervasive developmental disorder: A questionnaire based on Wing's subgrouping scheme. *Journal of Autism and Developmental Disorders*, *23*, 229-241.

COMMENT: The two studies, with relatively small samples, that investigated the quality of the WSQ seem to support the reliability and validity of the instrument. However, some problems with respect to the passive subtype were reported: the internal consistency for the passive subtype items was less than for the other subtypes and most instances of disagreement with regard to subtype diagnosis involved the passive subtype. In addition, this subtype proved to be difficult to differentiate from the aloof and active-but-odd subtype on measures of socialisation or communication. Since similar concerns were raised when other instruments or methods were used (see Roeyers, 1997), this may reflect a weakness of Wing's classification system, rather than a shortcoming of the questionnaire.

REFERENCES:

Castelloe, P., & Dawson, G. (1993). Subclassification of children with autism and pervasive developmental disorder: A questionnaire based on Wing's Subgrouping scheme. *Journal of Autism and Developmental Disorders, 23*, 229-241.

O'Brien, S.K. (1996). The validity and reliability of the Wing Subgroups Questionnaire. *Journal of Autism and Developmental Disorders, 26*, 321-335.

Roeyers, H. (1997). Subclassification of children with a pervasive developmental disorder: Assignment to social subtypes. *Journal of Developmental and Physical Disabilities, 9*, 347-357.

Wing, L., & Attwood, A. (1987). Syndromes of autism and atypical development. In: D.J. Cohen, & A.M. Donnellan (Eds.), *Handbook of Autism and Pervasive Developmental Disorders* (pp. 3-19). New York: Wiley & Sons.

Wing, L., & Gould, J. (1979). Severe impairments of social interaction and associated abnormalities in children: epidemiology and classification. *Journal of Autism and Childhood Schizophrenia, 9*, 11-29.

REVIEWER: Herbert Roeyers, Department of Clinical Psychology, Research Group Developmental Disorders, University of Ghent, Belgium.

CHAPTER 7

WORK AND EDUCATIONAL PSYCHOLOGY

7.01: APPROACHES AND STUDY SKILLS INVENTORY FOR STUDENTS.
AUTHORS: Entwistle, Tait, and McCune.

VARIABLES: Learning processes and associated motives and intentions. Optional additional scales measure conceptions of learning, learning orientations, and preferences for contrasting teaching environments.

DESCRIPTION: The Approaches and Study Skills Inventory for Students (ASSIST; Entwistle, Tait, & McCune, 1999) has developed out of work on the Approaches to Studying Inventory (ASI; Entwistle & Ramsden, 1983). The main part of the inventory includes 13 scales which measure students' intentions in learning and their associated learning processes. These scales are generally best interpreted in terms of three factors which refer to deep, surface and strategic approaches to studying in higher education. A deep approach involves an intention to understand ideas for oneself coupled with learning processes such as relating ideas and checking evidence. A surface approach is characterised by an intention to cope minimally with course requirements with related processes, lack of purpose, and fear of failure. Finally, the strategic approach combines the intention to achieve the highest possible grades with organised studying and alertness to assessment criteria. Additional items have been included in some analyses, which measure conceptions of learning, learning orientations, and preferences for contrasting teaching environments. Conceptions of learning refer to students' general ideas about the nature of learning (see, for example, Marton, Dall' Alba and Beaty, 1993). Learning orientations refer to students' broader attitudes and aims in relation to higher education, as opposed to their more specific intentions in studying (Beaty, Gibbs and Morgan, 1997). The teaching preferences items group into two scales, measuring preferences for teaching that encourages understanding versus teaching that involves transmitting information. These preferences relate to the deep and surface approaches to studying.

RELIABILITY: Internal consistency: Cronbach's alpha coefficients for the approaches scales and subscales and the teaching preferences ranged from .53 to .87 for a sample of 1284 students from 6 British Universities (Entwistle, Tait, & McCune, 2000). Reliabilities have not been calculated for the other parts of the questionnaire as each item refers to a different orientation or conception.

VALIDITY: In analyses by Tait, Entwistle and McCune (1998) scales from the strategic approach correlated positively with students' assessment scores and significant negative correlations were found with surface approach scales. These correlations are fairly small, ranging from .12 to .27. The deep approach scales did not correlate significantly with assessment performance, but they did show a significant positive relationship with students' self-ratings of performance, as did the strategic approach scales. As expected, the surface approach scales showed negative correlations with self-rating. The relationships with self-rating are stronger, with several correlations over .40. The validity of the inventory is further supported by the robustness of the factor structure across differing educational contexts and systems (Entwistle, Tait & McCune, 2000) and by the strong parallels found with other similar inventories (Biggs, 1993; Tait & Entwistle, 1996). The items in the ASI, on which ASSIST is based, were derived in part from students' interview descriptions of their everyday studying, thus enhancing the ecological validity of the scales (Entwistle & Ramsden, 1983).

COMMENT: To make good use of the ASSIST inventory it is important to bear in mind that the approaches refer to students' responses to a particular academic context. Although students may show a certain consistency in their approach, there will also be variability across different contexts, influenced particularly by the nature of the assessment. (Ramsden, 1997; Scouller, 1998). Any attempts to use the inventory to compare between courses should involve a careful consideration of these contextual factors and of previous contexts experienced by the students under study. It may be difficult to separate out the effects of these different elements. Use of the inventory for pre and post testing in relation to some educational innovation is not generally recommended, as pre-innovation measures will be affected by students' prior experiences and can only reflect how students *expect* to study on a course. Post-innovation measures will involve students reporting how they felt they *actually* studied and are thus not easily compared with measures made at the beginning of a course.

REFERENCES:

Beaty, L., Gibbs, G., & Morgan, A. (1997). Learning orientations and study contracts. In. F. Marton, D. J. Hounsell, & Entwistle, N .J. (Eds.) *The Experience of Learning.* (2nd Edition) Edinburgh: Scottish Academic Press.

Biggs, J.B. (1993). What do inventories of student learning processes really measure: a theoretical review and clarification. *British Journal of Educational Psychology 63*, 3-19.

Entwistle, N.J., & Ramsden, P. (1983). *Understanding Student Learning*. London: Croom Helm.

Entwistle, N.J., Tait, H., & McCune, V. (1999). *Scoring Key for Approaches to Studying Sub-scales within the Approaches and Study Skills Inventory for Students*. Unpublished, University of Edinburgh, Department of Higher and Further Education.

Entwistle, N.J., Tait, H., & McCune, V. (2000). Patterns of response to an approaches to studying inventory across contrasting groups and contexts. *European Journal of the Psychology of Education*, in press.

Marton, F., Dall' Alba, G., & Beaty, E. (1993). Conceptions of Learning. *International Journal of Educational Research*, *19*, 277-300.

Ramsden, P. (1997). The context of learning in academic departments. In. F. Marton, D. J. Hounsell, and Entwistle, N . J. (Eds.) *The Experience of Learning*. (2nd Edition). Edinburgh: Scottish Academic Press.

Scouller, K. (1998). The influence of assessment method on students' learning approaches: multiple choice question examination versus assignment essay. *Higher Education*, *35*, 435-452.

Tait, H., & Entwistle, N.J. (1996). Identifying students at risk through ineffective study strategies. *Higher Education*, *31*, 97-116.

Tait, H., Entwistle, N.J., & McCune, V. (1998). ASSIST: a reconceptualisation of the approaches to studying inventory. In Rust, C. (Ed.). *Improving Student Learning: Improving Students as Learners*. Oxford: Oxford Centre for Staff and Learning Development.

REVIEWER: Velda McCune, Department of Higher and Further Education, University of Edinburgh, Paterson's Land, Holyrood Road, Edinburgh, EH8 8AQ, Scotland, U.K. E-mail: Velda.McCune@ed.ac.uk

7.02: ATTITUDES TOWARD CAREER COUNSELING SCALE, THE.
AUTHORS: Rochlen, Mohr, and Hargrove.

VARIABLE: Attitudes toward career counseling-Perceived 'Value' and 'Stigma' attached to career counseling.

DESCRIPTION: The Attitudes Toward Career Counseling Scale (Rochlen, Mohr, & Hargrove, 1999) is a 16-item self-report scale assessing general attitudes toward career counseling. Factor analysis yielded two meaningful factors, namely perceived Value (*e.g.*, "Career counseling is a valuable resource in making a career choice"), and Stigma (*e.g.*, "Seeing a career counselor to discuss career issues is a very private matter that should not be discussed with anyone") attached to career counseling. Responses are scored on a 4-point scale ranging from (1) *Disagree* to (4) *Agree*. High scores on the Value subscale reflect an overall positive perception of the value of career counseling whereas high scores on the Stigma subscale represent a greater amount of stigma and shame linked to seeking career counseling.

SAMPLE: The samples used in the original instrument development project (Rochlen, Mohr, & Hargrove, 1999) were undergraduate students most of whom were between the ages of 18 and 22. The participants were primarily Caucasian, although minority students represented between 36 to 46% of the sample in each of the studies.

RELIABILITY: Internal consistency: Across five different samples, alpha estimates ranged from .80 to .83 for the Stigma subscale and .85 to .90 for the Value subscale. Test-retest: Both the Value and Stigma subscales yielded test-retest correlations of $r=.80$ over a 3-week period.

VALIDITY: Convergent -Value: In the original instrument development project, Rochlen et al., (1999) found that participants who valued career counseling tended to use the help of others in making important decisions, avoid making spontaneous decisions, report a greater likelihood of seeking help for a variety of concerns, report a greater likelihood of seeking career counseling, and had more positive attitudes toward general help-seeking. Moreover, students who reported benefiting from a career decision-making course had higher value scores than those who reported little gain from the same course. Convergent-Stigma: Rochlen et al., (1999) also found that participants who reported more stigma attached to career counseling tended to procrastinate in making decisions, express less likelihood of using career counseling services, avoid closeness in relationships, report seeing psychological support services in general as a secretive process used primarily for people with serious problems, and had more negative attitudes toward general help-seeking. Students who reported benefiting from a career decision making course reported less stigma toward career counseling than students who reported few benefits from the same course. Gender differences: Consistent with the general help-seeking attitude literature (see Fischer, Winer, & Abramowitz, 1983 for a review), women reported less stigma toward seeking career counseling than men. Value subscores were roughly equivalent among men and women (Rochlen *et al.*, 1999). **Discriminant-Value and Stigma:** Rochlen *et al.* (1999) demonstrated discriminant validity with data suggesting that the Value and Stigma subscales were not influenced by social desirability, perceptions of the degree to which society attaches stigma to psychotherapy, and whether people had selected a major or a career. In addition, vocational exploration and commitment as well as the tendency to foreclose on a career did not evidence a relationship with either subscale.

LOCATION: Rochlen, A.B., Mohr, J.J., & Hargrove, B.K. (1999). Development of the attitudes toward career counseling scale. *Journal of Counseling Psychology*, *46*, 196-206.

COMMENT: Although there has been extensive research on the correlates of general help-seeking attitudes (Fischer & Farina, 1995), surprisingly few efforts have been initiated to understand how people feel about particular types of counseling, including career counseling. The results of the five studies conducted in the original instrument development project show strong support for the potential utility of this attitude measure in furthering this important research area. With the importance of career choice and career-related success well documented (Betz & Corning, 1993), it seems useful to learn more about how different types of people perceive career counseling as well as whether we can improve people's attitudes and willingness to use this helping service.

LIMITATIONS: Because of the primarily homogenous sample used in the original instrument development project, using this measure with minority populations and non-college aged samples should be executed with caution. More research on the accuracy of the described factor structure as well as the validity and reliability data on different types of samples is highly encouraged.

REFERENCES:

Betz, N., & Corning, A. (1993). The inseparability of "career" and "personal" counseling. *Career Development Quarterly, 42,* 137-142.

Fischer, E.H., & Farina, A. (1995). Attitudes toward seeking professional psychological help: A shortened form and considerations for research. *Journal of College Student Development, 36,* 368-373.

Fischer, E.H., Winer, D., & Abramowitz, S.I. (1983). Seeking professional help for psychological problems. In A. Nadler, J.D. Fischer, & B.N. DePaulo (Eds.), *New Directions in Helping,* Vol. 3, (pp. 163-182). New York: Academic Press.

Rochlen, A.B., Mohr, J.J., & Hargrove, B.K. (1999). Development of the attitudes toward career counseling scale. *Journal of Counseling Psychology, 46,* 196-206.

REVIEWER: Aaron B. Rochlen, Department of Psychology, University of Maryland, College Park, MD 20742, U.S.A. E-mail: arochlen@Psyc.umd.edu

7.03: BULLYING-BEHAVIOUR SCALE (BBS).

AUTHORS: Austin and Joseph.

VARIABLE: Bullying and victimisation in schools.

DESCRIPTION: The Bullying-Behaviour Scale (BBS; Austin & Joseph, 1996) is designed to assess bullying behaviours in school. The item pool for the scale was derived from the Peer Victimisation Scale (PVS; Neary & Joseph, 1994) and involved changing the tense of the item from passive to active. Thus, the BBS scale consists of 6-forced choice items, three of which refer to being the perpetrator of negative physical actions (e.g., hit and pushed, picked on, bullied) and three referring to being the perpetrator of negative verbal actions (e.g., teased, horrible names, laughed at). As with the PVS (Neary & Joseph, 1994), the BBS is designed in the same format as the Self-Perception Profile for Children (SPPC; Harter, 1985). This allows the scale to be inserted within the SPPC in order to reduce the saliency of the items. Designed to be used in conjunction with the PVS (Neary & Joseph, 1994). When both scales are used in conjunction, researchers may be able to determine the grouping (e.g., Smith, Boulton & Cowie, 1993) into which each child should be placed. As such, children may be categorised as victims only, bullies only, or being both a bully and a victim simultaneously. Responses are scored according to the scoring instructions for scoring the SPPC sub-scales (i.e., sum of six items divided by six).

SAMPLE: Austin and Joseph (1996) do not recommend the BBS for use with children under 8 years of age, as the scale is administered with the SPPC which stipulates that 8 years is the appropriate cut-off age.

RELIABILITY: The BBS has been found to have satisfactory levels of internal reliability. Austin and Joseph (1996) report a Cronbach's alpha of .82 for the scale.

VALIDITY: As boys scored higher than girls on the BBS (mean scores of 1.98 and 1.77 respectively, t=3.26, p<.01), Austin and Joseph (1996) conducted separate analysis between scores on the BBS and the SPPC and Birleson Depression Inventory (BDI; Birleson, 1981) for each gender. For both boys and girls, higher scores on the BBS were associated with lower scores on all of the SPPC sub-scales, except athletic competence and physical appearance. For bys only, higher scores on the BBS were associated with higher scores on the BDI.

LOCATION: Austin,S., & Joseph, S. (1996). Assessment of bully/victimproblems in 8 to 11 year-olds. *British Journal of Educational Psychology, 66,* 447-456.

COMMENT: Although other questionnaires, such as the Bully/Victim Questionnaire (Olweus, 1978, 1991, 1993) are available to researchers interested in childhood bullying, the strength of the BBS, like the Peer Victimization Scale (PVS; Neary & Joseph, 1994), is in its brevity and structure. By being designed to slot into the SPPC, this not only helps to reduce possible manipulation of testing situations by bullies, but reduces the saliency of the items and allows for less socially desirable responding from the children. A further strength is that when used in conjunction with the PVS, which is similarly designed, assessments of categories of bullies and victims may be readily made. However, Austin and Joseph (1996) report that further work is required regarding the appropriateness of the chosen cut-off point for the purpose of classifications made with the BBS. Overall, the BBS is a useful instrument for any researcher attempting to assess accurately the levels of bullying behaviours in large samples of children. Although other instruments may be useful in assessing the extent and frequency of bullying behaviours in schools, the BBS addresses a real need for a discreet measure of bullying behaviours.

REFERENCES:

Austin,S., & Joseph, S. (1996). Assessment of bully/victim problems in 8 to 11 year-olds. *British Journal of Educational Psychology, 66,* 447-456.

Harter, S. (1985). *The Self-Perception Profile for Children: Revision of the Perceived Competence Scale for Children - Manual.* Denver, CO: University of Denver.

Neary, A., & Joseph, S. (1994). Peer victimization and its relationship to self-concept and depression among schoolchildren. *Personality and Individual Differences, 16*, 183-186.

Olweus, D. (1978). *Aggression in the Schools: Bullies and Whipping Boys.* Washington, DC: Hemisphere.

Olweus, D. (1991). Bully/victim problems among schoolchildren: basic facts and effects of a school based intervention program. In D.Pepler & K. Rubin (Eds.), *The Development and Treatment of Childhood Aggression*, (pp. 411-448). Hillsdale, NJ: Erlbaum.

Olweus, D. (1993). *Bullying at School: What We Know and What We Can Do.* Oxford: Blackwell.

Smith, P.K., Boulton, M.J., & Cowie, H. (1993). The impact of cooperative group work on ethnic relations in middle school, *School Psychology International, 14*, 21-42.

REVIEWER: Conor McGuckin and Christopher Alan Lewis, School of Psychology and Communication, University of Ulster at Magee College, Londonderry, Northern Ireland, BT48 7JL, U.K. E-mail: ca.lewis@ulst.ac.uk

7.04: CAREER THOUGHTS INVENTORY.

AUTHOR: Sampson, Peterson, Lenz, Reardon, and Saunders.

VARIABLE: Dysfunctional thoughts in career problem solving and decision making.

DESCRIPTION: The Career Thoughts Inventory (CTI; Sampson, Peterson, Lenz, Reardon, & Saunders, 1996) is a self-administered inventory designed to measure dysfunctional career thoughts and three further construct scales. All 48 items are used to assess overall dysfunctional career thoughts (*i.e.*, CTI Total score). Fourteen items are used to measure Decision-Making Confusion, which is an assessment of the inability to initiate or sustain the decision making process. Ten items measure Commitment Anxiety, which assesses anxiety and the inability to commit to a career choice. Five items measure External Conflict, which measures the inability to balance self-perceptions with the input from significant others. Responses are scored on a 4-point scale ranging from (0) *Strongly disagree* to (3) *Strongly agree*. Higher scores on all scales represent elevated dysfunctional career thoughts.

SAMPLE: Sampson *et al.*, (1996a,c) intended the CTI to be used as screening device for identifying high school students, college students, and adults possessing dysfunctional career thoughts, and assessing their needs. Furthermore, the CTI and corresponding workbook are intended to provide a structured format for facilitating learning of career decision making skills.

RELIABILITY: **Internal consistency:** Satisfactory levels of internal consistency were found by calculating coefficient alphas for each of four norm groups (*i.e.*, high school students, college students, adults, and clients) (Sampson *et al.*, 1996c). Alpha coefficients for these norm groups ranged from $\alpha=.93$ to .97 for the CTI total score; $\alpha=.90$ to .94 for Decision Making Confusion; $\alpha=.79$ to .91 for Commitment Anxiety; and $\alpha=.74$ to .81 for External Conflict. **Test-retest:** Sampson *et al*, (1996c) reported test-retest stability coefficients of $r=.86$ for 73 college students, and $r=.69$ for 48 high school students over a four week period for the CTI Total score. Test-retest correlation coefficients for the construct scales ranged from $r=.74$ to .82 for the college students, and from $r=.52$ to .72 for the high school students.

VALIDITY: Content: Each item and construct scale is linked directly to a content dimension of Cognitive Information Processing Theory (Sampson *et al.*, 1996c). **Construct:** A series of factor analyses conducted on samples of adults, college students, and high school students revealed the presence of a three factor model (Sampson *et al.*, 1996c), which corresponds to the three construct scales of the CTI. **Convergent:** The CTI Total score and construct scales have demonstrated satisfactory convergent validity with various measures of vocational identity, certainty, knowledge about occupations and training, indecision, neuroticism, and vulnerability across groups of high school students, college students, and adults (Sampson *et al.*, 1996c). **Criterion:** A sample of 199 clients seeking career services at two universities were found to have significantly higher CTI Total and construct scale scores than 149 nonclients (Sampson *et al.*, 1996c).

FURTHER EMPIRICAL USES: Recently, dysfunctional career thinking has been used to examine adjustment to learning disabilities (Dipeolu, 1997), choosing a college major (Kilk, 1997), career interests (Railey, 1997), perfectionism (Osborn, 1998), problem solving ability (Slatten, 1999) and career indecision (Saunders, 1997).

LOCATION: Sampson, J.P., Jr., Peterson, G.W., Lenz, J.G., Reardon, R.C., & Saunders, D.E. (1996). *Career Thoughts Inventory*. Odessa, FL: Psychological Assessment Resources, Inc.

COMMENT: The CTI appears to be a psychometrically sound instrument. It is proving to be a useful instrument for practitioners to quickly identify individuals who are likely to experience problems making career choices, and to assess the specific nature of dysfunctional career thoughts. Information gained from this instrument can help determine the amount of assistance each client needs. It is quickly administered (7-15 minutes), rapidly scored (5-10 minutes), easily interpreted, and with the help of the CTI Workbook (Sampson *et al.*, 1996b) can be easily integrated into counseling homework to facilitate learning.

REFERENCES:

Dipeolu, A.O. (1997). A study of the relationship between learning disabilities, dysfunctional career thoughts, and adjustment to disability (Decision-making confusion, commitment, conflict, anxiety, career thoughts inventory). (Doctoral dissertation, Florida State University, 1997). *Dissertation Abstracts International, 58*(07), 3938B.

Kilk, K.L. (1997). The relationship between dysfunctional career thoughts and choosing an academic major. (Doctoral dissertation, University of Northern Colorado, 1997). *Dissertation Abstracts International, 58*(08), 3038A.

Osborn, D.S. (1998). The relationship among perfectionism, dysfunctional career thoughts, and career indecision. (Doctoral dissertation, Florida State University, 1998). *Dissertation Abstracts International, 59*(10), 3746A.

Railey, M.G. (1997). The relationship between dysfunctional career thoughts and career interests with respect to offender status of female inmates and probationers. (Doctoral dissertation, Florida State University, 1997). *Dissertation Abstracts International, 58*(06), 3325B.

Sampson, J.P., Jr., Peterson, G.W., Lenz, J.G., Reardon, R.C., & Saunders, D.E. (1996a). *Career Thoughts Inventory*. Odessa, FL: Psychological Assessment Resources, Inc.

Sampson, J.P., Jr., Peterson, G.W., Lenz, J.G., Reardon, R.C., & Saunders, D.E. (1996b). *Improving your Career Thoughts: A Workbook for the Career Thoughts Inventory*. Odessa, FL: Psychological Assessment Resources, Inc.

Sampson, J.P., Jr., Peterson, G.W., Lenz, J.G., Reardon, R.C., & Saunders, D.E. (1996c). *Career Thoughts Inventory: Professional Manual.* Odessa, FL: Psychological Assessment Resources, Inc.

Saunders, D.E. (1997). The contribution of depression and dysfunctional career thinking to career indecision. (Doctoral dissertation, Florida State University, 1997). *Dissertation Abstracts International, 58*(07), 3953B.

Slatten, M.L. (1999). *Dysfunctional career thoughts and self-appraised problem-solving ability among substance abusers.* Unpublished doctoral dissertation, Florida State University.

REVIEWER: Jack C. Watson II, Department of Human Services and Studies, Florida State University, Tallahassee, FL 32306-4458, U.S.A.

7.05: CLASSROOM COMMUNICATION EASE SCALE (CCES), THE.

AUTHORS: Garrison, Long, and Stinson.

VARIABLE: Communication Ease for Deaf Students.

DESCRIPTION: The Classroom Communication Ease Scale (CCES; Garrison, Long, & Stinson, 1994) is a self-report procedure devised in response to increasing concern about the availability of instruments to adequately describe the communication abilities of hard-of-hearing and deaf students. Very few studies have examined deaf or hard-of-hearing students' performances with 'everyday' tasks, particularly in classroom contexts (Hyde & Power, 1992). Exceptions include the useful publication by Erber (1988) and the attempt by the designers of the CCES to determine students' self-ratings of their communication experiences in (College) classroom settings. The CCES was developed from an earlier 28-item, 4-point scale, the Perceived Communication Ease Scale (PCES) by Long, Stinson and Braeges (1991). The CCES consists of 84 items: 55 designed to assess deaf students' understanding of communication (the 'cognitive' dimension) and 21 to assess the 'affective' dimensions of communication in the classroom. Eight additional items are included to examine respondents' preferred modes of communication with teachers and peers. For each of the items, respondents have six (rather than four in the PCES) alternative responses. The items in the CCES attempt to focus on specific classroom activities and communication opportunities, particularly those relevant in mainstreamed education contexts. The readability of CCES items was examined to ensure that hard-of-hearing and deaf students did not have difficulty understanding the questions.

SAMPLE: The CCES was developed from a sample of 50 mainstreamed college students at the National Technical Institute for the Deaf in New York. They were described as "severely to profoundly deaf" and between 18 and 36 years.

RELIABILITY: The development of the CCES involved the use of the Rasch measurement model (Rasch, 1980) which doesn't assume equal scaling distances between response categories, but scaling differences are estimated from the data obtained in association with the 'difficulty' determined for each response alternative. The developers also used the BIGSTEPS reliability index (Wright & Linacre, 1991) in association with the Rasch procedure as a measure of internal consistency. The CCES study reports a strong set of reliability and internal consistency indices including Item Separation Indices of .90 and .92 for the 'cognitive' and 'affective' dimensions respectively.

VALIDITY: Examination of the content validity of the test items indicates that a substantial range of classroom communication situations and tasks is involved. There are, however, no items examining students' use of communication systems such as hearing aids or FM systems, or examination of the impact of classroom noise and lighting conditions: all of which have been demonstrated to be important for communication by deaf or hard-of-hearing students in regular classrooms. Further, no items are reported to examine the use of interpreters or note-takers in such situations. Students are not asked to describe or rate their own hearing loss within the Scale, although it has been demonstrated that there are significant differences between the listening abilities of moderately, severely and profoundly deaf students (for example, Erber, 1975 and Hyde & Power, 1992). Finally, the materials and the procedure were developed with college-age students (18 to 36 years) and it needs to be demonstrated that these materials are useable for hard-of-hearing and deaf students in mainstreamed school-age settings. Although valuable in its present form, the validity of the scale could enhanced if these features were considered.

LOCATION: Garrison, W., Long, G., & Stinson, M. (1994). The Classroom Communication Ease Scale: Development of a self-report questionnaire for mainstreamed deaf students. *American Annals of the Deaf, 139,* 132-140.

COMMENT: The CCES is a well-researched procedure for self report by deaf or hard-of-hearing students about the ease with which they communicate in regular (college) classroom situations. Further development of the Scale could include examination of students' (self-rated) level of hearing loss, their use of amplification systems and other systems designed to improve the signal-to-noise ratios that they receive, and consideration of influence noise and the use of note-takers and interpreters to enhance their communication ease in classrooms. Ongoing development of the CCES, including these additional parameters in secondary school settings, would enhance its existing value.

REFERENCES:

Erber, N.P. (1975) Audio-visual perception of speech. *Journal of Speech and Hearing Disorders, 40,* 481-492.

Erber, N.P. (1988). *Communication Therapy for Hearing-impaired Adults.* Melbourne: Clavis Publishing.

Garrison, W., Long, G., & Stinson, M. 1994. The Classroom Communication Ease Scale: Development of a self-report questionnaire for mainstreamed deaf students. *American Annals of the Deaf, 139,* 132-140.

Hyde, M.B. & Power, D.J. (1992) Receptive communication abilities of hearing-impaired students. *American Annals of the Deaf, 137,* 389-398.

Long, G., Stinson, M., & Braeges, J. (1991). Students' perceptions of communication ease and engagement: How they relate to academic success. *American Annals of the Deaf, 136,* 414-421.

Rasch, G. (1980). *Probabilistic Models for some Intelligence and Attainment Tests.* Chicago: University of Chicago Press.

Wright, B.D., & Linacre, J.M. (1991). *BIGSTEPS: Rasch Model Computer Program. (Version 2.0).* Chicago: MESA Press.

REVIEWER: Merv Hyde Centre of Deafness Studies and Research, Griffith University, QLD 4111, Australia

7.06: CLERICAL WORKER APTITUDE BATTERY.

AUTHOR: Porteous.

VARIABLE: Numerical Ability, Verbal Comprehension, Working Memory, measured by weighted combinations of Number Skill, Word Skill, Comprehension sub-tests.

DESCRIPTION: Three short (under ten minutes each) tests of Elementary Calculation And Decision Making, Grammar And Spelling Error Checking, and Verbal Comprehension from passages. Three tests scores are standardised according to accumulated and up-dated norms, and then transformed to a Deviation scale. Results are overall ratings for Clerical Ability and Clerical Accuracy. A spreadsheet program carries out the arithmetic.

SAMPLE: The test was constructed with Further Education college and School leavers. The norms are for 1,500 applicants for Clerical positions in local authority offices.

RELIABILITY: Internal consistency for each test separately in excess of .8: **Test-retest:** one sample of ten job applicants, $r=.75$ for overall composite rating.

VALIDITY: Three samples of existing clerical workers Overall ratings were ranked and correlated with job performance rankings: r>.80.

FURTHER EMPIRICAL USES: Available only as part of serviced assessment centre package

LOCATION: Psychometrica International Limited, Business and Technology Park, North Mall Cork, Ireland.

REFERENCES

Porteous, M.A. (1995). *Occupational Psychology*. London: Prentice Hall

REVIEWER: M.A. Porteous Applied Psychology Department, University College Cork, Cork, Ireland. E-mail: STAY8012@ucc.ie

7.07: CLINICAL POST-CONFERENCE LEARNING ENVIRONMENT SURVEY.
AUTHOR Letizia.

VARIABLE: Aspects of the learning environment in an educational conference setting.

DESCRIPTION: The Clinical Post-Conference Learning Environment Survey (CPCLES; Letizia. 1998) is derived from the Classroom Environment Scale (CES; Moos, 1974). The CPCLES is a self- report instrument consisting of 54 items designed to measure 3 dimensions and 6 subscales of the perceived learning environment. Responses are scored on a 7-point scale ranging from (1) *Never* to (7) *Always*.

SAMPLE: Letizia (1998) intends the instrument to be used to measure aspects of the learning environment in conference settings with an undergraduate nursing student and faculty population.

RELIABILITY: Internal consistency: Total alpha coefficient for the instrument=.96; subscale alpha coefficients ranging from .87 to .93. Inter item correlations ranging from .37 to .63. **Test-retest:** Person r correlation coefficients ranging from .92 to .99 when the instrument was re-administered to 10% of the population two weeks following the initial survey.

VALIDITY: **Construct:** Each of the six subscales was evaluated for internal consistency with the theoretical dimension in which it is placed; alpha coefficients ranging from .90 to .96.

LOCATION: Lelizia, M. (1998). Development and testing of the Clinical Post-Conference Learning Environment Survey. *Journal of Professional Nursing, 14,* 206-213.

COMMENT: Extensive educational research regarding the learning environment demonstrates the impact of the environment on the learning process. Documentation of student and faculty perceptions of the learning environment can be used to modify and improve conditions for positive learning experiences and potential learning gains.

REFERENCES

Lelizia, M. (1998). Development and Testing of the Clinical Post-Conference Learning Environment Survey. *Journal of Professional Nursing, 14,* 206-213.

Moos, R., & Trickett, E.S. (1974). *Classroom Environment Scale Manual.* Palo Alto: Consulting Psychologist Press.

REVIEWER: Marijo Letizia, Loyola University Chicago, Maywood IL, 60153, U.S.A.

7.08: COMPUTER UNDERSTANDING AND EXPERIENCE (CUE) SCALE, (THE).
AUTHORS: Potosky and Bobko.

VARIABLE: Computer experience, knowledge of computers.

DESCRIPTION: Self-report scale that contains 12 items to assess the degree to which an individual understands how to use a computer. Respondents are asked to rate their use, 'know how' and 'know what' regarding computers. A high score indicates more extensive knowledge of computers. The scale may be subdivided into two correlated subscales, which reflect technical competence (6 items) and general competence (6 items) regarding computers.

SAMPLE: Potosky and Bobko (1998) created the measure to assess overall computer expertise in non-psychiatric adult populations.

RELIABILITY: Internal consistency: Internal reliability estimates ranging from .87 (Potosky, 1996) to .93 (Potosky & Bobko, 1998) were obtained.

VALIDITY: Convergent: CUE scale scores were positively related to self-ratings of knowledge of computers, computer ownership, hours per day spent working at a computer, and whether or not a respondent had taken a course in computer programming or word processing (Potosky, 1996; Potosky & Bobko, 1998). **Discriminant:** Potosky and Bobko (1998) found that the overall CUE scale, as well as each subscale, were not significantly correlated with age or whether respondents were enrolled in a four-year college degree program. Although Potosky and Bobko (1998) reported a significant correlation between gender and CUE score, additional analyses indicated that males in this sample, on average, actually had more computer experience. The authors suggested that the reported gender difference was not necessarily due to the scale itself and may not generalise to other samples.

LOCATION: Potosky, D., & Bobko, P. (1998). The Computer Understanding and Experience Scale: A self-report measure of computer experience. *Computers in Human Behavior*, *14*, 337-348.

COMMENT: Satisfactory psychometric properties have been obtained for the CUE scale. Research is needed to establish the discriminant validity of the scale relative to measures of computer attitudes, computer anxiety, and computer efficacy beliefs. In addition, although the CUE scale appears to capture general 'know how' regarding computers, it subscales essentially refer to technical (*i.e.*, programming) and more general (*e.g.*, word processing) computer experience. Additional items regarding the use and understanding of internet applications may be needed, as it is not clear whether internet use would fall within the general use subscale or perhaps characterise a third type of computer understanding and experience.

REFERENCES:

Potosky, D. (1996). *Beliefs about Computers and Their Subsequent Effects on Response Distortion.* Unpublished doctoral dissertation, Rutgers University, New Brunswick, NJ.

Potosky, D., & Bobko, P. (1998). The Computer Understanding and Experience Scale: A self-report measure of computer experience. *Computers in Human Behavior*, *14*, 337-348.

REVIEWER: Denise Potosky, School of Graduate Professional Studies, Pennsylvania State University, Malvern, PA, 19355, U.S.A.

7.09: CONSIDERATE AND RESPONSIBLE EMPLOYEE (CARE) SCALE.
AUTHORS: Burt, Gladstone and Grieve .

VARIABLE: Work team safety attitudes, safety climate within a work group or division.

DESCRIPTION: Self-report scale which contains 21-items.   Factors analysis showed the 21–items load on a general factor.   Nineteen of the items concern positive employee safety related behaviours, while the other 2 items are negative employee safety related behaviours and are reverse scored.   Respondents are asked to rated each item using a 5-point scale as to the degree to which they agree with the behaviour (1=*Strongly disagree*, 2=*Disagree*, 3=*No opinion*, 4=*Agree*, 5=*Strongly agree*).   CARE scale scores can range from 21 to 105.   Higher scores on the CARE scale indicate more positive attitudes to safety related behaviours.

SAMPLE: The CARE scale is intended for use with work teams and measures the responsibility and consideration that might be expected from a worker towards their co-workers safety.   The scale is particularly suited to the assessment of safety climate in work teams in high-risk occupations such as forestry, construction, and petroleum exploration.   It could be used, for example, to contrast the safety climate in teams working the same operation within the same organisation, or to assess the impact of a safety related intervention on work group attitudes.

RELIABILITY: Internal consistency: It demonstrated satisfactory internal consistency ranging from .90 to .91 (Burt, Gladstone, & Grieve, 1998). **Test-retest:** Burt, Gladstone and Grieve (1998) reported a test-retest correlation of r=.62 among 40 operators in an aluminium smelter.

LOCATION: Burt, C.D.B. Gladstone, K., L., & Grieve, K. R. (1998). Development of the Considerate and Responsible Employee (CARE) Scale. *Work and Stress*, *12*, 362-369.

COMMENT: Care scale scores have shown means of 85.4, 79.2, and 88.5 in 3 samples, respectively 105 respondents from a range of occupation, 28 meat processors, and 40 aluminium smelter workers. Positive relationships have been found between CARE scale scores and measures of both group cohesion (Evans and Jarvis's, 1986 – Group Attitude Scale), and co-worker satisfaction (Balzer, Smith, Kravitz, Lovell, Paul, Reilly, & Reilly, 1990 – Job Descriptive Index).

REFERENCES:

Balzer, W., Smith, P., Kravitz, D., Lovell, S., Paul, K., Reilly, B., & Reilly, C. (1990). *User's Manual for the Job Descriptive Index (JDI) and the Job in General (JIG) Scale*. Department of Psychology, Bowling Green University.

Burt, C.D.B. Gladstone, K.L., & Grieve, K.R. (1998). Development of the Considerate and Responsible Employee (CARE) Scale. *Work and Stress*, *12*, 362-369.

Evans, N.J., & Jarvis, P.A. (1986). The group attitude scale: A measure of attraction to group. *Small Group Behavior*, *17*, 203-216.

REVIEWER: Christopher D. B. Burt, Department of Psychology, University of Canterbury, Private Bag 4800, Christchurch, New Zealand.   E-mail: cburt@psyc.canterbury.ac.nz.

7.10: COURSE EXPERIENCE QUESTIONNAIRE (CEQ), THE.

AUTHOR: Ramsden.

VARIABLE: Student evaluations of teaching quality at the level of whole course or degree.

DESCRIPTION: The Course Experience Questionnaire (CEQ) represents a development of work originally carried out at Lancaster University in the 1980s (Ramsden & Entwistle, 1981), and is designed as a performance indicator of teaching effectiveness at the level of whole course or degree. The CEQ is widely used as part of a national strategy of providing Australian universities with system-wide information which they can use to make informed judgements about the quality of the courses they are offering (Ainley & Long, 1994). Since 1992, it has been distributed to all Australian university graduates within a few months of course completion, as part of the Graduate Career Council of Australia Graduate Destination Survey. Thus, the scale has been designed to measure aspects of the learning environment across disciplines and institutions. The Course Experience Questionnaire consists of a full form (36 items, CEQ36), and a short form (23 items, CEQ23). The full form comprises five scales measuring key aspects of the learning context, namely Good Teaching, Clear Goals and Standards, Appropriate Assessment, Appropriate Workload, and an Emphasis on Independence, and a sixth outcome scale (Generic Skills) which measures the extent to which graduates perceive their courses as developing a number of generic skills and abilities, for example, problem-solving and team work. The 23 item short form excludes the Emphasis on Independence scale, and includes the full version of the Generic Skills scale, and shortened versions of the Good Teaching, Clear Goals and Standards, Appropriate Assessment, and Appropriate Workload scales.

SAMPLE: Tertiary level graduates or students.

RELIABILITY: Internal consistency: Demonstrates moderate to high levels of internal consistency for all scales, ranging from .67 to .88 (Ramsden, 1991; Wilson et al., 1997).

VALIDITY: Construct: The construct validity of both forms of the instrument is supported by extensive exploratory and confirmatory factor analyses conducted at both item and scale levels, using several large multi-disciplinary samples of university students (Ramsden, 1991; Richardson, 1994; Wilson et al., 1997). **Criterion:** The criterion validity of the instrument is demonstrated by the results of a series of correlational analyses conducted to test the relationship between scores on the scales of the CEQ and a number of external criteria related to teaching and learning effectiveness (Wilson et al., 1997).   All CEQ scales evidence significant positive correlations with a deep approach to student learning (emphasis on understanding and deriving meaning) and significant negative correlations with a surface approach to learning (emphasis on reproducing facts). Significant positive associations were found between scores on the learning environment scales of the CEQ and measures of learning outcomes - course satisfaction, academic achievement and generic skill acquisition. **Discriminant:** The discriminant validity of the short form is established by its demonstrated capacity to discriminate between programmes with distinct course objectives and teaching philosophies. A comparison of the pattern of differences in students' perceptions of their learning environments in traditional versus problem-based medical degree programmes, and traditional versus experiential and action learning based psychology degree programmes was conducted across an Australia wide sample. The results of analyses of variance revealed patterns in students' perceptions of their learning environment consistent with the pedagogic differences between programmes of study (Wilson et al., 1997).

LOCATION: Wilson, K.L., Lizzio, A., & Ramsden, P. (1997). The development, validation and application of the Course Experience Questionnaire. *Studies in Higher Education, 22,* 33-53.

COMMENT: The CEQ can be regarded as a valid, reliable and stable instrument, and is demonstrably useful as an educational evaluation tool. Both the long and short forms of the instrument demonstrate a high degree of stability and validity. Additionally, the CEQ measures constructs directly relevant to students' reported approaches to, satisfaction with, and outcomes of, their learning in university contexts. The CEQ's sensitivity to differences, along theoretically predictable lines, between traditional and problem-based and experiential programmes suggests its useful application in research studies seeking to establish the comparative educational efficiency of learning environments. It is important to stress that the CEQ is designed as a summative program evaluation tool, and is not designed to provide specific feedback regarding individual subjects or teachers. Thus, broad-based diagnoses of student perceptions of a degree programme should be followed up by more specific qualitative and quantitative investigations.

REFERENCES:

Ainley, J., & Long, M. (1994). *The Course Experience Survey 1992 Graduates.* Canberra: Australian Government Publishing Service.

Ramsden, P. (1991). A performance indicator of teaching quality in higher education: The Course Experience Questionnaire. *Studies in Higher Education, 16,* 129-150.

Ramsden, P., & Entwistle, N.J. (1981). Effects of academic departments on student's approaches to studying. *British Journal of Educational Psychology, 51,* 368-383.

Richardson, J.T.E. (1994). A British evaluation of the Course Experience Questionnaire. *Studies in Higher Education, 19*, 59-68.

Wilson, K.L., Lizzio, A., & Ramsden, P. (1997). The development, validation and application of the Course Experience Questionnaire. *Studies in Higher Education, 22*, 33-53.

REVIEWERS: Lizzio, A.J., & Wilson K.L., School of Applied Psychology, Griffith University, Mt. Gravah, Qld 4111, Australia. E-mail: A.Lizzio@mailbox.gu.edu.au

7.11: DECISIONAL PROCESS INVENTORY, THE.
AUTHOR: Hartung.

VARIABLE: Career decidedness, indecision.

DESCRIPTION: The Decisional Process Inventory (DPI; Hartung, 1994) contains 25 items designed to measure level of career indecision, defined in terms of progress and problems in moving through the Gestalt Career Decision Making Cycle (CDMC). The CDMC comprises three dimensions: career decision-making orientation (CDO; 11 items dealing with readiness to make a career choice), career decision-making closure (CDC; 7 items dealing with action to make a career decision), and career decision-making resistance (CDR; 7 items dealing with interruption of the decision-making process). Each item includes two response anchors for respondents to rate how they think and feel about making career decisions on a five-point, Likert-type scale. This produces items such as "The career information I have makes me want to: tune in 1 2 3 4 5 tune out." Summing the items for each scale yields a score range of 11-55 on CDO, of 7-35 on CDC, and of 7-35 on CDR. Higher scores on CDO indicate more readiness for making a career choice. Higher scores on CDC indicate more involvement in the career choice process. Higher scores on CDR indicate more difficulty in making a career decision.

SAMPLE: To date, the DPI has been used strictly in research with community college and undergraduate university students. The intended use of the DPI, however, is with adolescents, young adults, adults, and individuals at other stages of the lifespan who are considering career options or making career choices.

RELIABILITY: Internal consistency: Three studies of the DPI have reported satisfactory levels of internal consistency among the items and scales (Hartung, 1995; Hartung & Marco, 1998; Marco, 1998). The most recent study of the DPI attained Cronbach's alpha coefficients of .89 for CDO, .79 for CDC, and .81 for CDR.

VALIDITY: Construct: Factor analyses of the DPI items and scales have indicated that the DPI may best measure three latent dimensions of the Gestalt Career Decision-Making Cycle. These three dimensions are CDO, CDC, and CDR. The convergent validity data also give evidence of the construct validity of scores on the DPI. Convergent: The DPI has been shown to correlate in the expected directions with measures of career decidedness and vocational identity (Hartung, 1995; Hartung & Marco, 1998; Marco, 1998).

LOCATION:

Hartung, P.J. (1994). *The Decisional Process Inventory*. Unpublished psychological test. Northeastern Ohio Universities College of Medicine, Rootstown, OH 44272-0095, U.S.A.

Hartung, P.J., & Marco, C.D. (1998). Refinement and further validation of the Decisional Process Inventory. *Journal of Career Assessment, 6,* 147-162.

COMMENT: Initial research and development of the Decisional Process Inventory provides satisfactory and encouraging evidence for the basic psychometric properties of the scale. The DPI appears useful as a brief measure of career decidedness that yields data about three aspects of the career decision-making process: readiness to make a choice, action aimed at making a choice, and problems that may interrupt the choice process. Implications for using the DPI in career counseling have been described. Further research is needed to examine the test-retest reliability of the DPI, its ability to discriminate from other measures of similar purpose, its predictive validity, and the potential effects of social desirability associated with this self-report measure.

REFERENCES:

Marco, C.D. (1998). *A Gestalt perspective on career decision making: Validity of the Decisional Process Inventory.* Unpublished doctoral dissertation, The University of Akron, Akron, OH.

Hartung, P.J. (1995). Developing a theory-based measure of career decision making: The Decisional Process Inventory. *Journal of Career Assessment, 3,* 299-313.

Hartung, P.J., & Marco, C. (1998).   Refinement and further validation of the
    Decisional Process Inventory.   *Journal of Career Assessment*, *6*, 147-
    162.

REVIEWER: Paul J. Hartung, Behavioral Sciences Department, Northeastern Ohio
Universities College of Medicine, Rootstown, OH, 44272-0095, U.S.A.

7.12: EMPLOYEES' PERCEPTIONS OF CAREER MANAGEMENT PRACTICES.
AUTHOR: Crabtree.

VARIABLE: Employees' perceptions of how successfully they felt their organisation
developed and implemented career management practices.

DESCRIPTION: Self-report scale which contains 18-items representing employees'
perceptions of their organisation's career management practices. Respondents are
asked to rate how successfully they felt their Organization developed and
implemented career management practices on an 8-point Likert-type scale (0=*Not
Available in this Company, At this Location*; U=*Uncertain*; 1=*Extremely
Unsuccessfully*, 6=*Extremely Successfully*). Higher scores on the scale indicate
success at developing and implementing career management practices.

SAMPLE: Crabtree (1999) intended the scale to be used by organizations for the
assessment of their company's career management practices. The scale is intended
to be used by academic researchers in conjunction with other organisational and
individual variables.

RELIABILITY: **Reliability** alpha levels for the total scales are .95; .94 for Training and Development, .95 for Job Postings and Assignments, and .88 for Career Counseling and Mentoring. **Factor analysis** indicates a 3-factor, 15-item scale. The three factors or subscales are Training and Development (8-item), Job Postings and Assignments (4-items), and Career Counseling and Mentoring (3-items).

LOCATION: Crabtree, M.J. (1999). Employees' Perceptions of Career Management Practices: The development of a new measure. *Journal of Career Assessment*, 7, 203-212. Scale items are available from the author M. Jane Crabtree at Benedictine University, Lisle, IL.

COMMENT: These is a need for further research utilising the Employees' Perceptions of Career Management Practices with a variety of samples and with various organisational and individual variables.

REFERENCES:

Crabtree, M.J. (1999). Employees' Perceptions of Career Management Practices: The development of a new measure. *Journal of Career Assessment*, 7, 203-212.

REVIEWER: M. Jane Crabtree, College of Business, Benedictine University, Lisle, IL 60532, U.S.A. E-mail: jcrabtree@ben.edu

7.13: ENCOURAGEMENT AND CONTROL BEHAVIOR MANAGEMENT SCALES.

AUTHORS: Ooi, Sherwood, Murphy, Morris, and Morris.

VARIABLE: Nursing approach to interpersonal interaction to increase positive affect in institutionalized elders.

DESCRIPTION: Two scales were developed in a series of factor analytic procedures to measure commonly employed nursing management strategies - defined here as encouragement and control techniques used to care for elderly subjects with symptom distress in an institutional setting.   The summary Encouragement and Control scales were based on staff processes that occur 5 or more days per-week. In the exploratory sample, the mean 6-item Encouragement scale score was 1.95 (the number of areas for which the resident received a nursing intervention of this type). For the 5-item Control scale, the mean was less than one intervention per resident (.54).   In the confirmatory sample, average scores were higher: for Encouragement, it was 2.50 and for the Control scale, it was 1.25.

SAMPLES: In the exploratory study, a proportionate random sample of nursing home residents, aged 60 years or older, with markers of mental disorder from 45 facilities in Delaware state (*n*=808). In the confirmatory study, a random sample of nursing home residents (by unit), aged 60 years or older, both with and without markers of disorder at HRCA, a large, long-term care facility in Boston, Massachusetts (*n*=290).

RELIABILITY: A series of analyses were performed to study the comparability of factor structures derived from the Delaware dataset and that of the long-term care facility in Boston); and the psychometric properties of the concepts as originally defined. **Internal consistency:** In Delaware, for the Encouragement scale, the alpha reliability was .689, and for the Control scale, the reliability was .687. Higher reliability values were obtained when the analysis was limited to those with cognitive impairment. In the confirmatory sample, alpha reliabilities were higher; for encouragement: .76, and for Control: .74. **Test-retest:** Pending a test-retest correlation analysis of data from a recently completed, prospective 18-month study designed to test the impact of training staff to specifically employ encouragement and control intervention techniques.

VALIDITY: We determined that it was possible to obtain high concordance between trained observer and staff self-report of Encouragement and Control nursing processes at HRCA (average intra-class correlation of .89 for Encouragement and .73 for Control, items). However, the greater the lag time between observer rating and nursing self-report, the lower the reliability. To improve understanding of these nursing management processes, and to help clarify whether the same phenomena were measured at HRCA as in Delaware, multiple regression analyses were performed to identify independent predictors of Encouragement and Control indices. The focus was on delineating the kinds of cognitive, behavioral and mood measures that would be predictive of Encouragement and Control use in the Delaware (as compared to the HRCA) setting. The data showed extensive overlap in predictive factors for both samples. Although the multiple R for the equation in Delaware differed from HRCA (*e.g.*, Control, .41 vs. .56), similar measures (and beta coefficients) emerged as predictive of Encouragement and Control scales in both settings with minor exceptions.

A confirmatory factor analysis using LISREL indicated that the model specifying both scale structures was fundamentally sound, and the data fitted the model well. However, the existing scale structures did not fully explain all inter-correlations between items, suggesting the inclusion of another dimension that involved improving ways to monitor residents and/or manipulate sources of environmental stimuli.

LOCATION: Ooi, W.L., Sherwood, S., Murphy, M., Morris, S.A., & Morris, J.N. (1999). Development, testing and validation of two scales measuring nursing management of subjects with markers of mental disorder. *Journal of Clinical Epidemiology, 49*, 1381-1388.

COMMENT: The data revealed that two basic groupings of factors emerged from both data-sets, thus providing independent verification of the existence of different items (11 nursing process items) that would conceptually distinguish encouragement from control processes. The difference in alpha reliability values was attributable to lower average inter-item correlations in Delaware, and the fact that at HRCA, there was greater consistency in the implementation of these processes - staff had been trained to employ variations of the basic approach throughout the day. This translated into higher levels of Encouragement and Control at HRCA, and a comparison of mean encouragement levels at HRCA and Delaware reflected this difference in training. Additional studies have incorporated the principles of these nursing management strategies in the design and execution of their study protocols, and have found these scales to be useful in guiding protocol development and/or in data analysis and interpretation (Ooi, Morris, Brandeis, *et al.*, 1999; Camberg, Woods, Ooi, *et al.*, 1999; Hurley, Ashley, Woods, *et al.* in press; Ooi , Morris, Morris, *et al.*1998).

REFERENCES

Camberg, L., Woods, P., Ooi, W.L., Hurley, A., Volicer, L., Ashley, J., Odenheimer, G., & McIntyre, K. (1999). Evaluation of simulated presence: A personalized approach to enhance well-being in persons with

Alzheimer's Disease. *Journal of American Geriatric Society*, *47*, 446-452.

Hurley, A.C., Ashley, J., Woods, P., Camberg, L., Odenheimer, G., Ooi, W.L., McIntyre, K., & Volicer, L. (1999). Measurement of observed agitation in patients with dementia of Alzheimer's type. *International Journal of Mental Health and Ageing*, in press.

Ooi, W.L., Morris, J., Brandeis, G., Hossain, M., & Lipsitz, L. (1999). Nursing home characteristics and the development of pressure sores and disruptive behavior. *Age and Ageing*, *28*, 45-52.

Ooi, W.L., Morris, J.N., Morris, S., Belleville-Taylor, P., Murphy, K., Kiely, D., Gwyther, L., & Emerson-Lombardo, N. (1997). *Facility Resource and Administrative Factors that affect Family Involvement with Care in the Special Care Unit*. Paper presented, Amer Public Health Association Annual Meeting, Nov.1997, Indianapolis, IN.

Ooi, W.L., Sherwood, S., Murphy, M., Morris, S.A., & Morris, J.N. (1996). Development, testing and validation of two scales measuring nursing management of dubjects with markers of mental disorder. *Journal of Clinical Epidemiology*, *49*, 1381-1388.

REVIEWER: Wee Lock Ooi, Health Care Consult and Analysis, 8 DeForest Road, Newton, Massachusetts, MA 02462, U.S.A. E-mail: plce600@earthlink.net

7.14: ESSENTIAL SKILLS SCREENER: "AT-RISK" IDENTIFICATION (ESS).
AUTHORS: Erford, Vitali, Haas, and Boykin.

VARIABLE: Reading, Arithmetic and Writing skills in children ages 3-11.

DESCRIPTION: The Essential Skills Screener (ESS) is a standardized instrument used to quickly and reliably identify children who are 'at-risk' of educational problems or failure. It is designed to screen or identify children, 3-11 years of age, who may exhibit problems in preacademic or academic development (Erford, Vitali, Haas, & Boykin, 1995). The ESS assesses three age categories [Preschool (P), Elementary School (E), and Upper- Elementary School (U)], each consisting of one of three academic skill areas [Reading Essential Skills Screener (RESS), Math Essential Skills Screener (MESS) and Writing Essential Skills Screener (WESS)], for a total of nine tests. With a user-friendly format and an administration time of approximately ten minutes or less per category, the ESS is an efficient and practical way of identifying the needs of students within the school setting. The design of the ESS also allows it to be used as a criterion-referenced test by teachers to identify mastery-level achievement of students in one or more subject areas.

SAMPLES: The ESS is a norm-referenced test developed from a sample of 2,190 children residing in the states of Maryland and Virginia, U.S.A. The children were in grades preschool through six and ranged in age from three to eleven. Of the children sampled, 43% attended public elementary school, 37% attended private elementary schools and 20% attended private day care organizations. In terms of comparability with the United States census data, "the ESS standardization sample is approximately equivalent to national averages with respect to race and sex and only slightly over representative of urban/suburban children and children with educated fathers" (Erford *et al.*, 1995, p. 42).

Reliability: Internal consistency: Results for internal consistency were obtained from the standardization sample of 2,190 children and ranged from .87 to .95 (RESS-P, $r=.93$; RESS-E, $r=.93$; RESS-U, $r=.90$; WESS-P, $r=.95$; WESS-E, $r=.93$; WESS-U, $r=.87$; MESS-P, $r=.93$; MESS-E, $r=.94$; MESS-U, $r=.90$). These coefficients demonstrate strong internal consistency (Erford *et al.*, 1995). Test-retest: The authors tested 367 normal children, aged 3-11, and then re-tested them 30 days later. Correlations ranged from .83 to .93 indicating that the ESS scales are stable over time (Erford *et al.*, 1995). Reliability coefficients for each level of the ESS are as follows: RESS-P, $r=.89$ ($n=119$); RESS-E, $r=.93$ ($n=125$); RESS-U, $r=.90$ ($n=123$); WESS-P, $r=.91$, ($n=85$); WESS-E, $r=.86$ ($n=83$); WESS-U, $r=.83$ ($n=165$); WESS-P, $r=.91$ ($n=119$); MESS-E, $r=.86$ ($n=125$); MESS-U, $r=.90$ ($n=123$).

VALIDITY: Content: The ESS authors consulted authoritative and empirical sources to help identify the major domains of the three academic areas and items that would represent those domains. To further support content validity the authors employed item - total scale correlational procedures yielding significant ($p<.01$) correlations for all items with their respective scales, with the exception of two items on the RESS-P that had a significance level of $p<.05$. **Criterion-Related:** Various tests were administered to establish concurrent criterion-related validity yielding coefficients of .66 to .92, with the majority having a correlation coefficients of at least .77 (all correlations, $p<.01$). According to Erford *et al.* (1995), the RESS-P correlated .79 ($n=175$) with the Expressive One-Word Picture Vocabulary Test-Revised (EOWPVT-R; Gardner, 1990) and .89 ($n=175$) with the Test of Early Reading Ability-2nd Edition (Reid, Hresko, & Hammill, 1989). Erford (1997) reported the WESS-P correlated .76 ($n=125$) with the EOWPVT-R, and .82 ($n=125$) with the Developmental Test of Visual-Motor Integration (VMI; Beery, 1989). Erford (in press) also found the MESS-P to correlate .92 ($n=125$)

with the Test of Early Math Ability-2nd Edition (Ginsberg & Baroody, 1990).
Erford *et al.* (1995) reported the RESS-E correlated .82 (n=171) with the
Woodcock-Johnson reading domain (Woodcock & Johnson, 1989), .76 (n=171)
with the Wide Range Achievement Test-Revised Reading Sub-test (WRAT-R;
Jastak & Wilkinson, 1984), and .72 (n=171) with the Slosson Oral Reading Test -
Revised (Slosson & Nicholson, 1990). According to Erford *et al.* (1995), the
WESS-E correlated .75 (n=125) with the Woodcock-Johnson writing cluster, .78
(n=125) with the WRAT-R Spelling Sub-test, and .84 (n=125) with the Test of
Written Language-2nd Edition (Hammill & Larsen, 1988). The MESS-E (Erford
et. Al., 1998) correlated .80 (n=171) with the WRAT-R Math Sub-test, .74
(n=171) with the Woodcock-Johnson-Revised math cluster, and .73 (n=171) with
the KeyMath-Revised (Connelly, 1988) calculation cluster. Erford *et al.* (1995)
reported the RESS-U correlated .83 (n=200) with the WRAT-R Reading Sub-test,
.75 (n=200) with the SORT-R, and .79 (n=200) and .75 (n=200) with the Word
Identification and Passage Comprehension Subtests of the Woodcock Reading
Mastery Test-Revised (Woodcock, 1987), respectively. According to Erford,
Ivey, and Dorman, the WESS-U correlated .66 (n=275) with the Woodcock-
Johnson writing cluster, .80 with the WRAT-R Spelling sub-test, and .80 (n=275)
with the TOWL-2. The MESS-U correlated .78 (n=200) with the WRAT-R Math
Sub-test, .80 (n=200) with the Woodcock-Johnson-Revised math cluster, and .77
(n=200) with the KeyMath-Revised calculation cluster (Erford *et al.*, 1995)
Construct: Construct validity was measured through correlations with other tests,
measures of internal consistency, and age/grade differentiation. The first two
were positively reported above. Age and grade differentiation analysis revealed a
consistent pattern of differences between age and grade groups with a smooth
directional progression. According to Erford *et al.* (1995), "the presence of a
smooth, significant progression of age and grade means on the ESS tests provides
further evidence that the ESS measures the constructs of developmental academic
skills" (p. 54).

LOCATION: Slosson Educational Publications, Inc. P.O. Box 280, East Aurora, New York 14052, U.S.A.

COMMENT: The ESS is a well-developed, standardized instrument measuring pre-academic and academic abilities and disabilities. The authors provide detailed information on test construction, norms, reliability and validity. The manual also provides detailed directions for administration and scoring with examples of correct and incorrect answers. The manual provides age and grade norms (percentile ranks, standard scores, and age equivalents). With the growing population of children being tested, the ESS, with its ease of use, efficiency, and high reliability and validity for at-risk samples, is a welcomed addition.

REFERENCES:

Beery, K.E. (1989). *Manual for the Developmental Test of Visual-Motor Integration* (3rd Edition). Cleveland, OH: Modern Curriculum Press.

Connolly, A.J. (1988). *Manual for the KeyMath - Revised: A Diagnostic Inventory of Essential Mathematics*. Circle Pines, MN: American Guidance Services.

Erford, B.T. (1997). Reliability and validity of the Writing Essential Skills Screener-Preschool Version (WESS-P). *Diagnostique, 23,* 213-223.

Erford, B.T. (in press). Development and psychometric properties of the Math Essential Skills Screener-Preschool Version (MESS-P). *Educational Research Quarterly.*

Erford, B.T., Bagley, D.L., Hopper, J.A., Lee, R.M., Panagopulos, K.A., & Preller, D.B. (1998). Reliability and validity of the Math Essential Skills Screener-Elementary Version (MESS-E). *Psychology in the Schools, 35,* 127-135.

Erford, B.T., Ivey, E.A., & Dorman, S.L. (1999). The Writing Essential Skills Screener-Upper Elementary Version: A technical analysis. *Psychological Reports, 84*, 917-926

Erford, B.T., Vitali, G.J., Haas, R., & Boykin, R.R. (1995). *Manual for the Essential Skills Screener: "At-Risk" Identification.* East Aurora, NY: Slosson Educational Publications.

Ginsberg, H.P., & Baroody, A.J. (1990). *Manual for the Test of Early Mathematics Ability* (2nd Edition). Austin, TX: Pro-ed.

Hammill, D.D., & Larsen, S.C. (1988). *Manual for the Test of Written Language* (2nd Edition). Austin, TX: Pro-ed.

Jastak, S., & Wilkinson, G.S. (1984). *Manual for the Wide-Range Achievement Test - Revised.* Wilmington, DE: Jastak Associates.

Reid, D.K., Hresko, W.P., & Hammill, D.D. (1989). *Manual for the Test of Early Reading Ability* (2nd edition). Austin, TX: Pro-ed.

Slosson, R., & Nicholson, C. (1990). *Manual for the Slosson Oral Reading Test - Revised.* East Aurora, NY: Slosson Educational Publications.

Woodcock, R.W. (1987). *Manual for the Woodcock Reading Mastery Test - Revised.* Circle Pines, MN: American Guidance Services.

Woodcock, R.W., & Johnson, M.B. (1989). *Manual for the Woodcock-Johnson: Tests of Achievement - Revised.* Allen, TX: DLM.

REVIEWERS: David E. Cavan and Bradley T. Erford, Ph.D., Loyola College in Maryland, U.S.A.

7.15: ETHICAL CLIMATE QUESTIONNAIRE (ECQ).
AUTHORS: Bart and Cullen.

VARIABLES: Ethical climate in work settings; nine sub-components underlying ethical climate.

DESCRIPTION: The Ethical Climate Questionnaire is a self-administered tool addressing nine proposed components derived from a theoretical construct (Victor & Cullen, 1988). The multidimensional questionnaire originally comprised 26 items using an adapted 6-point Likert-type format; the more recent version (Cullen, Victor, & Bronson, 1993) is comprised of 36 items, with four items on each of the climate-types theoretically proposed. It uses a broad and general definition of ethics, that, essentially responds to "what one should do?" in a situation. The ECQ was developed to "...tap respondents' perceptions of how the members of their ...organization ...make decisions ...requiring ethical criteria (Victor & Cullen, 1988)." In particular, it was designed to "...identify organization decision-making norms..." (Victor & Cullen, 1988), with attention to descriptions of the general work climate in the organization. Based on earlier theoretical work, the authors desired to describe "forms or styles of behaviour in organizations" (Victor & Cullen, 1988), rather than what the respondent wished would occur, for example. An underlying assumption was respondents' ability to objectively observe "organizational behaviour."

SAMPLES: The original study by the authors (Victor & Cullen, 1987) assessed the 26-item ECQ among four convenience samples: MBA students ($n=75$), university faculty ($n=25$), military students in an MBA program ($n=29$), and trucking managers ($n=17$). The second study (Victor & Cullen; 1988) tested the 26-item ECQ on 872 employees in four firms, with an overall response rate of 74%, ranging from 52-84%. The respondents, representing CEOs of 40 organizations in a mid-sized midwestern city, originally participated in a seminar and volunteered for the study. From 20 volunteer firms, four were selected based on pre-set criteria; all respondents were full-time employees in these four firms. In a 1993 study (Cullen, Victor, & Bronson), the authors reported findings from three studies using twelve (12) organizations comprising 1,167 individuals; this study used the 36-item version of the ECQ. A follow-up study (Vaicys, Barnett, & Brown, 1996) randomly selected respondents from 1,000 members of the American Marketing Association, with a 20% (n=207) response rate among these marketers; the marketers represented 207 firms. A recent study of lodging personnel (Upchurch, 1998) consisted of random purposively selected respondents (n=500) from the 1994 Hotel Travel Index, with 198 usable surveys (39.6% rate) returned. This study used the older 26-item version of the ECQ among these general managers of lodging operations; the sample included three sub-groupings: full service, limited, and rooms-only operations.

RELIABILITY: The reliability from the studies noted above were established using Cronbach's alpha for internal consistency reliability on the original 26-item and 36-item versions of the ECQ. Initial analysis resulted in reliabilities on six factors ranging from .65 to.82. The 1988 study reported alphas ranging from .60 to .80 on five factors on the 26-item ECQ; the 1993 36-item study reported reliabilities ranging from .69 to .85 on seven factors; the 1996 study revealed six factors among the proposed nine using the 36-item ECQ, with reliabilities ranging from .62 to .89. The 1998 descriptive study (Upchurch) did not report reliability coefficients on three constructs tested by administration of the earlier 26-item ECQ. None of the studies above reported test-retest reliability results.

VALIDITY: No study above reported validity analyses. One study stated results of factor analyses were "suggesting" validity (Cullen, et. al.,1993), however, type of validity was not specified nor were studies reported that directly assessed validity.

LOCATION: Two versions of the ECQ were noted: an original 26-item version, and the more recent 36-item version. In addition, the second study (*i.e.*, 1988) using the original 26-item version reported a "modification" from the original (*i.e.*, 1987) ECQ version. Language translations were not reported in the above studies.

COMMENT: The studies reviewed above indicated a multidimensional instrument that obtained respondents' perceptions of behaviours regarding ethical decisions in their respective organizations. While the authors proposed a nine factor (or component) multidimentional scale, none of the studies confirmed all nine factors, with mixed results among those confirmed. The number of factors confirmed ranged from four to seven. As with any study among organizations, there was the continuing challenge of a) adequate sample, b) response rate, and c) theoretical isomorphism with the scale. These first two issues were noted in the studies above, as well as in additional theoretical discussions of both the ECQ and measures of organizations. Several of the above studies had low response rates (*i.e.*, 20%), small organizational samples (*i.e.*, one or several), and stated need for studies among larger samples of organizations. Theoreticians in instrumentation would expect discussion of the modified Likert-type scaling and its implications for test results. Several additional works identified measurement challenges in this field. Cullen, *et. al.*, (1993) discussed organizational level of analyses resulting from significant difference between groups, however, none of the studies above discussed the theoretical and statistical issues involved when one measured at the individual level, which all of these studies did, and then shifted to the organizational (or firm) level for analysis. No statistical transformations were reported in the studies above to ameliorate for this shift in analysis. This was a continuing challenge in the field of organizational studies requiring sensitivity to such resulting conclusions. In conclusion, the ECQ expanded available measures of the ethical climate as perceived by employees in their firms on a scale that attended to theoretical as well as psychometric properties. The above studies represented significant attention to the development and confirmation of a scale for ethical climates in organizations providing relevant psychometric information. A particular strength of the ECQ was the authors' attention to the theoretical foundation. Attention should also be given to other psychometric properties; additional studies will confirm the strongest factors of this multidimensional measure enhancing its psychometric standing.

REFERENCES:

Cullen, J., Victor, B., & Bronson, J. (1993). The Ethical Climate Questionnaire: An assessment of its development and validity. *Psychological Reports, 73,* 667-674.

Upchurch, R. A. (1998). Conceptual foundation for ethical decision making: A stakeholder perspective in the Lodging Industry (U.S.A.). *Journal of Business Ethics, 17,* 1349-1361.

Vaicys, C., Barnett, T., & Brown, G. (1996). An analysis of the factor structure of the Ethical Climate Questionnaire. *Psychological Reports, 79,* 115-120.

Victor, B., & Cullen, J. (1987). A theory and measure of Ethical Climate in organizations. In W. C. Frederick, Guest Editor, *Research in Corporate Social Performance and Policy,* 9, (pp. 51-71). Greenwich, CT: JAI Press.

Victor, B., & Cullen, J. (1988). The organizational bases of Ethical Work Climates. *Administrative Science Quarterly, 33,* 101-125.

Vidaver-Cohen, D. (1998).   Moral Climate in business firms: A conceptual framework for analysis and change. *Journal of Business Ethics*, *17*, 1211-1226.

REVIEWER: Charlotte McDaniel, Center for Ethics in Public Policy and the Professions, Emory University, Atlanta, GA 30322, U.S.A.

7.16: ETHICAL COMPETENCE QUESTIONNAIRE – POLITICAL.
AUTHOR: Kavathatzopoulos.

VARIABLE: Ethical autonomy according to Piaget's theory.

DESCRIPTION: Questionnaire which contains nine items representing different political ethical dilemmas. Each item contains four alternatives of which two represent autonomous thinking and two represent heteronomous thinking. Respondents are asked to identify themselves with the main character in the story and try to solve the dilemma. The alternative respondent feels to be the most important to consider for the solution of the dilemma is marked with the number '*1*' and the second most important is marked with the number '*2*'. The possible scores on the questionnaire can range between 0 and 27. Higher scores indicate higher ethical autonomy.

SAMPLES: Kavathatzopoulos (1994) and Kavathatzopoulos and Rigas (1998) intended the test to be used for the assessment of ethical competence in populations of politicians and other people active in politics.

RELIABILITY: **Internal consistency**: The Cronbach's alpha coefficient is .74 (Kavathatzopoulos, 1994; Kavathatzopoulos & Rigas, 1998), which indicates that the scale has sufficient homogeneity. **Test-retest:** The stability coefficient is .88 (Kavathatzopoulos, 1994), and .78 (Kavathatzopoulos & Rigas, 1998).

VALIDITY: Information about the validity of ECQ-P's scores is given by the confirmatory factor analysis. The factor parameters in front of the latent variable 'Autonomy' can be interpreted as validity coefficients since these coefficients were generally high. Furthermore, the validity of ECQ-P is also supported by its discriminatory power in distinguishing between politicians at different hierarchical levels. Participants at a higher political level scored significantly higher. The effect size was medium (Kavathatzopoulos & Rigas, 1998).

LOCATION:

Kavathatzopoulos, I. (1994). *Politics and Ethics: Training and Assessment of Decision-making and Problem-solving Competency.* (Uppsala Psychological Reports, No. 436). Uppsala, Sweden: University of Uppsala, Department of Psychology.

Kavathatzopoulos, I., & Rigas, G. (1998). A piagetian scale for the measurement of ethical competence in politics. *Educational and Psychological Measurement, 58,* 791-803.

LOCATION: There is a growing interest in ethical competence and especially in the assessment of ethical competence. However, existing moral development tests are based on some kind of moral or ideological content whereas ECQ-P assesses the psychological ability to handle ethical issues independent of respondent's values and principles.

REFERENCES:

Kavathatzopoulos, I. (1994). *Politics and Ethics: Training and Assessment of Decision-making and Problem-solving Competency.* (Uppsala Psychological Reports, No. 436). Uppsala, Sweden: University of Uppsala, Department of Psychology.

Kavathatzopoulos, I,. & Rigas, G. (1998). A piagetian scale for the measurement of ethical competence in politics. *Educational and Psychological Measurement, 58,* 791-803.

REVIEWERS: Iordanis Kavathatzopoulos, Uppsala University, Department of Human-Computer Interaction, Box 337, S-751 05 Uppsala, Sweden. E-mail: iordanis@hci.uu.se

7.17: ETHICAL COMPETENCE QUESTIONNAIRE-WORKING LIFE & BUSINESS.
AUTHOR: Kavathatzopoulos.

VARIABLE: Ethical autonomy according to Piaget's theory.

DESCRIPTION: Questionnaire which contains six items representing various business ethics dilemmas. Each item contains four alternatives of which two represent autonomous thinking and two represent heteronomous thinking. Respondents are asked to identify themselves with the main character in the story and try to solve the dilemma. The alternative respondent feels to be the most important to consider for the solution of the dilemma is marked with the number '1' and the second most important is marked with the number '2'. The possible scores on the questionnaire can range between 0 and 18. Higher scores indicate higher ethical autonomy.

SAMPLE: Kavathatzopoulos (1993, 1994a) and Kavathatzopoulos and Rigas (under preparation) intended the test to be used for the assessment of ethical competence in populations of business people in private and public sectors.

RELIABILITY: **Internal consistency:** The Cronbach's alpha coefficient was .61 (Kavathatzopoulos & Rigas, under preparation), which indicates that the scale has sufficient homogeneity. Earlier versions showed KR=.64 to .81 (Kavathatzopoulos, 1993, 1994a). **Test-retest:** The stability coefficient was .72 (Kavathatzopoulos & Rigas, under preparation).

VALIDITY: Information about the validity of ECQ-WLB's scores is given by the confirmatory factor analysis. The factor parameters in front of the latent variable 'Autonomy' can be interpreted as validity coefficients since these coefficients were generally high. Furthermore, the validity of ECQ-WLB is also supported by its discriminatory power in distinguishing between business people at different hierarchical levels. Participants at a higher level scored Significantly higher. The effect size was high (Kavathatzopoulos & Rigas, under preparation).

LOCATION:

Kavathatzopoulos, I. (1994a). Training professional managers in decision-making about real life business ethics problems: The acquisition of the autonomous problem-solving skill. *Journal of Business Ethics*, *13*, 379-386.

Kavathatzopoulos, I., & Rigas, G. (under preparation). *Assessment of Ethical Competence in Business as a Psychological Ability*. Uppsala University, Department of Human-Computer Interaction.

COMMENT: There is a growing interest in ethical competence and especially in the assessment of ethical competence. However, existing moral development tests are based on some kind of moral content whereas ECQ-WLB assesses the psychological ability to handle ethical issues independent of respondent's values and principles.

REFERENCES:

Kavathatzopoulos, I. (1993). Development of a cognitive skill in solving business ethics problems: The effect of instruction. *Journal of Business Ethics, 12,* 379-386.

Kavathatzopoulos, I. (1994a). Training professional managers in decision-making about real life business ethics problems: The acquisition of the autonomous problem-solving skill. *Journal of Business Ethics, 13,* 379-386.

Kavathatzopoulos, I. (1994b). *Politics and ethics: Training and Assessment of Decision-making and Problem-solving Competency.* (Uppsala Psychological Reports, No. 436). Uppsala, Sweden: University of Uppsala, Department of Psychology.

Kavathatzopoulos, I., & Rigas, G. (1998). A Piagetian scale for the measurement of ethical competence in politics. *Educational and Psychological Measurement, 58,* 791-803.

Kavathatzopoulos, I., & Rigas, G. (under preparation). *Assessment of Ethical Competence in Business as a Psychological Ability.* Uppsala University, Department of Human-Computer Interaction.

REVIEWER: Iordanis Kavathatzopoulos, Uppsala University, Department of Human-Computer Interaction, Box 337, S-751 05 Uppsala, Sweden. E-mail: iordanis@hci.uu.se

7.18: ETHICS ENVIRONMENT QUESTIONNAIRE.

AUTHOR: McDaniel.

VARIABLE: Ethics environment.

DESCRIPTION: The EEQ is a twenty-item self-administered questionnaire using Likert-type five-point format. As a unidimensional scale it obtains the respondents' opinion of the environment in which h/she works. In particular, it purports to measure the perception of ethics in the organization. Originally developed for health-care organizations, it also has been administered among a large sample of non-health care employees in multi-levels of a large organization. Interspersed negative wording is introduced to diffuse a potential response set on the part of respondents. Language employed is non-site specific and inclusive. It is, therefore, applicable to a cross-section of employees and settings. One would desire a high (4-5.0) score to indicate a positive perception of ethical environment in the organization; scaling results in a summative score. The three-page questionnaire includes a cover sheet with directions.

SAMPLE: The instrument was originally tested on a sample of more than four hundred and fifty (450) registered nurses in a cross-section of health care settings; additional testing in health care expanded the nurse sample, and included a smaller sample of physicians, clergy, social workers, and administrators with similar psychometric results. A recent 1997 sample included more than four thousand (4,000) employees in a non-health care setting in multiple levels and positions within the organization. The samples in health care and non-health care represent personnel from diverse regions of the U.S.

RELIABILITY: Internal consistency: The EEQ has reported internal consistency reliability on Cronbach's alpha coefficient of .93, with a recent internal consistency reliability, also on Cronbach' alpha coefficient, in non-health care of .94 (McDaniel, 1997, 1998). A correlation matrix showed that a large proportion (48%) of the test items correlated with each other. With scaling using Likert-type format, the internal consistency reliability is an appropriate analysis. **Test-retest:** Test-retest reliability is .88 among a sample of registered nurses with a four-month interval (McDaniel, 1997) between testing. The testing employed a Pearson product moment correlation analysis.

VALIDITY: The **content validity** was established using two recommended procedures: Development and Judgment-Quantification Stage. **Construct validity** employed the pre-set criterion of .70 for predicted relationships between measures on two previously established questionnaires. The resulting correlations were above .88 (p=.01). An accepted "common sense" approach was used to assess **criterion validity**, with a resulting correlation of .94 (p=.001) with established instruments. **Dimensional analysis** of two types was completed, an exploratory factor analysis and a confirmatory factor analysis. The exploratory factor analysis was used with an established ratio of 5-10 subjects per variable. The eigenvalue was 8.627 for the primary factor of the unidimensional scale, dropping to 1.3, then 1.0. **Confirmatory factor analysis** was conducted following the exploratory factor analysis in order to "...confirm the configuration..." from the initial analysis (Eagly & Chaiken, 1993). A significant majority of the twenty items, or eighteen items, loaded above .50. All twenty items loaded above a pre-set minimum criterion of .30, with all but two above .50. The validity of the measurement model was confirmed. Additional testing among non-health care employees confirmed the underlying measurement model and the unidimensional scaling of the EEQ. **Factor Scoring Adequacy** statistics were reported for the twenty items (McDaniel, 1997). For instance, the Kaiser-Meyer-Olkin Sampling Adequacy was .92, Bartlett's Test of Sphericity was 1327.6; twelve percent (12%) of the AIC Matrix was greater than .09, and forty-eight (48%) of the residuals was greater than .05. **Reading Level:** Reading level was assessed using the Grammatik IV (Reference Software International, San Francisco, CA) with Flesch-Kincaid scoring on a computer program. The level of reading was ninth grade level, which is a level appropriate for the targeted populations. **Administrative Burden:** Given the amount of time that personnel may donate to administration and test taking, the burden of administration was assessed to determine time investment. Two forms of administrative burden were assessed: burden for the respondent, and burden for the administrator. Ease of administration for respondents was noted to be high, with an average administration time of ten minutes (10) for self-administration. This assessment suggests a readily accessible instrument. The range of completion time across all respondents ranged from a low of five (5) minutes to thirteen (13) minutes, with the mean of ten minutes (10) as noted above. Respondents had no questions about directions and assessed the questionnaire directions as unambiguous. Ease of administration for the test administrator was also noted as high, which is the second assessment for burden of administration. No special skills or preparation were required; administrators noted no problems in the administration of the EEQ.

LOCATION: McDaniel, C. (1997). Development and Psychometric Properties of the Ethics Environment Questionnaire. *Medical Care, 35*, 901-914.

COMMENT: There are few valid and reliable questionnaires to measure ethics, especially in organizations and health care settings. This established instrument demonstrates a high degree of portability to multi-sites and occupations, including professional employees. Further testing and assessment should be conducted to confirm, or disconfirm, the unidimensional scale and its psychometric properties. Generalizations made to populations upon which the EEQ has not been directly tested should be assessed carefully; testing for stability over time needs to be continued. Language translations were not noted.

REFERENCES:

Eagly, A., & Chaiken, S. (1993). *Psychology of Attitudes*. Ft. Worth, TX: Harcourt Brace, Javanovich College Publishers, p.17.

McDaniel, C. (1997). Development and Psychometric Properties of the Ethics Environment Questionnaire. *Medical Care, 35*, 901-914.

McDaniel, C. (1998). Enhancing Nurses' Ethical Practice: Development of a Clinical Ethics Program. *Nursing clinics of North America, 33*, 299-312.

McDaniel, C. (1998). Ethical Environment: Reports of Practicing Nurses. *Nursing clinics of North America, 33*, 363-372.

REVIEWER: Charlotte McDaniel, Candler School of Theology, Center for Ethics in Public Policy and the Professions, Emory University, Atlanta, GA 30322, U.S.A.

7.19: FACETS OF JOB AMBIGUITY (QUESTIONNAIRE FOR MEASURING).
AUTHORS: Breaugh and Colihan.

VARIABLE: Three facets of job ambiguity.

DESCRIPTION: Self-report instrument designed to measure the following three facets of job ambiguity: work method ambiguity (*i.e.*, employee uncertainty with regard to the methods or procedures to be used for accomplishing the work), scheduling ambiguity (i.e, employee uncertainty concerning the scheduling or sequencing of work activities), and performance criteria ambiguity (*i.e.*, employee uncertainty concerning the standards that are used for determining whether one's job performance is satisfactory). The instrument contains nine positively worded items (three items to tap each facet). Responses are scored on a 7-point scale ranging from (1) *Disagree strongly* to (7) *Agree strongly*. Lower scores on the scale indicate a high degree of experienced ambiguity.

SAMPLE: The questionnaire can be used for measuring job ambiguity in all jobs and occupational groups.

RELIABILITY: **Internal consistency:** The reliability coefficients (Cronbach's α) for each facet reach satisfactory levels ranging from .77 for the work method subscale (Schmidt & Hollmann, 1998) to .97 for the performance criteria subscale (Breaugh & Colihan, 1994). Furthermore, the results of confirmatory factor analyses show that a three-factor-model provides a better fit to the data than a one-factor (global) ambiguity model (Breaugh & Colihan, 1994; Schmidt & Hollmann, 1998). However, an added specified two-factor-model, in which the items for measuring work method and scheduling ambiguity form one factor, reveals similarly good fit indices than the three-factor-model (Schmidt & Hollmann, 1998). **Test-retest:** Breaugh and Colihan (1994) report a median test-retest-reliability of .69 across two studies for time periods of one month and two weeks, respectively.

VALIDITY: **Convergent:** The three ambiguity subscales correlate with various measures of the information environment at work like co-workers as source of information, feedback from agents, and tenure with company (Breaugh & Colihan, 1994; Schmidt & Hollmann, 1998). Furthermore, the subscales are related to satisfaction with supervision (Breaugh & Colihan, 1994; Schmidt & Hollmann, 1998), satisfaction with work, performance ratings (Breaugh & Colihan, 1994), and organisational commitment (Schmidt & Hollmann, 1998).

LOCATION:

Breaugh, J.A., & Colihan, J.P. (1994). Measuring facets of job ambiguity: Construct validity evidence. *Journal of Applied Psychology*, *79*, 191-202. (English version)

Schmidt, K.-H., & Hollmann, S. (1998). Eine deutschsprachige Skala zur Messung verschiedener Ambiguitätsfacetten bei der Arbeit. *Diagnostica*, *44*, 21-29. (German version)

COMMENT: Several researchers (*e.g.*, King & King, 1990) have suggested that the lack of an instrument capable of measuring different facets of job ambiguity may have impeded both theory development and the application of job ambiguity research results. The present instrument remedies this defect. However, the factorial structure of the questionnaire needs further examination.

REFERENCES:

Breaugh, J.A., & Colihan, J.P. (1994). Measuring facets of job ambiguity: Construct validity evidence. *Journal of Applied Psychology*, *79*, 191-202.

King, L.A., & King, D.W. (1990). Role conflict and role ambiguity: A critical assessment of construct validity. *Psychological Bulletin*, *107*, 48-64.

Schmidt, K.-H., & Hollmann, S. (1998). Eine deutschsprachige Skala zur Messung verschiedener Ambiguitätsfacetten bei der Arbeit. *Diagnostica*, *44*, 21-29.

REVIEWER: Klaus-Helmut Schmidt, Institut für Arbeitsphysiologie an der Universität Dortmund, Ardeystr. 67, D-44139 Dortmund, Germany.

7.20: FILL-IN CONCEPT MAPS.

AUTHORS: Schau and Mattern.

VARIABLE: Connected understanding of discipline concepts.

DESCRIPTION: The fill-in concept map format was created to yield scores that measure connected understanding (understanding both concepts and the connections among concepts) of the discipline being assessed. This format is based on traditional concept maps where concept words or phrases are placed in geometric shapes (usually ovals or rectangles) and interconnected with linking words (represented by labelled arrows). Keeping an expert-drawn concept map structure intact, a fill-in map is created by removing some or all of the concept words and/or linking words. Students fill in these blanks either by generating the words to use (called "generate-and-fill-in") or by selecting the words from a set which may or may not include distractors (called "select-and-fill-in" or SAFI) (Schau, Mattern, Weber, Minnick, & Witt, 1997). To date, the SAFI version of this map format has been the more widely used. Fill-in concept maps are most often scored as the percentage of correctly filled-in responses, although they also may be scored in other ways.

SAMPLE: SAFI maps have been used as research and/or instruction assessment tools with middle-school science students (Schau *et al.*, 1997), undergraduate-level introductory astronomy students (Schau, Zeilik, Mattern, & Teague, 1999; Zeilik, Schau, & Mattern, 1999; Zeilik, Schau, Mattern, Hall, Teague, & Bisard, 1997), graduate-level introductory statistics students (Schau & Mattern, 1997a,b), and personnel enrolled in a hazardous waste training course (Stevens, 1997).

RELIABILITY: Internal consistency: Scores from carefully-developed SAFI concept map assessments show adequate or good levels of internal consistency.

Cronbach's alpha values for middle-school science students (Schau *et al.*, 1997) and for personnel enrolled in a hazardous waste training course (Stevens, 1997) were in the low .90s, while those for introductory astronomy students were in the low to mid .80s (*e.g.*, Schau *et al.*, 1999). **Test-retest:** There is no research exploring the short-term test-retest stability of these scores. Because connected understanding is a form of achievement, instructors do not care about stability across a course; instead, they desire a large mean increase in achievement from the beginning to the end of instruction.

VALIDITY: Each of the SAFI maps described in the cited studies was created using a thorough development procedure. Although these procedures varied somewhat among the studies, in each case they included extensive input from course instructors to ensure the inclusion of appropriate and accurate discipline content in the maps. As expected from a good achievement measure, scores from each of the SAFI maps showed large increases from the beginning to the end of the courses studied. For astronomy students, percent correct gains across the course ranged from 20% to 30% (*e.g.*, Schau *et al.*, 1999). For statistics students, gains were almost 50% (Schau & Mattern, 1997a,b). For adults in the training course, gains ranged from 13% to 20% (Stevens, 1997). Evidence indicates that scores from SAFI concept maps assess domain-relevant achievement. SAFI map scores correlate moderately or highly with scores from other traditional measures of achievement. For adults also completing classroom multiple-choice tests, these correlations clustered in the low .50s (Schau *et al.*, 1999; Stevens, 1997; Zeilik *et al.*, 1997). For middle school students, SAFI map scores correlated in the mid .70s with scores from a multiple-choice standardized science achievement test (Schau *et al.*, 1997). For statistics students, map scores correlated over .80 with total course points (Schau & Mattern, 1997a,b). One study provides evidence that scores from SAFI concept maps assess connected understanding. Astronomy students' SAFI map scores correlated in the low .50s with scores from a related ratings task (a traditional research assessment of connected understanding), a large effect size (*e.g.*, Schau *et al.*, 1999).

LOCATION: Examples of SAFI concept map measures can be found in the references included in this review. The maps used in each of these references are available from the authors. However, to be most effective as an assessment, instructors and researchers should create a new set of SAFI maps designed to target the connected understanding of greatest importance in their specific courses.

REFERENCES:

Schau, C., & Mattern, N. (1997a). Assessing students' connected understanding of statistical relationships. In I. Gal, & J.B. Garfield (Eds.), *The Assessment Challenge in Statistics Education* (pp. 91-104). Netherlands: IOS Press.

Schau, C., & Mattern, N. (1997b). Use of map techniques in teaching applied statistics courses. *The American Statistician, 51*, 171-175.

Schau, C., Mattern, N., Weber, R. W., Minnick, K., & Witt, C. (1997, April). *Use of fill-in concept maps to assess middle school students' connected understanding of science.* Paper presented at the annual meeting of the American Educational Research Association, Chicago, IL.

Schau, C., Zeilik, M., Mattern, N., & Teague, K. W. (1999, April). *Select-and-fill-in concept maps as a measure of undergraduate students' connected understanding of introductory astronomy.* Paper presented at the annual meeting of the American Educational Research Association, Montreal.

Stevens, P. A. (1997). *Using concept maps for assessing adult learners in training situations.* Unpublished dissertation, University of New Mexico, Albuquerque.

Zeilik, M., Schau, C., & Mattern, N. (1999).   Conceptual astronomy II:
Replicating conceptual gains, probing attitude changes across three
semesters. *American Journal of Physics, 67*, 923-927.

Zeilik, M., Schau, C., Mattern, N., Hall, S., Teague, K., & Bisard, W. (1997).
Conceptual astronomy: A novel model for teaching postsecondary
science courses. *American Journal of Physics, 65*, 987-996.

REVIEWER: Candace Schau, 12812 Hugh Graham Road N.E., Albuquerque, New
Mexico, 87111, U.S.A. E-mail: cschau@unm.edu

7.21: FORMAL AND INFORMAL POWER QUESTIONNAIRES (FIPQ), THE.
AUTHORS: Melià, Oliver, and Tomas.

VARIABLE: Social power in organisational settings: Formal and Informal power,
and French and Raven bases of power.

DESCRIPTION: An earlier form of the FIPQ was first developed by Melià (1984,
1985) and Melià and Peiró (1985), and was later improved by Melià, Oliver, and
Tomás (1993a). It measures the formal and informal power that a focal person
(*i.e.*, the person who answers the questionnaire) has over (sent power) and
receives from (received power) each of his/her role-set members. The role-set can
be described as the set of positions with which a focal person interacts while
he/she is accomplishing his/her organisational role (Kahn, *et al.* 1964). The FIPQ
works in three steps. Firstly, 10 open items allow the focal person to identify the
outstanding role-set members. Secondly, the Received Power Questionnaire
measures the power that each role set member has over the focal person. Thirdly,
the Sent Power Questionnaire measures the power that the focal person has over

each of his/her role set members. Both the Received and the Sent Power Questionnaires have the same structure. Each of them has 35 items, 5 items to measure each of the 5 bases of power formulated by French and Raven (legitimate, reward, coercion, expert and referent power), 5 more items to measure the sixth base of power (informational power) incorporated by Raven (Raven, 1993), plus 5 items to measure general power. All the items are in a 5-point Likert scale. The items are presented in 5 sets of 7 items randomly ordered. Melià (1984), Melià and Peiró (1984), Melià, Oliver, and Tomás (1993a, 1993b) and Peiró and Meliá (1999) have clearly identified that the bases of power are grouped in two dimensions. The first, named formal power, grouped legitimate, reward, punishment and informational power bases (the latter only included in the Melià, Oliver, & Tomás studies). The second, named informal power, grouped expert and referent power sources. General power items saturated in both dimensions.

SAMPLE: The FIPQ is designed to be used for the assessment of power in organisations. The FIPQ may be used on samples of managers, middle-managers, supervisors or workers.

RELIABILITY: Internal consistency: Melià, et al., (1993a) reported coefficients alpha for the received and the sent power questionnaires. Received Power Questionnaire: All items, alpha .95; Formal power (24 items), alpha .97; Informal power (11 items), alpha .90. Sent Power Questionnaire: All items, alpha .95; Formal power (23 items), .95; Informal power (11 items), .91. Peiró and Melià (1999) using a short form of the Received Power Questionnaire, obtained a coefficient alpha of .84 for formal power (7 items) and a coefficient alpha of .7 for the informal power (5 items).

VALIDITY: Content: FIPQ samples systematically the French and Raven 5 bases of power, the informational power and the general power. Criterion: It was assessed in several works using both objective and subjective relational criterions. The absolute hierarchical level and the relative hierarchical level were used as objective criterions. Dependence, contact and conflict were used as subjective criterions. All the correlations were as expected by the Bifactorial Theory of Power (*e.g.* Melià *et al.*, 1993a) found that the absolute hierarchical level of the role set members (*n*=436) is correlated .67 with received formal power, -.01 with received informal power, -.48 with sent formal power and -.13 with sent informal power). **Construct:** The structure and development of the FIPQ was based on the Bifactorial Theory of Organizational Power (Melià, 1984, 1985; Melià & Peiró, 1985; Melià, Tomás, & Oliver, 1992). Both received and sent power questionnaires support exactly the same expected bidimensional structure, with the exception of one item in the send power questionnaire. The main hypotheses of the Bifactorial Theory of Organizational Power are supported (*i.e.* the way in that bases of power are grouped, the association of formal power with the organisational hierarchy and the non-association between informal power and hierarchy, the asymmetrical property of formal power and the symmetrical property of informal power, the non-association of formal power with conflict but the negative association of informal power with conflict).

LOCATION: A summary of the content of the items may be found in Melià, Oliver, and Tomás (1993). For a full version of the questionnaire contact the first author.

COMMENT: There is evidence that supports the aggregation of the French and Raven bases of power into the Formal and Informal power dimensions and the satisfactory psychometric properties of the FIPQ. This questionnaire allows a detailed evaluation of the bases of social power in organisational networks.

REFERENCES:

Kahn, R.L., Wolfe, D.M., Quinn, R.P., Snoek, J.D., & Rosenthal, R.A. (1964). *Occupational Stress: Studies in Role Conflict and Ambiguity.* New York: Wiley and Sons.

Melià, J.L. (1984). *Role-set and the relationships between focal person and role senders: A study of the Proximity, Communication, Dependence, Power and Conflict.* University of Valencia.

Melià, J.L. (1985). El poder en las organizaciones humanas: Poder formal y poder informal, una teoría bifactorial. *Informació Psicológica, 20,* 39-42.

Melià, J.L., Oliver, A., & Tomás, J.M. (1993). A bifactorial theory of organizational power: Hypothesis and measurement. *Revista de Psicología Social Aplicada, 3,* 25-42.

Melià, J.L., Oliver, A., & Tomás, J.M. (1993). El poder en las organizaciones y su medición: El cuestionario de poder formal e informal. *Revista Latinoamericana de Psicología, 25,* 139-155.

Melià, J.L., Tomás, J.M., & Oliver, A. (1992). Teoría bifactorial del poder: Medición radial del poder social emitido. *Revista de Psicología General y Aplicada, 45,* 285-294.

Melià, J.L., & Peiró, J.M. (1984). Percepción de las relaciones de poder en ambientes organizacionales: Estudio empírico e implicaciones para un diseño de la estructura de poder. *Proceedings of the 1st Congress of the Colegio Oficial de Psicólogos* (pp. 135-144). Madrid.

Melià, J.L., & Peiró, J.M. (1985). Análisis empírico de un modelo bifactorial de poder e influencia en las organizaciones. *Proceedings of the National 2nd Congress of Work Psychology* (pp. 243-302). Terrassa.

Peiró, J.M., & Melià, J.L. (1999). Formal and informal interpersonal power in organizations: A bifactorial model of power. In Munduate, L. & Gravenhorst, K.M.B. *Proceedings of the Symposium on Power Dynamics and Organizational Change III. Innovations for Work, Organizations and Well-Being* (pp. 15-28). Espoo-Helsinki.

Raven, B.H. (1993). The bases of power: Origins and recent developments. *Journal of Social Issues, 49*, 227-251.

REVIEWER: Josep Lluís Melià, Faculty of Psychology, University of Valencia, Blasco Ibañez, 21, 46010 Valencia, Spain. E-mail: Jose.L.Melia@uv.es

7.22: GENERAL SAFETY QUESTIONNAIRE (GSQ), THE.

AUTHORS: Melià and Islas.

VARIABLE: The GSQ measures 7 safety related psychological variables: Safety Climate (CL), Supervisors and Middle Management Safety Response (S), Co-workers and Team Work Safety Response (CO), Worker Safety Behaviour (W), Base Risk (B), Real Risk (R) and Work related Tension (T).

DESCRIPTION: The General Safety Questionnaire (GSQ; Melià and Islas, 1992) is a 142-item questionnaire that measures separately the 7 variables mentioned above, and obtains descriptive and background information about the respondent, his/her job and the organisation. It also allows the description of the last three work accidents and other aspects like individual or collective protection equipment, as perceived by the respondent. The CL scale (15 items) measures the safety policy, safety structure and safety actions of the company. The S scale (7 items) measures the safety behaviour, safety attitudes and safety contingencies provided by the supervisors and middle managers. In a parallel way, the CO scale (8 items) measures the safety response of the co-workers and the W scale (13 items) the safety behaviour of the worker. Base Risk, measured by B scale (16 items), is defined as the inherent risk at the work site, independent of the safe or unsafe actions of the company, management or workers. Real risk, measured by the R scale (6 items), is the risk of having an accident given the base risk and the safe or unsafe actions of the company, the management and the workers. The T scale (15 items) measures the experience of tension associated with the work. Each of the 7 scales can also be used separately.

SAMPLE: The GSQ was designed to be used in organisational work settings, on workers, supervisors or middle managers exposed to any degree of risk.

RELIABILITY: Internal consistency: The CL scale presents a structure of three factors (*i.e.* Safety Structure of the Organisation, Safety Actions of the Organisation, and Safety Involvement of the Organisation) and an overall alpha coefficient of .84 (Islas, Oliver, Tomás, & Melià, 1992). Melià and Sesé (1997a) reported an alpha of .88 for this scale. The coefficient alpha of the S scale ranges from .84 to .88 (Melià & Sesé, 1997a; Melià, Sesé, Tomás, & Oliver, 1992; 1994). In a multisample factor analysis Melià and Sesé (1998) confirm the monofactorial structure of the S scale. The CO scale shows a bifactorial structure (*i.e.*, Social Safety Response of the Co-workers and Individual Safety Behaviour of the Co-workers) integrated into a second order factor (Melià, Oliver, Tomás, & Chisvert, 1993). Melià and Sesé (1997b) reported a coefficient alpha of .84. The W scale shows a three factor structure (*i.e.*, Safe Behaviours, Unsafe Behaviours and Specific Safe and Unsafe Behaviours) and an alpha between .75 and .77 (Melià, Rodrigo, & Sospedra, 1994; Melià & Sesé, 1997a). The B scale has a three factor structure (*i.e.* Risk Severity, Chemical Risk, and Mechanical Risk) and a overall alpha ranging from .86 (Melià, Rodrigo, & Sospedra, 1993) to .89 (Melià, Sospedra, & Rodrigo, 1993; 1994). The R scale has a monofactorial structure and an alpha of .84 (Melià & Sesé, 1997a). The T scale was developed independently but also included into the GSQ. The T scale has a monofactorial structure and an alpha of .85 (Melià, 1994, Melià & Sesé, 1999).

VALIDITY: The relationships within the GSQ scales and between other variables have been systematically studied in several researches. Islas *et al.*, (1992) reported correlations between the CL scale an other variables: .63 with S scale, .46 with CO scale, .27 with W scale, -.08 with R scale, -.08 with work accidents, and .46 with the degree of safety training. Melià and Sesé (1997a) reported correlations between the S scale and other scales: .64 with W scale, .56 with CO scale, -.11 with B scale, -.28 with R scale, -.40 with T scale and -.18 with work accidents. Melià, Rodrigo, and Sospedra (1993) found that Base Risk correlates .57 with Real Risk and .26 with accidents. Melià, Sospedra, and Rodrigo (1993, 1994) found that the Base Risk Scale discriminates among different kinds of industries with different levels of risk. Early results about the relationships among the safety scales included in the GSQ can be found in Melià, Oliver, and Tomás (1992) and Melià, Tomás, Oliver, and Islas (1992). Melià (1998) presents a path model of the psycho-social antecedents of work accidents that illustrates the main validity relationships among the scales included in the GSQ. The model, supported by the data, postulated that Safety Climate has effects on the supervisors' safety response; that supervisors' safety response has effects on the co-workers' safety response, and that co-workers' safety response together with safety climate and supervisors' safety response have effects on workers' safety behaviour. Safety climate, base risk and the worker safety behaviour have independent causal effects on real risk, and finally, real risk has causal effects on accidents. Melià (1994) presents the correlations between the T scale and some of the most used questionnaires about tension related with work. The T scale correlated .44 with the Job Related Tension Index (Kahn *et al.* 1964), and .68 with the Anxiety-Stress Questionnaire (House & Rizzo, 1972). Melià and Sesé (1999) obtained a correlation of -.46 between safety behaviour and tension, a correlation of .26

between tension and real risk and a correlation of .18 between tension and accidents.

LOCATION: A summary of the content of the items may be found in several of the above quoted papers. For a full version of the questionnaire contact the first author.

COMMENT: The psycho-social model of the causes of the accidents underlying the GSQ scales has been supported by the data and the reliability and validity coefficients obtained and replicated in several samples seems suitable. The GSQ is a useful instrument to diagnose the state of some of the most outstanding safety variables from a safety psychology point of view.

REFERENCES:

House, R.J., & Rizzo, J.R. (1972). Role conflict and ambiguity as critical variables in a model of organizational behavior. *Organizational Behavior and Human Performance, 7*, 467-505.

Islas, M.E., Oliver, A., Tomás, J.M., & Melià, J.L. (1992). Una medida de clima organizacional hacia la seguridad: Estudios psicométricos. *Revista Sonorense de Psicología, 6*, 31-40.

Kahn, R.L., Wolfe, D.M., Quinn, R.P., Snoek, J.D., & Rosenthal, R.A. (1964). *Occupational Stress: Studies in Role Conflict and Ambiguity.* New York: Wiley and Sons.

Melià, J.L. (1994). La medición de la tensión en el trabajo. *Revista de Psicología del Trabajo y las Organizaciones, 28*, 17-37.

Melià, J.L. (1998). Un modelo causal psicosocial de los accidentes laborales. *Anuario de Psicología, 29*, 25-43.

Melià, J.L., & Islas, M.E. (1992). *Batería de Cuestionarios de Seguridad Laboral.* Valencia: Cristobal Serrano.

Melià, J.L., Oliver, A., & Tomás, J.M. (1992). An organizational and psychological causal model of occupational accidents. *The European Work and Organizational Psychologist*, *2*, 212.

Melià, J.L., Oliver, A., Tomás, J.M., & Chisvert, M. (1993). El cuestionario de respuesta de los compañeros hacia la seguridad: Estudio psicométrico. *Revista de Psicología Social Aplicada*, *3*, 47-60.

Melià, J.L., Rodrigo, M.F., & Sospedra, M.J. (1993). Replicación del estudio del Cuestionario para la medida del Riesgo Basal: Fiabilidad, validez, estructura factorial y análisis diferenciales en una muestra de sujetos accidentados. *Psicológica*, *14*, 161-175.

Melià, J.L., Rodrigo, M.F., & Sospedra, M.J. (1994). Análisis psicométrico del Cuestionario de Conducta hacia la Seguridad: Fiabilidad, Validez, estructura factorial y anàlisis diferenciales. *Psicológica*, *15*, 209-225.

Melià, J.L., Tomás, J.M., Oliver, A., & Islas, M.E. (1992). *Organisational and Psychological variables as antecedents of work safety: A causal model.* Proceedings of the Conference on Safety and Well-Being at Work: A Human Factors Approach. Loughborough.

Melià, J.L., & Sesé, A. (1997a). La medida de la respuesta de los supervisores y mandos intermedios hacia la seguridad y la higiene laboral. *Revista de Psicología del Trabajo y de las Organizaciones*, *13*, 223-243.

Melià, J.L., & Sesé, A. (1997b). La mesura de la resposat dels companys de treball cap a la seguretat i salut laboral. *Anuari de Psicologia*, *4*, 71-92.

Melià, J.L., & Sesé, A. (1998). Análisis factorial confirmatorio multimuestra de la escala de respuesta de los supervisores y mandos intermedios hacia la seguridad a través de tres muestras. *Revista de Psicología Universitas Tarraconensis*, *20*, 91-108.

Melià, J.L., & Sesé, A. (1999). La medida de la tensión laboral y su influencia en la conducta de seguridad. *Ansiedad y Estres*, *5*.

Melià, J.L., Sesé, A., Tomás, J.M., & Oliver, A. (1992). Propiedades psicométricas y análisis factorial confirmatorio del cuestionario de respuesta hacia la seguridad de los supervisores y mandos intermedios. *Psicológica, 13*, 285-299.

Melià, J.L., Sesé, A., Tomás, J.M., & Oliver, A. (1994). Un estudio psicométrico de replicación sobre el cuestionario de respuesta hacia la seguridad de los supervisores y mandos intermedios. *Revista de Psicología Social Aplicada, 4*, 47-61.

Melià, J.L., Sospedra, M.J., & Rodrigo, M.F. (1993). Una segunda replicación del estudio del Cuestionario para la medida del Riesgo Basal: Fiabilidad, Validez, Estructura factorial y análisis diferenciales en una muestra de sujetos accidentados. *Revista de Psicología del Trabajo y de las Organizaciones, 9*, 251-263.

Melià, J.L., Sospedra, M.J., & Rodrigo, M.F. (1994). Medición del Riesgo Basal en Psicología de la Seguridad Laboral. *Anuario de Psicología, 60*, 49-61.

REVIEWER: Josep Lluís Melià, Faculty of Psychology, University of Valencia, Blasco Ibañez, 21, 46010, Valencia, Spain. E-mail: Jose.L.Melia@uv.es

7.23: HOSPITAL SOCIAL WORK SELF-EFFICACY SCALE (HSWSE),THE.

AUTHORS: Holden, Cuzzi, Rutter, Rosenberg, and Chernack.

VARIABLE: Self-efficacy regarding hospital social work.

DESCRIPTION: The Hosptial Social Work Self-Efficacy Scale (HSWSE; Holden, Cuzzi, Rutter, Rosenberg, & Chernack, 1996) is a 39-item, self-report scale comprised of five subscales: patient groups; written communications; team performance; critical case tasks; and stress management. The respondent is asked to indicate how confident they are today that they could successfully perform each of the 39 tasks. Their level of confidence is rated on a nine point scale (1=*Not at all confident*; 5=*Moderately confident*; and 9=*Totally confident*). Subscale and total scale scores are created by computing average scores across the items for each sub or total scale.

SAMPLE: The HSWSE is intended for use with social workers employed in hospital settings and with masters' level social work interns placed in hospital settings. It has been used with both groups.

RELIABILITY: Internal consistency: The Cronbach's alphas for the HSWSE Total scale have always exceeded .90. The Cronbach's alphas for the HSWSE subscales have typically exceeded .80. **Test-Retest:** Although the HSWSE is a state measure, the test-retest reliability was examined in the longitudinal study in which the scale was developed. As would be expected with a state measure the test-retest reliability of the HSWE declined with time (for total scale the correlations declined from .75 at 9 week, to .55 and .47 at 21 and 30 weeks respectively).

VALIDITY: Preliminary evidence was obtained regarding the construct validity of the HSWSE using an effect size estimate approach to construct validity. The predicted relationships between the HSWSE and, a slightly modified version of Sherer and Adams' Self-Efficacy Scale, Moos' Work Environment Scale (various subscales on the Real and Ideal versions), and Frans' Social Work Empowerment scale, have tended to be quite close to the observed relationships.

LOCATION: Holden, G., Cuzzi, L.C., Rutter, S. Rosenberg, G., & Chernack, P. (1996). The Hospital Social Work Self-Efficacy Scale: Initial development.

Research on Social Work Practice, 6, 353-65. Full scale with instructions and background available from: gary.holden@nyu.edu

COMMENT: While there is growing evidence for the satisfactory psychometric properties of the HSWSE, the studies to date have been with small samples of hospital social workers and hospital social work interns.

REFERENCES:

Cuzzi, L.C., Holden, G., Chernack, P., Rutter, S., & Rosenberg, G. (1997). Evaluating social work field instruction: Rotations versus year-long placements. *Research on Social Work Practice, 7,* 402-14.

Cuzzi, L.C., Holden, G., Rutter, S. Rosenberg, G., & Chernack, P. (1996). A pilot study of fieldwork rotations vs. year long placements for social work students in a public hospital. *Social Work in Health Care, 24,* 73-91. Co-published simultaneously in M. Mailick, & P. Caroff (Eds.), *Professional Social Work Education: Challenges for the Future,* Binghamton, NY: Haworth Press.

Holden, G., Cuzzi, L.C., Rutter, S., Chernack, P., & Rosenberg, G. (1997). The Hospital Social Work Self-Efficacy Scale: A replication. *Research on Social Work Practice, 7,* 490-9.

Holden, G., Cuzzi, L.C., Rutter, S., Chernack, P., Spitzer, W., & Rosenberg, G. (1997). The Hospital Social Work Self-Efficacy Scale: A partial replication and extension. *Health and Social Work, 22,* 256-63.

Holden, G., Cuzzi, L.C., Rutter, S. Rosenberg, G., & Chernack, P. (1996). The Hospital Social Work Self-Efficacy Scale: Initial development. *Research on Social Work Practice, 6,* 353-65.

REVIEWERS: Gary Holden, Ehrenkranz School of Social Work, New York University, 1 Washington Square North, New York, NY 10003 U.S.A. **and** Gary Rosenberg, Mount Sinai-NYU Medical Center and Health System, 1 Gustave L. Levy Place, New York, NY 10029 U.S.A. E-mail: gary.holden@nyu.edu

7.24: IMPACT OF INFORMATION TECHNOLOGY ON WORK, MEASURING THE.
AUTHORS: Torkzadeh and Doll.

VARIABLE: Four dimensions of information technology impact.

DESCRIPTION: A 12-item scale measuring the perceived impact of information technology on work at the level of the individual. Questions are grouped into four factors that measure how extensively information technology applications impact *task productivity, task innovation, customer satisfaction,* and *management control.* Each factor is measured by three questions. Respondents are asked to rate the extent of computer application impact using a 5-point Likert-type scale: 1=*Not at all* to 5=*A great deal.* The scores on the scale can range between 12 and 60 for the overall scale and between 3 to 15 for each sub-scale. Higher scores on the scale indicate a higher impact of a computer application on work for the end-user.

SAMPLE: Torkzadeh and Doll intended the 12-item scale to be used for assessing the multidimensional impact of computer applications at the level of the individual.

854 Work and Educational Psychology

RELIABILITY: **Internal consistency:** Reliability scores, using coefficient alpha, are .93 for *task productivity*, .95 for *task innovation*, .96 for *customer satisfaction*, and .93 for *management control* sub-scales. Overall reliability for the 12-item scale is .92. The reliability of the impact scales for different hardware platform, types of applications, modes of application development, and required usage conditions are also reported (Nunnally, 1978; Schoenfeldt, 1984). These reliability scores are high (Bailey & Pearson, 1983; Davis, 1989; Doll & Torkzadeh, 1988, 1990, 1998; Torkzadeh & Koufteros, 1994; Sethi & King, 1994).

VALIDITY: **Construct:** The construct validity is demonstrated using factor analysis (Kerlinger, 1978). There are no multiple loadings for any category. The four-factor model is a simple solution and explains 87.7% of the variation in the 12 items. Further, validity is demonstrated by examining correlations between the four impact sub-scales and related constructs thought to comprise the nomological network. These related constructs include an 8-item measure of perceived user involvement (Doll & Torkzadeh, 1990), a 12-item measure of user satisfaction (Doll & Torkzadeh, 1988), and a 30-item measure of system use (Doll & Torkzadeh, 1998). The scale's correlation matrix was analysed for convergent and discriminant validity. **Convergent:** Convergent validity is demonstrated by examining the correlations between measures of the same theoretical construct. The smallest within variable (factor) correlations are: *task productivity*=.79; *task innovation*=.79; *customer satisfaction*=.81; and *management control*=.73 (all significant at $p<.001$). **Discriminant:** Discriminant validity is demonstrated for each item by counting the number of times it correlates more highly with an item of another variable (factor) than with items of its own theoretical variable (Campbell & Fiske, 1959). The examination of the matrix for the 12-item instrument reveals zero violation (out of 66 comparisons) of the condition for discriminant validity. Each of the twelve items is more highly correlated with the other items in its group than with any of the items measuring other variables.

LOCATION: Torkzadeh, G., & Doll, W.J. (1999). The development of a tool for. measuring the perceived impact of information technology on work. *Omega, International Journal of Management Science, 27,* 327-339.

COMMENT: The impact of information technology on work life has been one of the most talked about issues over the recent years. There has been growing interest to study information technology impacts: on competitive advantage (Sethi & King, 1994), on time utilization (Sulek & Marucheck, 1992), on middle managers (Millman & Hartwick, 1987; Pinsonneault & Kraemer, 1993), on industry level competitive advantage (Segars & Grover, 1994), and on relative advantage (Moore & Benbasat, 1992). While the research on impact of information technology has been diverse, it (a) has narrowly focused on productivity impacts and (b) has ignored work at the level of the individual. This study uses a broader concept that is based on the impact of technology on the nature of work literature and focuses on impact at the level of the individual.

REFERENCES:

Bailey, J.E., & Pearson, S.W. (1983). Development of a tool for measuring and analyzing computer user satisfaction. *Management Science, 29,* 530-545.

Campbell, D.T., & Fiske, D.W. (1959), Convergent and discriminant validation by the multitrait-multimethod matrix. *Psychological Bulletin, 56,* 81-105.

Davis, F. (1989). Perceived usefulness, perceived ease of use, and user acceptance of information technology. *MIS Quarterly,* 319-342.

Doll, W.J., & Torkzadeh, G. (1988). The measurement of end-user computing satisfaction. *MIS Quarterly,* 259-274.

Doll, W.J., & Torkzadeh, G. (1990). The measurement of end-user software involvement. *Omega, International Journal of Management Science, 18,* 399-406.

Doll, W.J., & Torkzadeh, G. (1998). Developing a multidimensional measure of system-use in an organizational context. *Information and Management, 33,*171-185.

Millman, Z., & Hartwick, J. (1987). The impact of automated office systems on middle managers and their work. *MIS Quarterly,* 479-491.

Moore, G.C., & Benbasat, I. (1992). *An empirical examination of a model of the factors affecting utilization of information technology by End Users.* Working Paper, University of British Columbia.

Nunnally, J.C. (1978). *Psychometric Theory.* New York: McGraw-Hill.

Pinsonneault, A., & Kraemer, K.L. (1993). The impact of information technology on middle managers. *MIS Quarterly,* 271-292.

Schoenfeldt, L.F. (1984). Psychometric properties of organizational research instruments. In T.S. Bateman, & G.R. Ferris (Eds.), *Methods and Analysis in Organizational Research.* Reston, VA: Reston Publishing Co.

Segars, A., & Grover, V. (1994). Strategic Group Analysis: A methodological approach for exploring the industry level impact of information technology. *Omega, International Journal of Management Science, 22,* 13-34.

Sethi, V., & King, W.R. (1994). Development of measures to assess the extent to which an information technology application provides competitive advantage. *Management Science, 40,* 1601-1627.

Sulek, J.M., & Marucheck, A.S. (1992). A study of the impact of an integrated information technology on the time utilization of information workers. *Decision Sciences, 23,* 1174-1191.

REVIEWER: Reza Torkzadeh, College of Business, University of Nevada at Las Vegas, 4505 Maryland Parkway, Box 456009, Las Vegas, Nevada 89154, U.S.A.

7.25: LEARNING PREFERENCE ASSESSMENT, THE.

AUTHORS: Guglielmino and Guglielmino.

VARIABLE: Inclination and ability to engage in self-directed learning.

DESCRIPTION: The Learning Preference Assessment (LPA; Guglielmino & Guglielmino, 1991) is a new, self-scoring format of the Self-Directed Learning Readiness Scale (SDLRS). The SDLRS was developed by Lucy Guglielmino in 1977 and most of the research has been undertaken on the 58-item version of this instrument. Lucy and Paul Guglielmino collaborated to publish it in a self-scoring format in 1991. The instrument uses a 5-point Likert scale (*Almost always true, Usually true, Sometimes true, Usually not true, Almost never true*) items with 41 of the items positively phrased and 17 negatively phrased. The instrument measures the attitudes, values and abilities of learners relating to their readiness to engage in self-directed learning at the time of response. This readiness is assessed as a total score which is then converted into bands of 'high', 'above average', 'average', 'below average' and 'low ' readiness. The LPA/SDLRS is the most widely used instrument for the measurement of readiness for self-directed-learning (Long & Agyekum, 1988; McCune, 1988; Merriam & Brockett, 1997) and has been translated into French, German, Greek, Spanish, Japanese, Chinese, Korean, Finnish, Italian, Portuguese, Malay, and Afrikaans.

SAMPLE: The SDLRS was originally designed as a predictive or diagnostic tool for those preparing for self-directed learning in an academic field at high school, college or tertiary institutions (Guglielmino, 1977). The self-scoring format (LPA) has been used widely in business and industry (*e.g.* Guglielmino & Guglielmino, 1998; Durr, Guglielmino, & Guglielmino, 1994; Guglielmino & Klatt, 1994; Guglielmino, 1996) as well as in education for increasing awareness of self-directed learning and for self-assessment.

RELIABILITY: **Internal consistency:** Studies have demonstrated satisfactory to excellent levels with coefficient alpha and split-half between .67 and .96 (Brockett, 1985; Delahaye & Smith, 1995; Finestone, 1984; Graeve, 1987; Guglielmino, 1977, 1989; Hall-Johnsen, 1981; Hassan, 1981; Skaggs, 1981). **Test-retest:** Finestone (1984) and Wiley (1981) noted values of .82 and .79 respectively.

VALIDITY: **Content:** The content validity of the instrument was established by Guglielmino (1977) by using a modified Delphi technique, with a panel of experts, with three rounds of surveys. Finestone (1984) found a clear congruence between Guglielmino's original Delphi results and an extensive review of available literature on self-directed learning. **Construct:** As only a total score is used in the instrument, convergent validity has been found with androgyny in the Student's Orientation Questionnaire (Christian, 1982) with a value of .35 ($p=.01$) (Delahaye and Smith, 1995). Long and Agyekum (1984) also found support for divergent validity. Posner (1989) reported convergent validity ($p<.01$) with several constructs, including: *preference for challenge (.81), curiosity for learning (.79), perceived scholastic competence (.69), use of internal criteria for evaluation (.64), independent mastery (.56), and independent judgement (.54).* Russell (1988) provides support for **divergent validity** with an inverse linear relationship on preference for structure ($r=.31$, $p<.03$). McCune, Guglielmino and Garcia (1990) also found support for both convergent and divergent validity. **Criterion-related:** Hall-Johnsen (1981) and Hassan (1981) found significant positive correlation with learning projects undertaken and Graeve (1987) reported a significant positive relationships with hours spent on self-directed learning. Jones (1989) found a significant positive relationship with observable student behaviours related to self-directed learning readiness.

LOCATION: Organization Design and Development Inc., King of Prussia, Pennsylvania, U.S.A.

COMMENT: There has been extensive support for the LPA in the literature as an accurate and useful instrument for measuring readiness for self-directed learning (for example, see Adenuga, 1989; Brockett & Hiemstra, 1991; Caffarella & O'Donnell, 1987; Cunningham, 1989; Long, 1987; Long & Redding 1991). Delahaye and Smith (1995) found that the instrument was not affected by gender or by level of tertiary study. The most ardent criticisms have come from Field (1989) and West and Bentley (1989, 1991) who incited much debate about the construct validity of the instrument. The construct validity criticisms are puzzling, as the instrument relies on one total score. Further, Field's (1989) study was itself criticised because of flaws in sampling and statistical analysis (Guglielmino, Long & McCune, 1989). Bonham (1991) and Field (1989) both questioned the content validity of the instrument, contending that it merely measured a 'love of learning' or a positive attitude to learning. The content validity studies (Delahaye & Smith 1995; Guglielmino 1977) have thrown doubts on these criticisms. Brockett (1985) and Brookfield (1985) caution that the instrument is designed more for the 'educationally advantaged' and Delahaye and Smith (1995) have raised minor concerns over its use with the under 20 age group. An ABE (Adult Basic Education) form of the Self-Directed Learning Readiness Scale has been developed (Guglielmino, 1989), but literature about its use is limited. While bearing these cautions in mind, the LPA can be used with acceptable confidence to provide an accurate measurement of readiness for self-directed learning.

REFERENCES:

Adenuga, B.O. (1989). Self-directed learning readiness and learning style preferences of adult learners. In B. Delahaye, & H. E. Smith (1995). The validity of the learning preference assessment. *Adult Education Quarterly*, *45*, 159-173.

Bonham, L.A. (1991). Guglielmino's Self-directed Learning Readiness Scale: What does it measure? *Adult Education Quarterly*, *41*, 92-99.

Brockett, R.G. (1985). Methodological and substantive issues in the measurement of self-directed learning readiness. *Adult Education*, *36*, 15-24.

Brockett, R.G., & Hiemstra, R. (1991). *Self-direction in Adult Learning: Perspectives on Theory, Research, and Practice*. London: Routledge.

Brookfield, S. (1985). Analyzing a critical paradigm of self-directed learning: A response. *Adult Education Quarterly*, *36*, 60-64.

Caffarella, R.S., & O'Donnell, J.M. (1987). Self-directed adult learning: A critical paradigm revisited. *Adult Education Quarterly*, *37*, 199-211.

Christian, A.C. (1982). *A comparative study of the andragogical-pedagogical orientation of military and civilian personnel*. Doctoral dissertation. Oklahoma State University.

Cunningham, A. (1989). An examination of the self-directed learning readiness of selected students and undergraduates of masters degree programs of southern Baptist seminaries. In B. Delahaye, & H. E. Smith (1995). The validity of the learning preference assessment. *Adult Education Quarterly*, *45*, 159-173.

Delahaye, B.L., & Smith, H.E. (1995). The validity of the learning preference assessment. *Adult Education Quarterly*, *45*, 159-173.

Durr, R.E., Guglielmino, L.M., & Guglielmino, P.J. (1994). Self-directed learning readiness and job performance at Motorola. In H.B. Long & Associates. *New Ideas about Self-directed Learning* (pp. 161-174). Norman, OK: Oklahoma Research Center for Continuing Professional and Higher Education of the University of Oklahoma.

Field, L. (1989). An investigation into the structure, validity, and reliability of Guglielmino's Self-directed Learning Readiness Scale. *Adult Education Quarterly, 39,* 125-139.

Finestone, P.M. (1984). A construct validation of the Self-Directed Learning Readiness Scale with labour education participants. *Dissertation Abstracts International, 46,* 1160-1161A.

Graeve, E.A. (1987). Patterns of self-directed learning of registered nurses. (Doctoral dissertation, University of Minnesota) *Dissertation Abstracts International, 48,* 820.

Guglielmino, L.M. (1977). Development of the self-directed learning readiness scale (Doctoral Dissertation, University of Georgia). *Dissertation Abstracts International, 38,* 6467A.

Guglielmino, L. M. (1989). Development of an adult basic education form of the Self-Directed Learning Readiness Scale. In H.B. Long and Associates. *Self-Directed Learning: Emerging theory and practice.* Norman OK: Oklahoma Research Center for Continuing Professional and Higher Education of the University of Oklahoma, 63-75.

Guglielmino, L.M. (1996). An examination of self-directed learning readiness and selected demographic variables of top female executives. In H.B. Long & Associates. *Current Developments in Self-directed Learning* (pp. 11-22). Norman, OK: Public Managers Center, University of Oklahoma.

Guglielmino, L. M. (1997). Reliability and validity of the Self-Directed Learning Readiness Scale and Learning Preference Assessment. In H.B. Long & Associates. *Expanding Horizons in Self-directed Learning* (pp. 209-222). Norman, OK: Public Managers Center, College of Education, University of Oklahoma,

Guglielmino, L.M., & Guglielmino, P.J. (1991). *The Learning Preference Assessment.* U.S.A.: Organization Design and Development.

Guglielmino, P.J., & Guglielmino, L.M. (1998). Three studies of self-directed learning readiness in the People's Republic of China. In H.B. Long and Associates. *Developing Paradigms for Self-directed Learning* (pp. 61-73). Norman, OK: Public Managers Center, College of Education, University of Oklahoma.

Guglielmino, P.J., & Klatt, L.A. (1994). Self-directed learning readiness as a characteristics of the entrepreneur. In H.B.Long & Associates. *New Ideas about Self-directed Learning* (pp. 161-174). Norman, OK: Oklahoma Research Center for Continuing Professional and Higher Education of the University of Oklahoma.

Guglielmino, L.M., Long, H., & McCune, S. (1989). Reactions to Field's investigation into the SDLRS. *Adult Education Quarterly, 39,* 236-247.

Hall-Johnsen, K.J. (1981). The relationship between readiness for self-directed learning and participation in self-directed learning. (Doctoral dissertation, Iwoa State University, 1981). *Dissertation Abstracts International, 50,* 3446.

Hassan, A.M. (1981). An investigation of the learning projects among adults of high and low readiness for self-direction in learning (Doctoral dissertation, Iowa State University, 1981). *Dissertation Abstracts International, 42,* 3838A.

Jones, C.J. (1989). A study of the relationship of self-directed learning readiness to observable behavioral characteristics in an adult basic education programs. In B. Delahaye, & H.E. Smith (1995). The validity of the learning preference assessment. *Adult Education Quarterly, 45,* 159-173.

Long, H.B. (1987). Item analysis of Guglielmino's Self-directed Learning Readiness Scale. *International Journal of Lifelong Education, 6,* 331-336.

Long, H.B., & Agyekum, S. (1984). Teacher ratings in the validation of Guglielmino's self-directed learning readiness scale. *Higher Education, 13,* 709-715.

Long, H.B., & Agyekum, S. (1988). Self-directed learning: Assessment and validation. In H.B. Long and Associates. *Self-directed Learning: Application and Theory.* (pp. 253-266). Athens, GA: Adult Education Department of the University of Georgia.

Long, H.B., & Redding, T.R. (1991). Self-directed learning. *Dissertation Abstracts 1966-1991.* Oklahoma: Research Centre for Continuing Professional and Higher Education.

McCune, S.K. (1988). A meta-analysis study of adult self-direction in learning. A review of the research from 1977 to 1987. (Doctoral dissertation, Texas A & M University, 1988). *Dissertation Abstracts International, 49,* 3237.

McCune, S.K., Guglielmino, L.M., & Garcia, G. (1990). Adult self-direction in learning: A preliminary meta-analytic investigation of research using the Self-Directed Readiness Scale. In H.B. Long & others. *Advances in Self-directed Learning Research.* (pp. 145-156). Norman, OK: Oklahoma Research Center for Continuing Professional and Higher Education.

Merriam, S., & Brockett, R. (1997). *The Profession and Practice of Adult Education.* San Francisco: Jossey-Bass.

Posner, F.G. (1989). A study of self-directed learning, perceived competencies and personal orientation among students in an open alternative high school (Doctoral dissertation, University of Denver, 1989). *Dissertation Abstracts International, 51,* 813.

Russell, J.W. (1988). Learning preference for structure, self-directed learning readiness, and instructional methods (Doctoral dissertation, University of Missouri-Kansas City, 1988). *Dissertation Abstracts International, 49,* 29A.

Skaggs, B.J. (1981). The relationship between involvement of professional nurses in self-directed learning activities, loci of control, and readiness for self-directed learning measures. (Doctoral dissertation, The University of Texas at Austin, 1981). *Dissertation Abstracts International, 42,* 1906A.

West, R., & Bentley, E. Jr. (1989). Structural analysis of the self-directed learning readiness scale: A confirmatory factor analysis using LISREL modeling. In: Long, H. B. & Associates. *Advances in Research and Practice in Self-directed Learning* (pp. 157-180). University of Oklahoma.

West, R.F., & Bentley, E. L. Jr. (1991). Relationships between scores on the Self-Directed Learning Readiness Scale, Oddi Continuing Learning Inventory and participation in continuing professional education. In H.B. Long and Associates. *Self-directed Learning: Consensus and Conflict*, (pp. 71-146). Norman, OL: Public Managers Center, College of Education, University of Oklahoma.

Wiley, K. (1981). Effects of a self-directed learning project and preference for structure on self-directed learning readiness of baccalaureate nursing students. (Doctoral dissertation, Northern Illinois University). *Dissertation Abstracts International, 43*, 1A.

REVIEWERS: Brian Delahaye and Sarojni Choy, School of Professional Studies, Queensland University of Technology, QLD 4059, Australia.

7.26: MOTIVATED STRATEGIES FOR LEARNING QUESTIONNAIRE (MSLQ).
AUTHORS: Pintrich, Smith, Garcia, and McKeachie.

VARIABLE: Motivation and Learning Strategies.

DESCRIPTION: The Motivated Strategies for Learning Questionnaire (MSLQ; Pintrich, Smith, Garcia, & McKeachie, 1991) is a self-report scale, which contains 81-items designed to measure college students' motivational orientation and their use of learning strategies for a college course. Student motivation is measured by six subcales: intrinsic goal orientation, extrinsic goal orientation, task value, control of learning beliefs, self-efficacy for learning and performance, and test anxiety. The 31 items that measure student motivation are based on Pintrich's model of motivation that includes expectancy, value, and affect dimensions. The items measure students' motivation at the course level. For example, students are asked to self-report their goals and value beliefs for a specific course. Their beliefs about their skills to achieve and their anxiety about tests are also contextualized to a specific course. The learning strategy component contains 31 items that assess students' use of various cognitive and metacognitve strategy. The remaining 19 items measure students' time management strategies and use of different resources. Respondents are asked to use a Likert scale to rate each item on a seven-point scale: *Not at all true of me* (1) - *Very true of me* (7). Thirteen negative items are reverse scored so that possible scores on the scale can range between 0 and 75. Higher scores on the scale indicate a higher level of motivation towards learning activities and greater use of effective learning approaches.

SAMPLE: The MSLQ has been under development informally since 1982 and formally since 1986. Earlier versions of the test were administered to students enrolled in a "Learning to Learn" course at the University of Michigan. Three major waves of data collection were conducted from 1986 to 1988. During this time, data was collected from college students enrolled in a four-year, public, comprehensive university; a small liberal arts college, and a community college. In total, thousands of American college students have completed the MSLQ representing students from a wide range of academic disciplines (natural sciences, humanities, social science, computer science, and foreign language). The instrument is intended to be used at the course level and it assumed that a student's scores might vary depending on the course. Because the MSLQ is intended for use at the individual course level with individual students, the authors do not provide norms. The authors encourage users to provide students with feedback in addition to a description of their scores. Students are offered suggestions for improving their levels of motivation and use of learning strategies.

RELIABILITY: Internal consistency: Demonstrated adequate levels of internal reliability for the majority of the subscales, ranging from .52 to .93 (Pintrich *et al.*, 1991). Unfortunately, the authors do not report Cronbach's alpha values for each subscale in the test manual. Coefficients alphas for individual subscales are reported in Garcia *et al.* (1995) article. They report alpha values ranging from .52 *Help-Seeking* subscale) to .93 (*Self-Efficacy for Learning and Performance* subscale), which are consistent with Pintrich *et al.*'s (1991) earlier findings.

VALIDITY: Construct: Results from several confirmatory factor analyses reveal that the conceptual and measurement models of the MSLQ seem to have adequate construct validity. Goodness-of-fit and adjusted goodness-of-fit indices (GFI and AGFI) for the measurement model for the motivation scales (GFI=.77; AGFI=.73) and the cognitive strategies scales (GFI=.78; AGFI=.75) show the MSLQ scales demonstrate good factor structure (Pintrich *et al.*, 1993). MSLQ scores were not found to be related to college students' scores on the Marlowe-Crowne social desirability scale (Garcia & Pintrich, 1995), which supports the validity of this self-report scale. **Predictive:** Both the motivation and learning strategies scales show significant correlations with students' final course grades (Pintrich *et al.*, 1993). However, there appears to be an interaction effect between the predictive validity of the MSLQ and academic discipline. For example, the fifteen MSLQ subscales accounted for a total of 39% of the variance in final grades in the computer and natural sciences and accounted for 17% of the variance in final course grades in the social sciences, humanities, and foreign languages (Garcia & Pintrich, 1995). **Convergent:** No published data for college student population.

Bong (1998) reports satisfactory convergent validity with problem-referenced measurement and the MSLQ for a sample of 383 high school students.

LOCATION: Pintrich, P.R., Smith, D.A.F., Garcia, T., & McKeachie, W.J. (1991). *A Manual for the use of the Motivated Strategies for Learning Questionnaire (MSLQ).* National Center for Research To Improve Postsecondary Teaching and Learning. Technical Report No. 91-B-004. The University of Michigan, U.S.A.

COMMENT: The practical utility of the MSLQ may be the greatest strength of this instrument. The scale is easy to administer, is available at no cost, and can be completed in a relatively short amount of time. Another strength of the MSLQ is that it has undergone extensive research and the authors continue to base their revisions on current views of social-cognitive theory. The MSLQ can be compared to the Learning and Study Strategies Inventory (LASSI; Weinstein, Palmer, & Schulte, 1987), which is another widely used instrument for measuring college students' motivational and learning strategies. The LASSI assesses learning strategies at a general level, whereas, the MSLQ contextualizes motivation and learning strategies at the course level (Garcia *et al.*, 1995). Another contrast is that the MSLQ is conceptually grounded in Schunk and Zimmerman's (Schunk & Zimmerman, 1994; Zimmerman & Schunk, 1989) work on self-regulated learning (SRL). Consistent with Schunk and Zimmerman's SRL model, the MSLQ focuses on students' abilities to plan, monitor, and regulate their own learning.

REFERENCES:

Bong, M. (1998). *Effects of scale differences on the generality of academic self-efficacy judgments.* Paper presented at the Annual Meeting of the American Educational Research Association, San Diego, CA, April 1998. ERIC Document #422-379.

868   Work and Educational Psychology

Garcia, T., & Pintrich, P.R. (1995). *Assessing students' motivation and learning strategies: The Motivated Strategies for Learning Questionnaire.* Paper presented at the Annual Meeting of the American Educational Research Association, San Francisco, CA, April 1995. ERIC Document #383-770.

Pintrich, P.R., & De Groot. (1990). Motivational and self-regulated learning components of classroom academic performance. *Journal of Educational Psychology, 82,* 33-40.

Pintrich, P.R., Smith, D.A.F., Garcia, T., & McKeachie, W.J. (1991). *A Manual for the use of the Motivated Strategies for Learning Questionnaire (MSLQ).* National Center for Research to Improve Postsecondary Teaching and Learning. University of Michigan, School of Education, Technical Report No. 91-B-004.

Pintrich, R.R., Smith, D.A.F., Garcia, T., & McKeachie, W.J. (1993). Reliability and predictive validity of the Motivated Strategies for Learning Questionnaire (MSLQ). *Educational and Psychological Measurement, 53,* 801-813.

Schunk, D., & Zimmerman, B. (1994). *Self-regulation of Learning and Performance: Issues and Educational Applications.* Hillsdale, NJ: Lawrence Erlbaum Associates.

Weinstein, C.E., Palmer, D.R., & Schulte, A.C. (1987). *Learning and Study Strategies Inventory.* Clearwater, FL: H & H Publishing.

Zimmerman, B.J., & Schunk, D.H. (1989). *Self-regulated Learning and Academic Achievement: Theory, Research, and Practice.* New York: Springer-Verlag.

REVIEWER: Gypsy M. Denzine, Department of Educational Psychology, Center for Excellence in Education, Northern Arizona University, Flagstaff, Arizona 86011, U.S.A. E-mail: gypsy.denzine@nau.edu

7.27: OCCUPATIONAL ATTRIBUTIONAL STYLE QUESTIONNAIRE, THE
AUTHORS: Furnham, Sadka and Brewin.

VARIABLE: Causal attributions for occupational outcomes.

DESCRIPTION: 10-item, self-report measure presenting 5-positive and 5-negative hypothetical situations which are commonly experienced by employed individuals. Respondents are asked to imagine themselves in each situation and write down the most likely cause of the event. Respondents then rate the cause on nine separate seven-point scales assessing attributions of internality, stability, probability, externality, chance, personal control, colleague control, forseeability and importance. Scores for each scale are calculated by averaging each respondent's rating for the positive and negative situations. Revised versions of the measure are comprised of either eight positive and eight negative, or four positive and four negative situations, and contain scales assessing internality, stability, globality, externality and personal control.

SAMPLE: Original and revised measures were developed using participants who varied in occupational status, social class, and years of education. Measures should thus be appropriate for most work populations for research purposes.

RELIABILITY: Internal consistency: Moderate levels of internal consistency were reported for each of the nine scales in the original measure; coefficient alphas ranged from .52 to .84. Factor analysis revealed a three factor solution for positive items and four for negative items (Furnham, Sadka, & Brewin, 1992). The 16-item revised measure demonstrated two factor solutions for positive and negative items (Heaven, 1994), and moderate internal reliability (Heaven, 1994; Furnham, Brewin, & O'Kelly, 1994) with alphas ranging from .60 to.83. Alphas for the eight-item revised scale ranged from .32 to .85 (Furnham, Stewart, &

Medhurst, 1996). **Test-retest:** A test-retest reliability of .87 after a four week period was reported for the original measure (Furnham, Sadka, & Brewin, 1992).

VALIDITY: **Convergent:** In initial study, scale scores were shown to be predictably associated with occupational status and high salaries. Significant correlations with job satisfaction were observed for positive items, and with intrinsic job motivation for positive and negative items combined (Furnham, Sadka, & Brewin, 1992). Positive items in 16-item revised measure demonstrated significant correlations with work attitudes (Furnham, Brewin, & O'Kelly, 1994). Significant relationships were reported between positive items and intrinsic motivation, between negative items and socio-economic status and salary, and between all items and perceived social consensus using the eight-item measure (Furnham, Stewart,& Medhurst, 1996).

LOCATION: **Original measure**: Furnham, A., Sadka, V., & Brewin, C.R. (1992). The development of an occupational attributional style questionnaire. *Journal of Organizational Behavior, 13*, 27-39. **16-item revised measure**: Furnham, A., Brewin, C.R., & O'Kelly, H. (1994). Cognitive style and attitudes to work. *Human Relations, 47*, 1509-1521. **8-item revised measure**: Furnham, A., Stewart, S., & Medhurst, S. (1996). Occupational attributional style, attitudes to work and perceived social consensus. *Polish Psychological Bulletin, 27*, 153-166.

COMMENT: Although low reliability is characteristic of most attributional style instruments, the continued revision of the occupational attributional style questionnaire underscores the measure's questionable utility at this point. Consistent correlations with work-related variables attest to the potential value of the measure, however further refinements appear necessary before the occupational attributional style questionnaire will serve as a valid instrument.

REFERENCES:

Furnham, A., Brewin, C.R., & O'Kelly, H. (1994). Cognitive style and attitudes to work. *Human Relations, 47,* 1509-1521.

Furnham, A., Sadka, V., & Brewin, C.R. (1992). The development of an occupational attributional style questionnaire. *Journal of Organizational Behavior, 13,* 27-39.

Furnham, A., Stewart, S., & Medhurst, S. (1996). Occupational attributional style, attitudes to work and perceived social consensus. *Polish Psychological Bulletin, 27,* 153-166.

Heaven, P.C. (1994). Occupational attributional style and attitudes to work: An Australian study. *Australian Psychologist, 29,* 57-61.

REVIEWER: James A. Gruman, Department of Psychology, University of Windsor, Windsor, Ontario, Canada, N9B 3P4. E-mail: gruman@uwindsor.ca

7.28: OPTIMISM SCALE FOR STUDENTS, THE.
AUTHOR: Koizumi.

VARIABLE: Domain specific optimism for medium-term goals.

DESCRIPTION: Self-report scale which consists of one item. The scale adopts the present attainment in mathematics, or the present level of mathematical knowledge and skills, as the criterion, and deals with the degree to which it is expandable in the near future (one year) by the assumed best efforts. Following an explanation a line of 24 circles is drawn. Ten black circles in the left part of the line indicate the subjects' present ability level and the remaining 14 circles in the right part, in which respondents are asked to draw slanted lines to indicate their optimism in mathematics, are blank. The number of circles in which slanted lines are drawn is defined as the optimism score.

SAMPLE: Koizumi (1992) intended the scale to be used for students from primary school to junior or senior high school level.

RELIABILITY: Test-retest: Koizumi (1992) reported a test-retest correlation of $r=.72$ among 32 eighth-grade students after one month interval.

VALIDITY: The validity of the Optimism Scale for Students is supported by significant correlations with expected attainment in the future (expected attainment in arithmetic/mathematics in one year) in third-, fifth-, seventh-, and ninth-grade students (Koizumi, 1986). The optimism for medium-term goals is a different concept from the present ability. No significant relationships are reported between the optimism and the perceived present ability measured by the Harter's (1982) Perceived Competence Scale for Children (Koizumi, 1992).

LOCATION: Koizumi, R. (1992). The relationship between perceived attainment and optimism, and academic achievement and motivation. *Japanese Psychological Research*, *34*, 1-9.

COMMENT: The scale was developed to examine the academic achievement and motivation of students who are optimistic in spite of their poor grades, or of talented students who have moderate and steady expectations for the next step of achievement. Domain specificity and medium-term goals (one year) were introduced to assess these individual differences in the framework of perceived academic ability. Students would be categorised into four groups by two dimensions, perceived present attainment(H/L) and optimism(h/l). Koizumi (1992, 1999) shows that a developmental change is observed in group categorisation; Two (Hh, Ll), three (Hh, Lh, Ll), four (Hh, Hl, Lh, Ll), and four (Hh, Hl, Lh, Ll) groups were obtained in the third, fifth, seventh, and ninth grades, respectively. Characteristic features in terms of motivation- and achievement-related measures were observed among the groups in each grade.

REFERENCES:

Harter, S. (1982). The Perceived Competence Scale for Children. *Child Development, 53,* 87-97.

Koizumi, R. (1986). *Developmental Study of Perceived Ability.* Paper presented at the 42nd Annual Conference of Chugoku-Shikoku Psychological Association, Shimane, Japan.

Koizumi, R. (1992). The relationship between perceived attainment and optimism, and academic achievement and motivation. *Japanese Psychological Research, 34,* 1-9.

Koizumi, R. (1999). The development of optimism and perceived attainment from elementary school to junior high school. *Japanese Psychological Research, 41,* 209-217.

REVIEWER: Reizo Koizumi, Department of Psychology, Fukuoka University of Education, 729-1 Akama, Munakata, Fukuoka 811-4192 Japan. E-mail: koizumi@fukuoka-edu.ac.jp

7.29: PEER VICTIMISATION SCALE (PVS).

AUTHORS: Neary and Joseph.

VARIABLE: Victimisation from bullying behaviours in schools.

DESCRIPTION: The Peer Victimisation Scale (PVS; Neary & Joseph, 1994) is designed to assess victimization from bullying behaviours at school. It consists of 6-forced choice items, three of which relate to victimization from negative physical actions (e.g., hit and pushed, picked on, bullied) and three relating to victimisation from negative verbal actions (e.g., teased, horrible names, laughed at). The rationale for the development of the scale was to attempt to overcome some of the inherent problems with assessing such behaviours in schools. For example, Austin and Joseph (1996) report that whilst many children are reluctant to admit to being a victim of such negative behaviours (e.g., Rigby & Slee, 1990; Smith, 1991; Tattum, 1988), most questionnaire studies of bullying behaviours are conducted on a class basis (e.g., Whitney & Smith, 1993) which may inadvertently lead to socially desirable responding from the children once the nature of the study has been made known to the children. The reasoning for this is that despite assurances of anonymity from the researcher, any bully in the class group may subtly manipulate the situation and impede any disclosure of victimisation . As such, the argument is that the issue of bullying and victimisation should not be made known to the class. To further this aim, the Peer Victimisation Scale was designed by Neary and Joseph (1994) to be immersed within Harter's (1985) 36-item Self-Perception Profile for Children (SPPC) so as to reduce the saliency of the items concerning victimisation . Responses are scored according to the scoring instructions for scoring the SPPC sub-scales (i.e., sum of six items divided by six).

SAMPLE: Neary and Joseph (1994) do not recommended the PVC for use with children under 8 years of age as it is recommended that it be administered in conjunction with the SPPC, which stipulates that 8 years is the appropriate cut-off age.

RELIABILITY: The scale has been found to exhibit satisfactory levels of internal reliability. Austin and Joseph (1996) report a Cronbach's alpha of .83 for the PVS.

VALIDITY: Neary and Joseph (1994) report that when the PVS was used in conjunction with the SPPC, it was able to discriminate well between bullied and non-bullied children on the basis of self and peer-reports. This finding was replicated by Callaghan and Joseph (1995), thus confirming the convergent validity of the PVS with self- and peer-reports of bullying behaviours. Neary and Joseph (1994) also reported that higher scores on the PVS were associated with lower scores on all of the SPPC sub-scales, except for athletic competence, and higher scores on the Birleson Depression Inventory (Birleson, 1981).

LOCATION: Neary, A., & Joseph, S. (1994). Peer victimization and its relationship to self-concept and depression among schoolchildren. *Personality and Individual Differences, 16,* 183-186.

COMMENT: Although other questionnaires, such as the Bully/Victim Questionnaire (Olweus, 1978, 1991, 1993) are available to researchers interested in childhood bullying, the strength of the PVC is in its brevity and structure. By being designed to slot into the SPPC, this not only helps to reduce possible manipulation of testing situations by bullies, but reduces the saliency of the items and allows for less socially desirable responding from the children. A further strength is that when used in conjunction with the Bullying-Behaviour Scale

(BBS; Austin & Joseph, 1996), which is similarly designed, assessments of categories of bullies and victims may be readily made. Overall, the PVS is a useful instrument for any researcher attempting to assess accurately the levels of victimisation in large samples of children. Although other instruments may be useful in assessing the extent and frequency of bullying behaviours in schools, the PVS addresses a real need for a discreet measure of the extent of peer victimisation from bullying behaviours.

REFERENCES:

Austin,S., & Joseph, S. (1996). Assessment of bully/victim problems in 8 to 11 year-olds. *British Journal of Educational Psychology, 66*, 447-456.

Birleson, P. (1981). The validity of depression disorder in childhood and the development of a self-rating scale: a research report. *Journal of Child Psychology and Psychiatry, 22*, 73-88.

Callaghan, S., & Joseph, S. (1995). Self-concept and peer victimization among schoolchildren. *Personality and Individual Differences, 18*, 161-163.

Harter, S. (1985). *The Self-Perception Profile for Children: Revision of the Perceived Competence Scale for Children - Manual*. Denver, CO: University of Denver.

Olweus, D. (1978). *Aggression in the Schools: Bullies and Whipping Boys*. Washington, DC: Hemisphere.

Olweus, D. (1991). Bully/victim problems among schoolchildren: basic facts and effects of a school based intervention program. In D.Pepler, & K. Rubin (Eds.), *The Development and Treatment of Childhood Aggression*, (pp. 411-448). Hillsdale, NJ: Erlbaum.

Olweus, D. (1993). *Bullying at School: What We Know and What We Can Do*. Oxford: Blackwell.

Neary, A., & Joseph, S. (1994). Peer victimization and its relationship to self-
concept and depression among schoolchildren. *Personality and
Individual Differences, 16*, 183-186.

Rigby, K., & Slee, P.T. (1990). Victims and bullies in school communities.
Journal of the Australian Society of Victimology, 1, 23-28.

Smith, P.K. (1991).The silent nightmare: bullying and victimization in school peer
groups. *The Psychologist, 14*, 243-248.

Tattum, D.P. (1988). Violence and aggression in schools. In D.P. Tattum & D.A.
Lane (Eds.), *Bullying in Schools*. Stoke-on-Trent: Trentham Books.

Whitney, I., & Smith, P.K. (1993). A survey of the nature and extent of bullying
in junior/middle and secondary schools. *Educational Research, 35*, 3-25.

REVIEWERS: Conor McGuckin and Christopher Alan Lewis, School of
Psychology and Communication, University of Ulster at Magee College,
Londonderry, Northern Ireland, BT48 7JL, U.K. E-mail: ca.lewis@ulst.ac.uk

7.30: PERCEIVED OCCUPATIONAL DISCRIMINATION SCALE-FORM B.
AUTHORS: Chung and Harmon.

VARIABLE: Perceived occupational discrimination against Black Americans.

DESCRIPTION: This scale was derived from the Black Discrimination Scale
(Turner & Turner, 1975) and was designed to assess respondents' perception of
occupational discrimination against Black Americans. Respondents rate each of
26 occupations regarding discrimination against Black workers in those
occupations using a 4-point scale (*No, A little, Some*, and *A lot of*). The average
score of all items is used; therefore, scores range from 1 to 4 with higher scores

indicating perceptions of more occupational discrimination against Black Americans.

SAMPLE: Chung and Harmon (1999) intended the scale to be used for assessment with any person with a high school education.

RELIABILITY: Internal consistency: It demonstrated appropriate levels of internal consistency ranging from .93 to .95 in high school and college samples (Chung & Harmon, 1999). **Test-retest:** Chung and Harmon (1999) reported a test-retest correlation of .74 with a three-week interval.

VALIDITY: The scale was derived from another scale by Turner and Turner (1975). It has a negative correlation (ranging from -.41 to -.58) with the Perceived Occupational Opportunity Scale (Chung & Harmon, 1999). Ratings of discrimination in each occupation also correlated negatively with percentages of Black workers in those occupations according to census data (ranging from -.47 to -.63; Chung & Harmon, 1999).

LOCATION: Chung, Y.B., & Harmon, L.W. (1999). Assessment of perceived occupational opportunity for Black Americans. *Journal of Career Assessment, 7*, 45-62.

COMMENT: The psychometric data of the scale are limited because the scale was only published recently. On the basis of available data, the scale seems to have appropriate reliability and validity and is an improvement over previous scales. More data are needed using different samples, especially on the scale's test-retest reliability in high school students.

REFERENCES:

Chung, Y.B., & Harmon, L.W. (1999). Assessment of perceived occupational opportunity for Black Americans. *Journal of Career Assessment*, 7, 45-62.

Turner, B.F., & Turner, C.B. (1975). Race, sex, and perception of the occupational opportunity structure among college students. *Sociological Quarterly*, *16*, 345-360.

REVIEWER: Y. Barry Chung, Department of Counseling and Psychological Services, Georgia State University, Atlanta, GA 30303-3083, U.S.A. E-mail: bchung@gsu.edu

7.31: PERCEIVED OCCUPATIONAL OPPORTUNITY SCALE-FORM B.

AUTHORS: Chung and Harmon.

VARIABLE: Perceived occupational opportunity for Black Americans.

DESCRIPTION: This scale was derived from items in the Institutional Racism, Racial Climate, and Adverse Impact Scales (Watts & Carter, 1991) and was designed to assess respondents' perception of occupational opportunity for Black Americans. It includes 16 items that are responded to using a 5-point scale ranging from *Strongly disagree* to *Strongly agree*. Five items are reverse-scored. The average score of all items is used; therefore, scores range from 1 to 5 with higher scores indicating perceptions of more occupational opportunities for Black Americans.

880   Work and Educational Psychology

SAMPLE: Chung and Harmon (1999) intended the scale to be used for assessment with any person with a high school education.

RELIABILITY: Internal consistency: It demonstrated appropriate levels of internal consistency ranging from .78 to .87 in high school and college samples (Chung & Harmon, 1999). **Test-retest:** Chung and Harmon (1999) reported a test-retest correlation of .75 with a three-week interval.

VALIDITY: Content: Four independent judges confirmed the face validity of the items (Chung & Harmon, 1999). **Construct:** The items were derived from relevant scales by Watts and Carter (1991). The scale has a negative correlation (ranging from -.41 to -.58) with the Perceived Occupational Discrimination Scale (Chung & Harmon, 1999).

LOCATION: Chung, Y.B., & Harmon, L.W. (1999). Assessment of perceived occupational opportunity for Black Americans. *Journal of Career Assessment, 7,* 45-62.

COMMENT: The psychometric data of the scale are limited because the scale was only published recently. On the basis of available data, the scale seems to have appropriate reliability and validity and is an improvement over previous scales. More data are needed using different samples, especially on the scale's test-retest reliability in high school students.

REFERENCES:

Chung, Y.B., & Harmon, L.W. (1999). Assessment of perceived occupational opportunity for Black Americans. *Journal of Career Assessment, 7,* 45-62.

Watts, R.J., & Carter, R.T. (1991). Psychological aspects of racism in organizations. *Group and Organization Studies*, *16*, 328-344.

REVIEWER: Y. Barry Chung, Department of Counseling and Psychological Services, Georgia State University, Atlanta, GA 30303-3083, U.S.A. E-mail: bchung@gsu.edu

7.32: PORTEOUS CHECKLIST.
AUTHOR: Porteous.

VARIABLES: The items of the Checklist are grouped into 9 content sets; Parents, Peers, Employment, Authority, Self-centred Concerns, Boy-Girl, Oppression, Behaviour, Image.

DESCRIPTION: The Porteous Checklist is a general-purpose inventory of adolescent problems for use by teachers, counsellors, psychologists, and social workers. It consists of 68 common adolescent worries and takes about 30 minutes to complete. A reading age of approximately 8 to 9 years is required.

SAMPLE: The checklist has been constructed and refined over fifteen years. Over 5,000 adolescents in Secondary schools in England and Ireland and in special settings such as clinics and care centres have provided the data. Feedback from teachers has been an essential step in construction of the Checklist. Factor analysis and item analysis determined the final items and problem sets.

RELIABILITY: **Internal consistency** for each Problem area separately in excess of .8, for overall disclosure level $r=.89$. **Test-retest:** One sample $r=>.75$ reported in the manual.

VALIDITY: Several published and unpublished studies and professional practice have confirmed the high validities and relevance of the Checklist in various contexts of use.

FURTHER EMPIRICAL USES: In a class or group situation, pupils can indicate their concerns in complete confidence. In teaching social and inter-personal skills and relationships, a more objective awareness of their own and other people's worries may be useful to members of the class. Information on individual items and problem sets can be used to help young people be reflective on their problems. In the course of individual counselling, changes in disclosure or the content of worries can be studied. The Checklist has been used in a variety of research studies in child care and treatment settings and in cohort studies of cultural or developmental issues. Checklist can be hand scored or computer scored

LOCATION: Applied Psychology Department, University College Cork, Cork, Ireland.

REFERENCES:

Porteous, M.A. (1979). A survey of the problems of normal 15 Year Olds. *Journal of Adolescence*, *2*, 307-323.

Porteous. M.A. (1981). Personal beliefs and the experience of problems: A study in adolescence. *British Journal of Social Work*, *11*, 43-60.

Porteous, M.A. (1985). Developmental aspects of adolescent problem disclosure in England and Ireland. *Journal Of Child Psychology and Psychiatry*, *26*, 465-478.

Porteous, M.A. (1985). *The Porteous Problem Checklist*. Windsor: NFER-Nelson.

Porteous, M.A., & Kelleher, E. (1987). School climate differences and their relationship to pupil personal problem admission in Irish schools. *British Journal Of Guidance And Counselling, 15*, 72-81.

Porteous, M.A., & Aherne, H.A. (1990). A study of the concurrent validity of the Porteous Checklist. *British Journal Of Guidance and Counselling, 18*, 197-200.

Porteous, M.A. (1995). *The Porteous Problem Checklist*. (2nd Edition). Cork: University College Cork.

REVIEWER: M.A.Porteous, Applied Psychology Department, University College Cork, Cork, Ireland. E-mail: STAY8012@ucc.ie

7.33: PRIMARY TEACHER QUESTIONNAIRE (PTQ), THE.

AUTHOR: Smith.

VARIABLE: Teacher beliefs (early childhood education).

DESCRIPTION: A self-report scale assessing degree of endorsement of 42 statements of educational practice based on the 1987 position statement on developmentally appropriate practices (DAP) from the National Association for the Education of Young Children (Bredekamp, 1987). The PTQ consists of two subscales, the 18 item DAP Scale, which assesses endorsement of developmentally appropriate practices, and the 24 item TRAD Scale, which assesses endorsement of traditional classroom practices. Respondents are asked to indicate level of agreement with the statements, using a 4-point Likert-type scale: (1) *Strongly disagree*, (2) *Somewhat disagree*, (3) *Somewhat agree*, (4)

Strongly agree. Subscale scores may be reported as the sum of responses for each subscale, or combined as a Total score, representing overall degree of endorsement of DAP and rejection of TRAD, by reflecting the TRAD Scale scores (1=4, 2=3, 3=2, 4=1) and adding the DAP and TRAD-Reflected scores.

SAMPLE: Smith (1993) intended the scale to be used with early childhood teachers, kindergarten-3rd grade.

RELIABILITY: **Internal consistency:** Smith (1993) reported Cronbach's alphas of .80 for the DAP Scale and .86 for the TRAD Scale.

VALIDITY: **Concurrent:** demonstrated ability to distinguish between teachers who have had and those who have not had specific training in early childhood education (McMullen, 1997, 1999; Smith, 1993, 1997). **Convergent:** demonstrated satisfactory convergent validity with other measures of early childhood teacher beliefs and practices (McMullen, 1999), including the Charlesworth *et al.* (1991) Teacher Beliefs and Practices Scale, the Hyson *et al.* (1990) Classroom Practices Inventory, and the Burt and Sugawara (1993) Scale of Primary Classroom Practices, as well as the DeFord (1985) Theoretical Orientation to Reading Profile.

LOCATION: Smith, K.E. (1993). Development of the Primary Teacher Questionnaire. *Journal of Educational Research, 87,* 23 -29.

REFERENCES:

Bredekamp, S. (1987). *Developmentally Appropriate Practices in Early Childhood: Programs Serving Children from Birth through Age 8.* Washington, DC: National Association for the Education of Young Children.

Burt, D., & Sugawara, A. (1993). A scale of primary classroom practices. *Early Child Development and Care, 84*, 19-36.

Charlesworth, R., Hart, C., Burts, D., & Hemandez, S. (1991). Kindergarten teachers' beliefs and practices. *Early Childhood Development and Care, 70*, 17-35.

DeFord, D. (1985). Validating the construct of theoretical orientation in reading instruction. *Reading Research Quarterly, 20*, 351-367.

Hyson, M. C., Hirsh-Pasek, K., & Rescorla, L. (1 990). The Classroom Practices Inventory: An observational instrument based on NAEYC's guidelines for developmentally appropriate practices for 4- and 5-year-old children. *Early Childhood Research Quarterly, 5*, 475-494.

Ketner, C., Smith, K.E., & Parnell, M.K. (1997). Relationship between teacher theoretical orientation to reading and endorsement of developmentally appropriate practice. *Journal of Educational Research, 90*, 212-220.

McMullen, M. (1997). The effects of early childhood academic and professional experience on self perceptions and beliefs about developmentally appropriate practices. *Journal of Early Childhood Teacher Education, 18*, 55-68.

McMullen, M. (1999). Characteristics of teachers who talk the DAP talk and walk the DAP walk. *Journal of Research in Childhood Education, 13*, 216-230.

Smith, K.E. (1993). Development of the Primary Teacher Questionnaire. *Journal of Educational Research, 87*, 23-29.

Smith, K.E. (1997). Student-teacher beliefs about developmentally appropriate practice: Pattern, stability, and the influence of locus of control. *Early Childhood Research Quarterly, 12*, 221-243.

REVIEWER: Kenneth E. Smith, Education Department, University of Nebraska at Omaha, Omaha, Nebraska, 68182-0613, U.S.A.

7.34: RESEARCH SELF-EFFICACY SCALE (RSE), THE.

AUTHORS: Holden, Barker, Meenaghan, and Rosenberg.

VARIABLE: Self-efficacy regarding research.

DESCRIPTION: The Research Self-Efficacy Scale (RSE; Holden, Barker, Meenaghan, & Rosenberg, 1999) is a 9- item, self-report scale covering research activities such as database searching; writing a literature review; formulating hypotheses; designing and implementing strategies for sampling, data analysis, etc. The respondent is asked to indicate how confident they are today that they could successfully perform each of the 9 research tasks. Their level of confidence is rated on an 11 point scale (0=*Not at all confident*; 50=*Moderately confident*; and 100=*Totally confident*). Subscale and total scale scores are created by computing average scores across the items for each sub or total scale. The RSW takes approximately 5 minutes to complete. The readability estimate is Flesch-Kincaid grade level 11.2.

SAMPLE: The RSE is intended for use with BSW, MSW and DSW/PhD level social workers. It has been used with both BSW and MSW groups to date.

RELIABILITY: Internal consistency: The Cronbach's alpha for the RSE was .94 at pretest and posttest in the development study.

VALIDITY: A principal components factor analysis revealed that a single factor explained approximately 68% of the total variance. Preliminary evidence was obtained regarding the construct validity of the RSE using an effect size estimate approach to construct validity. The predicted relationships between the RSE and Frans' Social Work Empowerment scale and the Social Work Self-Efficacy scale, were quite close to the observed relationships. That is, five of the eight predicted correlations were not significantly different than the observed correlations.

COMMENT: Results from this development study provide some evidence for the psychometric properties of the RSE. If similar findings are found in replications and extensions, the RSE may prove to be a useful tool in educational outcomes assessment.

LOCATION: Items available in: Holden, G., Barker, K., Meenaghan, T., & Rosenberg, G. (1999). Research self-efficacy: A new possibility for educational outcomes assessment. *Journal of Social Work Education, 3,* 463-76. Full scale with instructions and background available from: gary.holden@nyu.edu

REFERENCES:

Holden, G., Barker, K., Meenaghan, T., & Rosenberg, G. (1999). Research self-efficacy: A new possibility for educational outcomes assessment. *Journal of Social Work Education, 3,* 463-76.

REVIEWERS: Kathleen Barker, City University of New York: Medgar Evers College, 1650 Bedford Avenue, Brooklyn, NY 11225 U.S.A. **and** Gary Holden, Ehrenkranz School of Social Work, New York University, 1 Washington Square North, New York, NY 10003 U.S.A. **and** Thomas Meenaghan, Ehrenkranz School of Social Work, New York University, 1 Washington Square North, New York, NY 10003 U.S.A.; **and** Gary Rosenberg, Mount Sinai-NYU Medical Center and Health System, 1 Gustave L. Levy Place, New York, NY 10029, U.S.A.

7.35: SCREENING OF PHYSICAL LOAD DURING WORK, QUESTIONNAIRE FOR THE.
AUTHORS: Klimmer, Kylian, Hollmann, and Schmidt.

VARIABLE: Physical work load is measured by an estimation of the timely average compression in the lumbar spine during work.

DESCRIPTION: Self-report scale of 19 items on uncomfortable body positions and manual handling of loads. Respondents are asked how frequently they, on an average working day, have to work in the positions described in the items. Body positions in the items are additionally shown as pictograms. The response format is a point scale ranging from (0) *Never* to (4) *Very often*. Frequency ratings from 15 of the items, describing especially loading positions, are weighted with compressive forces on the lumbosacral disc L5-S 1, which have been derived from a biomechanical model (the 'Dortmunder' by Jager, Luttmann, & Laurig, 1991), and are added up for an index of overall physical work load. Sample The questionnaire is suitable for samples with physically demanding work tasks which effect the back. It is not intended for assessing special physical requirements, such as small, monotonous movements of the hands like machine sewing or computer work.

RELIABILITY: Internal consistency: Because of the construction no internal consistency can be calculated. **Test-retest:** A test-retest reliability ranging between .74 and .63 has been calculated for intervals between 4 month and one year, respectively (Hollmann *et al.*, 1999).

VALIDITY: The physical work load index showed a correlation of around .30 with musculoskeletal complaints in central body regions and of around .17 with musculoskeletal complaints in distal body regions. When musculoskeletal complaints were partialed out, the index did not correlate with any other psychological variable of the study (psychosomatic complaints, job satisfaction, self-efficacy). The questionnaire was also able to separate different occupational groups with differing physical job demands.

LOCATION: **English version:** Hollmann, S., Klimmer, F., Schmidt, K.Ä.H., & Kylian, H. (1999). Validation of a questionnaire for assessing physical work load. *Scandinavian Journal of Work, Environment and Health, 25,* 105-114. **German version:** Klimmer, F., Kylian, H., Hollmann, S., & Schmidt, K.Ä.H. (1998). Ein ScreeningVerfahren zur Beurteilung kOrperlicher Bela stung bei der Arbeit. *Zeitschrift fur Arbeitswissenschaft, 52,* 73-81.

COMMENT: The questionnaire is the first available self-report instrument for assessing certain aspects of physical work load, which is based on a theoretical model that describes the relevance of different loading factors for the human body In the first validation attempt the questionnaire showed good reliability and validity. It is especially suited for studies on the combined effects of psychosocial and physical factors on occupational health.

REFERENCES:

Jager, M., Luttmann, A., & Laurig, W. (1991). Lumbar load during one handed bricklaying. *International Journal of Industrial Ergonomics, 8,* 261-277.

REVIEWER: Sven Hollmann, Institut fuer Arbeitsphysiologie an de Universitaet Dortmund, Ardeystrasse 67, D44 139 Dortmund, Germany.

7.36: SELF-EFFICACY QUESTIONNAIRE FOR SCHOOL SITUATIONS.

AUTHORS: Heyne, King, Tonge, Rollings, Pritchard, Young, and Myerson.

VARIABLE: Children's beliefs about their ability to cope with school situations.

DESCRIPTION: This scale was developed to assess coping self-efficacy expectations of children, who are identified as school refusers. A school refuser is a child who has been absent from school. The SEQ-SS measures a school refuser's beliefs about his or her abilities to cope with school situations and achieve the goal of school return. The authors conceptually grounded this instrument in Bandura's (1977) social-cognitive theory. From this theoretical perspective, a student's school coping efficacy mediates behavioral change, assuming the student has sufficient motivation and skill level. After a review of the school refusal literature, the authors developed a 12-item instrument. Students use the following 5-point Likert scale to respond to the twelve items: 1=*Really sure I couldn't*, 2=*Probably sure I couldn't*, 3=*Maybe*, 4=*Probably could*, and 5=*Really sure I could*. Total scores are derived by summing the scores (possible range 12-60), with higher scores indicating greater self-efficacy expectations.

SAMPLE: Data were collected from 135 students between 5 and 15 years of age (average=11.4, *SD*=2.4). School personnel, families, or social service agency referred all students to the School Refusal Clinic. School refusers were not those who engaged in truancy or school withdrawal (families uninterested in child's attendance at school). Students were administered the SEQ-SS during their first visit to the School Refusal clinic. The average school attendance rate for this sample was 35% (SD=38%). All socioeconomic categories were represented in the sample. The sample contained a few more boys than girls (58% were male). Sixty-two percent of the students met the criteria for a DSM-III-R or DSM IV

(American Psychiatric Association, 1987, 1994) anxiety disorder or adjustment disorder.

RELIABILITY: Internal consistency: Demonstrated an adequate level of internal reliability (.85) for the total scale. Coefficient alphas for the two subscales were both .81 (Heyne *et al.*, 1998). **Test-retest:** Evidence of stability was established by administering the SEQ-SS to nineteen children (average age=11) on two different occasions (range=6 to 11 days). Intraclass correlations for the full scale, Academic/Social Stress, and Separation/Discipline Stress scales were .90, .79, and .91, respectively.

VALIDITY: Construct: Results from a principal components analysis, with a varimax rotation, reveal that the conceptual and measurement models of the SEQ-SS seem to have adequate construct validity. Two factors, containing only items with a factor loading of .4 or higher, emerged. The two factors: (1) *Academic/Social Stress*, and (2) *Separation/Discipline* Stress, accounted for 53.4% of the cumulative variance. The highest loading item (.82) on the Academic Social/Stress scale was "How sure are you of being able to do tests?" Items on the Academic/Social Stress scale seem to measure situations involving a behavioral response (doing school work) and social situations (approaching the teacher). Whereas, items on the Separation/Discipline Stress scale are related to emotionally challenging situations (morning separation from parents) (Heyne *et al.*, 1998). The highest loading item (.84) on the Separation/Discipline Stress scale was "How sure are you that you could cope with being away from your mother or father during school time?"

LOCATION: Heyne, D., King, N., Tonge, B., Rollings, S., Pritchard, M., Young, D., & Myerson, N. (1998). The self-efficacy questionnaire for school situations: Development and psychometric evaluation. *Behavior Change*, *15*, 31-40.

COMMENT: This instrument contributes to the self-efficacy literature, which lacks instruments for children. While previous research was more clinical in nature, this instrument adds to the literature by focusing on cognitive factors related to school refusal. Conceptually and empirically, the SEQ-SS is consistent with social-cognitive theory. Consistent with Bandura's theory, many students did discriminate between situations in evaluating their efficacy expectations. Many students reported high efficacy expectations on some items and low efficacy expectations on others. One of the strengths of this assessment tool is the situation specific nature of the problems presented to the children. For example, school refusers are asked about their coping abilities related to being sent to the principal. This item is more useful than simply asking about coping abilities related to discipline situations in general.   The brevity and ease of administration are additional strengths of the SEQ-SS. The authors recommend that users interpret children's scores at the total scale, subscale, and item levels. The scale appears to have potential for diagnostic purposes, treatment planning, and research focusing on measuring changes in efficacy expectations (King, Tonge, Heyne, Pritchard, Rollings, Young, Myerson, & Ollendick, 1998). A limitation of the SEQ-SS is that several important psychometric aspects of the scale have yet to be investigated. For example, the authors report there is a need to gather data from non-school refusers in order to better understand the measurement model. In addition, there is a need to test the factor structure of the test with an independent sample. Finally, the authors do not report separate analyses based on gender or age. Because the test development sample was aggregated, the assumption is that the structure of the construct is the same for 5 and 15-year-old students. The SEQ-SS offers a promising approach to understanding the cognitive aspects of school refusal; however, further research with a wide variety of samples is needed.

REFERENCES:

American Psychiatric Association. (1987). *Diagnostic and Statistical Manual of Mental Disorders* (3rd Edition. Revised). Washington, DC: American Psychiatric Association.

American Psychiatric Association. (1994). *Diagnostic and Statistical Manual of Mental Disorders* (4th Edition. Revised). Washington, DC: American Psychiatric Association.

Bandura, A. (1977). Self-efficacy: Toward a unifying theory of behavioral change. *Psychological Review, 84*, 191-215.

King, N.J., Tonge, B.J., Heyne, D., Pritchard, M., Rollings, S., Young, D., Myerson, N., & Ollendick, T.H. (1998). Cognitive-behavioral treatment of school refusing children: A controlled evaluation. *Journal of the American Academy of Child and Adolescent Psychiatry, 37*, 395-403.

REVIEWER: Gypsy M. Denzine, Department of Educational Psychology, Center for Excellence in Education, Northern Arizona University, Flagstaff, Arizona 86011, U.S.A. E-mail: gypsy.denzine@nau.edu

7.37: "SPURNING SCALE" FOR TEACHERS.
AUTHORS: Cheuk and Rosen.

VARIABLE: Teachers' perceptions of their offers of help being rejected by their peers and/or students.

DESCRIPTION: The scale was constructed based on a model that proposes that rejection of help is stressful to the rejected helpers because the rejection carries unfavourable implications on the helpers' self-perceptions of being efficacious and caring in helping others. The 9-item scale measures the extent to which classroom teachers experience recurrent rejections of their help by their peers and/or students, assessing, for instance, respondents' perceptions that their peers or students avoid seeking help from them, that their peers or students did not use the help offered, and that their peers or students thought that the help was offered out of ulterior motive. Responses are scored on an 11-point scale ranging from (1) *Definitely does not describe me* to (11) *Definitely describes me.*

SAMPLE: The scale was intended to be used by classroom teachers.

RELIABILITY: **Internal consistency:** Satisfactory levels of internal consistency of the scale were obtained in studies designed to assess the psychometric properties of the scale (Cheuk & Rosen, 1994; Cheuk, Wong, & Rosen, in press), and in studies examining the relationships between being spurned and burnout and other variables (Cheuk, Wong, & Rosen, 1994; Wong & Cheuk, 1998), with alphas ranging from .81 to .85.

VALIDITY: Evidence for validity was obtained in Cheuk & Rosen (1994) by (a) a significant correlation between the spurning scores and burnout scores, (b) a significant correlation between the spurning scores and the scores indicative of job satisfaction, but an insignificant relationship between the spurning scores and scores reflective of an intent to switch to another job, and (c) a significant correlation between the spurning scores and scores on the Student Sub-scale of Wilson's Stress Profile for Teachers.

LOCATION: Cheuk, W.H., & Rosen, S. (1994). Validating a 'Spurning Scale' for Teachers. *Current Psychology, 13*, 241-247.

FURTHER EMPIRICAL USES: The scale was used in a study that examined the impacts of being spurned on burnout and the role of social support in minimizing the adverse effects of being spurned in a sample of grade school teachers in Macau (Cheuk, Wong, & Rosen, 1994). The scale was also used in another study with beginning high school teachers in Macau, aiming to replicate the adverse effects of being spurned on job satisfaction, to explore the impact of stress preparation, and to examine the moderating effects of coping style (Wong & Cheuk, 1998).

COMMENT: The scale has been used with some success in identifying the antecedents of spurning and its negative consequences such as burnout and job satisfaction. Given the possibility that some teachers may not be willing to admit being spurned, a behavioral indicator of spurning could be explored for assessing the validity of the present spurning scale.

REFERENCES:

Cheuk, W.H., & Rosen, S. (1994). Validating a 'spurning scale' for teachers. *Current Psychology, 13*, 241-247.

Cheuk, W.H., Wong, K.S., & Rosen, S. (1994). The effects of spurning and social support on teacher burnout. *Journal of Social Behavior and Personality, 9*, 657-664.

Cheuk, W.H., Wong, K.S., & Rosen. (in press). Further efforts in validating a spurning scale for teachers: The case of Hong Kong. *Educational Research*.

Wilson, C.F. (1980). *Wilson stress profile for teachers*. Unpublished manuscript (Available form C.F. Wilson, Department of Education, San Diego County, 6401, Linda Vista Road, San Diego, CA92111).

Wong, K.S., & Cheuk, W.H. (1998). Beginning teachers' experience of being spurned, coping style, stress preparation, and burnout. *Educational Journal, 26*, 117-129.

REVIEWERS: Wai H. Cheuk, School of Arts and Social sciences, The Open University of Hong Kong, 30 Good Shepherd Street, Homantin, Kowloon, Hong Kong, **and** Kwok S. Wong, School of Early Childhood, Hong Kong Institute of Education, Lo Ping Road, Tai Po, Hong Kong.

7.38: SUBMISSIVENESS TO ORGANIZATIONAL AUTHORITY SCALE, THE.
AUTHORS: DeZoort and Roskos-Ewoldsen.

VARIABLE: Attitudes toward inappropriate submission to authority in the workplace.

DESCRIPTION: Self-report instrument containing 10 items. Items are designed to assess a particular aspect of authoritarianism, specifically, individual attitudes toward compliance with inappropriate requests from superiors. Half of the items are reverse scored to reduce response bias and carelessness. Responses are indicated on a 7-point Likert scale (1=*Strongly disagree*, 7=*Strongly agree*) for each item. Higher scores indicate stronger attitudes in favour of inappropriate compliance.

SAMPLE: The scale is designed to measure general attitudes towards inappropriate compliance, not attitudes towards a particular workplace. It thus assesses individual differences in a specific attitude, and has broad potential applicability.

RELIABILITY: **Internal consistency:** It demonstrated high levels of internal reliability (.79 and .83) in initial study. Item-total correlations for individual items were moderate ranging from .32 to .58, and all items were shown to load on a single factor. **Test-retest:** Using a subsample of 108 students, DeZoort and Roskos-Ewoldsen (1997) reported a test-retest reliability of .76 after a three month interval.

VALIDITY: **Convergent:** It demonstrated satisfactory convergent validity with two measures of attitudes toward organizational authority, and with the avoiding and obliging subscales of the Rahim Organizational Conflict Inventory (Rahim, 1983) in initial study. **Discriminant:** Weak evidence of discriminant validity was demonstrated by insignificant correlations with the compromising, dominating, and integrating subscales of the Rahim Organizational Conflict Inventory.

LOCATION: DeZoort, T.D., & Roskos-Ewoldsen, D.R. (1997). The submissiveness to organizational authority scale as a measure of authoritarianism. *Journal of Social Behavior and Personality, 12,* 651-670.

COMMENT: Although scales exist that measure submissiveness to organizational authority, The Submissiveness to Organizational Authority Scale is unique in that it is designed to assess general (versus location specific) attitudes towards complying with (versus accepting) inappropriate (versus appropriate) organizational demands. Since no research has yet been generated by this scale, further investigation is necessary before the validity, reliability and utility of this instrument can be firmly established.

REFERENCES:

DeZoort, T.D., & Roskos-Ewoldsen, D.R. (1997). The submissiveness to organizational authority scale as a measure of authoritarianism. *Journal of Social Behavior and Personality*, *12*, 651-670.

Rahim, M.A. (1983). *Rahim Organizational Conflict Inventory - II, Form A*. Palo Alto, CA: Consulting Psychologists Press.

REVIEWER: James A. Gruman, Department of Psychology, University of Windsor, Windsor, Ontario, Canada, N9B 3P4. E-mail: gruman@uwindsor.ca

7.39: SURVEY OF ATTITUDES TOWARD STATISTICS (SATS)©.

AUTHOR: Schau.

VARIABLE: Students' attitudes toward statistics.

DESCRIPTION: The 28-item Survey of Attitudes Toward Statistics (SATS; Schau, Stevens, Dauphinee, & Del Vecchio, 1995) was designed for use in both research and instruction. It measures four components of introductory statistics students' attitudes toward statistics: affect (student's positive and negative feelings about statistics-6 items), cognitive competence (student's intellectual knowledge and skills when applied to statistics - 6 items), value (usefulness, relevance, and worth of statistics in the student's personal and professional lives - 9 items), and difficulty (difficulty of statistics as a subject to learn - 7 items). Students respond to each item on a 7-point Likert scale ranging from *Strongly disagree* to *Strongly agree*. Pre-course and post-course versions of the SATS are available. Several additional items in the SATS packet ask about the student's academic background and skills, demographic information, and anticipated course grade (Schau *et al.*,

1995). The SATS can be administered through the web or as a paper-and-pencil measure.

SAMPLE: The SATS was developed to be used with post-secondary students (undergraduate and graduate) taking introductory statistics courses.

RELIABILITY: Internal consistency: Scores from the SATS usually exhibit satisfactory levels of internal consistency. Cronbach's alpha values have ranged from: affect - .81 to .88, cognitive competence - .77 to .85, value - .80 to .88, and difficulty - .64 to .77 (Schau et al., 1995; Wisenbaker & Scott, 1997). Test-retest: There is no research exploring the short-term test-retest stability of these attitudes. Most researchers and instructors are interested in how much attitudes change across an introductory statistics course. Wisenbaker and Scott (1997) found stability coefficients from the beginning to the end of introductory statistics courses that ranged from .34 to .87, depending on the setting in which the course was offered (community college or research university), level of the students enrolled (undergraduate or graduate), length of the course, and instructor.

VALIDITY: Content: A panel of instructors and introductory statistics students identified through consensus the four attitude components and wrote the items assessing each. In addition, a content analysis of all other major statistics attitude surveys showed that each includes items supporting the importance of one or more of the components (Dauphinee, Schau, & Stevens, 1997). Internal structure: Using confirmatory factor analysis techniques, responses from undergraduate introductory statistics students obtained within the first two weeks of class fit the four-component structure well (Schau et al., 1995) and better than any of the other three models commonly used to score other attitudes toward statistics surveys (Dauphinee et al., 1997). Concurrent: With one exception, scores from the four SATS subscales correlated positively and statistically significantly with medium or high effect sizes with the two subscale scores from Wise's Attitudes Toward Statistics measure, a commonly used statistics attitudes survey (Wise, 1985). The pattern and size of these relationships varied (Schau *et al.* , 1995).

FURTHER FINDINGS AND USES: Instructors and students alike believe that attitudes toward statistics are important in regard to classroom climate and achievement. To date, little good research exists exploring these relationships using any statistics attitudes measure. Initial work with the SATS indicated that students' cognitive competence at the beginning of an undergraduate introductory statistics course is positively and strongly related to successful course completion; this relationship was much stronger for white female than for white male students (Del Vecchio, 1994). The relationships between attitudes and course achievement as assessed by test scores appears to be much more complicated (Wisenbaker & Scott, 1997). A revised version of the SATS that includes attitudes toward research is being developed for use with students enrolled in healthcare programs (*e.g.*, medical and nursing students). A second revised version is under development for use with undergraduate engineering students.

LOCATION: The SATS items can be found in Dauphinee, T.L., Schau, C., & Stevens, J.J. (1997). Survey of Attitudes Toward Statistics: Factor structure and factorial invariance for females and males. *Structural Equation Modeling, 4*, 129-141. The entire SATS packet is available on the web at http://www.unm.edu/~csorge/infopage.htm or by e-mail from cschau@unm.edu

REFERENCES:

Dauphinee, T.L., Schau, C., & Stevens, J.J. (1997). Survey of Attitudes Toward Statistics: Factor structure and factorial invariance for females and males. *Structural Equation Modeling, 4,* 129-141.

Del Vecchio, A.M. (1994). *A psychological model of introductory statistics course completion.* Unpublished doctoral dissertation. University of New Mexico, Albuquerque.

Schau, C., Stevens, J., Dauphinee, T.L., & Del Vecchio, A. (1995). The development and validation of the Survey of Attitudes Toward Statistics. *Educational and Psychological Measurement, 55,* 868-875.

Wise, S.L. (1985). The development and validation of a scale measuring attitudes toward statistics. *Educational and Psychological Measurement, 45,* 401-405.

Wisenbaker, J.M., & Scott, J.S. (1997, April). *Modeling aspects of students' attitudes and achievement in introductory statistics courses.* Paper presented at the annual meeting of the American Educational Research Association, Chicago, IL.

REVIEWER: Candace Schau, 12812 Hugh Graham Road N.E., Albuquerque, New Mexico, 87111, U.S.A. E-mail: cschau@unm.edu

7.40: TECHNICIAN APTITUDE BATTERY.
AUTHORS: Porteous.

VARIABLES: Numerical Ability, Verbal Comprehension, Spatial Ability, Visualisation Ability, and Error Checking.

DESCRIPTION: Five short (under ten minutes each) tests of Elementary Decimal Calculation And Decision Making, Basic Verbal Comprehension, Reasoning using Spatial diagrams, Symbol Search, and Diagrammatic Rotation. The tests scores are standardised according to accumulated and up-dated norms, and then transformed to a Deviation scale. Results are presented as overall ratings for Ability (Power) and Accuracy, and also as a twelve point graph for individual tests. A spreadsheet program carries out the arithmetic.

SAMPLE: The test was constructed with Further Education college and School leavers. Norms apply to 500+ applicants for Technical positions in three major American Multinational companies and Clerical positions in local authority offices.

RELIABILITY: Internal Consistency for each test separately in excess of .75. **Test-retest:** One sample of ten job applicants, $r=.75$ for Overall Composite rating.

VALIDITY: Two samples of existing technicians, Overall ratings were ranked and correlated with job performance rankings: $r>.80$. Ratings correlated with Ramsay Technical Knowledge test.

FURTHER EMPIRICAL USES: Available only as part of serviced assessment centre package.

LOCATION: Psychometrica International Limited, Business and Technology Park, North Mall Cork, Ireland.

REFERENCES:
Porteous, M.A. (1995). *Occupational Psychology.* London: Prentice Hall.

REVIEWER: M.A. Porteous, Applied Psychology Department, University College Cork, Cork, Ireland.

7.41: TOTAL WORKLOAD QUESTIONNAIRE, THE.
AUTHORS: Mardberg, Lundberg, and Frankenhaeuser.

VARIABLE: The combined load of paid work and unpaid duties, mostly related to home and family.

DESCRIPTION: Self-report questionnaire covering a broad range of aspects of (perceiving) the work situation including caring for childen and other persons and household tasks. Its 134 specific questions refer to the following areas: general background, job characteristics, perception of job characteristics, household, child care, other duties, the total work situation, other aspects of total workload. Respondents are asked about how they feel about certain aspects of their workload by rating their experiences at 7-point scales from, *e.g., Not at all* to *Very demanding,* or *Not at all* to *Very interesting.*

SAMPLE: Mardberg, Lundberg, and Frankenhaeuser (1991) intended the scale to be used in samples of women and men with dual roles: worker and parent.

RELIABILITY: Internal consistency: The internal reliability of the various indices of work aspects, obtained after factor analysis, ranged from .70 to .92, except one (Social contacts) which had an alpha below .70 (Mardberg, Lundberg, & Frankenhaeuser, 1990) in a study among 356 female and 509 male white-collar workers. In 12 cases, the coefficient alphas were higher for men, in 6 cases higher for women, and in 2 cases similar for both sexes. However, the sex differences in alpha values were small.

VALIDITY: Convergent: A satisfactory convergent validity is demonstrated by several studies (Lundberg, 1996; Lundberg & Frankenhaeuser, 1999) showing that TWL-scores correlate positively with psychophysiological measures indicating load and stress.

LOCATION: Mardberg, B., Lundberg, U., & Frankenhaeuser, M. (1991). The total workload of parents employed in white-collar jobs: Construction of a questionnaire and a scoring system. *Scandinavian Journal of Psychology, 32,* 233-239. **For more details:** Mardberg, B., Lundberg, U., & Frankenhaeuser, M. (1990). The total workload of male and female white-collar workers: Construction of a questionnaire and a scoring system. *Reports from the Department of Psychology, Stockholm University,* Sweden, No.714.

COMMENT: The TWL is a valuable tool for measuring relevant aspects of total work load and perceived total work load (including care and household) of men and women with multiple roles. Results showing correlations between total work load as measured by the TWL and elevated psychophysiological levels indicate the meaningfulness of the scale. Regarding the various subscales, it seems worthwhile to do some further validation studies.

REFERENCES:

Lundberg, U. (1996). Influence of paid and unpaid work on psychophysiological stress responses of men and women. *Journal of Occupational Health Psychology, 1,* 117-130.

Lundberg, U., & Frankenhaueser, M. (1999). Stress and workload of men and women in high-ranking positions. *Journal of Occupational Health Psychology, 4,* 1-10.

Lundberg, U., Mardberg, B., & Frankenhaeuser, M. (1994). The total workload of male and female white collar workers as related to age, ocuupational level, and number of children. *Scandinavian Journal of Psychology, 35,* 315-327.

Mardberg, B., Lundberg, U., & Frankenhaeuser, M. (1990). *The total workload of male and female white-collar workers: Construction of a questionnaire and a scoring system.* Reports from the Department of Psychology, Stockholm University, Sweden, No.714.

Mardberg, B., Lundberg, U., & Frankenhaeuser, M. (1991). The total workload of parents employed in white-collar jobs: Construction of a questionnaire and a scoring system. *Scandinavian Journal of Psychology, 32,* 233-239.

REVIEWERS: Marrie H.J. Bekker, Department of Clinical Health Psychology and Departmet of Women's Studies and Klaas Sijtsma, Dept. of Methodology, Tilburg University, PO Box 90153, 5000 LE Tilburg, The Netherlands.

7.42: WORK ADDICTION RISK TEST, THE.

AUTHOR: Robinson.

VARIABLE: Workaholic tendencies.

DESCRIPTION: The Work Addiction Risk Test (WART; Robinson, 1999) is a 25-item self-report inventory. Respondents are instructed to rate each item according to how well the item describes their work habits. Responses are scored on a 4-point scale: 1=*Never true*; 2=*Sometimes true*; 3=*Often true*; and 4=*Always true*. Summing the item responses across all items creates a total score, ranging from 25 to 100.

SAMPLE: The WART is intended for use with working adults.

RELIABILITY: Internal consistency: Robinson, Post, and Khakee (1992) reported coefficient alpha of .85 using a sample size of 151 participants. Robinson and Post (1995) reported a Spearman-Brown split-half reliability coefficient of .85 based on 442 respondents. Robinson (1999) reported a coefficient alpha of .88 based on 371 respondents. **Test-retest:** Based on 151 respondents, Robinson, Post, and Khakee (1992) reported a test-retest correlation coefficient of .83 after a two week interval.

VALIDITY: Content: Face validity was estimated by having 50 working adults match each item to the major symptoms of work addiction (overdoing, self-worth, control-perfectionism, intimacy, and mental preoccupation-future reference) (Robinson & Post, 1994) with acceptable matching reported. Robinson and Phillips (1995) selected 20 psychotherapists to critically examine test items as they related to work addition. The psychotherapists were instructed to identify the 25 items out of 35, 10 items unrelated to work addiction were nested in the original 25 items, which were related to work addition. The mean percent of correctly identified symptoms was 89%. **Convergent:** Robinson (1999) correlated scores from the WART with measures of Type A behaviors and state-trait anxiety. Correlation coefficients ranged from .20 to .50. The relationships between the constructs were in the hypothesized direction and expected magnitude.

LOCATION: Robinson, B.E. (1999). The work addition risk test: Development of a tentative measure of workaholism. *Perceptual and Motor Skills, 88,* 199-210.

COMMENT: Studies on the WART have been limited to a few studies with small and non-representative samples. Even though the validity and reliability evidence have been positive, much more evidence, particularly in the area of construct validity, needs to be conducted before the WART can be used for making decisions concerning individuals.

REFERENCES:

Robinson, B.E. (1999). The work addition risk test: Development of a tentative measure of workaholism. *Perceptual and Motor Skills, 88,* 199-210.

Robinson, B.E., & Phillips, B. (1995). Measuring workaholism: Content validity of the Work Addiction Risk Test. *Psychological Reports, 77,* 657-658.

Robinson, B.E., & Post, P. (1994). Validity of the Work Addition Risk Test. *Perceptual and Motor Skills, 78,* 337-338.

Robinson, B.E., & Post, P. (1995). Split-half reliability of the Work Addition Risk Test: Development of a measure of workaholism. *Psychological Reports, 76,* 1226.

Robinson, B.E., Post, P., & Khakee, J.F. (1992). Test-retest reliability of the Work Addiction Risk Test. *Perceptual and Motor Skills, 74,* 926.

REVIEWERS: Claudia Flowers, Department of Educational Administration, Research, and Technology, University of North Carolina at Charlotte, NC28223, U.S.A. E-mail: cpflower@email.uncc.edu **and** Bryan E. Robinson, Department of Counseling, Special Education, and Child Development, University of North Carolina at Charlotte, NC28223, U.S.A. E-mail: berobins@email.uncc.edu

7.43: WORK DOMAIN GOAL ORIENTATION INSTRUMENT.

AUTHOR: VandeWalle.

VARIABLE: Learning, proving and avoiding dimensions of work domain goal orientation.

DESCRIPTION: This instrument is grounded in the theory of goal orientation developed by Dweck and colleagues (Dweck, 1986; Dweck & Leggett, 1988). Goal orientation is an individual disposition for goal preferences in achievement settings. Work domain goal orientation is assessed with a 13-item instrument that has three subscales: (a) five items measure a *learning* goal orientation which is the desire to develop the self by acquiring new skills, mastering new situations and improving one's competence; (b) four items measure the *proving* dimension of a performance goal orientation which is the desire to prove one's competence and to gain favourable judgements about it, and (c) four items measure the *avoiding* dimension of a performance goal orientation which is the desire to avoid the disproving of one's competence and to avoid negative Judgments about it. A 7-point Likert-type response scale, ranging from 7 (*Strongly agree*) to 1 (*Strongly disagree*), is used for each item.

SAMPLE: VandeWalle (1997) developed the instrument for use with adults in reference to their work environment.

RELIABILITY: **Internal consistency:** The instrument has demonstrated satisfactory levels of internal reliability (Cronbach's alpha) in multiple studies. In samples from the United States, VandeWalle (1997) and Brett and VandeWalle (1999) reported the following respective alpha values: α=.89 and .78 for learning; α=.85 and .81 for proving; α=.88 and .88 for avoiding. For a sample of Dutch undergraduate students, Heimbeck, Sonnentag, and Frese (1999) reported alpha values of α=.85 for learning; α=.86 for proving; and α=.78 for avoiding. **Test-retest:** VandeWalle (1997) reported the following test-retest correlations over a 3 month interval for a sample of 53 students enrolled in adult evening classes at an American college: r=.66 for learning, r=.60 for proving, and r=.57 for avoiding.

VALIDITY: **Factorial:** Three studies have used exploratory factor analysis and confirmatory factor analysis to assess the fit of the data collected to a correlated three-factor model (VandeWalle, 1997; Brett & VandeWalle, 1999; and Heimbeck, Sonnentag, & Frese, 1999). All three studies report an excellent fit of the data to the three-factor model. **Convergent and Divergent:** Research has found the hypothesized patterns of convergent and divergent relationships with the following constructs: implicit theories of ability, mastery, competitiveness, and fear of negative evaluation (VandeWalle, 1997); feedback seeking (VandeWalle & Cummings, 1997), goal choice (Brett & VandeWalle, 1999); need for achievement (Heimbeck, Sonnentag, & Frese, 1999).

LOCATION: VandeWalle, D. (1997). Development and validation of a work domain goal orientation instrument. *Educational and Psychological Measurement, 57,* 995-1015.

COMMENT: Two features distinguish this instrument from extant goal orientation instruments: First, the instrument was developed to assess both the proving and avoiding dimensions of a performance goal orientation. Second, the instrument is domain specific in that it assesses work related goal orientation in contrast to the global level of goal orientation.

REFERENCES:

Brett, J.F., & VandeWalle, D. (1999). Goal orientation and goal content as predictors of performance in a training program. *Journal of Applied Psychology, 84,* 863-873.

Heimbeck, D., Sonnentag, S., & Frese, M. (1999). *Goal orientation: A comparison between two instruments and their relationship with achievement motivation.* Working paper, University of Giessen, Giessen, Germany.

VandeWalle, D. (1997). Development and validation of a work domain goal orientation instrument. *Educational and Psychological Measurement, 57,* 995-1015.

VandeWalle, D., & Cummings, L.L. (1997). A test of the influence of goal orientation on the feedback seeking process. *Journal of Applied Psychology, 82,* 390-400.

REVIEWER: Don VandeWalle, Organizational Behavior and Business Policy Department, Cox School of Business, Southern Methodist University, Dallas, Texas 75275-0333, U.S.A. E-mail: dvande@Mail.cox.smu.edu

7.44: WORKER EMPOWERMENT SCALE, THE.
AUTHORS: Leslie, Holzhalb, and Holland.

VARIABLE: Perceived level of worker empowerment with three subscale dimensions of personal orientation, work environment, and work relationships.

DESCRIPTION: The Worker Empowerment Scale (WES; Leslie, Holzhalb, & Holland, 1998) is an 18-item self-report scale measuring perceived empowerment of the worker in the work environment, with 3 subscale dimensions of personal work orientation, control of the work environment, and work relationships. Responses are scored on a 5-point Likert type format ranging from *Strongly agree* (4), through *Undecided* (2), to *Strongly disagree* (0). After adjusting 8 reverse scored items, an overall mean score of between 0 and 1 is computed with higher scores indicating stronger perceptions of empowerment.

SAMPLE: The WES scale was intended for use with social service workers to measure their perception of empowerment in the work environment.

RELIABILITY: Internal consistency: It demonstrated satisfactory levels of internal reliability with an overall scale alpha coefficient of .89 and alpha coefficients .83, .83, and .82 on the three six item subscales. Additionally, factor analysis produced a principle factor with an eigenvalue of 8.8, with each item loading on a single factor with values ranging from .49 to .75 demonstrating a single construct measure (Leslie, Holzhalb, & Holland, 1998).

VALIDITY: Face and content: It was established through review of a pool of potential items by a panel of 20 professionals, with expertise in the theoretical area. **Construct:** It demonstrated both convergent and discriminant construct validity through comparative analysis with concurrent administrations of the

Work Locus of Control scale (Rotter, 1966), and the Job Satisfaction Survey (Spector, 1985), with all hypothesized relationships being statistically significant at least at the less than .01 level of probability. **Predictive:** It demonstrated through an ability to predict known group membership with a statistical significance at the less than .05 level of probability (Leslie, Holzhalb, & Holland, 1998).

FURTHER EMPIRICAL USES: Recently, requests to use the WES have been received from researchers in the US, Israel, Italy, and France for use with work populations ranging from social work students to hotel employees. It is hoped that the validity, reliability, and usefulness of this scale will be expanded to include a wide range of workers in diverse work environments.

LOCATION: Leslie, D.R., Holzhalb, C.M., & Holland, T.P. (1998). Measuring staff empowerment: Development of a worker empowerment scale. *Research on Social Work Practice, 8,* 212-222.

COMMENT: The WES has provided a discrete measurement instrument which was shown to be different from either work locus of control or job satisfaction. This discrete measurement will allow for further systematic exploration of the impact of changes in the work environment, thus assisting administrators and researchers alike to evaluate organizational interventions.

REFERENCES

Leslie, D.R., Holzhalb, C.M., & Holland, T.P. (1998). Measuring staff empowerment: Development of a worker empowerment scale. *Research on Social Work Practice, 8,* 212-222.

Rotter, J.B. (1966). Generalized expectancies for internal versus external control of reinforcements. *Psychological Monographs, 80,* 1-28.

Spector, P. (1985). Measurement of human service staff satisfaction: Development of the job satisfaction survey. *American Journal of Community Psychology, 13*, 693-713.

REVIEWER: Donald Robert Leslie, School of Social Work, University of Windsor, 401 Sunset, Windsor, Ontario, N9B 3P4, Canada.

AUTHOR OF TEST INDEX

SUBJECT AND TEST INDEX

MELLEN STUDIES IN PSYCHOLOGY